Choosing and Using Fiction and Non-Fiction 3–11

A comprehensive guide for teachers and student teachers

Margaret Mallett

Routledge
Taylor & Francis Group

LONDON AND NEW YORK

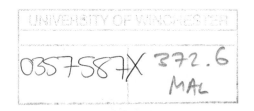
First published 2010 by Routledge
2 Park Square, Milton Park, Abingdon, Oxon, OX14 4RN

Simultaneously published in the USA and Canada
By Routledge
270 Madison Avenue, New York, NY 10016

Routledge is an imprint of the Taylor & Francis Group, an informa business

©2010 Margaret Mallett

Typeset in Perpetua and Bell Gothic by
Florence Production Ltd, Stoodleigh, Devon
Printed and bound in Great Britain by
TJ International Ltd, Padstow, Cornwall

British Library Cataloguing in Publication Data
A catalogue record for this book is available from the British Library

Library of Congress Cataloguing in Publication Data
Mallett, Margaret.
  Choosing and using fiction and non-fiction 3–11: a comprehensive
  guide for teachers and student teachers/Margaret Mallett. – 1st ed.
      p. cm.
  1. Reading (Early childhood).   2. Reading (Elementary).
  3. Children – Books and reading.   4. Book selection.   I. Title.
  LB1139.5.R43M248 2010
  372.41 – dc22   2009041556

ISBN10: 0–415–48458–8 (hbk)
ISBN10: 1–84312–322–3 (pbk)
ISBN10: 0–203–85496–9 (ebk)

ISBN13: 978–0–415–48458–9 (hbk)
ISBN13: 978–1–84312–322–4 (pbk)
ISBN13: 978–0–203–85496–9 (ebk)

Contents

CONTENTS

CONTENTS

CONTENTS

CONTENTS

(A comprehensive list of children's books and resources mentioned can be downloaded from www.routledge.com/9781843123224)

Figures

Boxes

Case studies

Acknowledgements

During a long career working with children, students and teachers many people have helped me and contributed to my thinking. My colleagues in the Education Department at Goldsmiths College and the students and teachers I have worked with taught me much about what it means to be a reflective practitioner.

Another huge source of interest and enjoyment has been my governorship of Castlecombe Primary School in Mottingham for over twenty years, where teachers, fellow governors and most of all the children have kept me practical and down-to-earth. I thank Tim Smith, Roger Ward and the teachers and children who have generously allowed me to draw on their work and reproduce examples of writing and drawing. I am also indebted to other teachers, children and schools who have contributed to the classroom case studies that pepper my book. Here I want to thank the following: my former student Siobhan Carolin, Myatt Garden Primary School (Brockley) and Orla and Nancy for writing exampes, Gill Robins and her Year 6 pupils at Sun Hill Junior School, Hampshire, for their drawing and writing and Lindsey Apps and Sharon Swanton and Year 2 at Hindsford CE Primary School (Atherton) for Case Study 32.1.

As a team editor for the English Association's journal for primary school specialists, *English 4–11,* I have been inspired and stimulated by the lively meetings, and especially those discussions devoted to choosing the best fiction and non-fiction illustrated books for awards each year. Most recent colleagues are John Paine, Marion Hampton, Eve Bearne, Liz Connolly, Pam Dowson, Rebecca Kennedy, Brenda Marshall, Dee Reid and Gill Robins.

I thank the publishers, authors and illustrators who allowed me to reproduce the front covers of and sometimes extracts from children's books. These are acknowledged in detail where they appear in the book.

Researching for and writing this book, with its exceptionally wide scope, has been challenging and has often intruded into family time; I appreciate the help of my husband, David, in keeping me on task and for spending many hours commenting helpfully on the evolving text.

Preface

Those of us who are passionate about reading know that it has enriched our lives. Fiction helps create and develop that inner world of the imagination where we can play with ideas and possibilities. As we read widely and grow older we appreciate these inner resources more and more as a great source of solace and entertainment in a sometimes harsh world. But reading and writing non-fiction can also draw on and develop our creativity. It sets us on intellectual adventures in the real world and the best texts are well researched and information-rich, but are also speculative and honest about what can only be provisional in our present state of knowledge.

There are two reasons for writing this book. First of all I simply want to share the fruits of my experiences with children's texts in all their forms during my years of classroom teaching, during my work with students and teachers, and during my research on projects to do with literature, language and learning. But, of course, 'text' has come to cover any representation of meaning and includes print in all its forms: illustrations, posters, films, website pages and information presented digitally. And children are required to read on screen as well as page. So a teacher's expertise now has to stretch across an expanding range of texts and there needs to be a definition of literacy that meets the increasing variety of semiotic resources (Bearne, 2009: 1). There is a move towards a freer, more flexible classroom culture in the United Kingdom, encouraged by two recent reviews of primary education: *Independent Review of the Primary Curriculum: Final Report* by Sir Jim Rose and *Children, Their World, Their Education: Final Report and Recommendations of the Cambridge Primary Review* by Robin Alexander (Rose, 2009; Alexander, 2009). This new atmosphere fosters collaboration between colleagues so that teachers work together to choose for the library and classroom collections. This book aims to support those seeking a richer understanding of the great variety of texts, fiction and non-fiction, which deserve a place in the classroom and school library. I sense, also, a new energy being directed towards talk about interesting questions and challenges – how to support children's visual literacy, how to regard those exciting, risky boundary-breaking books that are deliciously controversial and how to evaluate multimodal and multimedia texts. Collaboration is also important in the broader sense and there are a number of organizations which seek to bring together those who value children's literature of all kinds. I have space here just to mention three. The Seven Stories Centre for Children's Books, set up in an old mill in the Ouseburn valley in the North East, was the first archive of children's books in the United Kingdom. Find out about their collections, exhibitions, courses for teachers and students and workshops for children on their website (www.sevenstories.org.uk). Theatre groups specializing in young audiences can be a huge source of inspiration. The Polka Theatre, based in Wimbledon, provides creative explorations of favourite children's books, for example *Charlie and Lola's Bestest Play* based on Lauren Child's books and *Flat Stanley* by Jeff Brown. The theatre group strives to inspire children's imagining and feeling, but above all seeks to entertain. Yes – this is the important thing – once entertained by plays, even reluctant readers may be drawn into reading the books on which they are based. And then there is the work of the School Librarian Association in promoting well-stocked and supervised libraries for all age groups. Their latest projects and achievements can be viewed on the SLA weblog (www.sla.org.uk/sla-blog.php). Although I hope there will be something in this book for anyone who is concerned with children and their texts, a large part of my readership will be student teachers and teachers in the early years of their career. So there will be input on things more experienced teachers will already be familiar with.

A second reason for taking on this challenge is that I wanted to write a book on children's texts which gave equal status and attention to fiction and non-fiction – you've had a hint of this above. There are, of course, books about children's non-fiction, but there are far more about fiction and it is relatively unusual for someone to take on both kinds in similar depth and detail. It is non-fiction that has tended to be marginalized as 'children's literature' has so often been taken to mean 'children's fiction'. In his book *International Companion Encyclo-pedia of Children's Literature*, Peter Hunt includes only one chapter, out of over a hundred, on non-fiction (Hunt, 2004). Kimberley Reynolds concentrates exclusively on fiction in *Modern Children's Literature* commenting that, for reasons of space, there are no sections 'on information books and other forms of non-fiction' (Reynolds, 2004: 3). Of course writers are entitled to focus their work as they wish, but the present book aims to move towards a balance. One thing I am convinced about is that (even though I have attended to fiction and non-fiction in the two parts of the book), the boundaries between them are often leaky .The children's historical novel combines 'the known facts' with some imaginative speculation. Autobiographies and biographies are inevitably selective in what they include and remembering can itself be a creative process. What we want to read about are the subjects' more surprising, adventurous, and even startling experiences, and their feelings about those experiences. The thrill of the best autobiographies is not so very unlike what we experience when we read a story or novel. Some of the most exciting history books show incidents through the eyes of a fictional individual: a Greek warrior, a suffragette or a child on a journey. Then there is that lyrical kind of non-fiction which uses imagery and sometimes watercolour illustra-tions to show the poetic element in nature and science. *Think of an Eel* by Karen Wallace was part of the breakthough series Read and Wonder published by Walker. 'Non-fiction' or 'informational texts' are not inviting descriptions but, to my knowledge, no one has thought of a better term, as Margaret Meek lamented at the Write Away conference on non-fiction in May 2008. I think 'children's non-fiction literature' sounds better – but it is a bit of a mouthful. Non-fiction texts may be playful, entertaining, innovative, involving, even lyrical but, by definition, they have an informational purpose at their centre and this is what distinguishes them from fiction.

I should make it clear that this book is about making readers, but not about the initial teaching of reading, important as this is. Nor is it an academic analysis of children's literature (although there is something about this included), but rather it is about making wise choices from the tremendously wide and rich array of reading material available for children and about using the texts in the classroom. The scope is huge as I try to cover the riches of fiction including picturebooks, traditional tales, plays, filmscripts, poetry and novels, including the graphic novels that appeal so much to some children. Then there is the treasure-store of non-fiction, including information stories, the traditional information book, instruction materials, texts to persuade and reference materials. When an estimate of the number of texts published for children each year is over 6,000, it is not hard to see the challenge for those choosing for home and school use and enjoyment (Reynolds, 2004: 1). Not only are there books and other print materials, but there is also a burgeoning number of texts in other media – audio CDs, DVDs, CD-ROMs, software, websites and film and television. Choosing for children between about three up to about eleven from such a huge number of possible texts has meant being selective, brutally so at times. And remember there is an existing, huge stable of books and other texts to which what is newly available must be added. Particularly when it comes to choosing fiction, the new books and texts have to take their place amongst existing favourites and those texts which have had the staying power to become classics and therefore remain a staple of any collection. I have made my criteria for choosing explicit, but I am only too aware that I have inevitably missed out some gems and some of each of my reader's favourites.

There are suggestions for children's talk and improvisation, their artwork and writing to help deepen their response to the texts and I include some thoughts about assessing children's progress as readers. But these are indeed just suggestions. Nothing is so deadening to one's teaching creativity than trying to follow someone else's lesson plan. So feel free to use, modify and transform for your own purposes anything that is offered here that seems of help and value.

ABOUT THIS BOOK

Assigning books to age ranges

Books have long been shelved under age ranges in libraries and bookshops. But some books now have a small black and white image suggesting the ages they might appeal to: 5+, 7+, 9+ and so on. It is important that suggestions should be viewed with some flexibility. Referring to picturebooks, Antony Browne remarked that care needed to be taken over assigning them 'with their rich layers of meaning' to a particular age group. A trainee was concerned that a nine-year-old just beginning on chapter books might be upset to see '7+' on the back of a book they were considering choosing (Horn, 2008).

These points should be kept in mind and yet I believe we can group most texts loosely within an age band. In this book, children's books and resources are discussed under three main, slightly overlapping, headings. They are: 3–5-year-olds; 5–8-year-olds; and 8–11-year-olds. These link broadly with the UK categories: the Early Years Foundation Stage, Key Stage 1 and Key Stage 2. (However, I begin the oldest age range at 8 rather than 7.)

References

Professional and academic books are mentioned in the main text using the Harvard system of second name and date, and page number where direct quotations are made, and in the bibliography. Over 1,000 children's texts and resources are referred to in this book. These are listed with author, publisher and price (usually of the cheapest edition) on the publishers' website (www.routledge.com/9781843123224).

Figures

These include annotated lists of recommended texts, front covers or, occasionally, artwork from some of the children's books mentioned and examples of children's writing and drawing.

Boxes

Reviews of some useful, interesting and innovative children's books and resources, information about key professional or academic books and summaries of relevant research are boxed.

Classroom examples

These are mostly vignettes rather than full-length case studies but they bring some of the vitality of the classroom to the analysis and show some sound and imaginative approaches to using and appreciating the different kinds of text.

Part I
Fiction

Chapter 1

Introduction to Part I

When someone writes about fiction they are usually thinking about texts which draw on invention and the inner world of the imagination, often using figurative language to get meaning across. What do we look for in such texts? It depends on the reader's age, their maturity, interests and tastes but we might seek things like a strong plot, interesting and convincing characters, language that is alive and powerful and well-described settings providing virtual experience of other times and environments. But we would also want to find, in some books in the collection at least, things relevant to a wide range of human issues, tapping into feelings of love and hate, joy and sadness, life and death so that our feelings are engaged. And we want some books that amaze, startle or change our view of the world. If we want to gather less bookish young learners into the readers' fold, we need some books that are above all entertaining, whatever other merits they might have. So in the chapters that follow in this first part of the book, you will find much about 'classics' – whether novels, picturebooks or poetry – and much about more recent books of the type often called 'quality children's literature'. You will also find some suggestions for lighter reads and for 'popular culture' texts, including some that are multimodal and/or multimedia. All this is to come; here I want to consider what fiction, whatever its form, offers the growing child. Perhaps the place to start is at the very beginnings of the capacity for cultural activity. Here many teachers have found inspiration in Donald Winnicott's books – *Playing and Reality*, for example – in which he locates the origins of this capacity in a child's early play. Where early play is satisfying and creative the growth of a special 'space for living' that is not properly described as 'inner' or 'outer' but is in fact intermediate between the two is encouraged (Winnicott, 1971: 106). The child that plays happily and creatively is actually growing a space for the enjoyment of cultural experiences, including reading fiction, that will sustain through life. Parents and teachers can help expand and nourish this by providing a rich range of books and making them a natural and pleasing part of everyday life.

Stories are one of the types of fiction offered first to children. Since narrative is a basic way of making sense of experience the chronological structure of a story is familiar to even the youngest children. As Margaret Meek argues so convincingly, fictive narrative has much to teach older children too about 'the different ways that language lets a writer tell, and the many different ways a reader reads' (Meek, 1988: 21).

Novels and stories that appeal to the inner world of the imagination are of huge benefit to the growing child. They can help ease the loneliness of the human condition as stories offer accounts of other lives and what it is like to grow up in different circumstances and societies to our own. Stories can reach over time and space and find something universal to share about being human. It can be a comfort to find that others have felt lonely, worried and fearful and have had difficulty in thinking positively about themselves. Books about characters overcoming these things with resourcefulness are well liked by children, which helps explain the popularity of Jacqueline Wilson's Tracy Beaker series and J.K. Rowling's Harry Potter books. Reading books like these, even where as in the Harry Potter books they occur in a secondary world, can echo children's own preoccupations, allowing them to reflect on them at a distance from their everyday reality. So instead of facing problems as raw lived experience, the reader can take on the challenges vicariously. In the classroom, many issues are best raised through a novel or story. We must remember that in all sorts of subtle and complex ways fiction socializes young listeners and readers, by revealing what is valued, feared and disapproved of in their culture. Becoming aware of this is part of becoming a critical reader and a mature human being.

Another huge benefit of reading fiction is the exposure it gives to powerful, interesting and sometimes aesthetically pleasing uses of language. The language in a book may be conversational and full of convincing everyday dialogue and the rhythms of everyday speech or lyrical, fresh and original. It is the language used in a work of fiction that brings alive the adventures, feelings and dilemmas of the characters. This is why reading aloud is so important for all children. They can concentrate on the language and the story while the teacher reads. It is particularly important that less forward or reluctant readers have these opportunities. Hearing stories read aloud reveals how stories are crafted, which can help children find their own writing 'voice' too.

One thing I have kept in mind when recommending texts is that, like adults, children read at different levels at different times – to suit their mood. Nine-year-old Alice told me she loves the books of Michael Morpurgo and was taken to see *War Horse* at the National Theatre, 'but sometimes I like to read my *Beano*' she added. Children have a right, just like adults, to have preferences and to make choices about what they read. What we try to do is help them justify their opinions and judgements with reference to the text. It is not going to be the worthy and bland books, plays and films that are likely to entice the young. The disturbing, risky and frightening book has a place too in making readers.

A number of teachers and specialists in children's literature have shown us that texts themselves teach (Meek, 1988; Benton and Fox, 1985; Chambers, 1991). Children learn by reading, for example, what to expect from certain kinds of book and that characters do not always say what they mean and so you have to read between the lines or infer meanings. Texts often have different levels of meaning too and so returning to a text read when you were younger may 'mean' differently when you return to it later. Reader response approaches like that of Benton and Fox and Martin and Leather show convincingly how children bring their personal life experience to interpreting texts (Benton and Fox, 1985; Martin and Leather, 1994). But response can be deepened by well-chosen activities and a teacher's sensitivity and enthusiasm can make the difference for some young readers. How do teachers decide which activities are worthwhile? Here I have always found helpful two questions which I trace back to a book by Michael Benton and Geoff Fox, *Teaching Literature*, written way back in the 1980s. They are: 'Will this activity enable the reader to look back on the texts and to develop meanings already made?'; 'Does what I plan to do bring reader and text closer together, or does it come between them?' (Benton and Fox, 1985: 108).

4

Text

Alliteration – the repetition of consonant sounds in a sequence in prose or poetry for emphasis or effect.

Classic – books that last through more than one generation of readers.

Cohesion – the way different parts of a text connect to communicate.

Discourse – any stretch of language longer than a sentence.

Genre – a kind or type of text bound by rules and conventions.

Iconotext – where text and illustration are intended to complement each other.

Inference – grasping meaning that is implied rather than made fully explicit in a text.

Intertextuality – where allusions to other texts are made within one text.

Metacognition – the awareness a person has of how they have come to know something.

Metafictive – a term applied to a postmodern kind of book, picturebook or novel which in creating a story, at the same time, comments on the very process of its creation.

Metalanguage – a linguistic term meaning terminology to talk about language.

Metaliteracy – how children talk about the way in which they read literature. It is used by Arizpe and Styles, when they observed children's reading and comments on picturebooks (Arizpe and Styles, 2003).

Metaphor – a literary device identifying one thing with another; the qualities of the first thing carry over into the second. 'He was the lion of the group.'

Multimedia – a communication combining different media, as in a CD-ROM with moving images, sound and graphics.

Multimodal – a communication is multimodal when it combines image, writing and design.

Narrative – chronologically ordered text.

Polysemic – capable of different interpretations of the message and often used to refer to picturebooks which are multi-layered.

Postmodern – the art, literature and thinking which is in reaction to modernism. Primary teachers, pupils and parents are perhaps most likely to be confronted by postmodernism when they read contemporary picturebooks. (See Lewis, 2001: 94–101.)

Reader-response theory – to do with how readers respond to and make sense of texts. This set of ideas is associated with literary scholars like Wolfgang Iser (*The Act of Reading*, 1978) and Stanley Fish (*Is There a Text in this Class?*, 1980). The basic question is something like – how far is meaning in the text and how far is it the creation of the reader? (See Gamble and Yates, 2008: 16–17.)

Semantic levels – the different levels of meaning from straightforward to more sophisticated. More than one reading is often necessary to tap into the deeper meanings.

Semiotics – a branch of linguistics concerned with the transmission of meaning through signs and symbols.

Simile – a figure of speech which makes a comparison nearly always using either 'like' or 'as'.

Figure 1.1 Glossary: terms to do with fiction

Surrealist – this twentieth-century movement in art and literature is suggestive of the content of the unconscious mind. It intrudes into picturebooks where we find dreamlike and sometimes distorted images like those in McKee's *I Hate My Teddy Bear*.

Symbol – something representing something else. Symbols may be culture specific. (See Lewis, 2001: 114.)

Illustration

Bleeding (of pictures) – the extension of illustrations to the very edge of the page.

Colour (hue) and tone – the media chosen will affect the tone and atmosphere of the picture. Pen and ink, line and wash, watercolours and collage are traditional choices. But modern illustrators, like Lauren Child, use new technology to create their pictures, often scanning and manipulating images and mixing colours on the computer.

Composition – the way in which people and things are placed on the page.

Double spread – a picture which covers two adjacent pages.

Endpapers – pages at the beginning and end of a book on which there may be decoration or images to do with the themes of the book.

Hatching – a term used to describe the parallel lines used to darken areas of a picture as in the work of Charles Keeping and Edward Ardizzone.

Iconotext – where written text and illustrations are intended to complement each other.

Interanimation – where words and images work together to create meaning as in picturebooks, comic strips and graphic novels.

Landscape – a format in which the pages of a book or a canvass are a rectangle with the longer sides in a horizontal position.

Line – an illustrator aims to develop a distinctive way of drawing which makes their work immediately recognizable. An artist's line may be heavy and bold like that of John Lawrence (see for example *This Little Chick*) or light and sensitive like that of John Burningham (see for example *The Magic Bed*).

Modulation – an artist's varying of colour and tone.

Movable – a novelty book with movable parts: flaps to open, tabs to pull and perhaps wheels to turn.

Picturebook – a book which combines pictures and words in telling a story and which demands that the reader relates non-linear reading of pictures to a linear written text.

Point of view (position) – the 'point of view' shows the reader objects and happenings from a particular perspective and affects how the narrative is understood.

Portrait – a format in which the long sides of a rectangle are placed vertically.

Restricted palette – a palette limited to a small number of hues.

Salience – the emphasis placed on a particular element in a picture. This might be achieved by size or colour.

Vignette – a small picture to enhance or extend written text.

Figure 1.1 *continued*

Chapter 2

Children's literature
Some key strands

THE CRITICAL STUDY OF CHILDREN'S LITERATURE

The critical study of children's literature has become well established and has explored questions like 'What is children's literature?', 'How are children shown in children's literature over the centuries?', 'What are the ways in which children's literature can be studied?' Professor Peter Hunt, the scholar and critic, has illuminated these questions in his course, one of the first, on children's literature at Cardiff University and in his many lectures, presentations and books. A good one to start with is *An Introduction to Children's Literature*, which covers the history of, mainly, British children's literature and explains the different ways in which the subject can be approached. Writing here of the power of children's books he comments that their characters – 'Cinderella, Pooh Bear, the Wizard of Oz, Mowgli, Biggles, the Famous Five and Peter Rabbit – are part of most people's psyche, and they link up not simply to childhood and storying, but to basic myths and archetypes' (Hunt, 1994: 1). So children's writers both tell a story and transmit cultural values.

John Rowe Townsend's is another 'voice' relating the story of children's literature and putting it in an historical and social context. His *Written for Children: An Outline of English-Language Children's Literature*, the definitive edition of which was published in 1995, has become a classic. Townsend has firm and original views on particular authors and particular books and often expresses these in an entertaining way. According to Townsend, Dahl's books appeal to 'the cruder end of childish taste, to a delight in rumbustious rudery and in giving people one in the eye' (Townsend, 1995: 249).

Another distinctive contributor to our understanding of the history of children's literature is Brian Alderson, founder of the Children's Books History Society and former Children's Book Editor for *The Times*. He reaches many readers through his 'Classics in Short' to be found on the back pages of *Books for Keeps*. These articles are models of criticism and have included *The Wind in the Willows* by Kenneth Grahame (May 2005), *Mog the Forgetful Cat* by Judith Kerr (Nov. 2008) and *Johnny the Clockmaker* by Edward Ardizzone (March 2009). He manages to pinpoint just those qualities that make a book distinctive and memorable and he does so in an entertaining and insightful way. He notes, for example, Mog's 'thoroughgoing and endearing gormlessness'.

Nicholas Tucker considers children and their literature from a psychologist's viewpoint. In *The Child and the Book*, while suggesting some developmental stages, he insists on the individuality of the child. Personalities, interests, preoccupations, life experiences, fears and abilities differ so much from child to child that, while suggestions for reading are welcome, flexibility has to be shown.

Then there are more recent studies, for example *Modern Children's Literature*, edited by Kimberley Reynolds and based on a course run by the National Centre for Research in Children's Literature which has been running at the University of Roehampton since the 1970s (Reynolds, 2004). This book concentrates on a selection of children's books written in the twentieth and the early twenty-first centuries. Like other recent studies it sees children's literature as part of a country's culture: the books children read 'provide them with the images, vocabularies, attitudes and structures to think about themselves, what happens to them and how the world around them operates' (Reynolds, 2004: 3).

David Lewis applies insights from postmodernism and structuralism to the examination of children's books (Lewis, 2001). This book helps us see some of the picturebooks we are most likely to use in the classroom, including those by Browne, Burningham, Briggs, Cole, Hughes and Sendak, in a new light. Notions of 'excess' and 'boundary breaking', for example, concepts adapted from literary criticism of adult books, are applied. Referring to 'excess', which pushes at our expectations of what seems acceptable and poses the question 'How far is it possible to go?', Lewis suggests we find this in John Burningham's *Would You Rather?*, where some worrying and extraordinary possibilities of parents' embarrassing behaviour are pictured (Lewis, 2001: 95). 'Excess' is also built into the theme of *Angry Arthur* by Hiawyn Oram and Satoshi Kitamura; Arthur is so cross about not being allowed to watch late night TV that his rage brings on terrifying earthquakes and storms.

'Boundary breaking' occurs, writes Lewis, when 'characters within a story are allowed by their author to wander beyond the narrative level to which they properly belong' (Lewis, 2001: 94). So in *The Story of a Little Mouse Trapped in a Book* by Monique Felix a small creature desperately tries to escape the confines of the page upon on which she is pictured. Since the publication of Lewis' book there have been ever more picturebooks published with this 'boundary-breaking' feature. The work of Neil Gaiman and David McKean (*The Wolves in the Walls*), Lauren Child (*Beware of the Storybook Wolves*) and Mini Grey (*The Pea and the Princess*) all come into this category.

For those who wish to read further in the fascinating area of contemporary picturebook criticism I recommend Perry Nodelman's *Words about Pictures* and Maria Nikolajeva and C. Scott's *How Picturebooks Work*. It is the exciting, risk taking picturebooks that grip young learners and a teacher's deeper understanding of the possibilities of the genre can aid selection for the classroom.

LINKS BETWEEN CHILDREN'S LITERATURE AND CHILDREN'S DEVELOPMENT AS READERS

Some of those who have studied and written about children's literature have been able to make a link between the quality of books and the needs and development of young readers. Here I want to look at the work of some of those teachers, critics and scholars who have made a contribution to helping teachers become informed about fiction and about how to support and deepen children's response to it. *The Cool Web: The Pattern of Children's Reading*, edited by Margaret Meek, Aidan Warlow and Griselda Barton, was a landmark book of extraordinary merit and influence that was published in 1977. The fifty articles by authors and critics, with helpful linkage by the editors, added considerably to the status of children's literature as an academic area of study. In this book Barbara Hardy argues that narrative and storying are not something that only writers do, but something fundamental to the way every human being tries to make sense of what happens on a day to day basis. Gamble and Yates have explored the implications of this in Chapter 3 of their book *Exploring Children's Literature* (Gamble and Yates, 2008). Read a book about someone being injured to a class of primary school children and they will be eager to tell you the stories of how they bumped their head and had to go to hospital or what happened when their friend fell off the swing and damaged her front teeth and so on. Listening to and hearing stories develops children's sense of narrative and its power. Then they can exploit all this in their own storytelling and writing. We must remember that narrative can be oral, written or visual and that, today, children receive stories through different media, film, television and CD-ROMs and from websites as well as in print.

Another book that changed perceptions of what was involved in reading fiction and how the texts themselves could teach was Margaret Meek's *How Texts Teach What Readers Learn* (Meek, 1988). Once they are able to read for themselves children have to take on the role of the 'teller' and this involves stepping into the author's shoes, but they are also the 'told' – the audience trying to make sense of the story.

The work of Tony Martin and Bob Leather concentrates on children's growth as readers and on the essentially creative nature of reading fiction (Martin and Leather, 1994). These teachers and writers show what Wolfgang Iser's Reader Response Theory can offer in the classroom (Iser, 1978). Stories draw us in by reflecting what happens in our lives, but they take us beyond our own experiences, beyond what happens to us every day, and this is where the excitement lies. In their book *Readers and Texts in the Primary Years* these authors include a case study of a very young child sharing with his father Ruth Brown's story *A Dark, Dark Tale*. Three-year-old Dominic is able to fill in the gaps between the text and pictures with his own speculations (Martin and Leather, 1994: 19). This essentially creative approach to reading fiction is characteristic of all enthusiastic readers whatever their age. The way a story is written and told is hugely important; nine-year-olds were listening with great interest to their teacher reading *The Turbulent Term of Tyke Tiler*. As one child remarked, 'it is as if the people are talking'. By listening, even non-bookish young learners get to know how books work and about the role of language in making them work. So this moves them ahead in what has been termed rather grandly 'literary competence' (Culler, 1975).

All this is very much at the heart of the work and writing of the children's author, critic and educationist Aidan Chambers. He believes quality texts teach, but more than anyone else I can think of shows the powerful nature of the role of the informed and 'enabling' adult in supporting and encouraging young readers. In *The Reading Environment* he shares what he believes the adult can do in involving children with books (Chambers, 1991). His later book *Tell Me* is about how the teacher can develop 'booktalk' to awaken children's response and to give a light but useful structure to the conversation. Beginning with the sharing of 'enthusiasms', children then go on to explain 'puzzles' and finally to discover patterns of meaning and language in the books (Chambers, 1993). This emphasis on a personal response to stories is very much in the spirit of the work and writing of Wolfgang Iser in *The Act of Reading* (1978).

The ideas mentioned here have been explored in many lively conferences organized by colleges and other organizations. I will mention just one series of conferences – those run by the tutors of Homerton College, Cambridge, culminating in books like *After Alice* and *The Prose and the Passion*, edited by Morag Styles, Eve Bearne and Victor Watson.

The work of all those mentioned in this section informs the rest of the book, not least in the 'Using' element in each chapter.

REVIEWING CHILDREN'S FICTION

Who reviews children's fiction? Reviewers include critics, librarians, teachers, writers and illustrators of children's books, and sometimes children themselves. All these 'voices' are a safeguard against blatant commercialization of the market and against recipe written uniformity and narrow correctness.

Good reviewing requires considerable knowledge of children's books, acute judgement and the ability to write truthfully in an accessible way. One debate centres on the issue of how far the critic should concentrate on the merits of the text itself and how far the needs of the young readers should be kept in mind. The perceptive reviews of Margery Fisher remain a model of fine critical comment. Many, this writer included, looked forward to the arrival of each issue of her reviewing journal *Growing Point* until it ceased publication in 1992. The Signal *Book Guides* from Nancy and Aidan Chambers' Thimble Press are greatly missed too.

Books for Keeps and *The School Librarian* have long published reviews, arranged in broad age bands, by teachers and critics. The reviews of children's books and resources in *English 4–11* are nearly always by classroom teachers, who are often able to comment very directly on children's responses. *The Core Booklist* from the Centre for Literacy in Primary Education is another source of informed reviews. There is a long tradition of reviewing children's books in newspapers like *The Times* and the *Guardian* and in the educational media like *Child Education* and the *Times Educational Supplement*. Publishers and bookshops offer reviews, too, but their impartiality is less certain. Reviews on websites include those of the independent book store Love Reading4kids-online (www.lovereading4kids.co.uk), those sites on which the reviews of critics who write children's review columns in main newspapers appear, for example Nicolette Jones and Amanda Craig of *The Times*, and those on the sites of educational organizations like Booktrust (www.booktrustchildrensbooks.org.uk). The customer reviews on Amazon UK vary in coherence but the best are vibrant and thought-provoking and often show that what one person's children like, another's may not.

In the 1970s, there was concern that girls and members of minority groups should be represented more fairly in the books in school collections. One clear voice here was that of Rosemary Stones in her articles in *The Children's Book Bulletin*. The debates at the 'Diversity Matters: Changing Cultural Perspectives in Children's Publishing' conference in June 2006 show potential authors in some groups in the UK need to be encouraged to write and submit work of merit. Reviewers are developing ways of appraising multimedia productions which demand knowledge of how film, photography and graphics work.

While books for adults are written by adults for adults, books for children are written by adults for children. So as the intended readership, children should be encouraged to have a view on what is offered to them. Being required to write reviews too often or to an inflexible framework can make writing them a chore. Teachers who welcome short as well as the occasional long review and the use of pictures and graphics, and who encourage the sharing of reviews by having them read aloud, help put energy into book journal work. It is a good thing, too, that children's views on books are sought by those offering book awards, for example the BBC's *Blue Peter*, and on shortlisting candidates for the Children's Laureate.

Finally, if I can leave you with one thought, it is that teachers who share their own passionate enthusiasm for reading do much to inspire children to become readers. Tell and show them what turned you on to reading. Use all your ingenuity and imagination to draw them into texts. Once children understand what reading can offer them, how it can connect with their feelings and experiences, they are gripped. In nearly all the following chapters there are case studies and classroom vignettes which show how some teachers have achieved this.

SUMMARY

- Children's literature is a vast field of study in which a number of different disciplines meet, including education, literary criticism, psychology and social studies.
- The books read by children affect their ways of thinking about themselves and the world and are therefore an important part of cultural influence.
- Links between fiction and literacy have been forged by teachers and scholars – Meek, Martin, Chambers and others – who have shown the role both of texts and of the enabling adult in developing children as readers.
- Narrative is a fundamental part of human thinking and all of us make sense of our world through the act of storying.
- All reviewers of children's fiction draw on their knowledge of children's literature and some pull also on their understanding of the needs, interests and preoccupations of the young readers.

Chapter 3

Fiction in the classroom
Resources, organization of teaching and learning, some issues and assessment and record keeping

INTRODUCTION

Perhaps the recent emphasis on literacy in schools, crucial as progress here is, has put at risk some other things that have an important place in the English lesson. At its best the spirit of English teaching finds its home in the imagination-expanding discourse that happens when teacher and children are totally absorbed in responding to a story. An initiative by the Centre for Literacy in Primary Education, The Power of Reading, supports teachers in effective uses of literature in the classroom. Details of this project involving 750 primary schools are available on the CLPE website (www.clpe.co.uk). The United Kingdom Literacy Association's Teachers as Readers project looks at the creative use of literature as well as researching patterns in primary teachers' reading, both personal and professional (www.ukla.org).

Teachers in classrooms in which children have become a community of engaged, empathetic, insightful and critical readers and writers of fiction have nearly always attended to the quality of what Aidan Chambers calls 'the reading environment' (Chambers, 1991: 7). This chapter introduces what I consider to be important here.

RESOURCES

Some things to keep in mind when choosing resources for the classroom and school library are the need to include:

- books that have become timeless classics as well as books from more recent authors and thus from some newer 'voices';
- books on loan from libraries as well as a permanent collection;
- books made by teachers and children (which may be covered and laminated);
- multimodal print texts and multimedia texts, including audio CDs, DVDs, CD-ROM talking books and films of stories;
- 'popular culture' and 'genre' texts that offer a link between children's home and school reading experience;
- books and resources of different levels of difficulty to meet the needs of less forward young learners as well as outstandingly able ones;
- some books that will appeal mainly to boys and some that are likely to be chosen by girls, (though gender is not the only factor in children's preferences);

- dual-language texts for children learning a new language, which combine English and the languages spoken, read and written at home (Mantra Lingua are leaders in this area of publishing);
- books reflecting regional or local interest;
- quality texts from different parts of the world, not least traditional tales which can reinforce a shared heritage.

There are some other things that can be provided to support children's reading and writing of fiction. We look for signs of:

- involvement of children in the choice and evaluation of books and resources;
- the central library being the heart of the school;
- children being involved in the running of the library, with older children being given the opportunity to train as library monitors (there is more about this in Chapter 34);
- the provision of 'book weeks', author visits and special outings to do with books, films, plays to nurture interest (the British Library, for example, has well-organized workshops on all manner of topics);
- imaginative, annotated displays of books and resources, displays to which the children have contributed: author of the week; stories on a theme; poems; traditional tales; picturebooks;
- a corner or area of the classroom where children can read, browse and work.

THE READING AND LITERACY AREA

The arrangement and resourcing of this area will vary according to the age of the children but teachers try to make it inviting with simple seating and display areas. As well as print books, magazines and posters we would expect to find a computer giving access to websites, software, audio CDs, CD-ROMs and talking books. Age-related writing and drawing materials and book-making tools have an important place too. Those language and literacy areas that are used constantly throughout the day by teacher and children are most likely to be a vibrant and interesting part of the classroom.

THE SCHOOL LIBRARY

Some general information about use of the library, including classification systems and the role of children as library monitors as well as aspects relevant to non-fiction reading, is set out in Chapter 34. The fiction collection is a most important resource for every primary school and benefits from having a specialist librarian who is knowledgeable about children's stories, poems and plays as well as about organizational matters. However this has cost implications, and often schools appoint a teacher willing to build on a special interest in children's literature and put in time in the library, perhaps with the help of a classroom assistant. The School Library Association offers considerable help to schools setting up or maintaining a strong central library. This advice is available on their website (www.sla.org.uk).

The association also publishes a journal, *The School Librarian*, a quarterly which includes articles and reviews on fiction (and non-fiction) in both print and electronic texts.

THE ORGANIZATION OF TEACHING AND LEARNING

Now that teachers in the UK have more freedom to use their professional skills in organizing the reading and writing programme we hear of 'literacy time' or 'literacy and English' rather than 'the literacy hour'. But however creative an approach may be there are just five ways of organizing activities for the children: as a class, in groups, in pairs, teacher and pupil on a one-to-one basis or as individuals reading or working silently.

Class-based reading

Hearing a story read aloud binds the children in the class together. It also gives less able readers the chance to enjoy stories that they might otherwise miss. Every child, whatever his or her ability, needs the space to enjoy listening to the flow of the language and the patterning of meaning. You will find much on this throughout the book, particularly in Chapter 5 and Chapter 7.

Class-based work around fiction can involve groups reporting back on discussions and use of the interactive whiteboard to make notes of some key points. There will be times, too, when the whiteboard can be used to show poems and films for class discussion.

Group reading

Teachers have always put children of similar ability and experience into groups for some of their English and literacy work. The terms 'guided' and 'independent' were used by the creators of the Primary National Strategy's Literacy Frameworks of 1998 and 2006 to differentiate between groups working with teacher support and groups where the children read and worked on tasks on their own. Even though teachers are not now expected to work to these frameworks, group reading will continue to have a place whatever it is called. Typically, teachers arrange the children in groups of about four to six and ask them to read aloud in turn from their copy of the same text. The teacher joins the group from time to time to support reading and energize discussion. So in the average-sized class we might have three or four guided groups and one group reading independently. Where younger children, the under eights, are concerned some initial teaching of reading takes place, including reading aloud to the teacher.

When it comes to choosing books for guided reading, there is a strong case for teachers themselves doing the selecting, and for developing and using their own ideas for activities and tasks. But the collection might include some of the best commercial packs available today, which, unlike reading scheme books encountered in the past, often include stories in a range of genres by quality writers and illustrators. The ideas for activities around guided reading books in the White Wolves fiction range from A&C Black benefit from advice from the Centre for Literacy in Primary Education and the stories are written by authors of the calibre of Geraldine McCaughrean, Tony Bradman and Margaret Mahy. Other examples of guided book packs are Ginn's All Aboard reading books, Oxford University Press' Guided Reading Cards and Reading Tree fiction for all age groups and Heinemann's Guided Reading Cards. Another reading programme which uses authors of high reputation, including Clare Llewellyn, Tony Bradman and Jeannie Willis, is Project X from Oxford University Press. The use made in some of the units of animation, video-clips and CD-ROMs is intended to help motivate reluctant boy readers, although it is hoped that all children enjoy them. The philosophy behind the resources links with research projects on boys and literacy, for example the *Raising Boys' Achievement* study (Warrington, Younger with Bearne, 2006).

There are a number of helpful books for teachers about the resourcing and organization of guided reading. *Book Bands for Guided Reading: A Handbook to Support Foundation and Key Stage 1 Teachers* gives guidance on books for children of different reading abilities (Bickler, Bake and Bodman, 2007). *Guiding Readers: A Handbook for Teaching Guided Reading at Key Stage 2* provides a detailed rationale and annotated lists of books, including multimedia texts (Hobsbaum, Gamble and Reedy, 2006).

Group reading will, I believe, continue for a number of reasons. First, it is relatively economic of a teacher's time. Second, the group can be a less intimidating setting for discussion around a text. Third, there is potential for collaborative learning. But to work well the texts need to be of good quality and appropriate choices for a particular group, and the teacher needs to intervene skilfully and, I would say, more speculatively and conversationally than seemed to be the case in the time of the Framework (Skidmore, Perez-Parent and Arnfield, 2003: 47–52).

Work in pairs

This is one of the least formal and unthreatening of all the groupings. Pairing children for oral or written work can bring variety and energy to an English or literacy lesson. Children can choose or be allocated what is sometimes termed a 'response partner' and asked perhaps to discuss something – what they think of a character or why a sentence is punctuated in a particular way – something that moves the lesson on. Children need some guidance on how to make discussions truly part of the learning. For example, they need to listen to what their partner says and respond carefully to it. The task can be focused by the teacher suggesting some of the things to cover, perhaps writing them down on a flip-chart or on the whiteboard. Then the pairs can report back on what they agreed to the whole class. The great benefit of collaborative kinds of learning is that a context is created where thoughts and opinions are made explicit.

One-to-one reading

Reading to a teacher each week, or even each day, was once a central routine in the early years and primary classroom, particularly for the under sevens and for those older children with some reading difficulties. Then came the UK Literacy Frameworks in 1998 and 2006, the creators of which considered this routine not to be efficient use of a teacher's time. It was reasoned that if several children needed the same advice and support, why not give it to them together? But one-to-one reading is a routine worth preserving. These short reading episodes when a child has the teacher's undivided attention can be very motivating. There is an opportunity to make real progress without a child feeling inhibited by the presence of other children. I've heard teachers say something like, 'I've found a book I think you will really like. Let's read it together'.

Silent reading time

Children of all ages benefit from having the time and space to savour a book and to read at their own pace. There are a number of acronyms for this: USSR (Uninterrupted Sustained Silent Reading); ERIC (Everyone Reading In Class) and DEAR (Drop Everything And Read). Reading at home has to compete with time on the computer, texting and watching television as well as with outdoor activities. And so providing reading time in school sends out a clear message that reading is valuable in its own right. Newly independent readers can be helped in reading times to make the transition from reading aloud to reading silently. This routine also reinforces a culture of reading, of being part of a community of readers. Teachers also use the opportunity to observe the children's reading choices and their level of concentration. But it is probably not a time to engage in conversation. Aidan Chambers names 'reading time' as one of four essentials if we are to help children become readers. (The others are reading aloud, a well-chosen collection to choose from and response to reading in a teacher-led group.) He goes on to argue that positive attitudes towards reading are likely to result if it is maintained as a sacrosanct ritual 'that conditions our set of mind' (1991: 38).

SOME ISSUES AND QUESTIONS

When it comes to that huge treasure store we call 'children's literature' there are issues that the classroom teacher needs to keep in mind and to discuss with colleagues. Opinions on these issues are constantly modifying and changing and I have organized this part of the chapter under some of the questions I have heard teachers discussing during my visits to many schools over the years.

How can children's developing visual literacy be supported?

Visual literacy is to do with 'reading' images of all kinds and seeing the connections between pictures and print. Children are surrounded by visual images in entertainment, advertising as well as in books and magazines. So becoming literate is no longer a matter of just learning to read and write but is to do with interpreting and evaluating both static and moving images. Children bring to school considerable knowledge and experience about visual images since they are likely to watch television, view DVDs and are surrounded by print images.

When we think of visual literacy and fiction one genre in particular springs to mind as having a huge impact on children's reading development. This is, of course, that important cultural form the picturebook, which communicates meaning through a combination of images and written text. The prevalence and popularity of the graphic picturebook and story extends the age range exposed to ideas about aesthetics, making children much more aware of such elements as design, colour and style (Reynolds, 2004: 3). You will find more about this in Chapter 4 where I draw on the insights of those who are specialists in the children's picturebook and particularly on the work of David Lewis (Lewis, 2001). When reading a picturebook a child has the challenge of relating 'non-linear' reading of the pictures to the linear processing of words (Hunt, 2001: 289). Research into children's responses to picturebooks is covered in Chapter 4, where there is some discussion of the classroom research of Arizpe and Styles (Arizpe and Styles, 2003).

Lewis considers that the illustrations in books other than picturebooks affect how a reader approaches the written text (Lewis, 2001: 68). So, as part of their own knowledge about children's literature, teachers need to consider the implications of the way in which children's books, including classics, have been illustrated by different artists. This is also an interesting study for older primary children when they carry out author studies.

While thinking about visual literacy I would like to draw attention to the greater status of what are now termed 'multimodal texts'. These are texts – comics and graphic novels are examples – which, in their print form, combine design, pictures and writing to communicate meaning. There are signs of quite young children being tuned into multimodality in their reading and their creation of texts. The merits of their efforts to combine writing and pictures, and sometimes to design the page, have not always been appreciated (Bearne, 2009: 57). Multimodality is also a feature of multimedia texts and moving image texts. The digital camera has made it much easier for teachers and children to make their own short films and there is more about this in Chapter 14.

What are current views about commercial reading schemes and programmes?

Reading schemes and programmes consist of books and other materials arranged into difficulty levels for teaching reading from about age five to age ten or eleven. In the 1970s and 1980s there was much debate about whether children should be taught to read using a reading scheme with its controlled vocabulary, or using what are termed 'real' or 'trade' books. Reading scheme books at this time tended to have a rather stilted text and a restricted vocabulary. Apart from these criticisms on linguistic grounds there were also objections to the social messages in some of the books, which tended to show mainly just one group in our society. Gender roles were less flexible than in real life and some groups rarely saw themselves pictured or described in the books.

Now that many of the criticisms of these programmes have been addressed are there some remaining concerns? I have two reservations. First, if the teachers in a primary school become locked into one reading programme, however good, it can take something away from their professionalism and from the enjoyment of choosing books for their pupils. Second, although programme designers and editors try to bring some reading and visual variety within a programme or scheme, in some cases the books tend to look rather similar, as if from the same family. But some books written for reading programmes are by 'quality' authors and illustrators and, in my view, would deserve a place in the early years and primary school collections.

What does the teacher need to know about gender and fiction?

The attention given to gender differences and the educational consequences of how these are perceived change as our culture changes. In the 1970s and 1980s the stereotyping of girls and women in children's fiction was challenged. Publishers took note and both reading scheme books and trade books began to reflect a more plural society where females were no longer locked into domesticity or traditionally female jobs and professions. It is often said that girls like fiction and boys prefer non-fiction, but the true picture is more complicated. Girls often enjoy the narrative kinds of non-fiction and the sort that reveal feelings as well as facts (Myers and Burnett, 2004). And while there is some evidence that many boys feel more comfortable with non-fiction, classroom research challenges the view that fiction cannot be presented in a way that appeals to them. For me, some of the most convincing evidence showing that reluctant boy readers can be turned on to reading fiction comes from a classroom-based study carried out by Kimberley Safford, Olivia O'Sullivan and Myra Barrs, working with teachers of Year 5 and 6 classes in London schools (Safford, O'Sullivan and Barrs, 2004). The reluctant boy readers, who mostly could read but chose not to, responded in an extremely involved way to poems and stories with a strong emotional appeal. One of these was Charles Causley's poem 'What Has Happened to Lulu?', about a girl who appears to have been abducted, but where plenty of room is left for imaginative speculation. Reading and discussing the poem led to exciting drama, writing and use of 'email' as a way of exploring the themes. *There's a Boy in the Girls' Bathroom* by Louis Sachar, about a very troubled boy, inspired an enthusiastic response too. The success of the work was down to the selection of intriguing, exciting and unsettling books and poems combined with imaginative tasks suggested by the teachers, tasks involving discussion, drama and interactive ICT, all designed to help deepen the pupils' responses.

Are there some topics and some kinds of language which should not intrude into fiction for the under elevens?

Crude racial or social stereotypes and scenes of mindless violence have no place in the primary collection. But what about 'good' books which have disturbing themes and realistic language? It is not only a matter of knowing what teachers and children think about the books, the views of parents and the wider community have to be understood too while not allowing unreasonable limits to be put on what children are offered in school.

Looking at the language used first, some people object to spelling and grammatical errors and others to realistic dialogue which sometimes includes swearing. A teacher of older primary school children remarked to me: 'We think David Almond's book *The Savage* is riveting and original, but some of our parents have objected to the spelling and grammatical errors'. But Blue himself explains: '. . . I know the spelling isn't brilliant, but I was younger then'. The swearing arises when Blue writes about the terrible time of his father's fatal heart attack. Again the fact that the swearing is not gratuitous is explained. 'I'll just say it was all absolutely b***** horrible. And I'm sorry about the swearing but if you can't swear about something like this what's the use of swearing at all?' I think most older primary children would cope with this and enjoy a powerful and original story which reads aloud brilliantly.

There are some writers who seem able to tackle difficult topics in a way children can understand and empathize with. Anne Fine and Jacqueline Wilson are two authors that consistently do this. They know that there must be some light relief from the sad events in their stories, not everything can be at the same level of intensity. So there are flashes of humour in Wilson's stories about Tracy Beaker, a child in care who has so much to contend with. Even in *The Illustrated Mum*, which shows the painful consequences when adults are so taken up with their own difficulties that children have to rely on their own resources, the genuine affection between mother and daughter is revealed.

Then there are authors who write about issues and people in a way that seems offensive to readers at a time removed from the original writing. An example here is the anti-German sentiments of the boys in Robert Westall's *The Machine Gunners*, which reflects what people thought and would say during the war. The book caused a stir when it was first published by Macmillan in 1975, because of its realistic language and the boys' attitudes. But, as Nikki Gamble and Sally Yates write, the ideological content of the book is 'pacifist and not anti-German' (Gamble and Yates, 2008: 135). This can be explained to the older primary children who might read the book. Rightly or wrongly, in later editions, some of the language has been modified. But the important thing is to keep in print one of the most exciting books ever written for children on living through times of war.

In her article 'Write and Wrong', Anne Fine explains how she has come to think that rewriting books to reflect changing times is 'better than prohibition'. In her own revisions she has not only made common-sense adjustments, for example changing money amounts to fit with current values, but also removed some of Granny's remarks about black neighbours in her book *The Granny Project*, first published in 1983 (*Times 2* in *The Times,* 13 July 2007: 4). Similar tweaks to the language and attitudes have been made in the work of other children's authors, notably in that of Enid Blyton.

But no one would like everything that is a bit worrying, shocking even, to be removed from children's books. As Nicholas Tucker argues in his classic *The Child and the Book*, the best authors take children forward by challenging their comfortable ways of thinking, showing 'new avenues, new attitudes' (Tucker, 1981: 186).

BOX 3.1 ANNE FINE'S COMMENTS ON CHANGES TO NEW EDITIONS OF HER BOOKS

How do you know when you have gone too far in cutting and slashing? ... when you have taken out something you want to put back in — it is the first thing on your mind when you wake up in the morning. If you have forgotten it already, then you are happy to let it go . . . I'm still not sure I made the right decisions.

(Anne Fine, 2007)

What might teachers keep in mind when choosing books to work towards a shared heritage?

Good schools have always put much thought into including quality books – stories, novels, picturebooks and poems – from different parts of the world. One of the most helpful guides is *A Multicultural Guide to Children's Books 0–12* edited by Rosemary Stones. It provides a critical evaluation of books and materials, including dual-language texts (Stones, 1999a). More recently there have been efforts to encourage the publishing of work by ethnic minority writers living in Britain, a major theme of the 'Diverse Matters: Changing Cultural Perspectives in Children's Publishing' conference in June 2006 (Pandit, 2006). Some publishers have made a strong contribution here. Frances Lincoln have long included stories about children from widely differing backgrounds and experiences. Together with the Seven Stories Centre for Children's Books they have set up an annual competition called 'Diverse Voices'. This seeks out authors writing from or about different cultures and perspectives and whose work is published in Britain today (diversevoices@sevenstories.org.uk). Mantra publish stories in English alongside a range of other languages. The folk tale *Keeping Up with Cheetah* retold by Lindsay Camp is now available in the TalkingPEN Mantra Lingua series, which has sound effects and the opportunity to record your own retelling. The fine picturebooks from another publisher, Tamarind, show children from groups often under represented in children's literature. One important principle that all these publishers hold to is that the books should be interesting and likely to be enjoyed by the young readers for whom they are intended. The Centre for Literacy in Primary Education is one of a number of organizations which have made a huge contribution to advising schools on how to make their resources for the classroom rich and wide. As well as building a useful library for the use of teachers and student teachers, they organize courses and multicultural book fairs. Perhaps the journal which has done most to keep these issues in our minds is *Books for Keeps*. It is committed to reminding readers of 'the role of books in promoting cultural diversity and combating social and religious stereotyping' (Stones, 2002a). Diversity should extend to disabled children and children who are carers to their sick parents (Marcovitch, 2006: 10).

Perhaps of all the different fiction genres it is traditional tales which are redolent of a shared heritage for readers from whatever part of the world they have their roots. Judith Elkin's comments in 1983 still ring true: 'What better medium . . . is there for toleration, hope and understanding than their inherent honesty, goodness and abiding faith in humanity?' (Elkin, 1983: 10). As Chapter 5 explains, traditional tales began as stories told by communities and handed down orally. It was only later that they were written down. Folk tales are tales of the people and have strong links to a country and often a region within a country. And yet, like fairy tales, they are often preoccupied with universal themes that unite people over time and distance. Themes about the transformation of a person's fortunes and about good characters overcoming obstacles seem persistent. There are many stories from across the world which echo the themes in *Cinderella*, *Sleeping Beauty* and *Rumpelstiltskin*. But we must remember that there are subtle differences between these different versions, differences worth discussing.

MAKING PROGRESS AS A READER OF FICTION: ASSESSMENT AND RECORD KEEPING

One of the things looked for is increasing breadth of reading of print texts and other media. Depth of response to a particular kind of reading material is of great significance, too, in assessing progress. The sort of thing this involves is developing a sensitivity to the nuances of an author's meanings and intentions and becoming able to infer meaning when something is not stated explicitly. In more colloquial terms this is about becoming able to 'read between the lines'. As soon as children learn to read and write they start to develop a metalanguage, a vocabulary to use to talk about language. Words like 'letter', 'sentence' and 'story' are some of the earliest. As they move towards the later primary classes teachers help children understand and use terms to do with talking about literature – 'image', 'alliteration', 'narrative' and 'personification'. Having these terms can help children's progress in defending an opinion about a poem or story, and defending this opinion by pointing to parts of the story or poem to support it. These social aspects of making progress are also to do with listening and commenting on the views and reflections of others and help children along the journey towards critical reading.

But, above all, it is a child's attitude to reading that is of supreme importance. Teachers put much energy into nurturing a love of reading and an appreciation of what reading offers. Children need to develop this if they are to have the stamina to read the more challenging texts, including the sort of novels which stretch both the intellect and the imagination.

Here are some of the practical ways of gathering evidence of progress teachers find helpful, ways that bind assessment to the cycle of work:

- Compiling a diary of books read to the class and read by individuals to record breadth of reading.
- Providing reading journals to help children keep track of how wide their reading has been.
- Listening and sometimes tape recording children's talk around poems, stories and novels to help indicate depth of reading response, an ability to defend a preference and to listen to the contribution and reflections of others.
- Setting up small groups to discuss texts, enabling the teacher to judge progress in a sympathetic context. Sometimes the discussion can be focused by suggesting children move from what they like, to what they find perplexing and then to detecting the patterns and themes in a book. Many teachers find the 'three sharings' on these lines suggested in Aidan Chambers' book *Tell Me* of great help (Chambers, 1993).
- Assembling photographs of improvised drama extending a theme from literature.
- Assembling stills from short films that children have made. The British Film Institute have advice about how children's moving image texts can be evaluated.
- Inviting imaginative writing and drawing in response to texts, including reviews, writing in role and playscripts.
- Applying our greater understanding of how to evaluate children's print multimodal texts (Bearne *et al.*, 2005).

- Making displays of photographs of special events like author visits and book weeks and of books and children's writing and drawing.
- Making notes from talks with children about their reading.
- Making notes from the comments of parents about their child's reading.

Information drawn from a selection of all of the above can be summarized in a record keeping format. Teachers sometimes devise their own format or they use one of the commercial ones available. A format which has received worldwide praise is the Primary Language Record devised by the staff at the Centre for Literacy in Education. Here teachers use their observations and notes to comment on a pupil's achievements in speaking and listening, and in reading and writing in both English and across the curriculum. It has made a huge contribution to our understanding and use of formative assessment. Strengths include the link it makes between assessment and record keeping and planning, learning and teaching, its recognition of children's own thoughts about their progress in language and learning and the contribution that parents can make (Barrs, Ellis, Hester and Thomas, 1988/95).

SUMMARY

- The quality of 'the reading environment', including selection of books and resources and classroom organization, has a crucial role in making readers.
- The judgement of teachers who know both about books and about the abilities and interests of the children in the school may well be more illuminating than applying readability indices to texts.
- A collaborative approach, one where the teachers in a school meet regularly to discuss books and reading, can lead to helpful consideration of the continuing issues about fiction in the classroom.
- What counts as progress as a reader of fiction, involving both breadth and depth of reading and responding, can usefully inform an approach which makes assessment and record keeping part of the cycle of teaching and learning.

Chapter 4

Picturebooks

INTRODUCTION

The best picturebooks are highly sophisticated works of art which combine the visual and the verbal in interesting and ingenious ways. They are much more than books with illustrations – however skilfully those illustrations have been created. Picturebooks came into full bloom in the closing decades of the twentieth century and continue to be a major part of contemporary children's literature. If you visit a bookshop with a good children's section you will find hundreds of colourful and exciting picturebooks. But, even so, publishers are tending to favour tried and tested illustrators and authors and it is a struggle for newer talent to get published. This is sad because new 'voices' are needed if what is on offer is to stay fresh and stimulating.

Picturebooks have become the subject of academic study and debate and so, for example, writers reflect on whether it is the pictures that are central or whether they work through a special interaction between the verbal and the visual. They cover every imaginable topic and theme: sad, dramatic, intriguing, puzzling, celebratory and joyful. Illustrators use an exciting range of media, too, ranging from traditional oil and watercolour, to crayon, pastel, pen and ink, collage, to digital techniques, often combined with other media. There are many novelty picturebooks using imaginative paper engineering to create pop-ups, pull-outs and cleverly cropped pages, holes and wheels, some of which simply entertain, while others enhance the story. Perhaps more than any other kind of reading material, their semantic subtlety and the ways in which they play with meanings indicate that linking a picturebook too closely to one age group would be unwise. So while I have some suggestions for choosing for different age groups, I hold to a light touch here. In the 'Using' section I suggest ways in which teachers can help children with this important, but sometimes challenging, kind of reading. Here I draw on an important research project which resulted in Arizpe and Styles' book *Children Reading Pictures: Interpreting Visual Texts*. The importance of children's talk around picturebooks, of making their observations, understandings and insights about visual texts explicit, shines out from this study.

I can only provide an introduction but Figure 4.1 has suggestions for further reading.

FEATURES OF PICTUREBOOKS

'Picturebook' describes books with many different styles and formats. Some picturebooks are wordless, some have a minimal text and then there are the graphic and comic book stories that need to be gathered into the fold. Those with a comic book format use devices like

---

BOX 4.1 ANTHONY BROWNE'S COMMENTS ON PICTUREBOOKS

At his inauguration as sixth Children's Laureate, Anthony Browne commented that:

> Picturebooks are for everybody at every age, not books to leave behind as we grow
> older. The best ones leave a tantalising gap between the pictures and the words, a
> gap that is filled by the reader's imagination adding so much to the excitement of
> reading a book.

(Anthony Browne, 2009)

---

speech balloons, panels and boxes. Other picturebooks exploit paper engineering techniques so that there are pop-ups, fold-puts, wheels to twist and pads to press – all providing visual surprises and treats.

A quick, if crude, way of distinguishing between an illustrated book and a picturebook is to ask: 'Could the meaning of this narrative stand on its own if the writing was read aloud and the listener not shown the pictures?' If the answer is yes, we have an illustrated book. Nothing wrong with that – but it is not a picturebook, where the pictures contribute at least equally to the meaning.

Written text in a picturebook is usually succinct, but can take many forms – rhyming couplets, speech balloons, a playscript as well as continuous prose. And new printing technology has made possible glorious hues as well as typology of different sizes, strengths and orientation. The drama, inventiveness and sheer imaginative power of the artwork is a defining feature that few illustrated books match.

In the light of such richness of theme, artistic style and format, what is the main feature that identifies a picturebook? It is the picturebook's potential for powerful communication through the visual. Sometimes the pictures carry the whole story, but most picturebooks combine pictures and written text, the best in ingenious and harmonious ways. What are the implications of this for how young learners read them? Perhaps the main one is that, because much of the meaning of a picturebook is contained within the visual, young readers have to relate a non-linear reading of pictures to a linear processing of words (Hunt, 2001: 289).

There are some other features found in the best contemporary picturebooks, those sometimes referred to as being 'postmodern', and these are explained in scholarly detail in David Lewis' book *Reading Contemporary Picturebooks*. Here I mention three of the most important: first, the best contemporary picturebooks are 'multilayered' and can be read at different semantic levels. Second there is often 'intertextuality': the reference, often in subtle ways, in one text to other texts. A third feature is the 'metafictive' nature of some contemporary picturebooks. Lewis explains that the metafictive 'is to do with reference in picturebooks to the nature of fiction in creating it' (Lewis, 2001: 93). Take Lauren Child's *Beware of the Storybook Wolves*; young Herb worries that the wolves in his storybook might come out from the pages. And one night they do! They burst forth with copious other fairy-tale characters in a metafictive frenzy. Stories like this show young readers and listeners that fiction is created. The rules can be turned on their head and tidy beginnings, middles and ends are abandoned.

- 'Reading Contemporary Picturebooks' by Judith Graham in Kimberley Reynolds (ed.) *Modern Children's Literature* (Palgrave Macmillan)
  Includes perceptive analyses of some individual books, for example *Who's Afraid of the Big Bad Book* by Lauren Child.

- *Reading Contemporary Picturebooks: Picturing Text* by David Lewis (RoutledgeFalmer)
  Lewis explores what is involved in becoming visually literate. In doing so he illuminates some challenging concepts: excess, multiple meanings, inter-animation, intertextuality and metafictive.

- *How Texts Teach What Readers Learn* by Margaret Meek (Thimble Press)
  Some things about reading are learnt, not through instruction, but from the books themselves and the best picturebooks have the depth and subtlety to teach the lessons.

- *Words about Pictures: The Narrative Art of Children's Picture Books* by P.N. Nodelman (University of Georgia Press)
  Nodelman considers that there is often tension between the visual and the verbal, each limiting the other's meaning: 'Each speaks of matters on which the other is silent' (1988: 222). He argues that young readers have to learn to deal creatively with this tension.

- 'Picturebook Case Study: Politics and Philosophy in the Work of Raymond Briggs' by Lisa Sainsbury in Kimberley Reynolds (ed.), *Modern Children's Literature* (Palgrave Macmillan)
  Sainsbury argues that *The Snowman, The Bear* and *The Man* all explore 'the central relationship between child and visitor; between child and newly discovered other'.

- 'The Development of Illustrated Texts and Picturebooks' by Joyce Irene Whalley in Peter Hunt (ed.) *International Companion Encyclopedia of Children's Literature* (Routledge)
  This is an historical review of illustrated books as well as picturebooks.

- 'Books and the World of Literature', Chapter 7 in *Language and Literacy in the Early Years* by Marian R. Whitehead (Sage)
  The connections children make between the events and feelings shown in picturebooks and their everyday lives and the pleasure they get from their growing appreciation of literary shape and predictability are helpfully covered here.

Figure 4.1 *Texts about picturebooks*

CRITERIA FOR CHOOSING

What makes a book excellent is always hard to pin down and perhaps particularly so in the case of picturebooks, where there are so many formats, themes and artistic styles. I have gathered my thoughts here under three overlapping areas: design, the combination of pictures and language, and originality. But of course other factors come into play when choosing books for individual children, for the class or for the school library. Teachers aim to have available a good variety of picturebooks by different authors and illustrators and on different themes to suit the preferences and needs of children and to cater for different levels of reading progress.

Design

The best picturebooks are usually what Judith Graham terms 'complete designs', with a coherence between each element from format and layout to covers and end papers (Graham in Reynolds, 2004: 209). Eric Carle's *The Very Hungry Caterpillar* is an example of a picturebook with a pleasing structure using strategically placed holes and pages of different lengths to engage the reader. Design and idea marry perfectly. The variety of design choices has been enhanced by new printing technology which has made possible innovative typefaces and exciting colours. Print books have also been enriched by illustrators taking note of innovations in moving image media.

The combination of pictures and language

A picturebook needs a strong narrative if it is to work well as a story that can hold the attention of young readers or listeners. The authorial voice needs to be distinctive whether the written text is in rhyme, in continuous prose or consists of single words, phrases or short sentences.

Where the written text is minimal the pictures have to tell us the tale. But the relationship between the visual and the verbal can be complex and subtle; words and pictures may playfully contradict each other or spring surprises.

Originality

Both the artwork and the narrative need a personal, recognizable style if the creators are to form a bond with the reader. Children need to be entertained, stimulated, surprised sometimes, intrigued and reassured. The best books show new ways of seeing experience and the world. A book's originality lies in how this is achieved.

CHOOSING PICTUREBOOKS FOR DIFFERENT AGE GROUPS

Younger listeners and readers: picturebooks for 3–5-year-olds and 5–8-year-olds

Picturebooks are an excellent introduction to the world of literature for young children and, at the same time, are a first step into literacy. Children increasingly bring their cultural knowledge of fairy tales and nursery rhymes to their reading and listening. Their experience of narrative through moving image media enriches their appreciation of print books, and this is true the other way around too.

3–5-year-olds

In the list of suggestions for this age range (Figure 4.2) there are books inviting children to recognize and talk about familiar objects (the Ahlbergs' *The Baby's Catalogue*), books that

- *The Baby's Catalogue* by Allan and Janet Ahlberg (Puffin)
  This book is ideal for the stage when children like to point at and name objects: books, clothes and family things. But the book also teaches that there are many kinds of family.

- *Giraffes Can't Dance* by Giles Andreae and Guy Parker-Rees (Orchard)
  A rhyming text and bold bright illustrations combine to tell the tale of Gerald the giraffe, who cannot dance like other creatures. We all need to find our own 'song' to dance to in life and this book tells us not to despair if ours is different from that of others. The big book version makes sharing the story with the class practical.

- *Dogger* by Shirley Hughes (Red Fox)
  Dogger is Dave's old, worn, but much loved, soft toy dog. Nearly every young child knows how upsetting it is to lose something precious. The big book version is a practical resource for reading to the whole class or group.

- *Traction Man* by Mini Grey (Random House)
  This superhero action doll comes to life and has extraordinary adventures in the bath and on 'planet duvet'. Then Granny knits him a bizarre green outfit with a little hat. Can you be a superhero in such a naff suit? Older children would understand that clothes need not define our true selves.

- *The Big Red Bus* by Judy Hindley and William Benedict (illus.) (Walker)
  The bus gets stuck and the story of how it gets moving again is told mainly through the pictures. Children will probably have seen cartoons on television and will appreciate the comic strip features like speech bubbles.

- *Everyone Hide from Wibbly Pig* by Mike Inkpen (Hodder)
  Lift-the-flap book. This book, like the others in the series, invites children to join the little pig and his friends as they do everyday things. This title is based on an exuberant game of hide and seek. Children guess who might be hiding and then lift the flap to confirm.

- *This Little Chick* by John Lawrence (Walker)
  The cover of this large, bright picturebook shows a massive chicken with sculpted feathers looking down at a little yellow chick with bright red feet. The impact is created with an exceptionally bold, thick, black line outlining the brightly coloured images. Vinyl engravings, wood textures and watercolours help create a distinctive visual 'voice'.

- *The Goat and the Donkey and the Noise Downstairs* by Simon Puttock and Russell Julian (illus.) (Oxford University Press)
  The Goat and Donkey books create a young child's home with toys, books and pictures on the walls. Like the other stories in the series this one is about friendship. 'What is that noise downstairs?', wonders Goat. Could it be burglars? Goat investigates and finds the noise is Donkey making a sandwich. So they both settle down to a midnight feast.

- *I Want to Go Home!* by Tony Ross (Andersen Press)
  Children are often unsettled when the family move to a new home. Little Princess is able to move on when she realizes her family and belongings are all at the new castle and this is her real home now.

Figure 4.2 Picturebooks for 3–5-year-olds

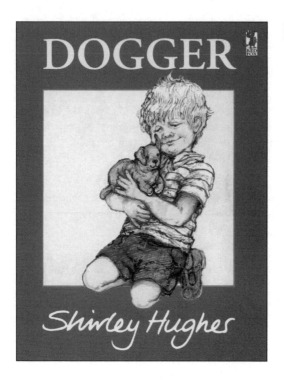

entertain and encourage joining in (Lawrence's *This Little Chick*) and books tapping into things that matter greatly to young children like losing a favourite toy (Hughes' *Dogger*). There are different formats to choose from too: lift-the-flap books (*Everyone Hide from Wibbly Pig*), books with comic book features like speech bubbles (Julie Hindley's *The Big Red Bus*) and books with innovative illustrations (Mini Grey's *Traction Man*).

5–8-year-olds

By the time they are about five, young readers and listeners can be offered picturebooks that make more demands on them (Figure 4.4). There are books which combine text, illustrations and comic strip in interesting ways; Shirley Hughes' *Chips and Jessie* was one of the first to use design to create meaning and humour. Longer exposure to moving image texts – television and film – will have increased the range and complexity of the visual jokes, so often found in picturebooks, that they can interpret. Many favourite picturebook stories have been produced in animated versions for film and television – the work of Raymond Briggs and Lucy Cousins, for example. Experience of the same story in different media helps make children active and creative readers, listeners and viewers. Children will have greater reservoirs of cultural knowledge to draw on now in interpreting and responding to what we offer them. Their knowledge of nursery rhymes and traditional tales helps them appreciate intertextual books like the Ahlbergs' *Each Peach Pear Plum* and Lauren Child's *Beware of the Storybook Wolves*. Books tapping into deep human feelings are important too, for example Bob Graham's tender book *How to Heal a Broken Wing* and Michael Foreman's *Mia's Story*.

- *Each Peach Pear Plum* by Allan and Janet Ahlberg (Puffin)
  When children know the words of nursery rhymes and fairy stories 'they bring the words to the page when they read for themselves' (Meek, 1988: 21). This interactive rhyming story works around an 'I-Spy' game which invites children to find the characters mentioned hidden in the pictures.

- *Mike Mulligan and His Steam Shovel* by Virginia Lee Burton (Frances Lincoln)
  Mike Mulligan and Mary Anne, his steam shovel, race against time to dig out a cellar for the new town hall. But can they compete with those using the new gasoline and electric machines? The book shows that if you are industrious you will find a place, even in a changing world.

- *Little Tim and the Brave Sea Captain* by Edward Ardizzone (Frances Lincoln)
  Young Tim lives near the sea and loves to watch the coastal steamers. This, the first Little Tim book, is about his adventures as a stowaway on Captain McFee's boat. What is Tim to do when he is discovered? This new edition allows young readers to savour Ardizzone's light line, cross-hatching and eye for detail.

- *Mia's Story* by Michael Foreman (Walker)
  Mia lives in the harsh conditions of the village of Campamento, San Francisco. When she rides off on a pony to seek her lost puppy a new life opens up to her. Handwritten journal entries are interspersed with double page spreads of watercolour, which help give young readers insight into a particular place.

- *Queenie the Bantam* by Bob Graham (Walker)
  Queenie, a bantam, is rescued from a lake by Caitlin's dad and joins the family. She lays some eggs but, like Jemima Puddleduck, she is not a reliable sitter! It is the family dog that hatches the eggs. The feelings of the animals and people are skilfully shown in the illustrations.

- *How to Heal a Broken Wing* by Bob Graham (Walker)
  Will finds a little bird with a broken wing on the pavement in the middle of a street bursting with busy, rushing people. He takes it home to help it heal and then releases it. So this tender book tells about what a child sees and cares about but what adults have failed to notice. The large format of the book lends itself to the double spread illustrations which communicate the atmosphere of a busy city landscape so powerfully.

- *Little Mouse's Big Book of Fears* by Emily Gravett (Macmillan Children's Books)
  This is a book that both entertains and helps children to come to terms with the worries none of us escape. Little Mouse explains his fear of the dark, his fear of slipping down the plughole and his fear of loud noises. Each page is a wonderful medley of newspaper cuttings, handwritten notes, pictures and pop-ups; then there are holes in the pages and chewed edges. There is a lot of inspiration for children's own writing and drawing.

- *The Incredible Book Eating Boy* by Oliver Jeffers (HarperCollins)
  Henry gulps down all sorts of books. When he eats dictionaries he feels cleverer. But then he starts to obtain so much knowledge that he gets confused.

Figure 4.4 *Picturebooks for 5–8-year-olds*

- *Splat the Cat* by Rob Scotton (HarperCollins)

  Many children wake with a feeling of apprehension when they are going to a new school or into a new class. So they will understand the concerns of Splat, the young cat in this story. The playful language is superb: Splat's tail 'wiggled wildly with worry' and when his Mum combs his hair she declares it 'Purr-fect'. Once at school, Splat finds he likes his teacher Mrs Wimpydimple but she does mention that cats chase mice . . .

- *Wonderful Life* by Helen Ward (Templar)

  This book is a remarkable creation – a vision of colour and unusual images. Snuff is an ift, an explorer and traveller through the universe, who is thrilled with all that he finds and investigates. There is something greatly heartening about Snuff's innocent enthusiasm. But travelling alone can have its bleak side, and his most valued discovery is someone to share his adventures with.

Figure 4.4 *continued*

Figure 4.5
Front cover of Wonderful Life *by Helen Ward*
Published by Templar Publishing, an imprint of The Templar Company plc (www.templarpublishing.co.uk). Illustration and text copyright Helen Ward

Older listeners and readers: picturebooks for 8–11-year-olds

Older children sometimes return to the picturebooks they read when they were younger to re-savour the stories and to bring a more sophisticated eye to them. It is the deep discussion that the best picturebooks inspire in older readers that the children's librarian and writer Elaine Moss considers so valuable. In *Picturebooks for Young People*, the third edition of which came out in 1992, she suggests books which explore social and ethical issues and family relationships (Morris, 2009: 8).

In choosing ten picturebooks for older children I have aimed to select examples that encourage discussion and which take children further in the development of their visual literacy (Figure 4.6). This is the age group when the deeper levels of meaning, in postmodern picturebooks, begin to intrigue and catch the imagination.

- *Seven for a Secret* by Laurence Anholt and Jim Copplestone (illus.) (Frances Lincoln)
  This story is told with great skill through letters from a young girl to her grandfather. We learn that Ruby lives in the city as her first letter begins 'Dear Grandpa, It's noisy in the city and I can't sleep'; her grandfather lives in the countryside. The more painful details of their lives are revealed as time moves on.

- *Gregory Cool* by Caroline Binch (Frances Lincoln)
  Gregory has gone to visit his grandparents in Tobago but finds it difficult to adjust to the customs and way of life there in spite of the warmth and kindness people show him. The illustrations, which have a warm and colourful palette, give a tremendous sense of place.

- *Fungus the Bogeyman* by Raymond Briggs (Puffin)
  This graphic picturebook about Fungus and the unsavoury, damp land where the bogeymen live uses language in interesting ways and is full of dark humour. Rather like the characters in Beckett's *Waiting for Godot*, Fungus struggles to find meaning in his life.

- *Her Mother's Face* by Roddy Doyle and Freya Blackwood (illus.) (Scholastic)
  Siobhan's mother died when she was a young child and now, aged ten years, she cannot recall her face. The epiphany comes when she meets a lady in a park who becomes her friend and predicts that Siobhan might see her mother's face again.

- *The Story of Frog Belly Rat Bone* by Timothy B. Ering (Walker)
  The Frog Belly Rat Bone of the title guards some special 'specks' of material from danger until they grow. Modern illustrations and the spiky hand lettering make the book distinctive. There is much to think and talk about here, including the symbolism in the tale and its unusual format.

- *The Colour of Home* by Mary Hoffman and Karin Littlewood (Frances Lincoln)
  It is hard for Hassan to cope with memories of his homeland. In his paintings the sunny colours of happier times give way to more recent memories and the blacks and reds of civil war. But he settles down and is eventually able to remember and paint the bright colours of home. This is one of a number of picturebooks from a publisher with an outstanding multicultural list.

- *Babymouse Queen of the World!* by Jennifer Holm and Matthew Holm (HarperCollins)
  Babymouse is bored by the romantic films favoured at Felicia Furrypaws' sleepover. So she joins Wilson the Weasel to watch more adventurous films – fantasies and horror stories. This picturebook, which has an interesting comic-strip format, taps into issues about popular culture and would lead to talk about films, leisure pursuits and friendships.

- *The Rabbits* by John Marsden and Shaun Tan (illus.) (Simply Read Books)
  This book begins with Shaun Tan's picturing of a beautiful landscape of sky and rock where reptiles roam. The threat to the landscape and source of its eventual destruction is an invasion of rabbit-like creatures. Why is the rabbit a symbol of invasion and perhaps possible ecological disaster? There are some deep themes for older primary school children to discuss.

Figure 4.6 *Picturebooks for 8–11-year-olds*

- *Sweets* by Sylvia Van Ommen, translated from Dutch by Sylvia Van Ommen and Neal Hoskins (Winged Chariot Press)
  Oscar the Rabbit texts his friend Josh the Cat and asks him to meet him in the park. Things take a philosophical turn when they wonder: 'Is there a heaven?' So fears and puzzles are mulled over between two close friends. The book's interesting format and references to Dutch culture will interest older readers.

- *Rose Blanche* by Ian McEwan and Roberto Innocenti (Red Fox)
  Rose lives in a German village during the Second World War. She follows a truck which stops behind a barbed wire fence where there are hungry looking children. Rose brings them food, but knows instinctively that she must not even tell her family about what she has seen. A spare text is accompanied by haunting pictures in a grey and brown palette; the book has an uncertain ending.

- *Varmints* by Helen Ward and Marc Craste (illus.) (Templar)
  This plea to think about the impact of changes to the environment starts with an image of calm and stillness. 'There was once only the sound of bees and the wind in the wiry grass, the low murmurings of moles in the cool dark earth.' The spare but poetic text is in hand lettering. Wonderful verbal images – the buildings 'scratch the sky' after 'they', the Varmints, come and spoil the peace. When the creatures peer out from the undergrowth we find a touch of Manga style in the illustrations.

Figure 4.6 *continued*

Figure 4.7
Front cover of Rose Blanche *by Ian McEwan and Roberto Innocenti (illus.)*
Reproduced with the permission of the publishers The Random House Group Ltd

Figure 4.8
Front cover of Varmints *by Helen Ward and Marc Craste (illus.)*
Published by Templar Publishing, an imprint of The Templar Company plc (www.templar publishing.co.uk). Illustration copyright Marc Craste. Text copyright Helen Ward

WORDLESS PICTUREBOOKS, CLASSIC PICTUREBOOKS AND PICTUREBOOKS BY NEW ILLUSTRATORS

The following three lists of suggestions aim to help teachers choose a variety of picturebooks for the classroom.

Wordless picturebooks

Wordless picturebooks have an important role in the development of visual literacy. They often transcend age and ability and are accessible to those speaking any language. They encourage

- *Up and Down* by Shirley Hughes (Red Fox)
  A little girl longs to be able to fly and, to her parents' alarm, she gets her wish. She has wonderful exhilarating experiences shown in energetic pictures. Children enjoy her daring adventures vicariously.

- *The Red Book* by Barbara Lehman (Houghton Miffin Harcourt)
  A young girl lives in a snowy city. One day she finds a book on the street and discovers in it a world very different from the one she has experienced. The evocative illustrations show the new world she has entered.

- *Black on White* by Tana Hoban (William Morrow)
  This sturdy board book will appeal to children at the start of the nursery age range. The series of black objects and animals, including a leaf, an elephant, a child and a fish, are each on a white background and this helps sharpen experience of shape.

- *Bow-Wow Bugs a Bug* by Mark Newgarden and Megan Montague Cash (illus.) (Walker)
  Here is a hugely entertaining graphic story for very young children. It has a touch of the surreal; we learn in the picture narrative that a yellow dog is confronted by a larger version of himself. The dogs are preoccupied by catching bugs. For a look at the cartoon approach in the books and to try some games, see www.bow-wowbooks.com.

- *Sunshine; Moonlight* by Jan Omerod (Frances Lincoln)
  These two classic wordless picturebooks show a family's morning and evening routines. *Sunshine* has a wonderfully bright palette: a series of small pictures home in on a little girl waking up as the sunlight streams through her window. She sits up and begins to read a book. *Moonlight* shows the family's evening routine of dinner, bath and then settling for the night. These universal activities are a good starting point for children's reflections.

- *The Arrival* by Shaun Tan (Lothian)
  This sombre graphic picturebook, for children aged ten or more, uses imaginative and detailed artwork to give a personal record of one person's journey to seek refuge in a new country. The sadness of leaving home and the difficulties of adjustment to new customs and realities are powerfully shown.

Figure 4.9 *Wordless picturebooks*

creative tellings, which can vary at each reading, and lead to close involvement and talk. Some of those suggested in Figure 4.9 could be offered to any age group.

Classic picturebooks

There were some hard choices to be made in selecting the books to include in all of the lists that are in this chapter – but none harder than those made here. All the books I have chosen have stood the test of time and have enduring qualities which we can see in their appeal over more than one generation. For reasons of space I have not annotated them, but offer the titles as a basis for discussion. These books are, in my view, part of our shared culture and every child should have the chance to enjoy them. They are: *The Jolly Postman or Other People's Letters* by Janet and Allan Ahlberg; *Mister Magnolia* by Quentin Blake; *The Tunnel* by Anthony Browne; *Granpa, Mr Gumpy's Outing* and *Oi! Get Off This Train* by John Burningham; *The Very Hungry Caterpillar* by Eric Carle; *Rosie's Walk* by Pat Hutchins; *The Tiger that Came to Tea* by Judith Kerr; *Not Now, Bernard* by David McKee; *Peace at Last* by Jill Murphy; *The Tale of Peter Rabbit* by Beatrix Potter and *Where the Wild Things Are* by Maurice Sendak.

Picturebooks by new illustrators

New illustrators use a fascinating array of styles, designs and formats. Many achieve their visual 'voice' by combining traditional media – oil paint, watercolour, crayon, pastel and collage – with digital manipulation in interesting ways (Figure 4.10).

USING PICTUREBOOKS

Understanding picturebooks, particularly the contemporary kind, involves filling the gap between the experience and understanding readers bring to a text and what they find there. It is this struggle that helps achieve what Iser calls 'a more or less organised imaginative experience' (Iser, 1978: 25). As Meek and others have shown so convincingly, the texts themselves teach much (Meek, 1988). Just looking at rich and interesting picturebooks, the sort where we find intellectual excitement converges with aesthetic pleasure, begins this reading journey (Arizpe and Styles, 2003: 21). How can teachers help? The role that reading picturebooks aloud can play, and how carefully planned and organized talk, drama, art and writing can help, is now considered first with reference to younger children and then to older ones.

Younger children

Reading aloud: where and when?

Where the youngest children are concerned, the most usual place for reading and talking about picturebooks is in the carpet area with the whole class. The social aspect is important because it is when children share imaginary experiences that they grow together as a community of young readers and listeners (Chambers, 1991: 57).

34

- *Penguin* by Polly Dunbar (Walker)

  Ben receives Penguin for his birthday but throws a tantrum when his toy will not speak. When a lion eats up the noisy boy, Penguin bites him on the nose and Ben falls out of the lion's mouth. Will young children be alarmed when Ben is eaten? I doubt it – in my experience they ask for the dramatic pages to be read and looked at again and again. This illustrator loves creating picturebooks for the very youngest children because 'their eyes are still wide open' (www.booktrustchildrensbooks.org.uk, accessed 30 April 2009).

- *Biscuit Bear* by Mini Grey (Random House)

  The chaos of toddler Horace's baking day is shown by scanned-in pictures of fingerprint and coffee stains. Mini Grey's playfulness with materials echoes the cooking experiments of the young child. Like all good books for the very young this one is far from cosy: it is sad when the family dog eats Biscuit Bear's friends.

- *Lost and Found* by Oliver Jeffers (HarperCollins)

  This book is a sequel to *How to Catch a Star* and the main character is the same young boy, whose thoughts and feelings come through so effectively through words and pictures.

- *Calm Down Boris* by Sam Lloyd, edited by Stella Gurney (Templar)

  Boris seems to lack a certain sensitivity to the feelings of others. For one thing he smothers people in kisses whether they like it or not. The pictures are in comic book style and the text runs all over the pages, echoing Boris' exuberance. There is a big furry mouth at the start of the book, which delights toddlers.

- *Whale* by David Lucas (Andersen Press)

  A beached whale is helped by the townspeople, who sing a rain song so that he can float away. In return the whale helps the people to rebuild the town, which he had squashed, with the help of nature – the sun and the wind – into something even better than before. Older readers will continue to reflect on the symbolism of the whale, its environment and its actions.

- *Small Mouse Big City* by Simon Prescott (Little Tiger Press)

  Simon Prescott uses a clear but light line and a palette of mostly soft watercolours in this version of Aesop's fable. Country Mouse is overwhelmed by the city but is rescued by Town Mouse, who tries to impress him with its advantages by taking him to galleries and cheese shops.

- *Dirty Bertie* by David Roberts (Little Tiger Press)

  This is the first in a series of deliciously 'rude' books about Dirty Bertie who delights in unsociable sounds and smells. Children find the book hilarious and join in with the refrain 'That's dirty, Bertie'. The cartoon-like illustrations are distinctive – Bertie has a large head and goggling eyes – and detailed – there are tiny Lego-men hiding in Granny's tea-cup.

- *Dexter Bexley and the Big Blue Beastie* by Joel Stewart (Doubleday)

  Dexter finds co-operation and friendship turn out to be the best solution to a monster's boredom. Comic strip is used in new and interesting ways with traditional materials and digital input. Best of all, Beastie springs off the page with his fierce blue hue.

Figure 4.10 *Picturebooks by new illustrators*

It adds zest and interest if children hear stories read in different places, including outdoors; stories like Rosen and Oxenbury's *We're Going on a Bear Hunt* and Eric Carle's *The Very Hungry Caterpillar* benefit from being read on a grassy area in the school grounds or garden. Some schools have become adventurous in seeking imaginative settings for reading stories; these include sleepovers in libraries, taking sleeping bags and soft toys to listen to stories like Martin Waddell's *Can't You Sleep Little Bear?* and *Peace at Last*. Most children could also cope with being just a little frightened within a controlled situation like a sleepover, and so some stories at the gentler end of 'scary' – Tom Maddox's *Fergus's Scary Night* and Jessica Souhami's *In the Dark, Dark Wood*, for example – could be included. Marian Whitehead urges us to read aloud spontaneously sometimes and to avoid 'just using the end of sessions when children are tired and families are arriving to collect them' (Whitehead, 2004: 162).

Using picturebooks which encourage 'joining in' and picturebooks to make sense of experience

Quite a lot of picturebooks for the very youngest children reflect this age group's need for the repetition that they find in songs and action rhymes. Every nursery class has a collection of these. Dale Penny has rung the changes with her sing-along story *The Boy on the Bus*, which can be sung to the familiar 'The Wheels on the Bus' tune. A boy drives a bus along a country road, stopping from time to time to collect animals. The growing list of animals and the sounds that they make are repeated and, of course, as well as being fun, this repetition is an aid to memory. Children are helped to join in by lyrical Caribbean speech rhythms in *So Much* by Helen Oxenbury. In all these books, the pictures are a guide to action. Other books which encourage 'saying aloud' are those in Emma Chichester Clark's Melrose and Clark series, and Lucy Cousin's Maisie books, for example the lift-the-flap book *Maisie Goes to Bed*.

Picturebooks also help children to make sense of everyday life. So reading Shirley Hughes' *Dogger* might remind a child of when they lost a precious toy. It works the other way around too: a child living through the experience of losing a toy may remember hearing *Dogger* read. This is from 'text to life' and 'life to text' in action. Tony Ross' *I Want to Go Home* taps into so many children's experience of moving house, and the anxieties associated with this; then it shows the positive side by revealing the differences between a mere dwelling and a home.

Wanting a pet is a well-known childhood yearning. Lauren Child's *I Want a Pet* is in big book format as well as small and ideal for sharing and discussing in the nursery and Reception class.

Stories based on fantastic happenings can sometimes be the best ones to illuminate human behaviour and experience. I find children talk a lot about John Burningham's *The Magic Bed* and not least about how to cope constructively with people's ill considered actions which affect us deeply. And so these 'creative supposings' link books with life and life with books (Whitehead, 2004: 141).

Resources for using picturebooks

What Marian Whitehead calls 'literature-enhanced play areas' can be the settings for listening and looking at picturebooks, talking about them and improvising around the themes. So the home corner can be transformed into Sendak's land in *Where the Wild Things Are* with the help of a frieze and a makeshift boat. Or a 'classroom' setting could be created with a flip-chart, lunch box and soft toy cats and a mouse to create a background for the reading of Rob Scotton's *Splat the Cat*. This not only encourages involved comment and questions but also role play and improvised drama.

A resource found in many lively classrooms is the story box, a box or bag containing items to accompany reading, and which can add interest and sometimes a *frisson*. I have a set of Steiff owls which work with several stories, not least Martin Waddell's *Baby Owls*. When she reads Helen Cooper's *Pumpkin Soup* Marian Whitehead brings out a soup ladle and a big pot. *Ouch! I Need a Plaster* by Nick Sharratt, about a nurse with ten plasters to give to children who have hurt themselves, can be enlivened if the children are given some plasters to put on their own toys. Worth considering, too, are story sacks normally containing a book, an audiotape version and a storyboard. These are available commercially or can be assembled by the teaching team.

Drama and role play

Some of the liveliest lessons I have seen over the years have been where the teacher takes up the role of a character from a story. Picturebook characters and plots lend themselves well to this sort of drama, as Case Study 4.1 suggests. Sendak's *Where the Wild Things Are* has universal imaginative appeal and so it is not surprising that reading it often leads to satisfying improvised drama. Colleen Johnson describes the work of a Year 2 teacher who takes on the role of a senior 'wild thing' to inspire creative reflection on the story. She gathers the children around her and says how much she misses Max now he has gone. The children say what they liked about Max – his sense of humour and his kindness. Then the children act

---

CASE STUDY 4.1 ROLE PLAY AROUND *BURGLAR BILL* BY ALLAN AND JANET AHLBERG (PUFFIN)

A Reception class had listened to a reading of *Burglar Bill*; the teacher and her student decided to extend reflection and enjoyment through role play. So, just before lunch one day, the teacher told the children that a visitor was coming to their classroom to talk to them that very afternoon.

The teacher settled the children, put out a chair and then brought in 'Burglar Betty', who was, of course, the student dressed in the sort of clothes that Betty wears in the book. The children entered into the role play with great seriousness and the comments came thick and fast: 'I didn't know burglars liked babies', 'I liked it when you gave the things back to the people', 'A burglar took some things out of our shed'. Questions were direct and thoughtful too: 'What is the baby called?', 'Have you given all the things back now?', 'How can you stop people stealing things?'

The role play created a space for the children to assimilate aspects of the story they found fascinating and stimulated their own thoughts. Of course they knew their visitor was really the student, but they 'suspended disbelief' in a rather mature way.

out scenes in pairs showing Max being kind or playful (Johnson in Fisher and Williams, 2004: 62–7). The children were able to say in a later discussion how Max, a human boy, was different from a wild thing. These insights came from looking at the pictures, reading the text and reflecting on them both. Improvisation can take children beyond the end of the picturebook story. So, for example, Max could make a return visit to the land of the wild things, or some of the wild things could visit Max.

Younger children's writing and artwork

Art, craft and writing can be combined when children aged about three to five years respond to a picturebook. Making a storybox scene in a cardboard box can be extended by writing signs and labels. Novelty books often inspire children's own creations. A book like *Calm Down Boris* by Sam Lloyd, with the huge hairy mouth on the cover, amuses young children hugely. They can be helped to make their own 'mouths' with furry material and felt pens and write their annotations. Designing a page about a favourite picturebook character with drawings and writing, perhaps in speech bubbles, is a first step towards multimodal work.

Children in the 5–8 age range are able to write short scripts to go with storybox scenes based on a picturebook. After hearing picturebooks read over a period of time some children are able to write their own multimodal book taking on the idea of visual jokes. Seven-year-old Grace, for example, used a recurring hand as a cohesive device in her picturebook. The teacher considered the books of Anthony Browne had played an important part in how Grace was able to use pictures to tell a story (Bearne, 2009).

Other books which show how visually adventurous picturebooks can be include those in Lauren Child's Charlie and Lola series. Print can be exciting too. After talking about how size, strength and orientation of print can emphasize parts of a story, children could handwrite or use templates for different kinds of print or use the computer to achieve interesting graphic effects in their own creations.

Interesting designs and formats appeal to many children in this age range and books like, for example, Emily Gravett's *Big Book of Fears* can be the inspiration for diary writing. Children could be asked to write an illustrated 'Day in the Life of Little Mouse'.

Older children

Reading picturebooks aloud is still important

Shared reading and talk about a picturebook of depth and quality remains valuable. In their classroom-based research project exploring the relationship between reading and writing for children between age eight and eleven, Myra Barrs and Valerie Cork noted that reading texts aloud enabled children 'to attend more closely to the language of the text'. They were able to attend to language patterns partly because reading aloud slows down the reading experience as compared with silent reading, which can be rapid (Barrs and Cork, 2001: 39). Sharing a picturebook leads to reflecting on the complementary roles of pictures and written text in the narrative.

Shared reading can lead to deep discussion

The balance between being entertained and being moved to deep thinking varies but some picturebooks have elements of both these dimensions and have the power to get older primary children thinking about important issues. Anthony Browne's *Piggybook* has flashes of dark humour alongside the serious point it makes about exploitation and selfishness. The chaos into which the father pig and the two sons descend once the mother has left has a grimly funny side and children notice the ironic comment about the 'important' jobs that these males do.

Some picturebooks are moving and troubling and these are best offered not to the whole class but to a group or an individual or even just placed in the school library for children to find for themselves. I think Rosen and Blake's *The Sad Book*, Anholt and Coplestone's *Seven for a Secret*, Ian McEwan's *Rose Blanche* and *Erika's Story* all probably come into this category.

As well as exploring the themes, plot and characters in picturebooks older children will have become more able to look at and talk about the choices and strategies used by the author/illustrator to get their meaning across.

CASE STUDY 4.2 TALKING ABOUT SAD AND SENSITIVE ISSUES RAISED IN A PICTUREBOOK: *ERIKA'S STORY* BY RUTH VANDER ZEE AND ROBERTO INNOCENTI (ILLUS.) (JONATHAN CAPE)

A group of six nine-year-olds listened to a reading of this picturebook based on the true story of Erika, a Jewish baby, who survived against the odds in the Second World War. She did so because her mother threw her from the train that was taking her family and many others to a concentration camp. She fell on soft grass and was discovered by a woman who became her adoptive mother. This book tells her story through a succinct but powerful written text and affecting pictures. The children made the following points in their discussion:

- The writing is spare but every word counts.
- The first page is stark and shocking as Erika did not know the name her biological parents had called her or her date of birth.
- The small pink bundle shown being thrown from the train – a bright area in an otherwise dark palette – was a symbol of hope.
- She had been lucky to have a kind adoptive family but not knowing about her true identity was still difficult to live with.
- A train passed through the countryside within sight of the adult Erika's cottage but a train could never be a neutral thing for her. The illustrator has somehow conveyed this.

BOX 4.2 *CHILDREN READING PICTURES* **BY E. ARIZPE AND M. STYLES: THE REPORT OF A RESEARCH STUDY (ROUTLEDGE FALMER)**

Arizpe and Styles began their research with this question: how do children of different ages between four and eleven respond to the same three classic picturebooks?

The books used were *On A Walk with Lily* by Satoshi Kitamura, and *Zoo* and *The Tunnel*, both by Anthony Browne.

The study took place in seven primary schools in different catchment areas. In-depth, semi-structured interviews were carried out with two boys and two girls from three classes in each school: early years, lower primary and upper primary. The researchers found that modern children are sophisticated readers of visual texts often able to integrate meanings from pictures and writing, understand different viewpoints, interpret visual jokes, tune into the moods and feelings of characters and make a personal response.

The main findings have strong implications for classroom practice: repeated reading of the same picturebooks helps refine children's construction of meaning; listening carefully to children is crucial in understanding their responses; articulating their understandings and viewpoints through talk and making their own drawings helps children to make progress in reading visual texts.

Drama

Like younger ones, older children benefit from the interactive way of working that drama makes possible. The thoughtful, exploratory and collaborative nature of improvisation can help illuminate the enigmatic even puzzling aspects of some picturebook stories. Improvisation involves three overlapping elements: the planning, the performance and the evaluation.

The initial discussion normally includes how the character would sound and how they would communicate non-verbally through gesture and facial expression. Then when a picturebook story is being dramatized, the visual aspects of the enactment are especially important. So, for example, how would the picturebook characters stand, move and relate to each other? Returning regularly to the text and pictures for clues is essential. The evaluation of each other's work within the performance would address questions like: how successfully were the characters brought alive? Was the language used appropriate and might improvements be made – adding language from the text? Are there points in the drama where non-verbal communication like facial expression, gesture and actions could have more impact? Has doing the drama alerted the children to the main themes of the picturebook and could how these thread through the enactment be strengthened? If the improvisation has been enacted in groups, constructive response from the 'audience', both other children and teacher, is an enjoyable part of the work.

Some of the devices of drama can be particularly helpful when they are used to explore a text. Bringing to life a picturebook's themes where the written text may be succinct means elaborating on what the characters may be thinking. Here a character can use soliloquy to share these thoughts or a narrator could speak while the character mimed. Frame freezing – freezing a key part of the improvisation – and hot seating – asking children to answer questions in role – can also be helpful.

Drama is a powerful medium to explore the imagined world of a picturebook. For example, understanding of the themes of abandonment and resourcefulness in Quentin Blake's *Clown* can be achieved through improvisation and script writing.

Older children's writing and artwork

Inspired and informed by picturebooks they have read and talked about, older children can make their own books, designing pages, using simple paper engineering like pop-ups and pull-outs and creating the visual jokes. By experimenting they will learn about the choices to be made: about the design of the writing on the page and whether to use hand lettering or particular typefaces and orientations and whether to have a comic book or traditional format.

Increasingly, teachers and support staff are becoming skilled enough to help children with film-making. Possible projects include making a film script and then short film of a picturebook story for an audience of younger children in the school.

Children still enjoy and learn from making storyboxes during this age span; a student teacher helped children make some atmospheric scenes together with scripts improvising on Anthony Browne's surrealist picturebook *The Tunnel*.

CASE STUDY 4.3 NINE-YEAR-OLDS USE A PICTUREBOOK AS INSPIRATION FOR THEIR OWN WRITING: *DIARY OF A WOMBAT* BY JACKIE FRENCH AND BRUCE WHATLEY (ILLUS.) (HARPERCOLLINS)

Lively discussion followed reading and the children were clearly amused by the wombat's relationship with its 'pets' – the humans who cared for it. The children wrote their own 'Week in the life of . . .' illustrated journals, choosing hamsters, guinea-pigs, hedgehogs, goldfish and rabbits. Even the more reluctant writers responded enthusiastically, showing they could write in an entertaining way and use visual humour too. Some children write best if they are given a structure, but one which is loose enough to allow for their creativity. (See Figure 4.11.)

ASSESSING AND RECORDING PROGRESS

In the case of younger children, their talk, writing and drawing reveal what they can understand about a character. We know their grip on unfolding plot is developing when they begin to have expectations about what might happen as the story proceeds. Sensitivity to the mood of a particular picturebook, whether it is a sad, nostalgic story or one full of playfulness and humour, often comes out in discussion. And developing preferences for particular books is a sign of increasing maturity. Above all, it is reading picturebooks which moves children on in their visual literacy. So we look for children's understandings of what the pictures tell us and

'The Diary of a Cat'

Jenna 9 years.

THE DIARY OF A CAT

MONDAY

I woke up on my lovely bed. I drank some milk and ate some of my food. A giant came up to me and picked me up. I hate it when they do that so I scratched him and ran through the square cut out the door. When I went outside I saw another cat and we started to play. After that I went back through the square-shaped thing in the door and went to bed.

TUESDAY

I went through the square thing in the door and figured out how to get onto the shed roof. I slept there in the sun all day. I woke up with a giant in front of me! The Giant picked me up and took me into the house. I was thinking about scratching him but he put me in my bed so I purred to say thank you.

WEDNESDAY

Slept all day in my bed. I couldn't be bothered to go up onto the shed roof today. I don't like rain it makes my fur all wet.

THURSDAY

I saw the giant near my bed. He had my ball and I thought he wanted to play with me but he kept on picking me up and throwing the ball away. I got bored of that so I just went to sleep.

FRIDAY

Felt ill today so slept. After all, it had been a very busy week for me!

Part of a very long 'Diary of a Guinea-Pig'

James 9 years.

Friday

Morning: Ate carrots. Went to the vets, sharp thing poked me in my tummy. It HURT!

Afternoon: Slept, Slept, Slept, snored until giant paw poked me.

Evening: Went for a check-up at the vets, said that I would have some babies, one boy, two girls.

Night: Slept carefully, snored.

Both these accounts are fluent and show good control over the narrative. Jenna's word-processed piece reminds me of Anne Fine's *The Diary of a Killer Cat*; she manages to sustain the role well and includes flashes of humour.

The other piece, 'Diary of a Guinea-Pig', is multimodal, using a combination of design, illustration and language to communicate clearly and entertainingly. The little pictures of the vet's needle and the hand are integrated into the text. The 'zzzs' to show snoring and the use of capitals for emphasis both show the influence of the modern picturebook and comic strip.

Figure 4.11 *Two 'pet' diaries*

what writing does best. Ways of thinking about how to assess and record this are being developed (Bearne, 2009). Early years specialists call these signs of progress 'critical moments' or, as Marian Whitehead suggests, 'breakthroughs of understanding' (Whitehead, 2004: 232).

So what sort of 'critical moments' do we look for when it comes to older primary school children? Older children who have been fortunate enough to read and share picturebooks regularly will be increasingly able to tune into the deeper layers of meaning that lie in the best picturebooks. Teachers note examples of where children infer meanings from things hinted at in text or picture. By the later primary years children will be becoming more aware of both the cultural knowledge readers bring to their reading and intertextuality. We know a 'critical moment' is coming up when children say something like 'This reminds me of that other book . . .' They will also, with encouragement, discover the patterns and connections which Aidan Chambers writes of (Chambers, 1993). It is in these later years, too, that children will have some understanding of the choices picturebook creators make about design and format and how these affect quality and interest.

All of these things have a place in the 'picturebook' section of a child's English, language and literacy folder or portfolio. Keeping such a folder in print or electronic form is compatible with an approach to assessment that emphasizes formative aspects, aspects that show 'progress in development'. So we might include some brief transcripts of a child responding in a group, some annotated writing and drawing samples and some photographs of drama or displays.

SUMMARY

- The children's picturebook has found its place as a valued cultural form.
- All possible topics are covered: everyday experiences, exciting adventures, imaginative fantasies and retellings of traditional tales; the range of design and media used is vast.
- Picturebooks make for enjoyable but demanding reading as children have to relate their 'non-linear' reading of the pictures to the linear processing of the words.
- The best picturebooks can be a push towards literacy because children experience a distinctive narrative rhythm and become able to predict what might happen next while being ready to be surprised.
- It is often said that some contemporary picturebooks are 'multilayered' and can be read at different levels. It is wise, therefore, to be flexible about recommending particular books to children by age criteria.
- Picturebooks often rely on young readers' cultural knowledge; familiarity of traditional tales, for example, helps appreciation of intertexuality.
- The contemporary, postmodern picturebook is 'metafictive': it encourages the reader to reflect on the nature of fiction and its conventions, sometimes by playing with or turning those conventions on their head.
- Picturebooks draw on and help develop children's visual literacy.
- Response to and appreciation of all that the picturebook genre offers can be developed and honed by shared reading, talk, drama, writing, book-making and artwork.
- A record-keeping system that emphasizes formative assessment is most likely to enrich future planning and therefore support progress.

43

Chapter 5

Traditional tales
Folk and fairy tales; myths, creation
stories and legends; parables and fables

INTRODUCTION

The term 'traditional tales' refers to that huge treasury of ancient stories from many cultures and traditions which have come down to us, first orally and then through written forms, through many generations. They tell us about universal and enduring aspects of human nature both at its best and at its worst, and they help children learn about what is feared or valued in their own and other cultures. They are rich, too, in metaphor and symbolism, which are the nourishers of that inner world of the imagination which is so important to the well-being of the developing child. As Judith Elkin comments: 'A story which has lived for hundreds if not thousands of years must possess a vitality which is imperishable and immutable' (Elkin, 1983: 10). In his essay 'Myth and Legend', Maurice Saxby comments on the fragility of the line between myth, legend and folk tale, suggesting that 'the more generic term "traditional literature" is ultimately more reliable and useful' (Saxby in Hunt, 2004: 258). Becoming familiar with them paves the way for 'the future delights of fantasy to come' (Melling, 2002: 9).

There are literally hundreds of books of traditional tales for sale. So how do teachers select from so many? Elizabeth Cook's *The Ordinary and the Fabulous* (1971) and Mary Steele's Signal Book guide *Traditional Tales* (second edition 1989) both have a deserved place on my bookshelf, but books go out of print and new ones appear and so the publication of Booktrust's *Folk and Fairy Tales: A Book Guide* by Deborah Hallford and Edgardo Zaghini in 2005 was welcome. For an historical account which explores whether 'the authenticity and the art of the storyteller' can be preserved in fairy tales published today, you cannot do better than read Brian Alderson's article 'Fairy Tales in the New Millennium' in *Books For Keeps* (Alderson, 2001).

Getting the best out of traditional tales requires readers and listeners to enter worlds which have their own rules and customs. When they do so young imaginations are stretched. Curiosity is encouraged, too, as many of the tales seem to be saying 'What if?' Teachers hope for a creative response from the children as it arises from the independent thinking and imagining that are a mark of a developing critical reader.

CRITERIA FOR CHOOSING

The qualities we look for in choosing traditional tales for the classroom are gathered here under design, language and illustration but with an eye for those with a special appeal for the imagination.

Design

No one wants a collection of books which stick to a particular design or formula, however praiseworthy it may be. So, we seek books of traditional tales for the library or classroom collection that are varied in size, in the patterning of the images and of the text on the page and in the use of print and graphics. The quality and impact of the cover will affect whether or not children take up the book in the first place and so it should be arresting and give a good idea of what the book is about. Clear print is necessary, particularly for newly independent readers. Big format books have a valued place in the collection for reading aloud to younger children, but small formats like Ladybird's First Tales are liked by many younger children starting to read on their own. Teachers have to keep an eye on cost, but children appreciate having just a few sumptuous books in the collection, books which are a delight to pick up because of their shiny covers, silky white pages, decorated end pages and illuminated letters. Carol Ann Duffy's large format fairy tale *The Princess' Blankets* is an example here.

Language

A storyteller in the oral tradition sets the scene for the tale and uses gesture and facial expression as well as words to convey the nature of the characters and the excitement, tension or passion of the story. Writers have only words to beguile and interest. The best keep something of the oral storyteller's dramatic skills. Kevin Crossley-Holland draws in listeners or readers with the opening words of 'The Sea-Woman' in his collection *The Magic Lands*: 'It was an empty, oyster-and-pearl afternoon. The water lapped at the sand and sorted the shingle and lapped round the rock where the girl was sitting'.

Powerful expressions of passion and feeling make the tale live in the imagination too. When the Sea-woman cries out, 'Oh! The moon's edge and a mother's ache was in that cry', we understand the depth of her anguish and yearning.

The skill of the translator is another consideration. Two well-regarded translators of fairy tales and legends are Naomi Lewis and Brian Alderson. Lyrical 'voices' like those of these scholars and storytellers need to have a strong place in the collection. But there is room, too, for modern 'popular culture' tellings with their cartoon strips and speech balloons. Marcia Williams, who has a keen ear for the rhythms of language, reaches many young readers through lively modern tellings in, for example, her books *Greek Myths* and *King Arthur and the Knights of the Round Table*. Then there are the postmodern fairy tales, the best of which use language and illustration to tease, twist and often satirize traditional fairy tales in amusing ways. I'm thinking here of the work of Allan and Janet Ahlberg and Jon Scieska and, more recently, of Mini Grey and Lauren Child.

Illustration

Brian Alderson finds some of today's illustrations over-elaborate and refers to the comment of the editor of *Books For Keeps* that some of the fanciest were rather reminiscent of expensive wrapping paper! The audience of the storytellers of long ago 'had the good fortune to be able to imagine for themselves our hero falling into the frumity and suchlike' (Alderson,

45

2001). He reminds us that when first written down, traditional tales were often illustrated by woodcuts with scenes and characters generalized enough to allow the viewer to use their imagination to fill out the picture. However, some artists in each new generation of children's book illustrators like to take on the challenge of making pictures for traditional tales. Sometimes a new eye on an old tale brings refreshing insight and food for thought. Stars over recent decades have been Nick Sharratt (*Red Riding Hood*), Anthony Browne (*Hansel and Gretel*), Bee Willey (*Indian Myths*), Tony Ross (*Zeus Conquers the Titans*), Charlotte Voake (*The Best of Aesop's Fables*), Brian Wildsmith (*The Lion and the Rat*), Gerald McDermot (*Anansi the Spider*) and Adrienne Kennaway (*Rainbow Bird*). Of course personal taste comes into this. I like Christina Balit's ornate, jewel-like pictures in Robert Leeson's *My Sister Shahrazad: Tales from the Arabian Nights*. Nevertheless a good selection of traditional tales calls out for the inclusion of the work of long established artists, artists who have enchanted more than one generation of children. I would choose two artists in this category – Arthur Rackham and Charles Keeping.

The manner in which a story is illustrated affects the way a child construes the story (Lewis, 2001: 68). Where a tale is a modern fairy or folk tale or a parody of an old one, modern dress and recognizable contemporary objects are appropriate. On the other hand it has become a tradition to show French fairy-tale characters in the eighteenth-century dress typical of the time when they were first written down. Elizabeth Cook notes that Hans Andersen's characters, too, usually wear the dress of the time of their writing, commenting, however, that the artist he chose, Vilhelm Pedersen, shows the dress 'in a simplified form (of it) which is subtly timeless'. Cook praises those illustrators selected by Andrew Lang for his Fairy Books series, artists who 'concocted a pseudo-medieval, psuedo-classical kind of drapery that suited these traditional stories perfectly' and suggest a timeless past (Cook, 1971: 53).

BOX 5.1 SOME VIEWS ABOUT WHY WE READ STORIES

According to Christopher Booker in *The Seven Basic Plots* (Booker, 2004) every story can be placed under the following story themes:

- Overcoming the Monster
- Rags to Riches
- The Quest
- Voyage and Return
- Comedy
- Tragedy
- Rebirth.

Neil Philip, however, takes issue with Booker because he believes story is not mainly to do with plot but that 'the essence of story is metaphor' (Philip, 2008: 10) . 'Great storytelling', he goes on, 'is a web that entraps the reader – or listener, or viewer – inside the tale, and then offers a way out of it, enlarged and renewed'. The best provide an imaginative experience which can change and mature a young reader.

FOLK AND FAIRY TALES

What is the difference between a folk and a fairy tale when there is much overlap in the way the terms are used and both come to us from ancient oral traditions? John Rowe Townsend argues that 'folk' refers to a tale's origin while 'fairy' is to do with its nature (Townsend, 1995: 7). Here I have tended to apply the term 'folk' to stories about the trials and tribulations of ordinary people and to some stories featuring animals with human traits. Fairy tales can be seen as a group of stories falling within the bigger folk tale category. But fairy tales are always threaded through with enchantment, and are peopled by magical folk: fairy godmothers, witches, elves, sprites, goblins and suchlike. So a particular folk tale may or may not be also a fairy tale.

Folk tales

Folk tales tend to come from a particular culture or community and reveal the values, fears and customs of particular people living in a particular place at a particular time. *Breaking the Magic Spell: Radical Theories of Folk Tales and Fairy Tales* by Jack Zipes has greatly contributed to our knowledge and understanding of the origins and meaning of folk and fairy tales. Here he writes of 'a time when folk tales were part of communal property and told with fantastic insights by gifted storytellers who gave vent to the frustrations of the common people and embodied their needs and wishes in the folk narrative' (Zipes, 2002a: 10). The books in Figure 5.1 are just a few of those many available which I believe to be of quality and which range across cultures and communities.

Fairy tales

Magic is a defining feature of a fairy tale, which is often peopled by magical folk like gnomes, elves, witches, wizards, giants, ogres, sprites and fairies. They are to do with quests, wishes and challenges, and can be about 'a reversal of fortune, often with a rags-to-riches plot that culminates in a wedding' (Bottigheimer in Hunt, 2004: 261). You will find fairy stories about transformation, reflecting a very human desire to escape from an unsatisfying existence into a better one. In *The Fairies in Tradition and Literature*, Katharine Briggs writes about fairies mentioned in medieval manuscripts, some only half an inch high, and the human sized fairies in the work of Shakespeare (Briggs, 2002).

This kind of traditional tale is typically a written version of an oral folk tale, as we know from the collections of Charles Perrault and the Grimm brothers. The themes found in fairy tales and their symbols and metaphors are persistent and this must surely mean that they tell us much that is universal in human thinking and feeling. There follow some comments on the work of two of the many contributors to the debate about the meaning and value of fairy tales, Bruno Bettleheim and Jack Zipes.

Bruno Bettleheim

In his book *The Uses of Enchantment: The Meaning and Importance of Fairy Tales* Bruno Bettleheim presents a psychoanalyst's view of the significance of fairy tales. Children, he argues, have

47

- *The Troll* by Julia Donaldson and David Roberts (Macmillan)
  Children at the nursery or Reception stage will enjoy this story about a troll's search for a meal of billy-goat. David Roberts pictures him as fierce looking with sharp teeth and yellow eyes.

- *The Gingerbread Man; Three Billy Goats Gruff; The Three Little Pigs* by A. Macdonald (ed.) and Anja Rieger (illus.) (Ladybird)
  The artwork is lively and bright and the large print would suit beginning readers.

- *Mama Panya's Pancakes: A Village Tale from Kenya* by Mary and Richard Chamberlain and Julia Cairns (illus.) (Barefoot Books)
  Mama Panya's son, Adika, invites everyone to a pancake party. But how will Mama Panya provide for so many? This is a spirit-lifting tale about resourcefulness and sharing.

- *The Magic Lands: Folk Tales of Britain and Ireland* by Kevin Crossley-Holland and Emma Chichester Clark (illus.) (Orion Children's Books)
  In this collection, which includes 'The Sea-Woman', 'The Lambton Worm' and 'The Green Children', the tales are told with a lyrical 'voice'. The excellent notes on the origin of the fifty-five different tales are helpful to teachers of older primary school children.

- *Swedish Folk Tales* translated by Holger Lundburgh and John Bauer (illus.) (Floris Books)
  This lively collection of folk tales has illustrations of remote and wild scenery full of mountains, lakes and trees and of darkness and light.

- *The Brothers Grimm: Popular Folk Tales* by Jacob Grimm and Wilhelm Grimm, translated by Brian Alderson and illustrated by Michael Foreman (Hamish Hamilton)
  The tune and rhythm of oral storytelling beats through these thirty-one stories, which include 'Snow White' and 'Rumpelstiltskin'. They do older primary children the courtesy of not missing out the cruel twists and turns of fate in some of the original tellings.

- *A Bag of Moonshine: Stories from Folklore of England and Wales* by Alan Garner (CollinsVoyager edition)
  Older primary children would enjoy hearing these stories read aloud. They are full of the creatures of folklore and myth associated with the regions from which the stories come.

Figure 5.1 *Folk tales and folk tale collections, roughly in order of challenge*

an inner world of the imagination which is not entirely comfortable. In fact they can have disturbing emotions and ambivalent feelings about those closest to them. The fairy tale helps bring some organization to children's inner life and seems to offer symbolic ways of coping. Entering into the world of magic, wicked stepmothers and quests can create a space within which children can deal with their feelings and concerns as they grow up.

Jack Zipes

Jack Zipes' books are not easy reads, but perseverance is rewarded for here is a scholar who has thought deeply about the meaning and cultural importance of traditional tales. In *Breaking the Magic Spell: Radical Theories of Folk Tales and Fairy Tales*, published in a revised edition in 2002, he examines three main European fairy-tale traditions, those represented by Charles Perrault, Jacob and Wilhelm Grimm and Hans Christian Andersen. He also writes insightfully about the fairy tales and the fairy-tale elements in the work of J.R.R. Tolkien, C.S. Lewis and J.K. Rowling and points out the continuing significant representation of fairy tales in bookshops and school libraries. 'Fairy tales for children are universal, ageless, therapeutic, miraculous and beautiful' (Zipes, 2006b: 1). However, Zipes believes that these products of the human imagination are at risk of becoming both instrumentalized and commercialized and he considers that the important connection between tale and community has sometimes been lost. This puts at risk the power of the tales to shape children's values and behaviour. In his book *Sticks and Stones: The Troublesome Success of Children's Literature from Slovenly Peter to Harry Potter* Zipes explores these concerns further and asks the question: how do children read fairy tales?

In his most recent book *Why Fairy Tales Stick: The Evolution and Relevance of a Genre* Zipes brings new energy and insight to the question of why fairy tales have such cultural and psychological power. The fairy and folk tales of a culture invade the mind and affect how the world is viewed and, indeed, how we take decisions and act within it.

CHOOSING FAIRY TALES

Teachers seek good retellings of fairy tales from different traditions for the central school library. And, in addition, each classroom needs a bookshelf with collections of the stories children are most likely to read and enjoy.

Younger children

Amongst the favourite fairy stories in nursery and Reception classes are 'Goldilocks and the Three Bears', 'Cinderella' and 'Sleeping Beauty'. These are represented in Figure 5.2 where I include collections like Mary Hoffman's *A First Book of Fairy Tales* and Margaret Mayo's *First Fairy Tales*. Naomi Lewis' *Hans Christian Andersen's Fairy Tales* tells some other favourite tales for this age group, for example 'The Ugly Ducking' and 'The Emperor's New Clothes'.

By about age six or seven children are becoming secure enough in the structure and characterization of the traditional telling to appreciate tales with a playful approach in which gender roles may be reversed or which end with a teasing twist. In their book *The Jolly Postman* the Ahlbergs have fine-tuned this kind of teasing and intertextuality. There have been many other improvisations on the tales, sometimes termed 'fractured fairy tales'. Favourites include Babette Coles' *Smartypants,* and what is now a classic – Robert Munsch's *The Paperbag Princess.* In Lauren Child's postmodern tale *Who's Afraid of the Big Bad Book*, young Herb falls into a book of fairy tales and causes some chaos. You should not deface books, of course, but it is

49

BOX 5.2 THREE EUROPEAN TRADITIONS: THE FAIRY TALES OF CHARLES PERRAULT, JACOB AND WILHELM GRIMM AND HANS CHRISTIAN ANDERSEN

Charles Perrault

This folklorist and writer collected fairy tales in the seventeenth century so that 'Cinderella', 'Little Red Riding Hood' and 'Sleeping Beauty' and many other less familiar tales have been enjoyed through the centuries. It is the humour and detail that make Perrault's tellings so vivid and memorable. They also tap into children's secret fears, conflicts between members of families and the universal challenges of growing up. For the entire collection, see *Charles Perrault: The Complete Fairy Tales,* illustrated by Gustav Dore, translated by Christopher Betts (Oxford University Press). Angela Carter's *The Fairy Tales of Charles Perrault* retells the tales for the modern adult reader in English. This version has become a classic in its own right enjoyed for its post-feminist, subversive flavour.

Jacob and Wilhelm Grimm

Born in the later part of the eighteenth century and writing in the first part of the nineteenth century, the Grimm brothers were folklorists and philologists who collected the tales they heard about giants and dwarfs, princes and princesses and fantasy animals. Favourites include 'Hansel and Gretel', 'Rapunzel', 'Snow White' and 'The Twelve Dancing Princesses'. Constant amendments were made by the brothers to the numerous editions of the stories and these tend to bring them in line with the values of middle-class people in Germany in the nineteenth century. For a collection of all the stories, see *Grimm: The Complete Fairy Tales*, Wordsworth special edition with illustrations by Arthur Rackham.

Hans Christian Andersen

While Perrault and the Grimm brothers retold stories they had heard, Hans Andersen wrote his own tales. *Tales Told for Children* appeared in Britain in 1846. He writes with the voice of an oral storyteller, often seeming to address the reader directly. Best known of his stories are: 'The Little Mermaid', 'The Princess and the Pea' and 'The Ugly Duckling'. Sadness threads through many of the stories and 'The Little Match Girl', with its bleak ending, is heart rending. For an edition containing 156 of Andersen's 168 stories, including the sad, dark and lesser known, see *Complete Hans Andersen Fairy Tales* (Gramercy Books). (See also the translations of the tales by Naomi Lewis and Brian Alderson, which stay true to Andersen's distinctive 'voice'.)

amusing to see the moustaches drawn on some characters and the absence of Prince Charming because he has been cut out for a birthday card.

There are some good collections for the over eights, including *The Enchanted Wood* – a selection of tales from different countries and pictured by such giants of illustration as Walter Crane, Arthur Rackham and Charles Robinson. Oscar Wilde's fairy tales, including 'The Selfish

Giant' and 'The Happy Prince', are full of the symbolism older children in the primary years can appreciate. This age group are ready, too, for some of the more challenging and interesting 'fractured' fairy tales like Jon Scieska and Lane Smith's *The True Story of the Three Little Pigs*.

Figure 5.2 lists traditional tellings in rough order of challenge and Figure 5.4 some examples of playful 'fractured fairy tales' — again in the order in which different age groups may appreciate them. These lists are, of course, one person's choices from a huge number of collections and single stories.

BOX 5.3 *THE PRINCESS' BLANKETS* **BY CAROL ANN DUFFY AND CATHERINE HYDE (ILLUS.) (TEMPLAR)**

A princess lived, once, who was always cold.

This large format picturebook has all the traditional fairy-tale elements: a beautiful but troubled princess, a worried king and queen, a sinister suitor and an 'all turns out well' ending. Duffy's poetic telling is perfectly complemented by Hyde's richly coloured illustrations. The themes of coping with human worries and fears and of the pitfalls along the way towards true love will be a good place to start. But what is the deeper meaning of the princess' condition? Older readers can be helped to see how words and pictures weave together to create the imaginative power of this story.

Postmodern fairy tales

Are these modern tales worthy of being called 'fairy tales'? David Lewis considers that, even in parody, fairy tales or folk tales need to be 'shaped to the generic outlines already laid down by tradition if they are to count as a new addition to the genre' (Lewis, 2001: 66). Readers expect, therefore, to find here princesses, magical beings, brothers and quests, and the numbers twelve, seven and three need to retain their power. And so Mini Grey's *The Pea and the Princess* follows the structure of the traditional telling with some entertaining quirks and reversals. Parody is 'metafictive' as, in Lewis' words, 'it does not accept as "natural and given" what is culturally determined' (Lewis, 2001: 87). And so it makes us think and puzzle and, interestingly, can help us understand the traditional versions more profoundly.

MYTHS, CREATION STORIES AND LEGENDS

These traditional tales require readers or listeners to make an imaginative leap into new worlds with their own customs and rules. As they listen to the stories read to them or read them themselves, children become increasingly familiar with the kinds of events and characters they are likely to encounter in such stories. They learn that some things which concern human beings reach across time and space and are explored in the stories of people from many cultures and traditions. Eve Bearne considers that myths and legends offer 'a unique language

51

- *A First Book of Fairy Tales* by Mary Hoffman, Anne Millard and Julie Downing (Dorling Kindersley)
  Here are fourteen classic tales from the European tradition. Mary Hoffman comments that it is 'a little bit of magic that stirs the imagination'. With her ear for language, she keeps the magic in these retellings, which include such favourites as 'Cinderella' as well as some less well-known stories. Other collections for the five to eights are: *First Fairy Tales* by Margaret Mayo and Selina Young (illus.); *Favourite Fairy Tales*, retold by Sarah Hayes and illustrated by P.J. Lynch; *Fairy Tales* by Berlie Doherty and Jane Ray (illus.); *Hans Christian Andersen's Fairy Tales* by Naomi Lewis (trans.) and Val Biro (illus.); *The Fairy Tales* by Jan Pienkowski.
- *Michael Foreman's Classic Fairy Tales* retold and illustrated by Michael Foreman (Pavilion)
  Children in the middle of the primary years would appreciate the involving retellings and atmospheric, dreamlike pictures in this collection. All the favourite tales are included, for example: 'Cinderella', 'Sleeping Beauty', 'The Ugly Ducking' and 'The Princess and the Pea'.
- *Hansel and Gretel* by Anthony Browne (Walker)
  This picturebook is a compelling and disturbing telling and picturing of the familiar tale. The forest is full of large and sombre trees and the tiny witch's house can be seen through them with its bright frontage.
- *Little Red Riding Hood* retold by Sam McBratney and Emma Chichester Clark (illus.) (Hodder)
  There is something unsettling about the girl's eyes and the pictures of the black cats she keeps as pets. And so while this book will appeal enormously to some young readers, others will be less enthusiastic. Good: we want books that give rise to strong reactions.
- *Snow White* by Josephine Poole and Angela Barratt (illus.) (Red Fox)
  In this picturebook retelling of the classic fairy tale, author and illustrator create a mysterious, romantic atmosphere. The unsettling side of the tale is indicated on the front cover: Snow White is shown in a white flowing dress contrasting with her dark hair and the dark trees of the forest behind her.
- *Andrew Lang's Complete 'Fairy Book' series* (Shoes, Ships and Sealing Wax Ltd)
  If you asked me to name retellers of fairy stories I remember from my own childhood, Andrew Lang's name would be high on my list. I recall reading his fairy tales gathered under colours: blue, red, green, yellow, pink, grey, violet, crimson, orange and lilac. Here they all are in an omnibus edition which is a splendid classroom resource.
- *The Selfish Giant* by Oscar Wilde, and Michael Foreman and Freire Wright (illus.) (Picture Puffin)
  Like the best stories this one is full of symbolic meaning: the giant builds a wall to keep children out and the eternal winter in the garden symbolizes his own frosty heart. The appearance of the small boy, the awakening of the garden when the children are allowed to enter it and their forgiveness make it a tale that sticks in the memory. Over eights will be most likely to appreciate it.

Figure 5.2 *Fairy-tale books, roughly in order of challenge*

- *Oxford Treasury of Fairy Tales* retold by Geraldine McCaughrean and Sophy Williams (illus.) (Oxford University Press)
  There are some older endings to the tales in this collection. Sleeping Beauty ends thus: 'As sharp as a needle, the sun broke through and shone on the royal palace'. The illustrations include some gorgeous vignettes of, for example, a spinning wheel, a frog, Cinderella's glass slipper and a shell.
- *My Sister Shahrazad: Tales from the Arabian Nights* by Robert Leeson and Christina Balit (illus.) (Frances Lincoln)
  A lyrical telling of tales, including 'Ali Baba and the Forty Thieves', 'Aladdin' and 'The Fisherman and the Jinni', this collection is illustrated with vibrant use of colour.
- *The Enchanted Wood: The Greatest Folk Tales and Fairy Stories* by Aesop, Jacob Grimm, Wilhelm Grimm, Hans Christian Andersen and Oscar Wilde and Walter Crane, Arthur Rackham and Charles Robinson (illus.) (Collector's Library Publishing Limited)
  This is a huge resource book for the library shelf in the classrooms of older primary children. At 712 pages it is a considerable tome which includes folk stories from all over the world.
- *Andersen's Fairy Tales* by Hans Christian Andersen (Wordsworth Editions Ltd)
  This unabridged version costing only £1.99 includes some of the sadder and more disturbing events. Andersen's imagery in tales like 'The Mermaid' makes the imagination active. 'Far out to sea the water is as blue as the bluest cornflower and as clear as the clearest crystal; but it is very deep, too deep for any cable to fathom, and if many steeples were piled on the top of one another they would not reach from the bed of the sea to the surface of the water. It is down there that the mermen live'. Other collections for older primary children include: *Celtic Fairy Tales* retold by Neil Philip and *Grimm's Fairy Tales* illustrated by Arthur Rackman.

Figure 5.2 *continued*

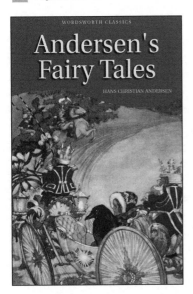

Figure 5.3
Front cover of Andersen's Fairy Tales
Reproduced with the permission of the publishers
Wordsworth Editions Ltd. (www.wordsworth-editions.com)

- *Little Red Riding Hood* by Stephen Tucker and Nick Sharratt (illus.) (Macmillan)
  Lift-the-flap edition for the three to fives. Little Red Riding Hood contacts her granny by mobile phone before making her way through the wood. The wolf escapes when he sees the woodcutter's axe and so the ending is not as frightening as some.

- *The Paperbag Princess* by Robert Munsch and Michael Martchenko (illus.) (Scholastic)
  A dragon ruins Princess Elizabeth's castle and burns her clothes. But her resourcefulness helps her win through. She convinces young readers that what you do is more important than how you look. But does her prince agree?

- *Mixed-Up Fairy Tales* by Hilary Robinson and Nick Sharratt (Hodder)
  Twelve fairy tales are each made into one long sentence and divided into four parts so that we have a split page. Each of the four parts can be turned over to make new combinations of the sentence. You can either create the classic telling or make some highly entertaining mismatches – Red Riding Hood eating the bears' porridge and so on.

- *Princess Smartypants* by Babette Cole (Puffin)
  The picture on the cover showing the heroine on a motorbike prepares young readers and listeners for an unconventional princess. *Prince Cinders*, also by Babette Cole, also teases with role reversal.

- *The Fly-by-Night (Twentieth Century Fairy Tales)* by Terry Jones and Michael Foreman (illus.) (Puffin)
  Imagine hearing a tap on your window at night and then seeing a black creature with golden eyes on the back of a flying cat. Then you join them, flying up into the night sky . . .

- *Three Little Wolves and the Big Bad Pig* by Eugene Trivizas and Helen Oxenbury (illus.) (Egmont)
  Young children know that wolves in stories are usually the bad characters and enjoy the fun of the reversal. Older children take on the more subtle messages, for example that, perhaps, there are bad deeds rather than bad people.

- *The Pea and the Princess* by Mini Grey (Random House)
  The traditional story is told from the point of view of the pea. Look out for the vegetable wallpaper and the Queen's pea-like eyes and pea necklace. After waiting to be felt by the princess under all the mattresses, the pea takes the initiative. This is a tale that is food for thought. (Two other teasing versions of the tale are: *The Princess and the Pea* by Susannah Davidson and Mike Gordon (illus.); *The Princess and the Pea* by Lauren Child.)

- *Fairytale News* by Colin Hawkins and Jacqui Hawkins (illus.) (Walker)
  The conceit of a paperboy is used to help explain about different kinds of journalistic writing and about headlines, special features, cartoons and news stories. Of course the news story headlines are amusing and include 'Golden-haired girl caught napping at three bears' cottage' and 'Boy makes fortune out of magic beans'.

- *The True Story of the Three Little Pigs* by Jon Sciezska and Lane Smith (Puffin)
  This is B.B. Wolf's version of events, which turns out to be less than reliable.

Figure 5.4 *Fairy tales with postmodern twists and teases*

Figure 5.5
Front cover of The Pea and the Princess
by Mini Grey
Reproduced with the permission of the
publishers The Random House Group Ltd.
Copyright Mini Grey 2003

which enables new and discriminating meanings to be made – especially by children' (Styles, Bearne and Watson, 1992: 143). Becoming familiar with myth and legend paves the way for appreciating the mythology in the Harry Potter books and in the work of Philip Pullman.

Myths and creation stories

Myths are ancient stories about gods, heroes and about the creation of this world and about other worlds that might be around us. The stories are often dramatic and to do with the extremes of human behaviour: love and hate, good and evil, of despair and hope and with creation. They have at their heart 'imagination, creativity and the urge to understand, to explain and to embellish' (Saxby in Hunt, 2004: 249).

Many myths, including Greek and Northern myths, concentrate on stories about the gods and how they interact with human beings. Greek myths take readers to Mount Olympus, the home of Zeus and the other gods. The dramatic stories include the tale of Persephone, the daughter of Zeus, who spent half the year on Earth and half in the underworld.

Northern myths also take us into a world where the paths of gods and human beings cross in dramatic ways. In his article about the Norse tales, 'The Northern Myths', Kevin Crossley-Holland notes that the rhythm of day and night and the rhythm of the seasons as well as changing weather conditions preoccupied these people, as they did in all early civilizations. So, for example, a Norse legend explains that thunder is the sound of the wheels of Thor's chariot moving across the sky (Crossley-Holland, 1982: 8).

The type of myth we call a 'creation story' explores the origins of the world and human existence. This is the case in Barbara Picard's *Tales of the Norse Gods*, where the first chapter is entitled 'The Beginning of All Things' and starts: 'This is the story the Norsemen told of how the world began' (Picard, 2001: 1). Originally, the people in many tribal and early communities believed that the explanations in their creation myths were literally true. These explanations are likely to have helped people to feel less afraid of and more at ease with the

- *The Secret of Pandora's Box* retold by Saviour Pirotta and Jan Lewis (illus.) (Orchard)
Like the other books in Orchard's First Greek Myths series, this one is in large clear print helpful to the newly independent reader. The excitement and menace of the story are caught as young readers learn how Pandora opens the box belonging to Epimetheus, the box that the gods have warned should never be opened. The pictures show the characters in Greek dress but have a modern quirkiness. (Other books of Greek myths for younger children include: *Greek Myths for Young Children* by Heather Amery and Linda Edwards; *Perseus and the Monstrous Medusa* by Saviour Pirotta and Jan Lewis and *Orchard Book of Greek Myths* by Geraldine McCaughrean and Emma Chichester Clark).

- *Rainbow Bird* by Eric Maddern and Adrienne Kennaway (illus.) (Frances Lincoln)
The luminous image of the firebird, with its electric blue head and outstretched green and red wing feathers, shines out from the front cover. The book tells the aboriginal fire creation myth from Northern Australia.

- *The Horse Girl* by Miriam Moss and Jason Crockcroft (Frances Lincoln)
'Freya loved horses. The clap of hoofs on cobbles or the chink of a harness in the moonlight were magic to her.' So why was she forbidden to ride them? Freya has a magical encounter which leads to the solving of her family problems.

- *Zeus Conquers the Titans and Other Greek Myths* by Geraldine McCaughrean and Tony Ross (illus.) (Orchard)
This book has pace and spirit and would suit newly independent readers. The lively illustrations of Tony Ross add to the enjoyment.

- *Indian Myths: Stories from Ancient Civilizations* by Shahrukh Husain and Bee Willey (illus.) (Evans Brothers)
This 32-page picturebook introduces children aged from about five to eight to Indian creation stories and to the sagas of the Mahabarata and Ramayana.

- *Greek Myths* by Marcia Williams (Walker)
Using her familiar cartoon strip to good effect Marcia Williams retells the stories, including 'Theseus and the Minotaur' and 'Heracles and his Twelve Tasks', with energy and humour. This author has also retold *The Iliad* and *The Odyssey*.

- *Tales from the Norse Legends* by Edward Ferrie (author), Gustav Mahler (composer) and Benjamin Soames (reader) (Naxos Audiobooks)
This double audio CD brings humour and excitement to the tales. Soames enlivens his reading by using different voices and the atmospheric classical music is an aid to young imaginations.

- *Shapeshifters: Tales from Ovid's Metamorphoses* by Adrian Mitchell and Alan Lee (illus.) (Frances Lincoln)
These thirty powerful myths from Ovid's tales would appeal to children from about eight or nine upwards.

Figure 5.6 *Books of myths, roughly in order of challenge*

56

- *The Game* by Diana Wynne Jones (HarperCollins)
  This modern story drawing on ancient myths would interest forward readers of about ten or eleven upwards. Hayley visits her relatives who live in a castle in Ireland. She is introduced by her cousins to 'The Game' – to a 'mythosphere' where myths and folklore intrude into everyday life.

- *Stories from Ancient Egypt: Egyptian Myths and Legends for Children* by Joyce A. Tyldesley and Julian Heath (illus.) (Rutherford Press)
  Here are creation stories and myths about Osiris, Isis and Horis. The illustrations include stylized black and white line drawings reminiscent of ancient Egyptian friezes and pictures. There are questions and extra information at the end of each story and even an invitation for readers to write their names in hieroglyphs.

Figure 5.6 *continued*

Figure 5.7
Picture from Greek Myths *retold and illustrated by Marcia Williams*
Reproduced with the permission of the publishers Walker Books Ltd., London SE11 5HJ. Copyright Marcia Williams 1991, 2006

world around them. Even now, the creation stories retain metaphoric power and young children find them absorbing.

So we look for the retellings which retain the drama of the oral tradition and which also encourage thinking, imagining and questioning. Tellings which illuminate the relationship of human beings with the natural world are worth seeking out. It is important to take account of the quality of the illustrations when choosing books because they can communicate much about landscapes, clothes, artefacts and customs, and reveal the feelings and attitudes of the characters.

- *The Girl Who Loved Wild Horses* by Paul Goble (Atheneum Books for Young People)
  The author of this legend has combined several stories told by the Indians of the Great Plains. A young girl who loves wild horses goes to live with them. What happens when she is made to leave them and to come back to her community?

- *Coll the Storyteller's Tales of Enchantment* by Lucy Coat and Antony Lewis (illus.) (Orion Children's Books)
  Coll Hazel, a young Druid bard, is sent to find the treasures of Avalon and to recover them from the clutches of the Viking invaders. Young listeners or readers are introduced to Celtic folklore, where human beings interact with a magical, supernatural world.

- *The Golden Hoard; The Silver Treasure; The Bronze Cauldron; The Crystal Pool: Myths and Legends of the World* by Geraldine McCaughrean and Bee Willey (illus.) (Orion Children's Books)
  These four collections, each include more than twenty stories which come from many different times and places (the title story in the fourth collection is from Melanesia), would be an asset to any primary school library.

- *Stories from the Billabong* retold by James Vance Marshall and Francis Firebrace (illus.) (Frances Lincoln)
  These ten legends from the Yorta-Yorta people of Australia are set in Dreamtime and illustrated by an Aboriginal artist in sand painting style. The retelling is vivid and the illustrations greatly add to the drama and atmosphere of the tales.

- *Irish Myths and Legends* retold by Ita Daly and Bee Willey (illus.) (Oxford University Press)
  There are quite a few collections of Irish myths and legends. These retellings of ten stories are told clearly and well with a conversational tone and are enhanced by the sympathetic illustrations of that favourite illustrator of traditional tales, Bee Willey.

- *King Arthur and the Round Table* by Geraldine McCaughrean and Alan Mark (illus.) (Macdonald)
  McCaughrean captures the magical and the mysterious in these timeless stories which are complemented by the dramatic and atmospheric pictures of Alan Mark.

- *Robin of Sherwood* retold by Michael Morpurgo and Michael Foreman (illus.) (Pavilion)
  Children are pulled into the story when it begins with the experience of a boy in the hurricane of 1987. A great oak falls and we enter the times and adventures of Robin Hood. This is a fine combination of a leading storyteller and an artist whose water-colours help the stories 'live'.

- *Myths and Legends* by Anthony Horowitz (Kingfisher)
  This substantial book of 247 pages gathers together thirty-five tales from around the world which reveal much about the time and place of each one. Horowitz has a distinctive storytelling 'voice' and these tales have a modern tone, bringing humour to the characterization and events.

Figure 5.8 *Books retelling legends, roughly in order of challenge*

> • *Arthur and the Seeing Stone*; *At the Crossing-Place*; *King of the Middle Marches* by Kevin Crossley-Holland (Orion Children's Books)
> This fine trilogy is never allowed to go out of print and now has the status of a classic. The stories move between the legends of King Arthur and the adventures of a young boy, Arthur de Caldicott, living at the end of the twelfth century. The stories appeal to many over nines today and will certainly shift young minds and imaginations into top gear.

Figure 5.8 *continued*

Legends

The very fact that quite a few collections include both myths and legends shows how leaky the boundary between them is. But I take it that legends are usually about heroes and heroines of long ago – King Arthur and his knights and Robin Hood, for example. These stories have been told from generation to generation so scarcely a decade passes without a new version of the Robin Hood or King Arthur story appearing on film or television. They may be about historical characters and events but tellers and then writers have embellished them and sometimes infused them with supernatural elements. The heroes and heroines in the legends of the people of a particular culture reveal the strong and weak elements of that culture. Viking society was not alone in recording both brave deeds and cruel ones in its legends.

Children will have their first encounter with epic heroes in legends and will find that stories of journeys and homecomings abound. And they will learn how a strong person can survive many challenges and how moral dilemmas are resolved. Growing familiarity with legends from every culture will not only enhance children's capacity to read and enjoy other forms, but will also enrich their language and vocabulary.

What do we look for in this kind of story for the elevens and under? The retelling has to be exciting and told with energy and pace. The best writers and illustrators are able to relate the dark and difficult things to be found in traditional tales in a way children can cope with. Good dialogue helps and gives the characters life. Geraldine McCaughrean, for example, is known for her thrilling way with direct speech. Illustrations, too, are important in conveying the romance and drama of the tales.

PARABLES AND FABLES

While the morality of parables is to do with religion, the ethical source of fables springs from secular judgements about human beings' selfishness and misuse of power. Many folklorists consider that fables are a kind of folk tale – see Ruth Bottigheimer's account 'Fairy Tales and Folk Tales' (Bottigheimer in Hunt, 2004: 272). But here, for reasons of clarity, I have given the fable separate treatment.

59

Parables

Often associated with the teachings of Jesus in the New Testament, parables are stories making a moral point. A knowledge of parables, such as 'The Good Samaritan', 'The Parable of the Talents' and 'The Prodigal Son', is helpful in reading books where some familiarity with them is assumed by the writer. The term can also be used to describe the form of some modern stories for adults and children. Dyan Sheldon's *The Whales' Song* and Anthony Browne's picturebook *The Tunnel* could both be read as modern parables.

The fact that parables are part of our culture is not enough to justify what Alan Brine calls 'a cosy literalism'. Rather we seek retellings that show us something of 'the imaginative, creative power of the stories' (Brine, 1991: 6). So a good thing to ask of any collection is: does it encourage creative questioning?

Fables

Like parables, these stories are usually concerned with illuminating a moral principle. But they differ from parables in a number of ways. Their philosophy does not have its origin in

---

- *The Usborne Children's Bible* by Heather Amery and Linda Evans (illus.) (Usborne)
  This children's Bible includes a clear retelling of the best-known parables in a way children from about age four years would understand. So, for example, we find here 'The Prodigal Son' and 'The Good Shepherd'.

- *Stories Jesus Told* by Nick Butterworth and Mick Inkpen (illus.) (Candle Books)
  Children understand the importance of keeping promises and of helping those less fortunate than themselves. And so they will appreciate these retellings of eight of Jesus' parables, including 'The Lost Sheep', 'The Good Samaritan' and 'The Prodigal Son'.

- *Parables* by Mary Hoffman and Jackie Morris (illus.) (Frances Lincoln)
  Children aged five to eight years will find the illustrations contextualize the stories: there are Middle Eastern landscapes and buildings. But the gestures and the expressions on the faces of the people tell most about the meaning of the stories and will appeal to young imaginations.

- *The Lion Graphic Bible* by Mike Maddox and Jeff Anderson (illus.) (Lion)
  Some children towards the end of Year 6 might appreciate this book, but there is some startlingly modern speech and it is probably best to stick with the parables as some more brutal incidents are recounted in the main text.

- *The Children's Illustrated Bible* by Selina Hastings and Eric Thomas (illus.) (Dorling Kindersley)
  Older children would find this book rich in helpful background information and historical context shown through both writing and illustration. The language is accessible to eight- to ten-year-olds but not banal. A comprehensive contents page helps young readers find the parables quickly.

 *Figure 5.9* Books containing parables

religious belief, but in the human instinct for survival and for power. The characters in fables are usually animals, some of which have unattractive human traits like selfishness and pride, as we find in both *Aesop's Fables* and the fable-like 'trickster' stories from the African tradition.

Insights from fables have become proverbial and we speak of 'sour grapes', and some of the features of fables are found in print cartoons like *Beryl the Peril* and in animated cartoons such as those featuring Wallace and Gromit. The boundaries between fable and folk tale are thin and some tales can be placed in either category. Fable and folk tale also thread through the work of some writers of children's novels, for example Richard Adams and Philip Pullman.

Geraldine McCaughrean confesses that fables, and particularly Aesop's fables, are her least favourite kind of traditional tale. She finds Aesop 'dour' (McCaughrean, 1996: 8). But Roger Mills comments that his young son 'seems to be developing an interest in creative writing . . . at school they have been writing fables and Hal, clearly thoroughly into this, told us with great pride of the fable of the Dog and the Frog which he had co-authored with another child' (Mills, 2009: 12). I have anecdotal evidence that the under eights in particular are very positive about the tales we call fables because of, rather than in spite of, their predictable structure and resolution.

For anyone carrying out a study of fables I recommend Brian Alderson's extension article on 'The History of Fable Publishing', which expands his 'Classics in Short 64' on 'The History

---

- *Chicken Licken* by Russell Punter and Anne Knonheimer (illus.) (Usborne)
  The rhyming, rhythmic lines – 'Chicken Licken', 'Henny Penny' and 'Foxy Loxy' – make it a good one to read aloud to three to fives and it would also suit newly independent readers.

- *The Lion and the Rat* by Brian Wildsmith (Oxford University Press)
  In the spirit of the fable genre, the creatures Wildsmith depicts show their animal nature, but we glimpse, too, something of human strengths and weaknesses. Wildsmith's rat has tiny paws and looks like a small, hairy bundle of energy but its expression and large eyes are earnest and full of feeling.

- *Aesop's Funky Fables* by Vivian French and Korky Paul (illus.) (Hamish Hamilton)
  Ten of Aesop's fables are retold with great energy and humour for five to eight-year-olds. Lively illustrations and written text which uses both rap-like verse and prose keep up the narrative pace.

- *Whadayyamean* by John Burningham (Cape)
  Two children take God to view what has become of planet Earth, once beautiful, now polluted. God entrusts the children to tell adults to stop spoiling the Earth and there is an upbeat ending: the world becomes a better place.

- *Aesop's Fables* by Jerry Pinkney (illus.) (Seastar Books)
  This straightforward telling of the classic tales with arresting illustrations came 34th in the Booktrust survey of the Best Children's Books of All Time, 2008.

Figure 5.10 *Books of fables, roughly in order of challenge*

of Aesop's Fables' (Alderson, 2007). The extended article traces fable publishing for children, with information about illustration, and can be viewed on www.booksforkeeps.co.uk.

In addition to the annotated suggestions in Figure 5.10 the following collections are recommended: *The Best of Aesop's Fables* by Margaret Clark and Charlotte Voake; *The Orchard Book of Aesop's Fables* by Michael Morpurgo and Emma Chichester Clark; *The Puffin Book of Fabulous Fables* by Mark Cohen and Mark Southgate.

USING TRADITIONAL TALES

In this part of the chapter I pinpoint which books seem the best read aloud and then go on to recommend a workshop approach which combines creative activities including drama, artwork and writing.

Reading aloud

The shared experience that reading aloud offers to every age group adds hugely to children's enjoyment of traditional tales. Their link with oral history makes listening to them read aloud particularly appropriate and satisfying and gives children the opportunity to think about how the rhythms and patterns of oral and written tellings differ. A teacher is usually the reader, but older children enjoy being narrators if given some preparation time. The use of audio tapes can help ring the changes. Most of the books mentioned in the 'Choosing sections' would 'read aloud' well. But here are some star books for reading aloud to different age groups.

Reading aloud to 3–5-year-olds

Children who have had traditional tales read aloud to them from an early age develop an imaginative 'space' to accommodate future tellings and readings. When it comes to fairy and folk tales, encountering traditional versions first will make it possible for them to appreciate amusing versions with a twist.

- The stories in Ladybird's First Favourite Tales series include *The Gingerbread Man: Based on a Traditional Folk Tale*, illustrated by Anja Rieger, which keeps up momentum with its rhythm and rhyme.
- *The Paperbag Princess* by Robert Munsch is often one of the first fairy tales with a twist children enjoy.
- *Greek Myths for Children* by Heather Amery and Linda Evans is big enough for a group of children to look at as well as listen to.
- *My First Aesop's Fables* by Martha Lightfoot retells some of the favourite tales, including 'The Hare and the Tortoise' and 'The Lion and the Mouse', using sharp stylized pictures that bring out the humour.

Reading aloud to 5–8-year-olds

Children enjoy traditional versions, but can also be interested in modern retellings of fairy tales and fables. Favourites for listening to include:

- *Mama Panya's Pancakes* by Mary and Richard Chamberlain.
- *The Rainbow Bird* by Eric Maddeson (in big as well as small book format).
- *A First Book of Fairytales* by Mary Hoffman *et al*.
- *Hans Christian Andersen's Fairy Tales* translated by Naomi Lewis.
- *The Tale of Johnny Town-Mouse* by Beatrix Potter has the simple but elegant language of the written form and helps with the acquisition of interesting vocabulary, which some children can gain by listening.
- *Aesop's Funky Fables* by Vivian French and Korky Paul (illus.) uses verse as well as lively prose, which make it fun to say the fables aloud.

Reading aloud to 8–11-year-olds

Older children still enjoy and benefit from hearing traditional tales read aloud and sometimes can, with some preparation, take on the reading role. As with other literature, prose and poetry, the listening experience allows children the space to appreciate the patterns of the language.

- Hans Andersen's tales are full of interesting characters and lively dialogue that encourages the reader to use different voices. Try choosing from a complete works, for example Gramercy Books' *Complete Hans Andersen Fairy Tales.*
- Wordsworth Classics' *The Complete Illustrated Fairy Tales* by Jacob and Wilhelm Grimm uses traditional language: 'Ah! Old water-splasher, is it thou?' said she; 'I am weeping for my golden ball which has fallen into the well'. Some of the stories are only a page long and so can fit into small spaces in the school day.
- *The Brothers Grimm: Popular Folk Tales,* translated by Brian Alderson, keeps the 'voice' of the ancient stories alive.
- Teachers like to ring the changes sometimes by using a CD telling a traditional tale. Edward Ferrie's *Tales from the Norse Legends* uses accessible language read by Benjamin Soames and with atmospheric background music.
- Kevin Crossley-Holland's *Arthur and the Seeing Stone* has a pace and drama that make it a good legend to read aloud. Sentences vary in length for dramatic effect: some are long while others are short.
- Rosemary Sutcliff's *Beowulf: Dragon Slayer* challenges even some older children in the primary years when they read it independently, but they may be able to appreciate the story read aloud.
- Mark Cohen and Mark Southgate's collection *The Puffin Book of Fabulous Fables* has tales from Aesop alongside similar stories from other cultures and traditions.
- *More Irish Folk Tales for Children* is an audio CD with four stories narrated by Sharon Kennedy, including 'The Magic Dancing Pig' and 'Annie O'Reilly'.

Workshops with opportunities for talk, drama, artwork and writing

There are several advantages to the workshop approach to exploring traditional tales. By 'workshop' I mean an extended session where there are writing and art materials available and some simple props and costumes. It is not, of course, just a matter of providing resources. Skilled teaching requires that a balance is achieved between providing some room for children's own choice of activities and giving enough direction and inspiration to keep the momentum up and help them reach high. This way of working and resourcing the learning often leads to discussion, improvisation and artwork being combined in interesting ways. Writing in particular benefits from being nourished by other creative activities. At the end of the series of workshops a final display of its fruits can be set up. Here are some suggestions.

3–5-year-olds

The active workshop approach suits the children in this age range well and the traditional tales read and thought about can shape and deepen their role play, artwork and talk.

- Retell the stories using a storyboard.
- Talk about the stories; even at this age it can be a conversation rather than a question and answer session. One of my students had quite a young child ask why Red Riding Hood did not realize the gruff voice from the cottage was not her grandmother's. Another child suggested 'Perhaps she thought her granny had a cough'.
- Encourage artwork – for example drawing or making a collage picture of princes and princesses and other characters from folk, fairy tales and fables. *Princess Smartypants* often inspires lively work – children so much like including the princess' unusual pets.
- Lois Ehlert's dual-language retelling of a Mexican folk tale *Cuckoo/Cucu* tells what happened to a cuckoo who was beautiful but vain. This book is full of visual treats and would be a good starting point for craft work and collage; it shows how young children could be helped to make their own cuckoos.
- Help children annotate their pictures with names and sentences which may be put in speech balloons.
- Ask each child to draw a different character from a folk tale or fairy story and make a frieze of a scene.
- Make storybox scenes from a favourite tale.
- Bake gingerbread boys and girls and help the children put on icing sugar eyes, orange peel mouths and sweets for buttons after reading a version of the 'The Gingerbread Man'.
- Acting out favourite stories in the home corner using some simple costumes and props is helped by a well-stocked dressing-up box and never goes out of fashion.
- The home corner or language area can be transformed into a scene from a story: Cinderella's room with broom and dusters; Sleeping Beauty's Christening feast; the Three Bears' house with a table and bowls of 'porridge'.

BOX 5.4 PARENTS CAN HELP INCREASE ENTHUSIASM FOR TRADITIONAL STORIES

Extract from a newsletter to Reception parents:

> We are continuing with our traditional stories this term and will be reading *Rapunzel*, *Snow White*, *Rumpelstiltskin*, *The Little Red Hen*, *Jack and the Beanstalk* and *The Enormous Turnip*.

> If your child has a version of one of these, or a relevant prop or toy, please could they bring it in and show it to us and add it to our display? We will be retelling the stories, acting them out and making puppets and props.

CASE STUDY 5.1 SIX-YEAR-OLDS DISCUSS DIFFERENT VERSIONS OF *LITTLE RED RIDING HOOD*

The teacher read out *Little Red Riding Hood* by Gill Guile from Brimax Books' Once Upon a Time series. The teacher, Tullia Schrauwers, comments: 'I like this story because Grandma hides in a cupboard. So no cutting open of the wolf to get Grandma out.' Then, in a geography lesson about maps later on, another version of the story from one of the flip-over books in Folens' Geography scheme for young children (alas out of print at present) was read out. This uses the tale to show Red Riding Hood's route through the forest. Tullia considers that even these young children were able to appreciate two different tellings and to talk about the differences in the detail. This is interesting to keep in mind when reading Arthur Applebee's research study, and suggests we might need to reconsider his view that children under about eight seem actually to believe fairy-tale characters exist and live somewhere. Only one version of a tale would be acceptable if the characters and stories are 'true' (Applebee, 1978).

5–8-year-olds

Children in this age range enjoy traditional tellings, but are likely to be secure enough in the structure and characterization of these to appreciate also teasing versions with a twist.

- Thus traditional tellings of folk and fairy tales can then be compared with some versions with a twist. Ask which they prefer and why (see list of fairy tales with a twist in Figure 5.4).
- Role play around the traditional and postmodern fairy tale can also help deepen understanding of genre features.
- *Aesop's Funky Fables* by Vivian French and illustrated by Korky Paul is ideal for reciting and performing because of the dramatic nature of the retelling using rap-like verse and prose.

CASE STUDY 5.2 CINDERELLA – WHAT HAPPENED NEXT? SEVEN-YEAR-OLDS SPECULATE ON CINDERELLA'S FUTURE

After hearing *Cinderella* read aloud a Year 2 class teacher set up some workshop sessions which were filled with drama, art and writing. The children were asked to imagine what Cinderella's palace would be like. Exciting artwork and some short but lively written accounts followed. James decides to make Cinderella extremely conciliatory, even asking the step-family to visit.

Three things strike me about this work. First, the writing benefited considerably from being embedded in other activities. Second, the invitation to extend the story helped children understand that stories are created: a teller or writer can choose what happens, what the characters say or do and when the story ends. Third, the lively display of artwork and writing set up in a corridor encouraged a culture of sharing stories.

James' letter from Cinderella to her Stepmother:

Dear Stepmother,

My palace has glittering pink walls. There are lots of pink and blue rabbits and tiny birds in the trees. It is a big house with gold floors and halls. There are big tables full of food and I eat all the time.

I have sparkling stairs made of ice and there is music all over the palace. It would be nice to see you and my stepsisters.

Cinderella

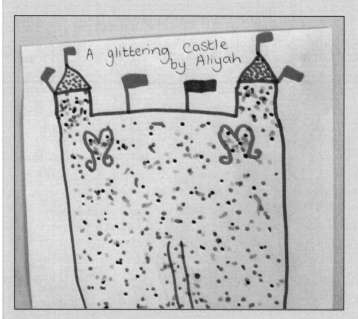

Figure 5.11 *Cinderella: a picture of what the palace might look like by Aliyah*

- *Lion Fables,* retold and illustrated by Jan Omerod, is a dual-language collection which can help broaden children's notion of what a fable is or can be.
- Art and role play can follow a reading of a traditional tale.
- Writing tasks might include:
  - If I had three wishes . . .
  - A conversation between two characters set out in script form, for example the Town Mouse explaining to the Country Mouse why he prefers where he lives.
  - A multimodal text, including speech bubbles of the thoughts of Red Riding Hood as she journeys through the forest.
  - What do you think would happen if the story went on?

8–11-year-olds

By the time they are aged eight and over, children can appreciate the more challenging of traditional retellings and the more ironic and ingenious 'fractured' fairy and folk tales. Given encouragement, they can improvise on the genre structure in drama or in their writing.

- Discussion can now include a consideration of how the design, language and illustration combine to make meaning in a particular tale.
- Some of the deeper symbolism in a fairy tale, fable or myth now comes within their reach. Mitsumasa Anno's *Anno's Aesop: A Book of Fables* has a postmodern take on the tales. How do readers make sense of the illustrations? Can Mr Fox read? These are the sort of questions young readers might ask.
- Children can also be helped to think and talk about the effect on the listener or reader of different versions of the same tale.
- This can be followed by short, prepared presentations about two or more different versions of a traditional tale, either by an individual or by pairs or groups of children.
- The merits of a particular illustrator's work could also be the subject of a short presentation, perhaps using the whiteboard or the overhead projector to show images.
- Children can speak 'in role' explaining the point of view of a particular character, whether this be Robin Hood, King Arthur or the Snow Queen. They can also answer questions 'in role'.
- Older children also enjoy being helped to script a story or legend and then to perform it for another class.
- What about writing? This is where the creativity of some children (by no means all) seems to run out. And yet there are some interesting things to try. Writing their own fairy or folk tale is often asked of older children. But they often need support and direction as they plan and write it.
- A task which sometimes inspires is the writing of a traditional tale for a younger class, followed by reading the tale aloud to the young audience.
- Some children's writing creativity is galvanized by an inspiring book. Marcia Williams' books on traditional tales – *Greek Myths* and *King Arthur and the Knights of the Round Table*, for example – show how serious subjects can be written as comic strip and with speech bubbles.

- Terry Deary's *Greek Tales: The Tortoise and the Dare*, with its new twist to Aesop's fable – the 'tortoise' is Cypselis, who has bet his twin sister against a goat in a race – might also enthuse young readers and inspire them to give their own 'twist' to another fable.
- A book like *Fairytale News* by Colin and Jacqui Hawkins can be the starting point for children's own 'front pages'.

CASE STUDY 5.3 A YEAR 6 CLASS DISCUSS A MODERN FAIRY TALE AND WRITE THEIR OWN, INSPIRED BY *THE TUNNEL* BY ANTHONY BROWNE (WALKER)

Anthony Browne's picturebooks 'trouble the text and they trouble the reader too' (Lewis, 2001: 66). This is certainly the case with *The Tunnel,* a multilayered book which can be read in different ways and at different levels of complexity. Ten-year-olds had read the book when younger and now returned to it as part of a class project on modern fairy tales. Class and group discussion covered the themes – sibling rivalry, gender differences and the power of love over evil. Also explored was how intertextuality is used to create a frame for the story and how the element of magic links the story with traditional tellings. The children wrote and then improvised their own versions of the story and made storybox scenes of key scenes. The workshop approach led to rich activities which put their imaginations into top gear.

ASSESSING AND RECORDING PROGRESS

What would count as making progress in reading and understanding traditional tales? Becoming able to predict and appreciate the structure of these highly patterned stories is one important step. In folk tales, for instance, we often have some poor people faced by a troubling situation which is resolved by their own resourcefulness, perhaps with the help of others. Characters are immediately recognizable too; in fairy tales we often find the worried king and queen, the beautiful but troubled princess, the courageous prince and the good and bad fairies. So as children reach the later primary years we hope they have become able to talk about the universal themes of traditional tales and about human nature and about human beings' responses to difficulties and challenges. It is when children are secure enough in the shape and patterns of the traditional forms that they can appreciate the teasing reversal of roles found in some postmodern tellings. But, interestingly, even here such universal themes of seeking adventure and achievement while needing some security of happiness at home usually remain.

When it comes to making a record of children's achievements, the English, language and literacy folder might include some of the following, dated and briefly annotated, as evidence of progress:

- a short film of some improvised drama;
- a photograph of a scene from an improvisation;

- a recording of a reading or a group discussion;
- a transcript of a child's retelling;
- a review or entry in a reading log or journal;
- writing with an alternative ending to a familiar tale or in the role of a character;
- a newspaper headline and report of a happening – 'Break-in at the Three Bears' house';
- an email or text message as part of a child's created modern traditional tale;
- a modern fairy tale, folk tale, legend or fable a child has created and illustrated;
- a photograph of a labelled display of books and reviews children have helped mount;
- a photograph of a storybox scene;
- a map of a fairy-tale journey: for example, Goldilocks' escape from the Three Bears' house;
- older children's big book of an illustrated tale for a younger class.

SUMMARY

- Traditional tales are ancient stories originally passed on in communities through the oral tradition and then told in written form.
- They are often divided into folk and fairy tales, myths, creation stories and legends and parables and fables, and tap into deeply rooted and often universal human beliefs, hopes and fears.
- The stories are often riveting, but their value is also to do with the metaphoric meanings and symbolism they contain.
- 'Folk' tends to refer to the origin of a tale while 'fairy' is to do with its nature.
- Folk tales are the stories of a people or community and often tell of the challenges and satisfactions of ordinary folk.
- Fairy tales are threaded through with magic and are inhabited by witches, giants, monsters, goblins and suchlike.
- Myths are about gods and how the world and all its objects and creatures were created.
- Legends tell of the adventures and activities of heroes and heroines, and are usually set in a time before records were kept.
- Parables are stories which make a moral point, often with religious import.
- Fables are stories, often about animals, which reveal important things about human behaviour.
- When it comes to using traditional tales in the classroom, reading aloud, dramatic improvisation, discussion and writing are all sound ways of developing children's responses.
- Evidence of progress lies in children's understanding of the structure of the stories, of the characters that people them and, above all, of the metaphoric and symbolic meanings.
- Annotated photographs of drama, and samples of writing and drawing help create a record of progress.

Chapter 6

Genre fiction, 'popular culture' texts and formats and media

INTRODUCTION

This chapter explores those books and materials for children sometimes referred to as 'genre fiction'. I include in these genres detective and mystery stories, science fiction, ghost and horror stories and have looked too at cartoon and graphic stories. All the texts gathered here have readily recognizable structures, events, characters and settings. Some are 'popular culture' texts, which link children's literacy experiences at home and school; others, like the science fiction stories of H.G. Wells, have become classics. The illustrations in these texts, now often digital artwork, generally have distinctive, recognizable qualities which help identify them with the genre or sub-genre. I also look at some of the different formats used, including comic strip and moving image media.

CHOOSING GENRE FICTION TEXTS AT DIFFERENT AGES AND STAGES

Detective and mystery stories

What is the difference between a detective and a mystery story? For me, a key feature of a detective story is an official attempt to solve a crime, while a mystery story may involve a crime but need not involve the police. However, both usually have resourceful and courageous children as central characters. This is their appeal, as we know from Erich Kastner's book *Emil and the Detectives*, published in 1930 and a forerunner of the genre read today. Children vicariously enjoy the power and status of the characters in the books. Both detective and mystery tales are in essence page turning adventure stories and this is why I have grouped them together here.

You might feel that detective and mystery stories, especially those published in series, are predictable, each having similar ingredients – secrets, gangs, disguises, treasure, old buildings and chases – but this is just the point. Like adults, children want an escape from the everyday; and so the familiar pattern of the genre reassures and comforts in an uncertain world. This is not to say that there are not some stories with surprising and unsettling themes for children in the mood for a challenge.

Pre-school and nursery, 3–5-year-olds

Even the youngest children like books about a mystery and there are picturebooks to introduce children to the detective and mystery genre. In Satoshi Kitamura's *Sheep in Wolves' Clothing* three sheep go for a swim, leaving their coats with some golfers. And yes, the golfers are wolves! The coats and the wolves vanish and the sheep call on a detective, their friend Elliott Baa, to help them. This is a story that intrigues children from about age four and makes them laugh. Then there is the classic tale by the Ahlbergs, *Burglar Bill*, which tells the story of two burglars, Bill and Betty, who reform once they have a baby to care for. In *Olivia and the Missing Toy* by Ian Falconer, the little pig is sad and angry when her soft toy disappears. Where can it be? At first, she tries to blame her family. But when she hears a noise one night she bravely creeps downstairs to see the shadow of a creature with her beloved toy in its jaws. A dog has chewed the teddy, but Olivia patches it up and all is well.

5–8-year-olds

The best detective and mystery stories for this age group can help make eager readers. Some fully involve readers in the search for clues alongside the children in the story: Dina Anastasio's *Twenty Mini Mysteries You Can Solve* are good for reading aloud and discussion with the younger end of this age range. The answers to the mysteries are at the end of the book.

The books in the Nate the Great series – *Nate the Great and the Missing Key* by M.W. Sharmat, for example – also give readers puzzles to solve. Short sentences suit newly independent readers and there is a lot of humour. The stories in another collection, Jurg Obrist's *Case Closed!*, invite young readers to help Daisy Pepper and Ridley Long, two detectives, to solve their cases. It is the quirky illustrations that provide the visual clues; in 'Ms Blaze and the Mysterious Ghost' why does one of the suspects have a bandage over one eye?

In *Detective Dan* by Vivian French and Alison Bartlett, the first of a children's detective series, Dan gets his friend Billy to help him find the culprit when his sardine sandwiches start disappearing. Part of A&C Black's White Wolves Guided Reading series, the Detective Dan books would suit even less confident readers in the age range.

Not all the best books for children are hot off the press. There are some classics written in the past which we hope will stay in print. The tales in Betsy Byars' *The Eighteenth Emergency* about the problem-solving abilities of Mouse and Ezzie are still a good read. Getting caught in quicksand and coping with a threatening shark are nothing compared with what might happen if you annoy 'Hammerman'. Reading this book aloud can lead to talk about dealing with bullies.

8–11-year-olds

Detective and mystery stories often tempt more reluctant readers and older children who want mature themes, but also need accessible reading material. Some of the Barrington Stoke titles, for example *The Secret Room* by Hazel Townson, are popular with this group.

And now that Enid Blyton's books have been republished children can escape into the adventures of the Famous Five and Famous Seven. All the usual ingredients are here: buried treasure, a gang of children and a dog, relative freedom from adult supervision and fast-moving stories in which the children solve mysteries, often involving a crime. The stories are predictable and will not extend children's vocabularies and language development very much, but they are sought out by children who like a fast-moving mystery.

Some detective stories have an historical setting. One of Terry Deary's Time Detective series, *The Princes in Terror Tower*, explores the mystery of what happened to two little boys imprisoned in the Tower of London in the reign of Richard III. John Pilkington's Elizabethan mysteries, *Rogue's Gold* and *Traitor!*, tell of the adventures of a group of actors and their rivalries with actors from another theatre.

If you are looking for a book for football fans which also involves some crime detection, track down *Big Match Manager* by Tom Sheldon. Hardwick City want to win the league but their best striker has been kidnapped.

Now for some more challenging books for older, abler primary school readers. Children doing author studies might be entertained by 'The Adventure of the Dented Computer' by Simon Chester, in Dennis Hamley's collection *An Oxford Anthology of Mystery Stories*. Narrated by the main character, a great admirer of the work of Sherlock Holmes, we learn that his author study is focused on 'The Hound of the Baskervilles'. But how is the class bully able to produce such an excellent effort? Could he have copied chunks from websites? The other children doubt it because 'Teachers spot downloaded stuff'. Some of the very best children's writers choose the mystery genre. Joan Aiken's story 'The Green Arches', in *Mystery Stories* chosen by Helen Cresswell, draws us in with a skilful beginning: 'There were three things needed before the charm would work. Rather like making a cake when you need eggs, flour, sugar: it had to be rainy, the day had to be Friday and I had to have had the Dream the night before.'

You need stamina to get through a long book; *The Mysterious Benedict Society* by Trenton Lee Stewart has a complex and interesting plot developed over 480 pages. Would you reply to a newspaper advertisement asking you to help save the world? Reynie, Sticky, Kate and Constance do.

Knife by R.J. Anderson is a difficult book to push into a category. It is a most original fantasy with a resourceful heroine who happens to be a fairy. Knife lives with the Oaken

Figure 6.1
Front cover of The Secret Room *by Hazel Townson and Martin Salisbury (illus.)*
Reproduced with the permission of the publishers Barrington Stoke Ltd. Copyright 2000

community in an old tree. Things change for her when she is appointed the group's Hunter and, as part of her duties, has to spy on human beings in a nearby house.

Children who like the Harry Potter stories might appreciate Anderson's creation of a fascinating and coherent, and sometimes chilling, alternative world.

Science fiction

The 'science' in children's science fiction books is in the area of fantasy rather than hard science and will be familiar to children who watch *Doctor Who* and *Star Trek*. We can trace this interest back to the 1950s when children were introduced to space, space travel and people from other planets in cartoon strips such as those in the *Eagle* featuring Dan Dare, Pilot of the Future and Captain Condor in the *Lion* comic. Children also listened to Charles Chilton's Journey into Space series on BBC radio. Where children's texts are concerned, I have placed them in the science fiction stable if they explore such things as monsters, aliens, space travel, futuristic time travel and if the characters use technologies yet to be discovered.

Pre-school and nursery, 3–5-year-olds

Young children today know about space ships and aliens from television programmes and the books and games of older siblings. Early books on these themes with some humour appeal most, for example Colin McNaughton's *Here Come the Aliens!*

Nicholas Fisk is a fine writer of science fiction for older children but his book *Broops! Down the Chimney* is an entertaining book for younger ones. The clear bright illustrations in Mike Brownlow and Michael Brownlow's book of just thirty-two pages, *Little Robots*, introduces the world of science fiction to the very young. Another early robot book is Nick Sharratt's *Super, Shiny Robot!* A ten-page board book, this has on each page a robot picture with a flap, a wheel or a pull-up. The book is excitingly visual, showing robots with clock eyes and springs for hair. The other favourite book about robots for these very young children is Fiona Watt's *'That's Not My Robot . . .'*. The text is brief but amusing, with sentences like 'That's not my robot – its eyes are too shiny'.

For this age group, and for slightly older children, there are two exhilarating books about imaginary journeys through space worth considering. Satoshi Kitamura's *UFO Diary* is

---

BOX 6.1 *HERE COME THE ALIENS!* BY COLIN MCNAUGHTON

A fleet of spaceships heads this way
They're fifty zillion miles away,
But getting closer every day–
The aliens are coming.

Each alien has its own strange looks and unpleasant habits. There is a terrific joke at the end. What frightens the aliens and makes them go away? They see a photograph of the class of children reading the book.

73

about a UFO which finds a strange blue planet. He makes a friend and the vibrant and atmospheric illustrations picture their exciting afternoon exploring heaven and Earth. *Maybe One Day*, by Frances Thomas and illustrated by Ross Collins, takes young readers or listeners on a wonderful imaginary journey through space as Little Monster wants to be an explorer when he grows up. It is an imagination-stretching fantasy, but it also gives some solid information. 'Did you know Jupiter has sixteen moons?' Little Monster asks his father.

5–8-year-olds

Many science fiction books for children around age seven or eight take up Mary Shelley's 'creation of a monster' theme. In *Frank N. Stein and the Great Green Garbage Monster* Ann Jungman tells how the monster brought to life by young Frank in a flash of lightning turns out to have an enormous appetite. Can the monster's constant need for food help with the world's rubbish problems?

Robots feature in a lot of stories too. Bob Wilson in his book *Helpful Helen the Robot* tells the story of a robot that goes off course when Tom's father gives it instructions too quickly. Children find it entertaining when things get in a muddle.

Another book for children just becoming more confident about reading alone is Russell Punter's *Stories of Robots*, in which Andrew Hamilton's cartoon illustrations with speech bubbles add to children's enjoyment. Some children, at the older end of this age range, like *A Bad Case of Robots* by Kenneth Oppel and Peter Utton. Tina builds a robot for her science lessons, but things go wrong. This theme of robots malfunctioning turns up a lot in robot books for this age range. *The Robot Dinner Lady*, a book of short stories in the Jake Cake series by author-illustrator Michael Broad, includes a tale about a robot dinner lady who gets cabbage stuck in her wiring.

Figure 6.2
Front cover of Space Ace *by Eric Brown and Tony Ross (illus.)*
Reproduced with the permission of the publishers Barrington Stoke Ltd.
Copyright 2005

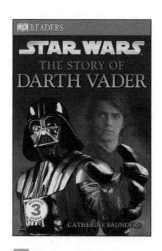

Figure 6.3
Front cover of Star Wars: The Story of Darth Vader *by Catherine Saunders*
Page design copyright Dorling Kindersley 2008.
Copyright Lucasfilm Ltd. Reproduced with the permission of the publishers The Penguin Group

Thinking about space travel now, a delightful and amusing cartoon-strip book for this age range is Lee Hobbs' *Old Tom Goes to Mars*. (See the 'Using . . .' section on pp. 90–3 for ideas to develop discussion and artwork using a text as a starting point.)

8–11-year-olds

Science fiction texts for older primary children range from the light and amusing to the thought-provoking and exciting. There are a lot of 'Captain Teggs' fans at the younger end of this age range who wait eagerly for the next book in Steve Cole's Astrosaurs series. Captain Teggs is an 'astrosaur' – a dinosaur that goes into space on energetic missions in his DSS Sauropodin; for example, in *Astrosaurs: The Sun Snatchers* he sets off to help a community in a land of three suns.

Dinah Capparucci's *Aliens Don't Eat Dog Food* is about some boys who cause considerable confusion whenever they take on a challenge. 'It's quite obvious that aliens exist. Quite a lot of people have been abducted by them, especially in America.' It is the sort of book that might well tempt boys and girls who do not think of themselves as 'book people'. *Space Ace* by Eric Brown and illustrated by Tony Ross is another book that seems to appeal to the more reluctant reader. Print science fiction that is based on film heroes, for example Catherine Saunders' *Star Wars: The Story of Darth Vader*, also often convinces children that the print book can be modern and exciting in design and content.

Although written back in the 1980s, the books in Gillian Cross' Demon Headmaster series continue to fascinate many young readers towards the top end of this age range. The stories demand that we suspend disbelief and accept a headteacher with remarkable but disturbing powers which mean he can dominate the minds of others. In *The Demon Headmaster Takes Over* the head's aim is to control the hyperbrain, a worldwide computer with the power of thought. Can books written some decades ago still work as futuristic stories considering that there have been so many advances in science and technology? Somehow the books survive well – taking on still topical things like genetic engineering.

Terry Pratchett's books show a new imagination at work and because of their humour have been labelled by some as 'comedic fantasy'. Some children, towards the end of Year 6, enjoy the Bromeliad trilogy: *Truckers*, *Diggers* and *Wings*. They appeal to a certain sort of sense of humour; the storylines are about the adventures of the nomes, small dynamic people who live under the floorboards of a department store and then when this is to be demolished face a number of challenges. While his characters live in an imagined world they have familiar hopes, fears and affections which make the stories more than a place for ingenious plots and ideas.

A story I still find unnerving and rather unpleasant is that sci-fi classic *Grinny* by Nicholas Fisk about the infiltration of aliens into an ordinary household. But many children around ten years find it compelling. One teacher who read it aloud to her class said they were 'spellbound'. At root it plays on the ancient 'good against evil' theme, but in a darkly imaginative way. Great Aunt Emma, who has a fiercesome grin, comes to stay with Tim and Beth and their parents. While GAE has a good short-term memory, there are obvious things which she seems not to know or understand. Most telling of all she does not smell human. The children continue their everyday lives, in sharp contrast to their worries about their bizarre visitor. Fisk adds to our unease by making the parents unconcerned and unable to see the terror that is threatened.

Another disturbing story about alien infiltration is 'The Star Beast' by Nicholas Stuart Gray, included in Dennis Pepper's *Alien Stories, Volume 2*. 'It was not easy to tell what sort of creature, but far too easy to tell that it was hurt and hungry and afraid. Only its pain and hunger had brought it to the door for help.'

Ghost stories

There is excitement in being frightened and the archetypal ghost stories by M.R. James build disquiet then fear. The main genre element of the ghost story is its representation of the supernatural, often signalled by the return of the dead, but the truly disturbing episodes we find in ghost stories for adults are toned down in books for children.

Preschool and nursery, 3–5-year-olds

The Haunted House by Kazuno Kahara has bold illustrations which help tell the story of how a resourceful little girl and her cat confront the ghosts in their new house. *Fergus's Scary Night* by author and illustrator Tom Maddox introduces children to all those cultural images that writers use to suggest that something frightening might be about to happen: a full moon, bats and a darkening landscape. The animals are telling 'spooky stories' in the barn, but Fergus the puppy does not believe in ghosts. And yet some strange things do seem to be happening . . . This is a gentle introduction to the genre with a reassuring ending.

5–8-year-olds

Children are by this age starting to understand the power of the imagination, not least their own, when it comes to ghost stories. Once children are about age five and have some notion of the sort of things that pop up in these tales, they like to be just a little scared. Jessica Souhami's story *In the Dark, Dark Wood* is typical of the tale that builds up some fear and anticipation, reaching a climax with a monster, or in this case a ghost, springing out of a double spread. None of Souhami's monsters are too terrifying to look at and a nursery class asked me to read this book again and again, always making the same squeaks of delight when the ghost appeared. Jan Pienkowski's *Haunted House* also amuses as well as giving young readers frightening surprises as they take a virtual walk through an old house.

Some children towards the end of these years and beyond would be fascinated by the story in *The Ghost Dog* by Pete Johnson and illustrated by Peter Dennis. In a nutshell, Daniel and his friends try to frighten big Aaron with a pretend ghost dog. The tale raises the unsettling question: Can stories come true? It also tells us something about the comfort friendship brings.

Ghost stories can sometimes explore the 'what ifs' of life. What would it be like to have a ghost as a friend that helps you with all that you have to cope with during the school day? Terrance Dicks explores this in *Jonathan's Ghost*, in which the ghost is Dave's, a casualty of the Second World War. The suspense grows as teachers become suspicious of Jonathan's apparent achievements. *Goodbye Mog*, the last in Judith Kerr's series of stories about the well-loved pet cat, imparts the comforting message that we do not forget loved ones when they die. When the family take on a troublesome kitten, Mog's ghost comes back to help sort out the problems.

My Brother's Ghost by Allan Ahlberg is another sad ghost story about the return of a ten-year-old boy as a ghost to comfort his sister after he has died (see Box 6.2).

8–11-year-olds

By this age most children can cope with more frightening stories and some prefer the ghost story genre over other kinds. Terry Deary's collection of short stories *Ghost for Sale* includes one about a 'haunted' wardrobe. Is the old lady who sold it really as trustworthy as she seems? In *The Ghost of Able Mabel* by Penny Dolan, Sam tries to retrieve his grandfather's gold from an inn. The problem is that the inn is haunted by an awkward spirit called Able Mabel. Children at the younger end of this age range would find B. Strange's *Too Ghoul for School* full of action and teasing language play. There is a troublesome ghost, Edith Codd, who dwells in the old plague pit beneath St Sebastian's School. When she tries to close the school down – one of her tactics is to turn the science teacher into a zombie – three boys, James, Alexander and Lenny, try to stop her.

For a longer read you might consider Julia Jarman's *Ghost Writer*, a 160-page 'spooky spine chilling adventure' about a Victorian ghost in an old classroom cupboard which was part of the original school put up in 1841. 'There was a cupboard at the back of Room 9 and sometimes it opened – for no reason that anyone could see . . .' Only Frankie can see the messages left on the board, but he finds it hard to decipher them as he is dyslexic.

Ivan Jones' Ghost Hunter series, for about age eight and under, became well known not just through the print books but also because of the BBC serialization of the stories and the audio cassette edition read by Dominic Taylor. Who is the ghost hunter that threatens to vaporize and bottle in a jam jar the ghost of William Povey and add him to her collection? In *The Ghost Hunter* we learn that the villain is Mrs Croker. But how can young Roddy and his sister Tessa save William, their unusual friend, from a really ghastly fate? The ten ghost stories in *Dust 'n' Bones* by Chris Mould are each just a few pages long. Some are quite frightening but most have some humour.

BOX 6.2 *MY BROTHER'S GHOST* BY ALLAN AHLBERG

A teacher writes: 'I wish Allan Ahlberg could have seen their faces when I read the last line' (Amazon UK site, accessed 4 September 2009). Yes, some stories just need to be read aloud and shared. Frances' description of her brother is succinct and moving: 'My best friend and biggest pest of course sometimes. The sharer of my secrets, the buffer between me and Harry.'

This is how Allan Ahlberg describes the appearance of Tom's ghost: 'It was Harry who saw him first. He grabbed my sleeve but said nothing. I looked . . . and there was Tom. He had his hands in his pockets, his jacket collar up. His hair was uncombed, as wild as ever. And he was leaning against a tree'. Children deserve books that use language so powerfully that they convey profound truths about human experience and feeling.

For children ready to go on from R.L. Stine's Goosebumps series, Oxford University Press have published two solid collections of ghost stories, selected by Dennis Pepper for this age range and above: *The New Oxford Book of Ghost Stories, Volume 1* and *The New Oxford Book of Ghost Stories, Volume 2*. The tales are by such quality writers as Philippa Pearce ('The Running Companion') and Jan Mark ('In Black and White'). There are some fine ghost stories in Kevin Crossley-Holland's *Enchantment: Fairy Tales, Ghost Stories and Tales of Wonder*; the stories come from all over the British Isles. 'Samuel's Ghost', about a ghost who must find his missing fingernail to be at peace, is one of the sadder tales. In her introduction to *Traditional Stories from the Caribbean*, Petronella Breinberg points out that 'haunting stories' reflect the history of the place where they are told. Older primary children would cope with all but the most frightening.

Ghost stories are usually less terrifying than stories in the 'horror' stable but there are still some sensitive children we have to keep in mind when offering the stories. Philippa Pearce argues that the best 'can stretch the imagination in ways otherwise impossible', and that 'fear engendered is often akin to awe' (Pearce in Watson, 2001: 285).

Horror stories and 'scary' books

Horror stories are far less subtle than ghost stories and tend to be about violent acts and hideous objects and creatures. Their explicit intention is to shock and repulse. Is this a suitable genre for children? Horror stories for children omit the extreme events of the adult form. But as Victoria de Rijke points out, censors respond inconsistently to horror in visual or written forms. 'If horror writing were to compare with levels of explicit digital violence and gore in computer games, it would be banned outright' (de Rijke in Hunt, 2004: 507).

So to go back to my question – 'Is this a suitable genre for children?' – I think we have to give the young readers the choice. Ask a class of children what they like to read and 'scary' books are usually mentioned. Why is this? I think it may be because the stories push at the boundaries of experience and expectation. There is also pleasure in 'being scared, just enough' and the best frightening stories develop aspects of the imagination, perhaps kinds that cannot be nourished in other ways (Impey, 1990: 11).

We have to take account of the age of the children when choosing; the very young may not always separate fantasy and reality and can be frightened by things they read or see. Nicholas Tucker comments that young children can be disturbed by a fierce story with an aggressive looking monster. But we must not forget that children are individuals and 'a book which terrifies one may delight another' (Tucker, 1989: 8). The important thing is that children should be in control and able to cope with the stories we offer them. Part of being in control involves knowing in advance what a genre is likely to include in the way of characters and events. Becoming able to suspend disbelief helps the older reader 'enjoy horror' (de Rijke, 2004: 516). Nine-year-old Natasha seemed to be saying something similar to me: 'Scary stories are exciting and you get frightened but nothing actually happens to you' (Mallett, 1997: 16).

Pre-school and nursery, 3–5-year-olds

Young children sometimes come across things that frighten them in books and it can be difficult to anticipate what they might be. Fifteen-month-old Henry found the large black spider that

> ## BOX 6.3 THINGS TO KEEP IN MIND WHEN CHOOSING SCARY STORIES
>
> - For younger children, the fear should be overt and not vague and hidden.
> - Check illustrations are not too disturbing.
> - Be aware that some things that do not trouble most children might be too much for a few.
> - Things should be more or less resolved by the end of the story.
> - Frightening stories can enhance children's sense of their own power, helping them to recognize their fears and anxieties and to make them explicit (e.g. *The Monster Bed*).
> - With older children in mind, there have to be some frightening moments to make the book exciting; humour can be a balancing element at any age (*The Ankle Grabbers*).
>
> This list draws on Impey (1990) and Tucker (1989).

springs out at the end of Rod Campbell's *I'm Not Scary* picturebook alarming. So it was put on a shelf out of the way; but Henry sometimes gets it down, opens it gingerly, closes it quickly and then puts it back on the shelf. Fascinated and repelled, he has found a way of being in control.

Children come across arresting images and notions in fairy and folk tales. *Hansel and Gretel* taps into a child's fear of abandonment and of being eaten. The monsters in Maurice Sendak's *Where the Wild Things Are* beg Max to stay with them and promise to eat him up because they love him so much! Other picturebooks take children into adventures and situations that both excite and worry. *Mr and Mrs Pig's Evening Out,* a picturebook by Mary Rayner, delighted a nursery class, who loved the pictures of the pigs in pyjamas with their tails sticking out. But would some children be frightened when Mrs Wolf turns out to be the babysitter? And might this fear return when they are left with a babysitter (Tucker, 1989: 8)? Children are often more robust than we suspect and do not always make this sort of connection.

The Monster Bed by Jeanne Willis and *The Gruffalo* by Julia Donaldson both help children by showing that facing your fears head on can sometimes be the best policy.

5–8-year-olds

When I asked whether five-year-old Orla would like a picturebook her mother said: 'Anything except a book that is about or has a picture of a wolf.' Then I found that a lot of picturebooks and short illustrated stories do include wolves. *Wolf Child* by Susan Gates is a transformation story: Small Wolf is changed into a human child when a shooting star falls from the sky. The Wolf family are devastated and so Wise Wolf uses a magic bone to make Small Wolf's fur, tail and claws reappear.

Turning to novelty books, one with great imaginative appeal is *The Foggy, Foggy Forest* by Nick Sharratt. Opaque pages form a misty background through which images can be glimpsed. Is it an elf or an ogre? For a peril-filled journey using pop-up images try Martin Taylor's *The Lost Treasure of the Mummy*.

For the upper end of this age range, Helen Paiba's *Scary Stories for Eight-Year-Olds* would be good for reading aloud. The tales are not too long, collected from around the world and are illustrated with distinctive humour by Tony Ross.

The books in the Chillers series are gripping but not too alarming, and at around eighty pages in length, suitable for the older end of this age range.

BOX 6.4 *DARKNESS SLIPPED IN* BY ELLA BURFOOT (MACMILLAN)

The little girl in this picturebook finds darkness 'eats up all the light'.

In an attempt to make darkness 'real' and not vague and amorphous, the book gives darkness a shape – a head and eyes – so that there is a focus for the little girl's fears. When I was helping select illustrated books for awards, I found some people thought this book was an imaginative way of helping children confront their fears while others felt the creature pictured actually made darkness all the more terrifying.

8–11-year-olds

A master of surrealism, Anthony Browne has produced a number of picturebooks where fantasy veers towards the horror category. *The Big Baby* is about a man who drinks a bottle of youth juice and becomes a baby with an adult-sized head. The images are disturbing and the detail fascinating, but older primary children seem able to find them amusing. Other picturebooks disturb – for example David McKee's *I Hate My Teddy Bear*, Maurice Sendak's *In the Night Kitchen* and Raymond Briggs' *Fungus the Bogeyman*.

But when we think of horror stories for the nines and over we tend to think first of the Goosebumps series by R.L. Stine, a series with monsters, magic and strange happenings that thrill and frighten (see Box 6.5).

BOX 6.5 THE GOOSEBUMPS SERIES BY R.L. STINE (SCHOLASTIC)

The page-turning qualities of R.L. Stine's Goosebumps series made them the most borrowed children's books in libraries in the late 1990s (Stones, 1999b). Referring to *The Blob That Ate Everyone*, ten-year-old Selcuk comments: 'I love the story. It is about a boy who likes typing scary stories, he finds an old typewriter and his story comes true. The blob trashes the whole neighbourhood.'

Another series in which the books have the elements of horror is Creepe Hall, written by Alan Durant and illustrated by Hunt Emerson. Included are *Creepe Hall*, *Return to Creepe Hall* and *Creepe Hall for Ever*. As is to be expected in Gothic tales, there are haunted houses, werebeavers, vampires and a child caught up in dangerous territory. This Gothic brand of fantasy reaches a new intensity of unnerving events and images in a book like Leander Deeny's *Hazel's Phantasmagoria*. This follows a familiar course of events: child is sent by parents to stay with a relative, relative turns out to be unpleasant, child tries to escape and meets up with all manner of terrifying characters. Even where older primary children are concerned, tolerance of frightening situations and characters varies with the individual. Peter Hollindale comments that the humour in *Hazel's Phantasmagoria* is a bit at odds with 'some very dark and questionable areas' that the book visits (Hollindale, 2008: 23).

I'm not sure that I would read children Louise Cooper's stories in *Short and Spooky! A Book of Very Short Spooky Stories* before Year 6. Just because the stories are short does not mean that they are not alarming. I find the story 'I Wish . . .' particularly chilling; Jack and John are unkind to younger brother Joe. Not so unusual, but what happens here is truly devastating. A collection of longer tales, again for the top end of this age range, is *Shock Forest and Other Stories* by Margaret Mahy, which looks at the unsettling effect some landscapes and buildings can have.

Justin Somper's Vampirates series is about twin fourteen-year-olds, Connor and Grace, who run off to sea. They are shipwrecked and each child is taken on to a different ship,

---

- *This Is the Bear and the Scary Night* by Sarah Hayes (Walker)
  Rhyming couplets and appealing illustrations by Helen Craig make this storybook a good introduction for the under fives to ways of dealing with fear and anxiety. An owl carries a little boy's teddy bear away in her talons. It gets dark in the park and the bear has to be brave. All is well in the end.

- *Scary Stories for Eight-Year-Olds* by Helen Paiba (Macmillan)
  These stories about monsters and witches are from around the world and illustrated distinctively by Tony Ross. (There are also collections by the same author for nine and ten-year-olds.)

- *Killer Mushrooms Ate My Gran* by Susan Gates (Puffin)
  'When Maggot arrived at Gran's house, she was trying to read a mushroom.' This is the intriguing first sentence in this most original book for children from about age eight years. There are some truly frightening moments – the mushrooms have terrifying spores that threaten to harm Gran and take over the world. The dialogue is brilliant and the book is full of surprises; for example, Gran has a courageous fiancé – Jack Dash.

- *The Thing in the Sink* by Frieda Hughes (Hodder Children's Books)
  Imagine something peering at you from the bath overflow! Peter wants a pet for the school project but 'the Thing' was not what he had in mind. This most imaginative story is well illustrated by Chris Riddell and would appeal to young readers of about eight or nine. (See also her *Three Scary Stories*.)

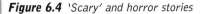

Figure 6.4 'Scary' and horror stories

Connor with pirates and Grace with vampires; and so each child faces different experiences and challenges. These adventure stories show something of the importance of loyalty and friendship and of being resourceful and courageous when danger looms. The books are long – *Blood Captain* is 544 pages – and use interesting and sometimes demanding language and imagery. And so it will be the abler, more mature young learners who enjoy these books before the teenage years.

Finally there are stories which tap not into the supernatural, but rather into terrifying real or possible events; Victoria de Rijke calls this the 'fear of the Real' (de Rijke in Hunt, 2004: 514). War stories often present this 'fear of the Real'; *The Boy in the Striped Pyjamas*, by John Boyne, tells of nine-year-old Bruno's meeting with Shmuel, who is the boy in the striped pyjamas of the title, an inmate of a concentration camp.

In *Rose Blanche* by Ian McEwan, a young girl attempts to help the starving children in a concentration camp. Unusually for a children's book, the ending is uncertain.

FORMATS AND MEDIA

Genre fiction uses a particularly varied repertoire of formats and media. Many of the texts discussed so far have been written narratives, with some illustrations. Here I go on to consider narratives in print comic and graphic text format, and think about the 'moving image' media which are so much part of children's reading experience in their leisure time. These essentially visual formats and media have been developed and enriched by digital technology and are now perceived much more positively – allowing children to bring to the classroom valuable skills and awareness about visual kinds of literacy.

You may find it helpful to refer to Figure 6.5 as you read the next sections.

Print comics and magazines, cartoon-strip storybooks, graphic picturebooks and novels

Some specialists in children's literature place all the texts mentioned in the sub-heading above in the 'comic book' stable. According to this view, graphic novels are comics that are longer, in book form and have a thematic unity that shorter comic strips may lack. So, writes Philip Pullman, 'Tintin is (a graphic story) and Dennis the Menace isn't' (Pullman, 1995: 8). Technology has enhanced and developed non-book print texts as it has film and moving image texts. Some print texts are multimodal, using three dimensions: design, words and pictures (see Box 6.8). We find multimodality in fictional narrative and also in the non-fiction texts considered in Part II of the present book; non-fiction authors and illustrators use colour, orientation, size and strength of print to communicate. The spatial organization of material and ideas means a different way of understanding how texts are constructed and socially mediated (Bearne, 2009: 8). What seems possible changes all the time and we would expect that new forms of texts, the nature of which may be difficult to imagine now, will constantly come into being.

Comics, cartoon strips and magazines

Cartoon images are widely used and familiar to the youngest children. They are evident in medical leaflets, safety cards on aeroplanes and in traffic signs – because they communicate

Cartoons – moving image narratives which were first made for cinema and then for television. The images can be created by drawing individual picture 'cells' in sequence (Disney's *Snow White*), by filming models (*Thomas the Tank Engine*) or by computer animation (*Toy Story*).

Comic strips – print narratives where each box or panel (which may differ in size or orientation) contains an illustration and often speech bubbles and explanatory narrative.

Digital literacy – a term associated with the new media age in which children encounter, understand and sometimes create animated films, computer graphics and sound.

Graphic texts – communicate through both writing and illustration, but word and image enjoy at least the same status and sometimes the pictures dominate or replace written text altogether.

Manga texts – comic storybooks originating in Japan, where they are still published in huge numbers. They are highly visual texts with stylized illustrations – characters often have accentuated eyes and expressions. (See Figure 6.9.)

Media texts – the programmes, films, images and websites carried by different forms of communication. Books can also be seen as media 'as they provide us with mediated representations of the world' (Buckingham, 2003: 3).

Medium – refers to the kind of communication channel through which meaning is made, be it a print resource or an electronic form.

Multimedia – refers to the combination of media to communicate meaning. The media may include written text, images both static and moving, sound and links.

Multimodal – refers to the forms in which meaning is communicated. A multimodal print text communicates through a combination of writing, image and design. Electronic texts may use these modes and a range of media, including sound, music and film. (See Box 6.8.)

Reading paths – these differ: when faced with continuous print readers use the sequence which unfolds to glean the relationship between events. If the text is multimodal the reader is not always offered a clear path to follow and can choose to let their eye alight on a block of writing, an image or on a particular colour or typeface (Kress, 2003).

Text – a constantly expanding term which now covers much more than what we find in print materials. Writers on the expanding concept of literacy suggest we see a text as a unit of communication which, in addition to continuous print, may take the form of a conversation, a radio or television programme, a blog, an image (static or moving), a text message or a cartoon.

Figure 6.5 *Glossary: terms to do with formats and media*

swiftly and universally. The children's comic and cartoon storybook has long had great appeal for many children, not least because this is an essentially graphic medium which uses pictures to make a narrative. The use of panels and layout, the shape, size and orientation of pictures all contribute to the meaning. For those who would like to read further, I recommend Katia Pizzi's chapter, 'Contemporary Comics', which gives a helpful overview and a succinct history of the comic over the twentieth century (Pizzi in Hunt, 2004: 385–95).

Figure 6.6 *Front cover of* Doctor Who Adventures
Parallel Worlds special, Issue 108, 26 March–20 April 2009. Reproduced with the permission of BBC World Wide

While the cartoon strip is ubiquitous in our culture and constantly developing, the print weekly comic which was such popular reading some decades ago – *The Eagle*, *Tiger* and *Wizard* – has largely disappeared. The *Beano*, edited by Alan Digby, survives as a weekly comic with popular cartoon strips including Dennis the Menace and Minnie the Minx. But on the whole, in the UK at least, publishers seem to have assumed that children prefer their comics on the computer screen, producing only annuals and monthly magazines. A lot of magazine type material for children contains comic strip alongside other kinds of writing and illustrating. There are many print spin-offs from popular television series like *Doctor Who* and *Star Wars*.

Cartoon strip in children's storybooks

Many picturebook creators use cartoon strip to great effect. One of the first and best was Janet Ahlberg, whose illustrations of the picturebooks she created with Allan Ahlberg have become classics. The cartoon-strip stories of Marcia Williams show that this form can be used for sad tales and events as well as for happy and comic ones. In *Bravo, Mr William Shakespeare!* a restricted palette and facial expressions communicate a bleak mood and atmosphere.

More recently, children's Manga-type comic storybooks covering mystery, adventure, science fiction and horror have become popular in the UK. In Franklin Watts' I Hero series Sonia Leong, the artist of titles like *Pirate Gold* and *Gorgon's Cave*, creates dramatic action-filled pictures and gives the characters she draws stylized features, including prominent eyes.

BOX 6.6 MARCIA WILLIAMS' USE OF COMIC STRIP TO RETELL CLASSIC STORIES

In an interview for *English 4–11* Williams discussed why comic strip is such an effective form for promoting literacy by encouraging enthusiasm for stories. Important factors seem to be:

- The best comic strips 'teach' young readers to integrate information by combining what is gleaned from different modes: pictures, text and speech balloons.
- 'Multimodal texts', whether print or a 'moving image' medium, link with children's experience of texts outside the classroom.
- The comic or cartoon-strip form lends itself to teasing and entertaining and helps create a relationship between illustrator and young readers.
- It can communicate the full range of human situations, dilemmas and emotions. Thus line and colour can create mood and atmosphere.

See Mallett (2008b).

Graphic picturebooks and novels

The graphic picturebook or novel is a modern art form which is far from easy to define. According to Lovereading-4kids.uk it is 'a novel whose narrative is conveyed through a combination of text and pictures, usually but not always in comic strip' (www.lovereading4-kids.uk, accessed 17 March 2009). Picturebook and storybook illustrators like Briggs and

BOX 6.7 *THE SAVAGE* BY DAVID ALMOND AND DAVID MCKEAN (ILLUS.) (WALKER)

In this graphic novel we learn early on that Blue deeply resents the bully who mocks him after the death of his father. He finds refuge in writing a story about a feral child who resembles a wild animal.

This is an innovative children's novel, not least because of the balance between a riveting story and David McKean's exciting graphic illustrations in ominous dark greens and blues. Look at the stunning cover picture of the defiant, lean wild boy! I actually think this book may be the making of readers in the same way as *The Catcher in the Rye* and *A Kestrel for a Knave* have been. The language is rhythmic, alive and accessible: 'There was a wild kid living in Burgess Woods. He had no family and he had no pals and he didn't know where he come from.'

A teacher remarked to me that she had found some colleagues and some parents had reservations about the non-standard spelling and concern that the Savage carries knives. Could this be a useful talking point? Over the years the books that have absorbed and truly engaged are those that press at the boundaries of convention and carry children into areas of harsher reality.

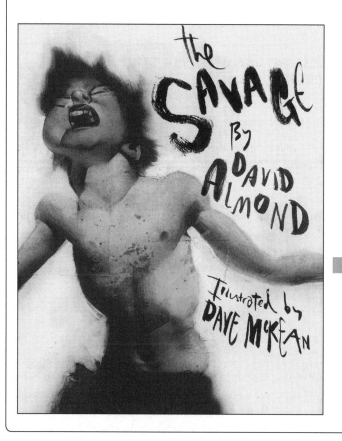

Figure 6.7
Front cover of The Savage *by David Almond and Dave McKean (illus.)* Reproduced with the permission of the publishers Walker Books Ltd. London SE11 5HJ. Cover illustration copyright 2008 Dave McKean

Williams who use cartoon strip to great effect have been mentioned above. Neil Gaimon and David McKean are at the forefront of innovative graphic picturebook creation. In their ground-breaking picturebook *The Wolves in the Walls*, paper and digital methods are combined.

It is not just genre fiction that appears in cartoon-strip or graphic format. What do you think of the many graphic versions of classic texts? Helen Oxenbury has copiously illustrated Lewis Carroll's *Alice's Adventures in Wonderland* to attract young readers who might not manage the original full-length novel. *Jane Eyre* and *Macbeth* are two of the quick text titles in the Classical Comic series.

David McKean's illustrations in David Almond's extraordinary graphic novel *Savage* are powerful, energetic and an integral part of the story (see Box 6.7). Neil Gaiman's novel *Coraline*, a disturbing story about a young girl living a parallel life alongside her real one, was published first as a novel and then in graphic form and an animated version appeared in cinemas from April 2009.

Brian Selznick's *The Invention of Hugo Cabret,* is another ground-breaking illustrated novel with some features reminiscent of picturebooks. The 500 pages take the reader through a highly imaginative reading experience. The story is intriguing and full of secrets and surprises which are shown through powerful charcoal drawings as well as a fast-moving written text. Novels that integrate so many ways of communicating are demanding to read, but this book might be appreciated by the older and abler primary school child.

Futuristic picturebooks

These books are innovative in concept, illustration and story line and aim to stretch the imagination in new ways. See Figure 6.8 for annotation of David Kirk's *Nova's Ark*.

Genre fiction communicated by 'moving image' media

Children see the moving image at an early age, usually through watching television programmes like the BBC's *In the Night Garden* and *The Teletubbies*. Two books are of particular help here. In *Young Children's Literacy Development and the Role of Televisual Texts*, Naima Brown shows how watching television programmes with very young children can lead to lively activities including role play, storytelling and, later on, writing. David Buckingham, in a number of books and papers, including *Media Education: Literacy, Learning and Contemporary Culture*, argues that children's visual knowledge and experience should be the basis for classroom work. In *Literacy and Popular Culture: Using Children's Culture in the Classroom*, Jackie Marsh and Elaine Millard argue that these texts are highly motivating for many children and have a valid place in the literacy programme (Marsh and Millard, 2000). One theme for film study in school is how different 'moving image' films are constructed. In *Shrek* (Dreamworks, 2001), *Finding Nemo* (Walt Disney Pictures, 2003) and *Toy Story 1* and *2* (Walt Disney Pictures, 1995/6) sophisticated computer generated digital images are used to produce complex and subtle narratives. *Wallace and Gromit* uses plasticine models to create animation and achieve subtle characterizations and relationships.

In an interesting account, 'Moving Stories: Digital Editing in the Nursery', Jackie Marsh looks at the activities of four-year-olds making an animated story using iMovie2 (Evans, 2004:

Comics and magazines

- *Derek the Sheep* by Gary Northfield (Bloomsbury)
  This comic book brings together some of Derek's adventures from the *Beano* for the enjoyment of children aged about five to seven years.

- *Casper the Friendly Ghost* by Leslie Carbarga and Jerry Beck (Dark House Publishers)
  An American comic book with an iconic little ghost who often befriends children, is rejected by their parents and then finds favour through his helpful deeds.

- *Doctor Who Adventures.* Parallel Worlds Special, Issue 108, 26 March–1 April 2009 (BBC Worldwide)
  This weekly magazine attracts readers from about age five upwards. Each issue has cartoon stories. (See Case Study 6.2.)

Cartoon-strip picturebooks and storybooks

- *Ghost Riders* by Alex Gutteridge (A&C Black)
  The Chiller series has comic book illustrations by Barry Wilkinson.

- *Ricky Ricotta's Giant Robot* by Dave Pilkey and Martin Ontiveros (Young Hippo)
  Digital pictures in cartoon format provide a distinctive reading experience. This would suit children of about seven and older children who need an accessible text but a sufficiently mature story.

- *Old Tom* by Leigh Hobbs (Happy Cat Books)
  (See Case Study 6.1.)

- *Bravo, Mr William Shakespeare!* by Marcia Williams (Walker)
  These versions of the Bard's plays show the power and versatility of the cartoon-strip form. In *King Lear* bleak landscape and tragic characters are shown with great skill.

Graphic picturebooks, storybooks and novels

- *The Boffin Boy* by David Orme (Ransome Publishing)
  These stories have simplified Manga-style illustrations and speech balloons.

- *Bambi* Cine-Manga Titles for Kids (Tokyopop Press)
  The familiar story about the young deer that loses its mother is presented with stylized illustrations.

- *Pirate Gold* by Steve Barlow and Steve Skidmore and Sonia Leong (Franklin Watts)
  (See Figure 6.9.)

- *The Wolves in the Wall* by Neil Gaiman and David McKean (Bloomsbury)
  What can Lucy hear at night? Wolves come out of the walls, wolves shown in David McKean's highly imaginative but nightmarish pictures: cruel jaws are drawn in pen and ink and appear against disturbing collages.

- *The Savage* by David Almond and David McKean (illus.) (Walker)
  (See Box 6.7.)

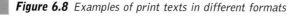

Figure 6.8 *Examples of print texts in different formats*

- *Stormbreaker* by Anthony Horowitz (Walker)
  The more reluctant young reader who responds to a strong visual element in their reading may be enticed by this graphic version of the novel.

Futuristic picturebooks

- *Nova's Ark* by David Kirk (Grosset & Dunlap)
  This tells the story of how a young robot and a dog called Sparky make a set of carved animals. The visual appeal is enormous and younger children, around age seven, might like the picturebook version with a toy included: *Nova's Ark Boo and Toy Set.*

Figure 6.8 *continued*

Figure 6.9
Front cover of Pirate Gold *by Steve Barlow and Steve Skidmore and Sonia Leong (illus.)*
Reproduced with the permission of the publishers Franklin Watts. Copyright 2008

31–44). Two organizations which help with advice and resources for the use of film in school are the British Film Institute (www.bfi.org.uk/education) and Film Education (www.filmeducation.org).

Moving image texts and texts on screen enable the combination of varied modes and media – sound, vocalization and movement as well as the visual and the written. Reading on screen calls on varied and different reading pathways and processes that contrast with reading continuous print (Bearne, 2009: 2).

Children making their own films with support from the teacher and ICT experts is becoming more common. On the Film Street site we read that 'Film making is a great leveller as special needs children can join in' (www.filmstreet.co.uk). This kind of activity

> ## BOX 6.8 MULTIMODALITY IN PRINT AND MOVING IMAGE TEXTS
>
> A multimodal text combines a number of modes of communication. Print multimodality combines design, words and pictures and may use speech balloons and different typefaces, print colours and sizes to add meaning. Screen texts can add or use instead a combination of music, sound and moving images. Digital technology has hugely increased the number and variety of texts on screen. So we have websites, DVDs, PlayStation games, virtual reality representations, hyper-textual narratives and, of course, email and texting. The range and worth of children's multimodal writing are celebrated in Bearne *et al.* 2005 and Bearne 2009.
>
> Also worth reading are the following: Bearne, E. *et al.* (2007) *Reading on Screen.* Leicester: UKLA. Bearne, E. (2009) 'Multimodality, Literacy, and Texts: Developing a Discourse'. *Journal of Early Years Literacy,* Summer, 2009, pp. 2–65. Bearne, E. *et al.* (2005) *More than Words 2: Creating Stories on Page and Screen.* London: QCA/UKLA. Evans, J. (ed.) (2004) *Literacy Moves On: Using Popular Culture, New Technologies and Critical Literacy in the Primary Classroom.* London: David Fulton (Chapter 1). Kress, G. and van Leeuwen, T. (2006) *Reading Images: The Grammar of Visual Design,* second edition. London: Routledge.

can lead to more motivated young learners and to creative thinkers and talented writers. Other sources of moving image texts include Doctor Who (www.bbc.co.uk/doctorwho/), Odeon cinemas (www.odeon.co.uk) and Moviemail (www.moviem.co.uk).

(All sites were accessed on 7 April 2009.)

USING GENRE FICTION IN THE CLASSROOM

Part of the teacher's skill is to choose just the right activity to explore a particular text, as the case studies in this section show. Not only do we want the activities to be enjoyable and satisfying, we aim also to make children critical readers of both print and moving image texts.

Reading aloud

Mystery, science fiction, ghost and horror stories can all be gripping enough to make for an exciting shared experience. When the children 'are balanced on that knife edge between pleasure and fear' you know you have tapped into something deeply felt (Impey, 1990: 9). Three excellent 'read alouds' for the under fives are the picturebooks *In a Dark Dark Wood* by Jessica Souhami, *Sheep in Wolf's Clothing* by Satoshi Kitamura and *Here Come the Aliens!* by Colin McNaughton.

Julia Donaldson's Gruffalo books are often read to younger classes because teachers have found that the response is usually so fulsome. The theme of how to overcome fear clearly appeals. Five to eights would find much to think about in Allan Ahlberg's moving story *My Brother's Ghost.*

Louise Cooper's selections in *Short and Scary* and *Short and Spooky* are helpful to teachers of older primary children seeking short 'read alouds'. Another collection worth considering is the two volume *Alien Stories* selected by Dennis Pepper. 'The Star Beast' by Nicholas Stuart Grey is riveting and told in wonderfully evocative language. Full-length children's novels on genre fiction mentioned in this chapter that have been found to be successful for reading to the whole class include Nicholas Fisk's *Grinny*, Penelope Lively's *The Ghost of Thomas Kempe* and, more recently, the stories in Justin Somper's *Vampirates* series.

Talk and drama

Part of this chapter has been about books which tap into fears and such books can be an excellent starting point for young readers and listeners to discuss fears and anxieties 'at a distance'. In addition to the books already mentioned the following are worth considering for the under sevens: *No Worries* by Marcia Williams; *The Park in the Dark* and *Owl Babies* by Martin Waddell; *Dark, Dark Tale* by Ruth Brown (see also Box 6.3).

Talk and discussion can help older children to become critical readers of genre fiction and of 'popular culture' texts: comics, cartoon strips, graphic stories and novels. For suggestions for using talk to understand, evaluate and use 'moving image' texts, see *Look Again!*, a resource published in 2003 by the British Film Institute (BFI).

Genre fiction texts lend themselves to drama work in which atmosphere, tension and climax and resolution feature. Workshops, sometimes enlivened by a visiting author, script writing following improvisation around ghost and horror stories and short films made with a digital camera all generate enthusiasm.

CASE STUDY 6.1 AN INTERACTIVE WORKSHOP: SEVEN-YEAR-OLDS TALK ABOUT LEIGH HOBBS' CARTOON-STRIP BOOKS AND HIS OLD TOM CHARACTER AND DO SOME DRAWINGS

Leigh Hobbs began by showing a large image of Old Tom, the cat which is the flawed but endearing hero of *Old Tom, Old Tom Goes to Mars* and other titles in the series. Leigh explained cartoons are about capturing just those characteristics that most define personality. Soon they were drawing the chubby orange cat, with one good eye and one weird one and his fish skeleton toy. Holding up some of the children's drawings, Leigh showed how just one little mark or line — a raised eyebrow perhaps — can change a character's expression, to reveal mood or attitude. Quite a lot of the humour, Leigh explained, came from the mismatches between his illustrations and the written text.

Finally, the children drew their own cartoon characters and Leigh suggested they might like to weave a story around them. (See Mallett, 2007c.)

Art, design and technology and writing combine in the 'storybox' approach

The storybox approach works well with the dramatic scenes from mystery, 'scary' and science fiction stories. Helen Bromley has shown the potential of recreating a scene from a story in a box – a shoebox, for example – with very young children (Bromley, 2004). Figures that pop up add suspense and surprise in 'scary' stories. Stories to inspire include *The Aliens Are Coming!* by Colin McNaughton, *The Foggy, Foggy Forest* by Nick Sharratt and *Harry and the Robots* by Ian Whybrow. The work could be extended by making multimodal texts with writing and drawing, writing character profiles and scripts for a puppet play and, in the case of science fiction themes, making robots out of scrap metals. The approach can be adapted for older children.

Comparing the same story in different media

Children are as likely to turn to a book after seeing a television version as the other way around. Stories in the genre fiction stable are often chosen for television and film and can encourage discussion about how the moving image makes a special impact, one different from a print illustration. Questions to tackle after viewing and reading might include:

- How is the story introduced in each medium?
- How effective is the moving image in building up tension?
- Are there any parts of the book which are better served by a written account and an illustration rather than by a moving image?
- What role do sound effects and music play in the screen version?
- Do you like to see the characters made flesh in the film, or do you prefer to use your own imagination?

BOX 6.9 *LOOK AGAIN! A TEACHING GUIDE TO USING FILM AND TELEVISION WITH THREE TO ELEVEN-YEAR-OLDS* (2003) (BFI EDUCATION, WITH SUPPORT FROM THE DFES, EDUCATION@BFI.ORG.UK)

This book is an inspirational resource for teachers of children from age three to eleven. Based on the belief that to be fully literate today's children need to understand and use moving image media, it supports lessons across the whole curriculum, offering a wealth of practical suggestions and some interesting classroom case studies. Eight teaching techniques are set out for helping children analyse film and television. Talking about films and television programmes and thinking about how they are made and for whom guides children towards making progress as critical readers of moving image media.

The book is peppered with interesting case studies, including a Reception class project in which the children viewed films about superheroes like Spiderman and Superwoman. They looked at the presentation of one superhero across a range of media and invented their own superhero.

- How does the written story make the characters convincing?
- How much of the dialogue in the book is taken over in the film?
- If you were the author of the book, how satisfied would you feel with the film version?
- Do you think it best to see the film first and then read the book or vice versa?

After discussion children could make notes under columns such as 'Advantages of the story in book form' and 'Advantages of the story on screen'.

Then the groups could report back to the whole class to debate the findings.

Writing their own science fiction, ghost or horror stories

Even the more reluctant young writer is often willing if not eager to write the genre fiction kind of story. Particularly in the case of older children, discussion can help identify the genre features of the kind of story being considered. Main points can be written on a flipchart or on a whiteboard note pad. There is nothing as potent as writing your own story to clinch not only understanding, but appreciation of the genre. I find children's writing is energized if embedded in other activities like art, discussion and drama. The writing outcomes in the two case studies that follow seem to reinforce this.

Two case studies

Children can enjoy reading and writing, but for many it is enriched and made meaningful by embedding it in other activities. Case Studies 6.2 and 6.3 show teachers creating interest and supporting learning, using art, drama, technology and contemporary texts.

ASSESSING AND RECORDING PROGRESS

Children's progress has to do with becoming able to read, talk about and appreciate a wide range of genre fiction as well as becoming able to attempt to create their own. Teachers will find helpful evidence by listening to children's talk about texts and reading their writing. Increasingly, children's ability to read visual texts and to produce multimodal texts is part of assessment and we have some way to go to develop a framework for this (Bearne *et al.*, 2004). A team at BECTA is working towards a critical approach to assessing visual and ICT texts (http://schools.becta.org.uk/).

When it comes to recording progress, the reviews that children write about genre texts, their writing and drawing in the different genres of mystery, horror and ghost stories and experiments with making cartoon strips have a place in the English, language and literacy portfolio. As with other kinds of writing and illustrating, date and brief annotation is helpful. Photographs of drama work and annotated book displays as well as films of improvisations are other valid ways of recording progress. Children's views on their achievement and ideas for 'next steps' also have a place.

CASE STUDY 6.2 A YEAR 2 SCIENCE FICTION PROJECT: MAGIC FLYING MACHINES

The children brought from home *Doctor Who Adventures* and *Star Wars* to spark off talk about flying machines and space travel. Then the teacher set up a 'thought shower' about the unusual things they might see if they went on a magical space journey. Atmospheric music suggestive of space and planets played in the background and each child talked through one thing they imagined they might see. They drew on this discussion in their writing and also on ideas that came up during exciting activities across the curriculum. For example, in their Design and Technology lessons model space ships were designed and created for display. And in Drama the children dressed up as professors with cloaks and hats and improvised preparations for space journeys. Writing and drawing were introduced when the children's imaginations had been put into top gear. Central to the dynamic of this work was the inspiration provided by the stories and images in the magazines.

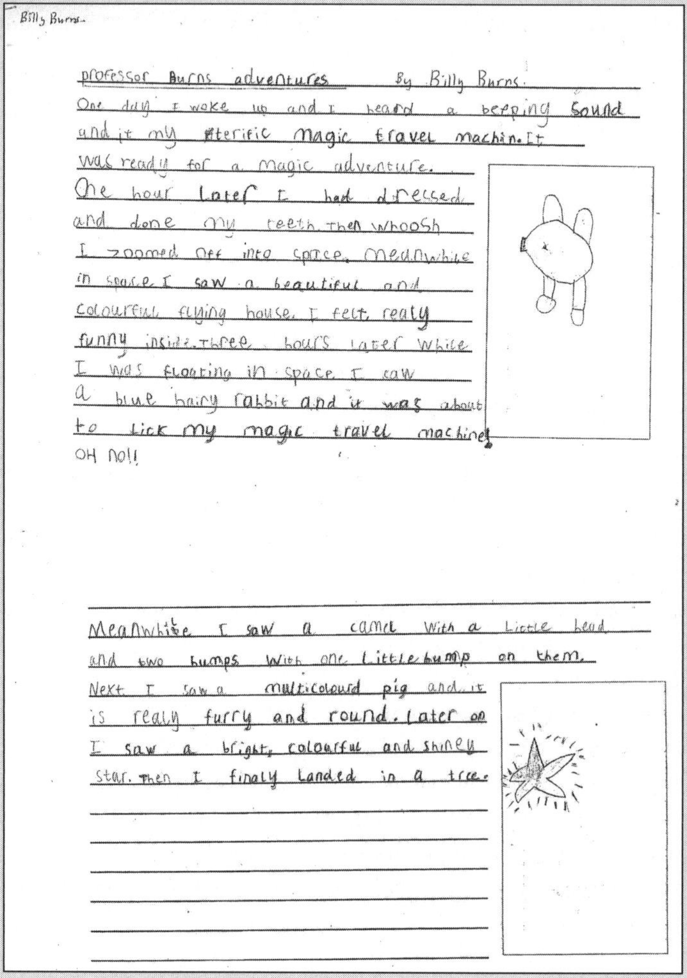

Billy Burns

Professor Burns adventures   By Billy Burns.
One day I woke up and I heard a bepping sound and it my pterific magic travel machin. It was ready for a magic adventure.
One hour later I had dressed and done my teeth then whoosh I zoomed off into space. Meanwhile in space I saw a beautiful and colourful flying house. I felt realy funny inside. Three hours later while I was floating in space I saw a blue hairy rabbit and it was about to lick my magic travel machine. OH no!!

Meanwhile I saw a camel with a little head and two humps with one little hump on them. Next I saw a multicoloured pig and it is realy furry and round. Later on I saw a bright, colourful and shiney star. Then I finaly landed in a tree.

Figure 6.10
Example of the Magic Flying Machines writing

CASE STUDY 6.3 A YEAR 6 CLASS USE CONTEMPORARY MEDIA TO EXPLORE A CLASSIC SCIENCE FICTION STORY: *WAR OF THE WORLDS* BY H.G. WELLS (STERLING)

This exciting science fiction project shows the impressive range of language and literacy work, in English lessons and across the curriculum, which children towards the end of the primary years can achieve. The teacher generated great enthusiasm by using contemporary media to illuminate a classic written text; in this case H.G.Wells' *War of the Worlds,* but the approach would transfer to other classic texts.

A stimulating start

Such an activity-packed project over several weeks can only be summarized here and I urge you to read the fuller account in Gill Robins' article in *English 4–11.*

There was a dynamic start: children arrived at school to be presented with press passes. They attended a 'press conference' led by Dr Xavier Delfosse (a teacher in role), who had discovered a new planet named Gliese 581c. He gave the 'journalists' information about the planet's size, position in the universe and its light years from Earth. The most exciting revelation was that it fitted into the Goldilocks zone – not too hot and not too cold – and therefore was possibly capable of sustaining life. The copious questions that followed showed the children were hooked on the notion of a new and possibly inhabited planet.

Choosing a format to write the reports

Before they wrote up reports for their newspapers and magazines, children were shown some genuine press releases about new planet discoveries from Times Online, *Los Angeles Times* and Associated Press. This led to research in information texts and on the internet about the scientific aspects of space exploration and the Universe.The children were given a free choice of the form in which the information would be given: a newspaper report, a scientific journal entry, a television or radio broadcast or a webpage.

There were interesting discussions about how you adapted language to intended audience, how you decided on a good angle and how the visual and verbal would be combined. Nearly all the children chose to present the information as a television, radio or web report because they were 'more fun to prepare':

Rachel: Good evening and welcome to News Today.

Hollie: I'm Hollie Webb.

Rachel: And I'm Rachel Harris.

Hollie: Reporting for News Today.

Rachel: For the first time, astronomers in Chile have discovered a 'super Earth' outside of our solar system that is potentially habitable. About five times the mass of Earth, the planet orbits a cool, dim, 'red dwarf' star located in the constellation of Libra, the team from the European Space Observatory said in a press release today.

What would happen if aliens arrived on Earth?

The children were invited, in their role as journalists, to meet Commander Alexis Higgins from Civilian Security Service (again the teacher in role) and to view a mysterious steel sphere that had landed in the school field. Was this a sign of an impending invasion by aliens from the newly discovered planet? Back in the classroom the whiteboard was used to note down a plan of action taking account of the most critical areas: physical needs, communication, safety, behaviour, media and belief.

Then came news that the town's security status had been raised to Red Alert and an aggressive invasion seemed imminent. The children explored their reactions through MSN conversations with a friend. Each pair was given a paper mock-up of an MSN screen.

Here is a snippet:

*Cheeky: Hey Monkey. Wats up? RU scared about the aliens?
Monkey: Yeah. I'm worried about wot they could do to me. You?

Reading the text of *War of the Worlds*

The children reflected together on what an alien invasion might involve as they read the first chapter of a Classic Start version of *War of the Worlds*. They recorded key themes, feelings and character details in their reading journals. Later they wrote narratives describing their 'personal experience' of the invasion. As they wrote, the opening of Jeff Wayne's soundtrack was played.

The written narratives were powerful. What people would feel as well as observe was recorded. 'I could hear the cry of tiny babies. Large, scaly, red and orange aliens floated everywhere on hover machines.' 'The alien's skin turned lighter because of the extreme coldness of Earth . . . As drops of cold liquid fell onto his hand, a piece of flaky skin got carried away in the turbulent breeze.' As the children and teacher read the story, they thought about how their narratives would develop. They also involved parents and friends of the school with special knowledge of the services that would be crucial if there was an alien invasion – including the Fire Service, the Church and the Police. Artwork was another motivating element; one choice was to plan a diagram of a Glesian and its vessel and fighting machine. Critically there was a continuing interplay between the reading and the other activities. From Chapters 6–9 the children learnt from Wells' description of how the Martians in his story moved and worked in teams and this led to discussions about communication. Chapters 10–15 tell of the tension between the narrator and the curate and this was explored through some 'hot seating'. One 'alien' sent an email home saying: 'I'm trying to help them look after their environment, but they looked at me with anger blazing in their eyes . . .'

As the reading of the book progressed towards Chapter 20, the children started to think of satisfying endings to their own narratives. This completed the structured part of the project. Now it was time for the children to communicate their responses and interpretations of the book. Amongst the choices were to make bookcovers, sculpture, collages and watercolours and to write poems.

Assessing the project

Most of the children chose to take up the art activities rather than perfecting their narratives and the teacher continues to ponder on this. The rich range of activities – only some of which have been mentioned in this short account – helped hugely with the children's reading of and enjoyment of a Victorian text which might otherwise not have been accessible to all of them. The move from single subject disciplines to a more integrated approach seemed to free the children to think creatively and to use skills they had acquired – not least in previous art, science, DT and ICT lessons – during the primary years.

Figure 6.11 *Eleven-year-old Elise's illustration of a space ship from Planet Gliese 581c*

Materials used: Sasaki, C. and Wells, H.G. (2007, illus. Akib, J.) *Classic Starts: The War of the Worlds Retold from the H.G. Wells original.* Sterling Publishing.

Music. Audio CD: Wayne, J. (2000) *Jeff Wayne's Musical Version of The War of the Worlds.* Columbia. ASIN:boooo4sknf.

For a longer version of this case study, see Robins (2009).

THE CAMBRIDGE/HOMERTON RESEARCH AND TEACHING CENTRE FOR CHILDREN'S LITERATURE

Concepts of what a text can be are changing rapidly. Professor Maria Nikolajeva, the director of this Centre opened in February 2010, and her team aim to give as much attention to comics, television programmes, films and video-games as to established forms of children's literature. She remarked: 'Children's literature and culture are not created in a vacuum; you need the social context' (*The Times*, 2010). Multimodal and multimedia texts are very much part of children's social environment now and deserve critical attention (www.educ. cam.ac.uk/centres/childrensliterature).

SUMMARY

- Genre fiction and popular culture texts are a useful bridge between home and school literacies.
- But if we want children to avoid being victims of commercialization and the unacceptable side of mass media influence, we need to help them to become critical readers.
- Mystery and detective stories show children as resourceful and courageous and this may be their main attraction.
- Science fiction is a form of fantasy inviting speculation about space travel and technology of the future.
- Ghost stories are concerned with the supernatural and particularly with the appearance of the spirits of the dead, while horror stories more deliberately aim to frighten and shock.
- Comics, magazines, cartoon-strip storybooks, graphic and futuristic picturebooks and novels add to children's repertoire and greatly help their visual literacy development.
- Moving image texts – televisual, film and internet access – also develop kinds of visual literacy and constantly change and help widen the concept of what literacy involves.
- Such texts can be an inspiring starting point for all kinds of activity: talk, drama, art, design and craft, writing and film making.
- Ways of assessing children's progress in visual kinds of literacy and of assessing print multimodal texts and 'moving image' texts are being developed.
- The spatial organization of material in some of these texts, whether in print or on screen, has implications for how texts are constructed and socially mediated.

Chapter 7

Longer stories and children's novels
An introduction

THE IMPORTANCE OF LONGER STORIES AND NOVELS

As children move through the primary years teachers hope that they become hooked on books and eager to tackle and persevere with longer stories. How do we help children build this desirable reading stamina? First and foremost it is a matter of provision and so the following chapters look at some appealing longer stories for class and school libraries. But don't forget to search your memory for stories you enjoyed and keep reading new stories for children to extend the repertoire from which you choose.

Longer stories and novels written for children are sustained fictional narratives with plots elaborate enough for characters to develop through events and challenges. I have found it helpful to group the large body of longer stories and novels under four main categories: animals; realistic (domestic, adventure and school); historical; and fantasy. We owe it to our pupils to introduce them to exciting and imaginative writing ; if you are sufficiently swept up by a long story to persevere with it, then you have made progress on the reading journey. In addition to the traditional print book we have audiobooks, stories in the form of film and electronic books. All offer a distinctive experience and children can be enthralled by graphics and the moving image. However, a print novel provides a unique and sustained reading experience.

GENRE FEATURES OF LONGER STORIES AND CHILDREN'S NOVELS

Longer stories and novels for children have a story 'structure', 'shape' or 'grammar'. At its most basic a story structure has a beginning or 'orientation' in which the setting is established and the main characters introduced, a middle and an end, where conflicts are resolved or, at any rate, partially resolved. Some narratologists and linguists include a 'special event' after the 'orientation' stage which energizes the tale and sets a series of events in motion (Gamble and Yates, 2008: 62). The point at which Tom accepts Willie into his care as an evacuee in *Goodnight Mister Tom* seems to be a 'special event' leading to all sorts of happenings. Robert Longacre calls this 'special event' an 'inciting moment'; he, along with others, also places a 'climax' just before the resolution of the story (Longacre, 1976).

'Story structure' may suggest that the events in a story are in chronological sequence. This is not always the case. For example, Nina Bawden's book *Carrie's War* starts with Carrie as an adult bringing her family to the place where she was evacuated as a child. All writers bring their own views and opinions to a story, consciously or not, which is one of the reasons why we provide children with a rich variety of different authors and books. Children become increasingly able to detect intentions and bias.

Writers have important choices to make, for example whether to tell the story in the first or the third person. A story written in the third person can offer several viewpoints about events, while writing in the first person shows everything from one perspective and can connect reader and writer in an inviting way. Quite a lot of stories for children are written entirely or partially in the form of letters between two or more characters. Michael Morpurgo's book *The Wreck of the Zanzibar* is written in letter and diary format, with some first-person narration. In other books using the 'letter' device, the reader has only one half of the correspondence and has to infer what the other character has written.

Are there particular themes we associate with children's longer stories? A common one is the tension between love of home and familiar surroundings and the need for independence and adventure. So there is often a home-away-home pattern (Nodelman, 1996; Gamble and Yates, 2008). Other themes often explored include friendship, loyalty, the tension between good and evil, fairness and unfairness and the human cost of war.

There are some language features associated with the story genre. For example, they are often written in an accessible style with much everyday sounding conversation. This does not mean that some young readers cannot cope with a more literary style, like that of Rosemary Sutcliff, for example.

Dialogue, including slang and dialect, is sometimes used to reveal a character's social group, personality and period. So Dickon's Yorkshire dialect is important in establishing character and period in Frances Hodgson Burnett's *The Secret Garden*.

Finally, like all texts, novels for children need cohesion to create what linguists call 'textuality' – the sense that what we have is a text rather than just a series of random sentences. The linguists who have contributed most to our understanding of cohesion are Michael Halliday and Ruqaiya Hasan, whose ground-breaking book *Cohesion in English* was published in 1976. It provides a detailed analysis of the many kinds of connectives and cohesive ties and the ways they are used in particular kinds of text. The two main kinds, however, are grammatical and lexical. Grammatical cohesive ties include, at sentence level, the use of conjunctions (and, but) and adverbs (soon, there). And, at text level, pronouns (he, she, they) can help a reader make referential connections to an earlier part of the text. 'Lexical' cohesive ties are especially important in stories; lexical cohesion is achieved by the choice of vocabulary, often to create images linked to a particular theme. So in Philip Pullman's *The Firework-Maker's Daughter*, images of heat, flame and warm colours – 'red fire and flame licked and cackled' – pervade the book.

Where a story is communicated through film, cohesion will be partly achieved visually. So a film story set on the coast will include moving images of waves, boats and sea birds.

CHOOSING LONGER STORIES AND CHILDREN'S NOVELS

What are the qualities to look for when choosing longer stories and novels for children? First they need to sustain interest and keep readers wanting to read on. So we need to take children's preferences and choices into account even if they include texts unlikely to please thoughtful critics of children's literature. Doesn't James Britton say somewhere that reading the second rate is sometimes not the first step to damnation but the beginning of a journey as a reader leading to the enjoyment of more satisfying and demanding books? Maybe, too, teachers need not worry if children are for a time locked into the work of one author. The important thing is that teachers look out for opportunities to introduce them to literature of enduring quality. We should not be surprised that views about whether or not a book is of enduring quality vary. But here are some thoughts about the qualities they might have. We should not, of course, expect any individual book to have all of the qualities described below:

- a strong story with a good plot, plenty of action and some suspense;
- characters for whom children can develop some empathy;
- the evocation of a memorable sense of place or setting;
- links to children's everyday lives and to their experience in the inner world of the imagination;
- emotional power – tapping into humour, worries and sadnesses as well as joyful and happy times;
- the ability to inspire young readers to think and imagine;
- constructive moral and ethical messages – books have a bias because each is a creation of an individual with their particular passions, beliefs and prejudices;
- convincing dialogue and vivid and flexible use of language, bringing the story and the characters alive on the page;
- high aesthetic standards, including the quality of the paper, print and cover design and illustrations which enhance the mood and atmosphere of the story.

There are two other considerations which teachers bear in mind when choosing books for their class. The first is 'readability'; no readability test I have encountered seems to be better than the judgement of a group of teachers in a school who have made themselves expert about children's literature and who know the interests, reading histories and abilities of the children. Children often rise to the challenge of more difficult syntax and vocabulary if the story and characters are riveting.

The second consideration is the balance of the whole collection and the range and variety of the longer stories provided. This would include the classics, newer works and books set in different historical, social, geographical and cultural settings. The balance of the collection also requires the provision of different media for presenting stories; these would include audiobooks, DVDs, television adaptations and electronic books.

Chapter 8

Animal stories
Animal autobiographies, talking animals and stories based on close observation of living creatures

INTRODUCTION

Animal stories in all their variety hold a strong place in children's literature. Two texts in particular have informed my analysis and you may wish to seek them out for further reading. The first is Simon Flynn's account 'Animal Stories', which explores issues of 'identification' and 'defamiliarization' and traces the development of the animal story through the centuries (Flynn in Hunt, 2004). The second is John Rowe Townsend's account 'Articulate Animals', which includes his reflections on the humanized animals in Kenneth Grahame's *The Wind in the Willows* (Townsend, 1995: 94–102).

ANIMAL AUTOBIOGRAPHIES

Here the animal is the storyteller. The best bring an immediacy to situations and events and carry children close to the animal's thoughts, preoccupations and fears. Children soon learn that the articulate animal is a literary device, something they find in the world of play and stories. However we must bear in mind that a child's response to a character is not straightforward. Some critics, Simon Flynn for example, are particularly wary of the notion of readers 'identifying with' characters and points out that it is naïve to think that all children love animals all the time. Some go through a period of being thoughtless or even cruel (Flynn in Hunt, 2004: 420). But, very generally, teachers find that children enjoy animal stories and empathize with animal characters.

For the five to eights, some of the most entertaining books with an animal narrator are those in Anne Fine's Killer Cat series.

Asked to name an animal autobiography for the over eights, many would think first of Anna Sewell's *Black Beauty*, published in 1877. Written by an author passionate about wanting to stop the cruel treatment of cab horses, it has its didactic moments. But it is also a riveting tale to which children often have a strong empathetic attachment. I would read this book aloud to children from about age eight and expect many young readers to manage it independently at about nine or ten years. Perhaps the animal 'autobiography' that has made most impact since *Black Beauty* is Michael Morpurgo's *War Horse*. The early months of the horse in *War Horse* are less idyllic than Beauty's; 'My earliest memories are a confusion of hilly fields and dark, damp stables, and rats that scampered along the beams above my head.' The National Theatre programme suggests that the play based on the novel is most suitable

---

BOX 8.1 *THE DIARY OF A KILLER CAT* **BY ANNE FINE (PENGUIN)**

We see all the incidents – killing birds, attacking next door's rabbit, grabbing small rodents – from the feline point of view. 'It is practically my JOB to go creeping round the garden after sweet little eensy-weensy birdypies that can hardly fly from one hedge to another', declares Tuffy. The dialogue in the book is superb, whether it is Ellie giving the cat little talks – 'Oh Tuffy! I know you're a cat but please, for my sake stop (killing birds)' – or Ellie's father shouting: 'Come out of there, you great fat furry psychopath. It's only a 'flu jab you're booked in for – more's the pity!'

Figure 8.1
Front cover of The Diary of a Killer Cat *by Anne Fine and Steve Cox (illus.)*
Reproduced with the permission of the publishers The Penguin Group. Copyright 1994

---

for children of twelve years and older. But one child's mother told me that she had ignored this guidance as her nine-year-old had already read the book. Some older primary school children will be ready to meet the challenge of such books that are powerful, insightful and linguistically alive.

TALKING ANIMALS

Why do children find anthropomorphic stories so satisfying? The most obvious reason is that the sight and thought of a dressed and talking animal is entertaining . John Rowe Townsend considers this kind of book can descend into 'sentimentality and whimsy' and show a preference for furry, cuddly creatures while making the more 'snappy creatures' the bad ones (Townsend, 1995: 94). However I have found that authors of the better books in this genre get beyond whimsy and tap into children's deepest longings – to seek adventure and yet have the safety of home to return to, to achieve what they would like to do and be sure of the loyalty of friends in an uncertain world (Flynn, 2004: 428).

103

Dick King-Smith, a former farmer and teacher, knows how to select just those sort of animal characters and plots that tell us something about human longings and behaviour. So often his message is that even the most difficult problems can be solved with determination and the help of friends. This is the theme of *The Sheep-Pig* and *The Hodgeheg*. Like a number of King-Smith's books, *The Hodgeheg* appeals to the five to eight age range but some pre-school children are ready to listen to it read aloud. Other tried and tested favourites include: *Sophie's Snail*, about a child who keeps a miniature 'farm' of small creatures; *Saddlebottom*, which tells of a pig with his saddle patch on his rear instead of his back; and *The Fox Busters*, about three remarkable hens who fight back against the fox. All these stories draw children into the narrative, and their sometimes stretching vocabulary and depth of theme help young readers make progress.

The Water Horse suits more confident readers and has enormous imaginative appeal. The book is an ingenious take on how the Loch Ness Monster reached its home. Kirstie and Angus find a strange egg which hatches out into a tiny sea monster with a horse's head and a crocodile's tale. The problems start when the children discover their tiny monster will not stop growing. *Harriet's Hare*, a tale about a girl whose loneliness is ended by meeting Wiz from the planet Pars, also seems to suit the slightly older reader of about nine years.

Another King-Smith book for fluent readers is *The Guard Dog*, about a little mongrel dog with two ambitions: to find a home and to be a guard dog. This book taps into a growing child's worries about how to establish an acceptable place in the world.

A book enjoyed by children of any age between about six and ten is Anne Fine's *The Chicken Gave It to Me*. This fable, about a space travelling chicken which is trying to save mankind, is an exhilarating read and the book also confronts some serious issues of animal welfare.

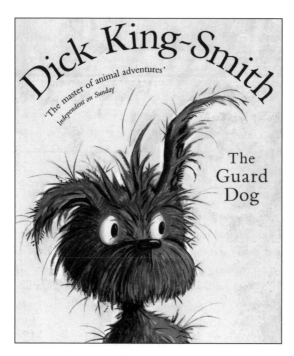

Figure 8.2
Front cover of The Guard Dog *by Dick King-Smith*
Young Corgi. Reproduced with the permission of the publishers The Random House Group Ltd

Although written way back in 1952, *Charlotte's Web* by E.B. White, the American writer, has been a much loved book ever since it was first published. The death of the spider after young readers have come to love her is sad, but something of Charlotte lives on through her offspring. Young readers or listeners learn that just as the seasons change, so everything in nature has a cycle of birth, life and death. There are also changes in childhood and, as Fern grows older, her first passionate attachment to animals changes as other interests compete. So although this is a fantasy the animals teach us much about the changes that are part of growing up.

Mrs Frisby and the Rats of NIMH by Robert O'Brien tells the two intertwining tales of a mouse whose home is in a field about to be ploughed up and of some super rats which are trying to escape from a laboratory. Can Mrs Frisby find a new home to raise her family and nurse her sick son back to health? Will the genetically modified rats be able to use their unusual intelligence to escape and establish their own community?

In contrast, Dodie Smith's *The Hundred and One Dalmatians* is a light and entertaining book in which, as Townsend puts it, 'anthropomorphism runs wild' (Townsend, 1995: 222). There is room, however, in the collection for books which are sheer fun without any deep theme. Another animal story offering light-hearted fun and a good story is Gene Kemp's *The Prime of Tamworth Pig*, although it does touch on how friends can help us overcome problems.

By age nine or ten many children will be ready to read one of the great 'talking animals' classics: Kenneth Grahame's *The Wind in the Willows*. The beautifully described natural settings add greatly to the appeal of the book; the riverbank is the home of the Water-Rat where Mole goes to live one Spring morning, and the Wild Wood, which so much frightens Mole at first, is full of dangerous stoats and weasels. This is a book in which characters tend to be presented as either 'good' or 'bad'. But Toad has both good and bad points and we enjoy his daring adventures. Some critics have pointed to a darker side of the book: Julia Briggs appreciated the exuberance of the animals but notes that 'women and lower classes are silently excluded from this Arcadia' (Briggs in Hunt, 1994: 181). But children appreciate an absorbing story and learn about the value of friendship and loyalty. There are many editions with different illustrators. If you value the original illustrations of E.H. Shephard – so atmospheric and lyrical – you will find these in the anniversary edition published by Egmont.

One of the most original animal stories of the second half of the twentieth century, and one enjoyed by adults as well as children, is Richard Adams' *Watership Down*. This fantasy is about a community of rabbits and their quest to find a new warren. The book tells of the thrilling and dangerous conflict between these rabbits and the evil General Woundwort and his warren, run like a totalitarian society. Some have felt it shows a conservative, even anti-feminist view of society (Carpenter and Prichard, 1984: 563). Others praise Adams' creation of a language, history and folklore for the rabbits. This is a long and demanding book, but read aloud by the teacher or parent, some primary-aged children would be able to learn of the importance of loyalty to others and the ability to endure hardship for a worthwhile cause.

STORIES BASED ON CLOSE OBSERVATION OF LIVING CREATURES

Some stories follow the events in a creature's life in a realistic way, sticking always to its natural behaviour and attributes. There are no animals in clothes or having a chat in these books! We cannot know what it feels like to be an animal, but as John Rowe Townsend remarks, 'the more the author knows about the animals he is writing about, the better qualified he will be to attempt that perilous imaginative leap into the animal mind' (Townsend, 1995: 94).

There are a number of 'real creature' books which appeal to children of about eight years and older. High on my list would be *The Midnight Fox* by Betsy Byars, which tells the story of a boy who has lived in the town and has to adapt to living in the countryside. How is Tom to choose between loyalty to the fox he has befriended and his obligations to Uncle Fred and Aunt Millie, his farming relatives who have given him shelter and who see the fox as their enemy? Here children are shown something profound about the relationships between animals and human beings and about the difficult choices that sometimes have to be made.

Can a creature be both a working animal and a pet? This is the issue explored in Berlie Doherty's story *Snowy*, in which Rachel is forbidden to take the family's canal boat horse to school when other children are showing their friends their pets. Longings and wishes can be very powerful in the growing child and this is what young readers respond to most in this story.

Michael Morpurgo never sentimentalizes animals or what happens to them. Tips, the cat in *The Amazing Story of Adolphus Tips*, about the impact of the Second World War on one family, is not allowed to keep her litters. Some children find the constant drownings difficult to endure, as does her owner Lily, and so when Tips is allowed to keep one of her litters they rejoice. Another book by Morpurgo about the relationship between a child and an animal is *The Butterfly Lion*. Tenderly illustrated by Christian Birmingham, this book is impossible to classify with its poetic quality where dream and reality often merge. Young readers feel tremendous empathy with Bertie at the point in the story where the lion he has rescued from the veld is sold to a circus.

Finally, pony books deserve some mention. Those written for the eight to twelves have a conventional narrative pattern: a girl longs for a pony, after much struggle she gets one, she learns to ride and care for it and then something happens to threaten this idyll. All is well in the end of course and things are usually rounded off by a big success – often in a show (Haymonds in Hunt, 2004: 482). As well as telling an exciting story, pony books nearly always give a lot of information about riding in gymkhanas and caring conscientiously for the animal. The best pony books, in my view, are those that tell a good story and have characters of some depth and subtlety. Some of those that meet these criteria are Christine Pullein-Thompson's *Wait for Me Phantom Horse*, Josephine Pullein-Thompson's *Ride to the Rescue*, K.M. Peyton's *Fly-by-Night*, Joy Cowley's *Shadrach Girl* and Stacy Gregg's *Mystic and the Midnight Rider*. An Amazon reviewer of the latter wonders whether the possum could have been replaced by a fox for British readers. I think not: young readers are quite capable of taking on such differences.

Fewer boys become attached to ponies but some might enjoy Walter Farley's Stallion series. In *The Black Stallion*, the boy and the horse both survive a shipwreck and the lad faces the challenge here of training a powerful and undisciplined creature.

Around 7 or 8

- *The Diary of a Killer Cat* by Anne Fine (Corgi)
  A hilarious account written as if killer kitten is talking.

- *Charlotte's Web* by E.B. White (Puffin)
  Classic tale of the friendship between a pig and a spider.

- *Harriet's Hare* by Dick King-Smith (Yearling)
  Meeting a talking hare transforms Harriet's life.

From about age 8 or 9

- *The Midnight Fox* by Betsy Byars (Faber & Faber)
  Loyalty to a wild creature versus loyalty to farming relatives.

- *The Amazing Story of Adolphus Tips* by Michael Morpurgo (HarperCollins)
  A lost cat and the impact of the Second World War on a Devon village.

- *Black Beauty* by Anna Sewell (Penguin)
  The story of the life and travails of a horse set in Victorian times.

- *The Wind in the Willows* by Kenneth Grahame (Egmont)
  Classic tale of the adventures of animals living in a rural idyll.

- *The Butterfly Lion* by Michael Morpurgo (Collins)
  Lyrical book about a boy's love for the lion he rescued from the veld.

- *War Horse* by Michael Morpurgo (Egmont)
  The story of a horse taken from a farm to serve on the battlefields of the First World War.

Figure 8.3 *Longer stories and novels about animals, roughly in order of challenge*

Chapter 9

Realism
Domestic, adventure and school stories

INTRODUCTION

'Realism' is, according to John Rowe Townsend, a 'holdall word which can be defined and redefined indefinitely' (Townsend, 1995: 251). Here I follow Townsend in using it to indicate that sort of fiction where the events portrayed could happen in real life. Books in this category are usually set in the present or recent past. Here I discuss them under domestic (books based around home and family), adventure and school. The books by critics and educationists which I have found helpful in writing this chapter include Ann Alston's *The Family in English Children's Literature*, Nicholas Tucker and Nikki Gamble's *Family Fictions: Contemporary Classics of Children's Fiction* and some of the chapters in Peter Hunt's *International Companion Encyclopedia of Children's Literature*, including Gillian Avery's 'The Family Story', Sheila Ray's 'The School Story', Janet Fisher's 'Historical Fiction' and Dennis Butts' 'Shaping Boyhood'.

DOMESTIC OR FAMILY STORIES

There is a long history of writing about families in children's literature, whether these families are supportive and loving or chaotic and miserable. Until the 1960s 'a middle-class viewpoint was taken for granted in the English family story' (Avery in Hunt, 2004: 456). There was an exception: in 1937 one of the best-loved classic family stories about a poor but contented family, Eve Garnett's *Family At One End Street*, was published and won the Carnegie Prize. Puffin brought out an edition in 2004 with Eve Garnett's original illustrations and with an introduction by Julia Eccleshare. Children from about age seven or eight enjoy having this read aloud. What is the appeal of a book written more than seventy years ago? I think there is something intriguing about a large, lively family in which the seven children have 'to-wear-each-others-clothes-right-down-to-the baby'. And children being reared in more cautious times no doubt marvel at the freedom of the Ruggles children to go about on their own and sometimes get into scrapes. There is also a strong sense of place and of the wider family in the story. Not everyone is a fan. Some find the book patronizing in its portrayal of the less well off. But, as Gamble and Yates point out, most domestic stories before this one concentrated on better off families and we need books about other families too. Even the family who have descended into more straightened circumstances than they were used to in E. Nesbit's *The Railway Children* are able to have help with the housework (Gamble and Yates, 2008: 85).

There is certainly more diversity in the 'family' books by contemporary writers, where depicted situations range from 'normal conflicts that are attendant on growing up, to serious issues such as abandonment and abuse' (Gamble and Yates, 2008: 131).

At around seven or eight children appreciate the 'normal conflicts' in *The Battle of Bubble and Squeak*, which taps into the longing of so many children to have a pet. To the mother in the story the gerbils beloved by Sid, Peggy and Amy are 'smelly little rats'. Dramatic tension reaches a height when the ginger cat nearly eats Bubble and Squeak.

Turning to family books for the over nines, these include Louise Fitzhugh's *Nobody's Family Is Going to Change*. On the front cover of the 2008 reprinting by Square Fish publishers the following question is printed: 'What can you do if your parents simply refuse to accept your hopes and dreams?' In this case Emma and Willie try to rise above parental expectations based on gender. The boy in Betsy Byars' *The Cartoonist* has a different problem and escapes from an inadequate mother by finding refuge in his attic room, where he draws and hangs up cartoons. Young readers share Alfie's dismay when he finds out that his mother has offered his room to his older brother and his wife.

There are involving stories about family separation. In Nina Bawden's *Carrie's War*, the Second World War causes the separation; Carrie and Nick are evacuated from London to Wales in 1939 and have to live as a family with a grumpy shopkeeper and his timid sister. This rich tale has many themes but how to cope without your 'real' family is a poignant one. In Bawden's *Peppermint Pig*, set in the early twentieth century, Poll and her family are separated by difficult circumstances from the father of the household and have to move from the city to the countryside in Norfolk. For the children and especially Poll, the bright spot in a harsh existence is a little pig called Johnny which becomes almost a member of the family. Johnny's fate causes Poll to grow up quickly. In the stories of some other writers, the pace of events is faster than in these two novels. It would be sad if this meant some young readers did not persevere with Bawden's books and benefit from their richness – the insights about growing up, for example. They do also sometimes have a dated turn of phrase and I find some children appreciate their merits when they are read aloud so that the teacher can make explaining the language a discussion point.

There are two contemporary writers who have taken on the difficulties many modern families face as a consequence of poverty, change of circumstances, elderly dependent relatives, divorce and inadequate parenting: Anne Fine and Jacqueline Wilson. Anne Fine writes of the individuals in families as others might see them; she is particularly convincing when telling us about the small meannesses children are capable of when their siblings annoy them. For example, in *Madame Doubtfire*, Lydia, Natalie and Christopher quarrel fiercely over who should give an upsetting letter to their father. In his analysis of her work in *Family Fictions*, Nicholas Tucker notes Fine's ability to depict 'the natural, electrical storm of being alive when young or else when surrounded by the young' and the temporary lulls in the dramas (Tucker and Gamble, 2001: 51). Fine's stories often take on difficult and painful issues in a way older primary children can understand and cope with. *The Granny Project* confronts young readers with an ever relevant and unsettling social problem: how can we best care for elderly relatives? She is able to make the characters convincing and rounded, not least by using her brilliant facility with convincing dialogue. There are no easy answers to some problems: Granny is not portrayed as a dear old lady, but as a real person with needs and the capacity to be irritating and selfish.

There are a number of books by contemporary writers which show the humorous side of family life. The titles in the Alistair Fury series by Jamie Rix use the device of a diary; in *The Revenge of Alistair Fury: Exam Fever* we find Alistair anxious to stop his mum and dad 'discovering I am the thickest in the family'.

When it comes to portraying some of the exceptionally difficult things some children have to cope with – dysfunctional families, foster and care homes, abuse and the mental ill health of adults around you – in a way older primary school children can deal with, few equal Jacqueline Wilson. Her most endearing and infuriating heroine is probably Tracy Beaker. *The Story of Tracy Beaker* is told in the first person, as if we are reading ten-year-old Tracy's diary. Through this fictional diary we find what happens when fostering does not work out and a child enters a children's home. Tracy escapes her troubled life in two ways: by fantasizing about being rescued by a glamorous relative and by writing her life story. As well as encountering countless Tracy fans from children as young as seven right through to eleven in school, I have read the many glowing responses on the Amazon UK Tracy Beaker site (accessed 9 January 2009). The Tracy Beaker stories tap into children's own painful experiences and show them how a resourceful and feisty girl can overcome the challenges in her life. Wilson's *The Illustrated Mum*, relates how Dolphin manages to cope with her mother's depression and emotional self-absorption as well as enduring some bullying at school. Another difficult subject is well tackled in *Sleepovers*: Daisy worries about introducing her group of friends to her physically and mentally handicapped sister.

Figure 9.2
Front cover of Sleepovers *by Jacqueline*
Wilson and Nick Sharratt (illus.)
Young Corgi. Reproduced with the
permission of the publishers The Random
House Group Ltd. Copyright 2008

BOOKS ABOUT CHILDREN LIVING IN OTHER CULTURES AND TRADITIONS

This is a category of realism which we need to include in the collection if we are to represent the variety of ways in which children experience life in different countries and amongst different communities here and abroad. There are many good picturebooks on the market, often written and illustrated by writers who have lived in ethnic minority communities in the United Kingdom, and some of these are mentioned in the annotated lists in Chapters 4 and 5. When it comes to longer books, I have found that factual texts about children's lives are, on the whole, less successful than fictional accounts. This seems partly because writers of non-fiction find it hard to tackle the difficulties and considerable suffering of children in some countries. It is the good writer of fiction who finds a way to tell of these things. The books in Figure 9.3 help young readers develop sympathetic insight into the lives of children growing up with challenges and hardships as well as telling interesting stories.

ADVENTURE STORIES

In Victorian times, adventure stories, like R.L. Stevenson's *Treasure Island* (1883), tended to reflect the traditional world of men and boys. The roots of contemporary adventure stories are even further back in books like *Robinson Crusoe* (1719). Such stories show a young person facing danger and conflict and events usually develop thrillingly and at a fast pace (Watson,

111

- *The Breadwinner* by Deborah Ellis (Oxford University Press)
  This story is set in Afghanistan during the time of Taliban rule. Parvana shows great courage and resourcefulness when she has to take a job to help her family survive.

- *Abela* by Berlie Doherty (Andersen)
  This is about two girls living very different lives whose stories collide. Abela grew up in Tanzania where she had a hard life while Rosa grew up in comfort.

- *Spilled Water* by Sally Grindley (Bloomsbury)
  Eleven-year-old Lu Si-Yang's father dies and this event changes the young girl's life completely. She moves from a contented life in the countryside to the city and enslavement. Sally Grindley based Lu Si-Yang's story on a newspaper cutting about a real girl in a similar situation.

- *Homeless Bird* by Gloria Whelan (Frances Lincoln)
  Koly is caught up in a series of events when her family want her to go ahead with an arranged marriage. Mature young readers of ten and over will learn about life in India as well as savouring an absorbing story.

- *Letters from Alain* by Enrique Perez Diaz and Francisco Solé (illus.) (Aurora Metro Publications)
  Shortlisted for the Marsh Award for books in translation, this story is about twelve-year-old Arturo who lives on the island of Cuba. His friend, Alain, sails away on a perilous journey to America in a small boat with his family. Alain's dog returns – an ominous sign. But then Arturo starts to receive letters from Alain.

- *Pearl Diver* by Julia Johnson (Stacey International)
  At the young age of six years Saeed is taken by his father on a pearling dhow that works the Arabian Gulf. The pearl industry predates the search for oil. The book tells of Saed's first summer at sea and his learning about different ways of seeing the world as well as the world of work.

- *Rickshaw Girl* by Mitali Perkins (Charlesbridge Publications)
  Naima lives in a Bangladeshi village and has to face the restrictions placed on female children in her culture. Then she decides to dress as a boy and to learn to drive her father's rickshaw.

- *Safe at Home* by Sharon Robinson (Scholastic)
  When his father dies, ten-year-old Elijah has to make a new life and he experiences some bullying. But when he learns to like baseball (instead of his beloved basketball) he begins to make new friends.

- *Then* by Morris Gleitzman (Puffin)
  This book continues the story begun in Once about Felix and Zelda who struggle to survive in Nazi Germany. Amongst brutality they find kindness.

Figure 9.3 *Books about children living in other cultures and traditions*

LETTERS
FROM ALAIN

ENRIQUE PEREZ DIAZ

Illustrations by Francisco Solé

2001: 6). Many adventure stories can be read online. For example, the whole of *Treasure Island* can be found at www.ukoln.ac.uk/services/treasure (accessed 12 January 2009). There are adventure stories set in fantasy worlds too – for example those by Alan Garner, Ursula Le Guin, Philip Pullman and Terry Pratchett, which are covered in Chapter 11. Here the emphasis is on the more realistic adventure stories and on the books children are likely to enjoy reading today. To give children something of the excitement of *Robinson Crusoe* and *Treasure Island*, Angela Wilkes and illustrator Peter Dennis have written versions of these books (and with these titles), based on the work of Defoe and Stevenson, for young readers of about eight years. Readers nearing age eleven might enjoy the challenge of reading the Templar Publishing edition of *Treasure Island* (2005), which is atmospherically illustrated by Robert Ingpen.

Stepping forward to the 1930s, we find a series of adventure stories written by Arthur Ransome, which are still in print; the first story in the series is *Swallows and Amazons*. This timeless classic tells of the adventures of four children called John, Susan, Titty and Roger who have a boat called *Swallow* – the *Swallow* of the book's title. The children sail this boat on a lake in the Lake District and have a series of adventures often involving their rivals, the Amazons called Nancy and Peggy. Some children will find the slow pace difficult as so many contemporary books in print and other media are swift moving. There is no exploration of the tensions between parents and children here – but these themes are well covered in contemporary books, as we saw in the previous sections. What appeals is the space the story creates for children to enjoy vicariously the easy companionship between boys and girls and ordinary activities like cooking, swimming and camping. As in Enid Blyton's books, adults are kept very much in the background and this is also an attraction for many young readers. Unlike the simple language of Enid Blyton's adventure stories, however, which is somewhat lacking in lyricism, Ransome's prose is pleasing – very much the sort of language we want children sometimes to experience and savour. Nevertheless Enid Blyton's adventure stories have stood the test of time. Her adventure series include the Secret Seven and the Secret Series, but it is the Famous Five stories that are amongst the most successful ever written for children commercially and also in terms of reader satisfaction. From the 1930s to the late 1950s she published hundreds of books, raising the fear amongst teachers and librarians that some children might have a reading diet dominated by one author, and worryingly an author whose style and language use seemed to some over-simple. The accusations of social class, gender and racial stereotyping are also well known and recent editions of her adventure stories have been edited to meet these criticisms. Since the sale of her copyright to the entertainments industry, much of her work is now available in other media than print. David Rudd suggests that we view Blyton as 'a storyteller in the oral tradition, relating safe but exciting tales in which children feature as heroes'. Their appeal also probably has to do with her placing the children at the centre of the stories, left by adults to solve their own problems (Rudd in Watson, 2001: 92). The very first book in the series, *The Famous Five: Five on a Treasure Island*, is about the children's search for treasure in a shipwreck off Kirrin Island and involves the five – Julian, Dick, Anne and their cousin Georgina and her dog Timmy – in finding clues to discover the treasure. Children can often read the stories independently from about age eight years. Further evidence of the popularity of the series is its high position, third, in Booktrust's 2008 survey of the Best Children's Books (www.booktrustchildrensbooks. org.uk).

What about the adventure stories of contemporary writers? New books in some ways reminiscent of books in the tradition of Henty and Buchan are emerging constantly. The Alex Rider series by Anthony Horowitz includes *Stormbreaker* (now a film), *Eagle Strike* and *Ark Angel* – thrillers about the adventures of a young boy recruited into MI6. In *Stormbreaker*, the first of the series, Alex Rider's guardian dies in suspicious circumstances. The stories have suspense, energy and some humour.

Children from about age seven enjoy both the story and the author's quirky illustrations in Harry Horse's exciting story *The Last Polar Bears*. Written in the form of fascinating letters to a grandchild, this charts a grandfather's treacherous journey on the *Unsinkable* to Walrus Bay at the North Pole. Another writer whose adventure books, about two brothers Hal and Roger, are liked by children towards the end of the primary years is Willard Price. The boys travel all over the world, often to dangerous and exotic locations, to help their father find wild animals for his zoo. *Amazonian Adventure* takes them to the Pastaza River in the Amazonian jungle, but what happens when it becomes clear someone is trying to stop them from collecting the creatures? The pair face sharks and killer whales in the tropical waters of the Great Barrier Reef in *Diving Adventure*. In *Arctic Adventure* the boys face freezing temperatures and a lack of food. The stories are action packed and exciting but they are also underpinned by the author's knowledge and understanding about all aspects of the natural world and its inhabitants.

As Dennis Butt observes, the Robinsonnade form is developed in some books by contemporary authors, including a hugely successful adventure story, *Kensuke's Kingdom*, by Michael Morpurgo, with excellent illustrations by Michael Foreman (Butt in Hunt, 2004: 350). Likely to be enjoyed most by nine to eleven-year-olds, it tells a dramatic story about a family who sail off on a yacht which later sinks.

The work of Geraldine McCaughrean is rich and exciting and is difficult to place in categories or even age ranges. Many of her books, including *A Little Lower than the Angels*, *Gold Dust* and *Plundering Paradise*, are vivid fast-moving adventure stories with strong characters and ingenious plots. However, each tale has a particular historic setting and each gives a powerful sense of place at a particular time. Therefore I have discussed them under the section on 'Historical novels' (pp. 118–19).

SCHOOL STORIES

Read a historical review, like Sheila Ray's for example, and you will find that until comparatively recently school stories have been mostly set in single sex, secondary boarding schools (Ray in Hunt, 2004). But there are school stories for the primary school age group. The books of Elinor Brent-Dyer, who began writing in the 1920s, and which are still in print, have a keen readership among girls from about age eight or nine. One of the first of her sixty-odd Chalet School stories, *The School at the Chalet*, tells how Madge Bettany, the older sister of Joey, one of the main characters in the books, sets up a school in the Austrian Tyrol. The books have survived because of Brent-Dyer's storytelling skills; the pace is brisk as young readers follow the girls' adventures in the school and in the surrounding alpine scenery, sometimes encountering mysteries and danger. Without being heavy handed, this author also shows the impact of the Second World War and readers follow the pupils and teachers to Guernsey and then to Wales.

Some of Enid Blyton's school stories have come out in new editions. Egmont Books have published some of the Malory Towers titles, including the very first, *First Term at Malory Towers*. The stories relate the adventures of the girls and their outbursts and mishaps. New editions of Blyton's Naughtiest Girl series have been published by Hodder. In the first book, *The Naughtiest Girl in the School*, Elizabeth Allen is portrayed as a spoilt child who behaves badly at her boarding school in the hope that she will be sent home. She tests everyone's patience, teachers and pupils but then she makes friends. Why are Enid Blyton's books, written some time ago, so much liked by young girls today? What comes over to me from talking to children and from the customer reviews on the Amazon UK site is that they give young readers the chance to enjoy boarding school life vicariously. They can go with Darrell Rivers and her friends at Malory Towers as they tiptoe down to the beach for a midnight feast; they can enjoy reading about the special friendships pupils form at boarding school, where the day does not end at 4.00 p.m.

What about boys' schools? Anthony Buckeridge's Jennings series, which includes *Jennings Goes to School* and *Jennings and Darbishire*, is set in Linbury Court Preparatory School. House of Stratus have brought out new editions of some of the titles. Young readers today will enjoy the language: 'fossilized fish hooks', 'frightful bish' and 'jolly wizard'. The adventures of the ever enthusiastic Jennings and the laugh-out-loud exploits, not least his encounters with Old Wilkie, a master of barely thirty years, have kept the books in print for over fifty years.

115

Around age 7 or 8

- *The Battle of Bubble and Squeak* by Philippa Pearce (Puffin)
  The children love their gerbils, their mother does not . . .

- *The Famous Five: Five on a Treasure Island* by Enid Blyton (Hodder & Stoughton)
  Fast-moving adventure story, first of a series, about a search for treasure on Kirrin Island.

- *The Family at One End Street: And Some of Their Adventures* by Eve Garnett (Penguin Classics)
  The story of a family who have little money but where the children have much love and freedom.

- *The Last Polar Bears* by Harry Horse (Puffin)
  Letters to a grandchild from grandfather as he makes a treacherous journey to the North Pole to see polar bears.

Around age 8 or 9

- *Dear Mr Henshaw* by Beverley Cleary (Scholastic)
  We hear through his letters to an author about a boy's difficult life with an often absent lorry-driving father.

- *The Turbulent Term of Tyke Tiler* by Gene Kemp (Puffin)
  Tyke is mischievous but is a kind friend to Danny. Surprise ending.

- *There's a Boy in the Girls' Bathroom* by Louis Sacher (Bloomsbury)
  Bradley rubs everyone up the wrong way at home and at school. Can he be helped?

- *The Story of Tracy Beaker* by Jacqueline Wilson (Corgi)
  Tracy's life is transformed when a writer visits her children's home.

- *Sleepovers* by Jacqueline Wilson (Young Corgi, Random House)
  How can Daisy cope with her group of friends meeting her disabled sister when the sleepover is at her house? A difficult subject is tackled well and there is much insight shared about female friendships.

- *Swallows and Amazons* by Arthur Ransome (Red Fox)
  Four children sail their boat in the Lake District. This story does not go at a swift pace but it is engrossing.

- *The Revenge Files of Alistair Fury: Exam Fever* by Jamie Rix (Corgi Yearling, Random House)
  How is Alistair going to manage to do well in the exams? Amusing treatment of an anxious-making challenge.

- *Kensuke's Kingdom* by Michael Morpurgo (Puffin)
  A Robinsonnade desert island survival story.

- *The Granny Project* by Anne Fine (Corgi)
  What do a family of children do when, to their dismay, their parents want their grandmother to go into a nursing home?

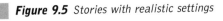
Figure 9.5 Stories with realistic settings

> • *Stormbreaker* by Anthony Horowitz (Walker)
> First in the Alex Rider series. This exciting, fast-moving thriller introduces Alex Rider, a young boy recruited into MI6. It begins with the suspicious death of Alex's guardian.

Figure 9.5 *continued*

The book about a mixed primary school which has made most impact is, of course, *The Turbulent Term of Tyke Tiler* by Gene Kemp. This book won the Carnegie Medal in 1977 and has been in print ever since, partly because of the irrepressible personality of Tyke and also because it is such a good action-packed story with a surprise at the end.

Another character who has made a strong impression on some young readers, mostly those over nine years and often boys, is Bradley in Louis Sachar's book *There's a Boy in the Girls' Bathroom*. Bradley picks fights and teases and bullies the other children in the school. Can Bradley change? Will Carla the school counsellor be able to help him? These are the questions that keep children turning the pages. Like Sachar's other children's books this one has an American flavour – after all the author lives in Texas – but it has wide appeal. For an undemanding read, children aged eight to ten often enjoy R.L. Stine's Rotten School series, which has a jokey, comic-book flavour. *The Good, the Bad and the Very Ugly* begins with Bernie saying: 'You are probably wondering why I – Bernie Bridges – decided to change my behaviour.' He wants to please a girl he likes, but the events in the slimy slug race foil his plan. (The Harry Potter series and the Demon Headmaster books are discussed in Chapters 11 and 6).

Why do many children find the school story in all its variety so attractive? First of all it taps into a common experience: all schools have rules, customs and routines. Second, the setting of a school story means that it can be a microcosm into which the demands of the wider society do not intrude. So the stories can concentrate on the narrower world of the school and on relationships with friends and the sometimes unfathomable teachers. Third, there is generally a culture of 'fair play', which can be reassuring for children whose world is less ordered.

Figure 9.6
UK front cover of There's a Boy in the Girls' Bathroom *by Louis Sachar*
Reproduced with the permission of the publishers Bloomsbury Publishing PLC

Chapter 10

Historical fiction
Historical novels, time-slips and war stories

INTRODUCTION

Is the historical novel worthwhile and rewarding reading for children today? Towards the end of the twentieth century such novels seemed to fall a little out of favour. John Rowe Townsend comments: 'Sadly, it has become more difficult for historical fiction to get published and if published to stay in print' (Townsend, 1998). The situation was also noted in the report on the first of a series of surveys by the Children's Literature Research Centre team at Roehampton University entitled *Young People's Reading at the End of the Century* (Reynolds (ed.), 1996). These researchers linked the relative decline of the historical novel to the enthusiasm children had been developing for fantasy novels and the realistic novels of writers like Anne Fine and Jacqueline Wilson. But there are some welcome signs: new editions of books like Alison Uttley's *A Traveller in Time* and Jill Paton Walsh's *Fireweed* are emerging from publishers like Jane Nissen, Red Fox and Heinemann. This is good news because historical novels help readers to reflect on human relationships and the human condition and how events and circumstances can affect these. The best stretch the imagination by showing us the lives of people in earlier times and, in the process, illuminate life in our own times. It also seems likely that historical novels create a context for children to 'explore concepts of time and of change and continuity' (Hoodless, 1998: 87). If we count adventure stories set in a particular time in the past as part of the historical fiction collection, there are quite a large number of such titles to be found in the children's section of bookshops. These stories pull us in and make us want to turn the pages while also introducing readers to the realities of life, and encourage them to speculate in an informed way about the feelings of those who lived before them. It is also true, as Peter Bramwell points out, that 'setting a text in the past can make it possible for child characters to move and behave more freely' than is possible in contemporary society – something which will be attractive to young readers (Bramwell, 2004: 108).

HISTORICAL NOVELS

One of the outstanding writers of the historical adventure novel is Geraldine McCaughrean, whose thrilling tales are often set in exotic places as well as in the past. This author is prolific and you and your class will have your own favourites. In *Plundering Paradise* Nathan and his sister leave their rather dreary school to travel with Tamo White, a Pirate King's son, to

Madagascar. The children marvel at the landscapes, colourful plants and interesting animals on the island, which are all brought to life in McCaughrean's vivid writing. But the brutality of the pirates is not hidden and a main theme is the clashing belief systems the children have to confront. *Gold Dust* also takes young readers into a distinctive setting (a small Brazilian town) and specific time (the South American goldrush in the eighteenth century). Inez and Maro wake up one morning to find a man digging a hole in the street outside. 'What's he doing?' said Inez. 'Search me. Maybe he wants to plant something.' But the activity is much more ominous than this exchange suggests. The children set off with their teacher to save their town from the destructive activities of the gold diggers. McCaughrean makes such situations, even those in remote times, real for young readers. On her website, she writes that she does not have 'any age in mind when I'm writing', but I think the novels I mention here are best for the over nines (www.geraldinemccaughrean.co.uk/chbs.htm, accessed 17 January 2009).

If teachers are reading a novel to enrich the study of a period in history, it is best if the story is fixed in a clear time frame to provide a more than superficial understanding of a period. Rosemary Sutcliff's novels set in Roman Britain – *The Eagle of the Ninth*, for example – have remained in print because of their authenticity and their exploration of the timeless themes of honour, courage, friendship, loyalty and determination, which continue to appeal to young readers. The historical fiction of this writer is renowned for its lucid, elegant writing and exciting tales, but I have found even older primary children can find the books challenging. Reading them aloud to the class makes them accessible to a wider range of young learners.

Some of the best historical novels support children's growing understanding of our social history. *Street Child* by Berlie Doherty is most importantly a powerful and moving adventure story about Jim's escape from the workhouse after his mother dies. This story has been made into a playscript and is discussed in Chapter 14. Other novels, including those written by authors contemporary to the period, tell us of lives, feelings and customs in earlier periods. *The Railway Children* by E. Nesbit informs us about food, housing, transport and the lives of people of different circumstances in Victorian times while telling a story with a good dollop of human warmth.

Each book in Usborne's Historical Houses series takes up the story of a young person living at Number 6 Chelsea Walk at a particular time in the past. *Mary Ann and Miss Mozart* by Ann Turnbull tells the story of a girl living in the eighteenth century who wants to be an opera singer – a difficult ambition for a girl to achieve at this time. The quest of the suffragettes to achieve votes for women is brought alive for young readers by Polly's involvement with the movement in *Polly's March* by Linda Newbery.

TIME-SLIPS

Time-slips, books in which someone passes into another time and place, are by definition fantasies. But the conceit does not rule out the creation of another period in meticulous and helpful detail following painstaking research into the incidents, customs and beliefs of another time. Even young children, from about age six or seven, soon come to recognize and feel comfortable with the time-slip device, as the popularity of the Magic Tree House books by the American writer Mary Pope Osbourne suggests. In the first book in the series, *Valley of the Dinosaurs*, two young children, Annie and Jack, encounter prehistoric animals, savour ancient landscapes and experience danger-filled adventures after which they are glad to be restored to the tree house. Although the books are enjoyed as lively adventure stories, the author has made it possible for children to learn from the historical settings, for example about medieval castles and medieval customs and food in *Castle of Mystery*.

Time-slips can happen in both directions – children being transported to the past as were Annie and Jack or a child from the past or future arriving in the present time.

Does the cave-boy 'really' exist or is he in the little boy's imagination in Clive King's *Stig of the Dump*? Either way this does not matter, as generations of children, from about age seven, have hugely enjoyed the adventures of Barney and Stig in the rubbish filled chalk-pit (Townsend, 1995: 240).

But many of the best time-slip stories tend to be appreciated after about age eight or nine. One of the very best is Alison Uttley's *A Traveller in Time*, first published in 1939 and brought back into print with other classics by Jane Nissen Books. Penelope, a girl living in the early part of the twentieth century, goes to stay in her great aunt's old manor house in Derbyshire and finds herself slipping back to the times of Elizabeth I and Mary Queen of Scots. The book enthrals partly because of the Babington plot to depose Elizabeth and put Mary on the English throne. We find here some insights on the strangeness of time, the possibility of revisiting previous periods as time travellers and the probability that once things have happened they cannot be changed.

Philippa Pearce's *Tom's Midnight Garden* also haunts us with musings about time and memory. The scene when Tom realizes that the old lady living at the top of the building is his friend Hattie in the garden is one of the most moving in children's literature.

Figure 10.1
Front cover of Stig of the Dump *by Clive King*
Puffin Books. Reproduced with the permission of The Penguin Group

Figure 10.2
Front cover of Tom's Midnight Garden *by Philippa Pearce*
2008 edition. Reproduced with the permission of Oxford University Press. Copyright OUP

120

Penelope Farmer's *Charlotte Sometimes* is a time-slip story that is also about the aftermath of war. Charlotte slips back forty years to just after the end of the First World War. The story is based on a real and disturbing incident and is an outstanding book because of both the period feeling it creates and the involving characters.

If you are looking for a more recent time-slip story, to suit girls of about ten or older, try Kate Saunders' *Beswitched*. How will Flora Fox cope without her iPod, mobile and laptop when she finds herself transported to St Winifreds in 1935?

WAR STORIES

War stories for young readers, based on real events during conflicts, are a special category of historical fiction. Gillian Lathey asks: 'Surely we should protect children from the inhumanity of war for as long as possible?' (Lathey in Reynolds, 2004: 59). However, she goes on to justify war stories for the young by pointing out that war affects children and changes their lives, often profoundly, and so children's authors are right to explore this in a way children can understand and deal with. For an exploration of the different kinds of modern war story for children I recommend the analysis in 'War' by Carol Fox and Peter Hunt (Hunt, 2004: 499–505).

Michael Morpurgo's *War Horse* and Michael Foreman's illustrated story *War Game* are set against the background of the First World War, but it is the Second World War which has given rise to 'a volume of children's fiction far in excess of that inspired by any previous conflict' (Watson, 2001: 737). Ian Serraillier's *The Silver Sword* has remained in print since it was first published in 1954. It reveals the devastation war causes and the harm it does to people's lives. Another book, *Once* by Morris Gleitzman, for children of age ten and above, tells of a child's difficult journey during the Second World War.

Many of the most successful Second World War stories tell of the experiences of evacuees, children taken to temporary homes in the countryside to escape the bombings in the cities. The adjustment children from urban backgrounds had to make to cope with a rural environment and the sheer upheaval evacuation caused are shown vividly in Michelle Magorian's *Goodnight Mister Tom*. The author provides just the right amount of period detail to take children into a 1940s setting: the flagstoned floor and the large black range in Tom's kitchen. Above all, it is the emotional pull of the book and the tender relationship that develops between Willie and Mister Tom that make the book memorable. This same emotional element makes another book about evacuees, Nina Bawden's *Carrie's War*, compelling for older primary children. It concentrates on human relationships and gives insight into the social history of the war: we learn about the food the evacuees ate, their leisure activities and how Carrie and Nick were perceived and treated. *Josie Under Fire*, a book by Ann Turnball in the Historical House series, also homes in on the social aspects of a period in the past. The story is set against the terror of the London blitz. It explores how the decision a member of a family makes, the decision to become a conscientious objector, affects other people in the family. In a period of understandable patriotic fervour, twelve-year-old Josie is subject to bullying at school because of her brother's beliefs.

Robert Westall's books about the Second World War – *The Machine Gunners*, *The Kingdom by the Sea* and *Blitzcat*, for example – are usually offered or read to children aged ten and over.

121

Historical fiction for the under eights

Picturebooks so often have the power to give younger children the flavour of past lives and events. The Ahlbergs' *Peepo!*, set in the 1940s, shows rooms with 'coal buckets', 'clothes horses' and 'hairnets'. *Seeing Red*, by Sarah Garland, tells of an incident in which young Trewenna and other Cornish women scare away invading French soldiers at the time of the Napoleonic Wars. They show their traditional red petticoats so that they are mistaken for red-coated English soldiers. In both books the narrative and illustrations combine, giving teachers and children a strong invitation to talk about, in one case, how people lived in the recent past and, in the other, about how resourcefulness and imagination can influence events.

BOX 10.1 *GOLDIE AT THE ORPHANAGE* BY MARTHA SANDWALL-BERGSTRÖM AND EVA STALSJÖ (ILLUS.) (FLORIS)

This involving story tells of Goldie's bleak early childhood in an orphanage. Young readers learn that now that Lotta and Goldie were seven years old, 'in those days they were old enough to start work'. The information that orphaned boys and girls could be bought at auction will draw strong responses from some children. This compelling tale has no conventional happy ending: Goldie and her friend are parted and face an uncertain future after being auctioned. Anticipating that young readers will now be hooked, and some certainly will be, the book ends with a footnote promising that the story is 'to be continued in *Goldie at the Farm*'.

(This review was first published in *Books for Keeps* 148, September 2004 and is reproduced here with the permission of Richard Hill and *Books for Keeps*.)

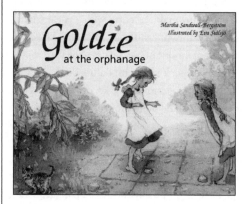

Figure 10.3
Front cover of Goldie at the Orphanage
by Martha Sandwall-Bergström and
Eva Stalsjö (illus.)
Reproduced with the permission of the
publishers Floris Books. Copyright 2004

- *The Railway Children* by E. Nesbit (Puffin Classic)
  Three Victorian children have to adjust to a move to a house near a country railway station.

- *The Silver Sword* by Ian Serraillier (Red Fox)
  A group of children search for their parents over war torn Europe after the end of the Second World War.

- *Goodnight Mister Tom* by Michelle Magorian (Penguin)
  A gripping and moving story about Willie, who is evacuated from a London slum during the Second World War and has to adapt to rural life and to living with the embittered but good-hearted Mister Tom.

- *Mary Ann and Miss Mozart* by Ann Turnbull (Usborne)
  An eighteenth-century girl who wants to become an opera singer faces many challenges before achieving success.

- *A Traveller in Time* by Alison Uttley (Jane Nissen Books)
  Penelope finds herself slipping back to the time of Elizabeth I and Mary Queen of Scots.

- *Carrie's War* by Nina Bawden (Puffin)
  About two children's experience of evacuation to a mining area in Wales, but also tackles wider themes to do with growing up.

- *Charlotte Sometimes* by Penelope Farmer (Red Fox)
  Charlotte wakes up after her first night at boarding school to find she has slipped back forty years to just after the First World War.

- *The Eagle of the Ninth* by Rosemary Sutcliff (Oxford University Press)
  One of Sutcliff's books that brings Roman Britain alive for the young reader.

- *Gold Dust* by Geraldine McCaughrean (Oxford University Press)
  This story is a tale of the South American goldrush. Two children, Inez and Maro, struggle to save their town from the ruinous activities of the gold diggers.

- *Blitzcat* by Robert Westall (Macmillan)
  A black cat is caught up in the drama and tragedy of the Coventry blitz and she undertakes a remarkable journey.

- *Beswitched* by Kate Saunders (Scholastic)
  Modern schoolgirl Flora Fox finds herself in the shoes of another Flora who attends a traditional girls' boarding school in 1935.

Figure 10.4 *Historical novels for the over eights, roughly in order of challenge*

Chapter 11

Fantasy stories and novels

INTRODUCTION

Fantasy stories, or at least stories containing fantasy elements, comprise a very large and important group within the body of children's literature. It is a group which takes in traditional tales, time-slips, anthropomorphic animal stories and science fiction, all of which are covered in earlier chapters, and takes in too the novel-length books considered here. 'Fantasy' is often contrasted with 'realism'. 'Realism' – many say – is to do with what has happened, or at least could happen without the events coming into conflict with the laws of nature. 'Fantasy' authors and illustrators in contrast are free to disobey these laws and can give their imagination full reign. Fantasy stories can take us into alternative worlds, bring magic into this world and introduce extraordinary beings. I'm sticking to this quite crude but reasonably useful distinction, while accepting that all fiction involves the workings of the imagination and that in some stories boundaries between fantasy and reality may be blurred.

A visit to any good bookshop will reveal the huge and ever-growing number of books falling within the fantasy category and these stories are well represented in publishers' lists too. How does the teacher select from so many? Some tell a good story with accessible narrative and a fast pace and, for some children, are a warm invitation into reading. You will find some of these in the lists of books to help develop reading stamina in reluctant readers (Figures 12.2 and 12.3). But in a necessarily selective account, I have been concerned to pick out some of the best writers and most memorable titles which have survived over the years and which I think are likely to continue to be read. I look first at longer fantasy stories for the seven to eights and then at those for the nines and above. Both age boundaries are leaky of course.

CHOOSING FANTASY STORIES AND NOVELS AROUND AGE SEVEN OR EIGHT

By this age children will have enjoyed reading fairy stories, both traditional and modern, and will be familiar with devices like the granting of wishes, magical events and extraordinary beings. Here I turn to the fantasy stories which, while having some of these features, are more sustained and more demanding of the young reader.

E. Nesbit, Mary Norton, Clive King and Dick King-Smith: fantasy intruding on the real world

Quite a lot of what is written for this age group brings fantasy into the real world, the world as we experience it every day. This is sometimes called 'low fantasy' to distinguish it from 'high fantasy', which creates and explores secondary worlds (Gamble and Yates, 2008: 120). E. Nesbit, in her books *Five Children and It* and *The Phoenix and the Carpet*, creates a domestic setting for the strange events experienced in the stories. In the first, the Bastable children unearth a sand fairy in a gravel pit and are granted wishes, while in the second, the same children are whisked away on a carpet to interesting and sometimes exotic places. Mary Norton, too, brings fantasy to a story set in a family house. In *The Borrowers*, miniature people live their lives under the floorboards. The problems start when Arrietty, the young daughter of Pod and Homily, meets and befriends a human boy.

Another enduring classic is *Stig of the Dump* by Clive King, where a cave-boy finds a pathway into Barney's world when he is staying with relatives who live near an abandoned chalk-pit. The efforts of the two boys to communicate and Stig's fascination with the rubbish tipped into the pit continue to intrigue children. The appearance of a strange presence in the midst of ordinary life also occurs in *Harriet's Hare* by Dick King-Smith. In a corn circle in a field, Harriet meets a talking hare who announces that he has come to visit Earth from the planet Pars. This kind of encounter often occurs when the child in the story is finding their real life troubled. Barney's parents are having problems and Harriet is struggling with loneliness. The appeal of these books seems to be to do with the empathy children feel for the main characters. Most children experience some domestic problems and growing up has its lonely moments. These things can sometimes be more comfortably explored and reflected on through fantasy.

Children are also drawn to books in which children enter new worlds, whether an enchanted forest, a magic island or, as in *The Lion, the Witch and the Wardrobe*, an icy kingdom reached through a wardrobe.

Enid Blyton: accessible stories with some imaginative appeal

Two Blyton fantasy books which still have enormous appeal for younger children are *The Magic Faraway Tree* and *The Adventures of the Wishing Chair*. Not only are bookshops packed with them, but also they are consistently high in the sales lists on book websites like Amazon UK. And they attract an unusually high number of reader responses on the sites. Many parents report that their children, as young as four or five, choose them to be read aloud as their bedtime stories. Why do they like them so much? Probably it is partly because the stories are accessible in theme, vocabulary and syntax. But to have become such favourites, they must have some imaginative appeal as well. In *The Magic Faraway Tree* children seem to especially like the characters – Silky, Moonface and Mr Saucepan – that Joe, Beth, Frannie and Rick (or as Blyton named them – Joe, Beth, Fanny and Dick) meet as they climb the enchanted tree. At the top of the tree they enter the fantasy lands that circle it. The simple device of the magic chair in *The Adventures of the Wishing Chair* also works well.

In these books, Blyton creates a world in which there is escape for the reader from daily routines and problems and where there are always happy endings. But, above all, as far as many children are concerned, she tells a good story.

Roald Dahl: teller of riveting stories

Roald Dahl's tales are original, imaginative and full of humour, albeit rather cruel humour sometimes. Adults are often the butt of children's dislike. In *Matilda*, for example, the child glues her father's head to his hat and writes out the head teacher's bad deeds on the board. Often the adults deserve their fates, not least the obnoxious aunts in *James and the Giant Peach*. A lot of teachers, including the present writer, loathe *The Twits*, in which an unsavoury elderly couple do dreadful things to each other – worms are served up for dinner as spaghetti. But children roar with laughter and some say it is their favourite Dahl book. John Rowe Townsend falls short of recommending that we ban Dahl's books from library shelves but thinks we should let children discover them for themselves rather than us introducing them. He remarks: 'They appeal, I think, to the cruder end of childish taste: to a delight in rumbustious rudery and in giving people one-in-the-eye' (Townsend, 1995: 249). Many teachers, and even Townsend, join children in liking *The BFG*, a kindlier Dahl tale about the Big Friendly Giant who helps Sophie stop wicked giants from eating up the children of England.

For me, the quirky, energetic illustrations of Quentin Blake add enormously to the worth of Dahl's books. The artistic collaboration between this author and illustrator was the subject of an exhibition at the Seven Stories Centre for Children's Books.

BOX 11.1 *SKELLIG* BY DAVID ALMOND (HODDER CHILDREN'S BOOKS)

What do you think of when you hear or read the word 'angel'? Perhaps not Skellig as described in David Almond's intriguing story. 'He was covered in dust and webs like everything else and his face was thin and pale.' This strange, unworldly creature found in the family garage intrudes into a familiar domestic setting. Two things make this a difficult time for young Michael. First his family have just moved house, often an unsettling experience for children. Second they are trying to cope with the serious illness of his baby sister. It is against this anxious background that Michael encounters a supernatural being. So the problems over differentiating between fantasy and reality come into sharp focus. As Ian Brinton puts it, David Almond takes us 'into a world both familiar and strange' (Brinton, 2004: 1). The depth of Michael's fear and concern about his baby sister can be inferred from the skilful way Almond shows the situation from the boy's point of view. No wonder young readers or listeners are relieved and joyful when the baby recovers. The same concern and kindness Michael shows to the baby he also sheds on Skellig and the angel transforms into a young and beautiful being. Vivid language, not least convincing dialogue, a suspenseful plot and enormous imaginative appeal make this a riveting read.

CHOOSING FANTASY BOOKS AROUND ABOUT AGE NINE AND ABOVE

There are hundreds of fantasy books on the market for this age group; some have the potential to become modern classics while others are of more ephemeral interest. But, like adults, children read texts of different levels of complexity and challenge and of different degrees of merit according to changing mood and changing contexts.

Penelope Lively and Philippa Pearce: time, memory, change and a sense of place

Two authors who write particularly well about the past intruding on the present are Penelope Lively and Philippa Pearce. In *A Stitch in Time*, Penelope Lively tells the intriguing story of Maria, who becomes consumed with concern and interest about a Victorian girl who once lived in the house where the family are staying on holiday.

The past pops up in a more amusing way in Lively's *The Ghost of Thomas Kempe*, about an apothecary who wants young James to be his assistant. Philippa Pearce's masterpiece, *Tom's Midnight Garden,* is one of the most important children's books of the twentieth century. While telling a good story is crucial in keeping up children's interest, there is also a need for books, like this, which encourage the reader to reflect as they read. The sheer skill and linguistic power of this writer help the young reader to experience a strong sense of place, to appreciate, alongside Tom, the atmosphere of the house in his own time and that of the beautiful garden from the past, visited when the clock strikes thirteen. It communicates human feelings exceptionally well; particularly affecting is the warmth of the friendship between Tom and Hattie. The themes of the book – friendship, time, memory and change – seem to appeal to children at age about ten or eleven perhaps partly because they are at the stage when their thoughts are turning to the step forward that starting secondary school signals.

J.R.R. Tolkien, C.S. Lewis, Lewis Carroll, J.M. Barrie and Philip Pullman: high fantasy

What qualifies as 'high fantasy' is debatable. I am thinking of sustained works of the imagination and select as examples the books of authors who create imaginary worlds with distinctive rules, characters, landscapes and customs.

J.R.R. Tolkien

It is *The Hobbit* which is most likely to appeal to children still in the primary years. At 400 pages, this story requires readers of some endurance, and independent readers of this story younger than eleven are comparatively rare, but the tale of the epic journey of the hobbit Bilbo Baggins to raid the treasure of a dragon is absorbing. It is one of those books enjoyed by adults as well as children and some may be fortunate enough to have a parent or teacher read it aloud.

C.S. Lewis

Children at the primary stage are more likely to read C.S. Lewis' books about the magical land of Narnia than any of the other sustained fantasies on the market, with the exception of the Harry Potter books (Booktrust survey, 2007). In *The Lion, the Witch and the Wardrobe*, a fascinating but grim secondary world is reached through the back of a wardrobe. Some consider the religious symbolism in the Narnia books sits too strongly within one belief system, with Aslan as the Christ figure overcoming evil given life by the wicked queen and her

127

supporters. Children, though, are drawn by these exciting adventure stories where children around their own age are leading characters and there are copious, intriguing and fantastic creatures that some find reminiscent of Tolkien's – dwarfs, thinking wolves, fairies and fauns.

Lewis Carroll

The Alice books may begin to appeal to children after the age of nine, but it has to be admitted that some children never take to them. Those who do enjoy the nonsense that often makes sense, the language play and the humour. Above all Alice herself is an appealing and resourceful heroine trying to survive in a topsy-turvy world. She thinks about all that happens and tries to understand what others mean. Lewis Carroll's Alice stories are usually combined in one volume as *Alice's Adventures in Wonderland and Through the Looking Glass*, although the former was first published in 1865 and the latter in 1871 and they are peopled by different characters – the Mad Hatter, the March Hare and the Cheshire Cat in the first and Humpty Dumpty, Tweedledum and Tweedledee and the Red Queen in the second. Many artists have taken on the challenge of illustrating these wonderful characters and the classic illustrations of John Tenniel have stood the test of time. The Walker edition of *Alice's Adventures in Wonderland* is illustrated by Helen Oxenbury with an Alice who looks like a modern girl with her casual blue dress. But the dream-like atmosphere of the book is not sacrificed and younger children may prefer these pictures to Tenniel's.

J.M. Barrie

Townsend considers parts of *Peter Pan and Wendy*, particularly where Wendy mothers the Lost Boys, sentimental (Townsend, 1995: 80). But many children still appreciate it in book form and performed on the stage as a fast-moving adventure story with strong and interesting characters, not least Captain Hook, Tinkerbell the fairy and the ticking crocodile. Many illustrators have felt drawn to the challenge of picturing the tale. Michael Foreman's illustrations, in the Chrysalis edition, communicate the exuberance of the children's adventures. In a shorter version of the story, published by Hodder, Shirley Hughes emphasizes the Edwardian setting of the story. The sequel by Geraldine McCaughrean, *Peter Pan in Scarlet*, is a successful attempt to take the Darling children back to Never Never Land, where the Lost Boys need help.

Philip Pullman

Pullman's books in His Dark Materials trilogy – *Northern Lights*, *The Subtle Knife* and *The Amber Spyglass* – create a parallel world, universe even, which is like and unlike our own. The notion of each of us having a daemon and the inclusion of another rational species – intelligent polar bears – are two of the intriguing creations of Pullman's imagination. The first book, *Northern Lights*, is the most accessible for children still in the primary years.

To get some impression of the response to Pullman's work a visit to Amazon UK shows hundreds of reader reactions. Most are positive; one ten-year-old writes: 'Daemons are a fantastic idea and I wouldn't mind having one myself.' Pullman himself has said that the idea of daemons was the best he ever had (quoted in Rustin, 2004: 10). When asked during an interview set out on Kids' Reads why daemons tended to be the opposite sex to their humans, Pullman replied that each of us has something of the other gender in us (Pullman interview 'Philip Pullman' on kidsreads.com, accessed 2 February 2009).

One big claim caught my eye: 'This is the stuff for young minds of the twenty first century – move over C.S. Lewis, Tolkien and J.K. Rowling' (Julia Platt, Amazon UK site, accessed 2 February 2009). Perhaps we have to wait another decade or so to be sure. The negative comments are often to do with what seems to be his attitude to organized religion and his belief that it can be harmful, even tyrannical. He also thinks that few people are totally good or totally evil and so he would rather we think in terms of good and bad actions (www.philip-pullman.com, accessed 1 February 2009). Like other 'high fantasy' books, Pullman's are often enjoyed by both adults and children in their print form, in audio CD and in film and theatre.

J.K. Rowling and the Harry Potter saga

The seven extraordinarily popular stories in this saga cover the seven years that Harry Potter is a pupil at the Hogwarts School of Witchcraft and Wizardry. All are underpinned by the usual fantasy novel theme – the struggle between light and dark forces. Behind the dark forces lurks Harry's main enemy, Lord Voldemort. The first of the stories, *Harry Potter and the Philosopher's Stone*, is the Potter book most often enjoyed by primary school children. Orphaned Harry's miserable time with the Dursleys, his realization that he is a wizard and his transportation to a new exciting life appeal considerably to children, some as young as age seven or eight. The later books become progressively longer, with increasingly complicated narratives, calling for sustained concentration. The popularity of the stories is explained, at least partly, by 'the powerful blend between school story, adventure story and fantasy' (Watson, 2001: 322).

The stories go at a fast pace but the characters of Harry and his friends are well developed. Rowling's inventiveness and storytelling skills have generated the kind of enthusiasm that helps children build the very stamina they need to go on to wider and deeper reading challenges.

Terry Pratchett: comedic fantasy

Longer stories and novels which fall into the 'fantasy' category can be full of wit and humour as well as suspense and strangeness. The three books – *Diggers*, *Truckers* and *Wings* – that make up Pratchett's Bromeliad trilogy combine a good plot, amusing characters and witty comment. The tales about the nomes, fast-moving creatures about four inches high, take us from their threatened home under the floorboards of a departmental store, to a quarry on the 'Outside' which they wrongly believe is abandoned. The third in the trilogy, *Wings*, reaches the height of the power struggle and sees 'Thing' put on a space shuttle – so Pratchett's fantasies draw on modern science and technology. Like Pratchett's other books those in this trilogy are very popular with some adults and with children of about age ten and over, less so with those who do not appreciate the distinctive humour.

129

Younger children can enjoy hearing books normally managed independently by the over nines if they are read aloud.

Around 7 or 8

- *The BFG* by Roald Dahl (Puffin)
  One of Dahl's kindlier tales about the generous giant. Other favourites are *James and the Giant Peach*; *Charlie and the Chocolate Factory*; *Danny the Champion of the World*; *The Fantastic Mr Fox*.

- *Peter Pan in Scarlet* by Geraldine McCaughrean (Oxford University Press)
  Wendy and the lost boys return to Neverland ... The full-length sequel to J.M. Barry's *Peter Pan* suits older, forward readers best, but the shortened version, illustrated so imaginatively by David Wyatt (McCaughrean calls him 'a master craftsman') and with a dramatic and inviting red cover, brings in a wider readership.

- *Ninnyhammer* by Dick King-Smith (Young Corgi)
  Peter finds a white stick in the stream near his family's farm. Ninnyhammer is grateful for the return of his magic wand and from then on the fortunes of Peter's troubled family improve dramatically. A good story which also gives young readers food for thought: people are not always what they seem to be at first.

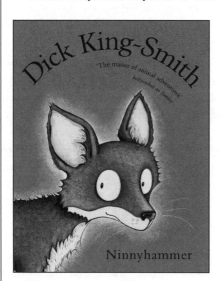

Figure 11.2
Front cover of Ninnyhammer *by Dick King-Smith*
Reproduced with the permission of the publishers The Random House Group Ltd. Copyright 2007

Around 8 or 9 upwards

- *Skellig* by David Almond (Hodder)
  In a family setting but stretches out to strange and mysterious happenings when a young boy finds an angel in the garage. Gripping and moving.

Figure 11.1 *Fantasy novels*

- *The Shrinking of Treehorn* by Florence Parry Heide (Puffin)
  Get an edition which, like this one, is tellingly illustrated by Edward Gorey. A longer, much more involved play on the theme of adult indifference to the concerns and fears of children than in the well-known picturebook *Not Now Bernard*. Treehorn is a boy who becomes smaller and smaller. He overcomes this and stops the shrinking – but then finds himself turning green.

- *The Ghost of Thomas Kempe* by Penelope Lively (Egmont)
  When the attic of an old house is disturbed to make James a bedroom in the family's new house, the spirit of a seventeenth-century apothecary is released. He wants James to be his apprentice. When the mischievous ghost knocks down fences, spills drinks and so on, James gets the blame and has to find a solution. Children love the humour in this story.

- *Northern Lights* by Philip Pullman (Scholastic)
  In this first novel in the His Dark Materials trilogy readers accompany Lyra, a child who lives with scholars in an Oxford college, on her strange and exciting journey to the North Pole. This is a highly original and absorbing story set in a parallel world.

Figure 11.1 *continued*

Figure 11.3
Front cover of Magic Tree House: Lions on the Loose *by Mary Pope Osborne*
Red Fox. Reproduced with the permission of the publishers The Random House Group Ltd

Figure 11.4
Front cover of The Windspinner *by Berlie Doherty*
Young Corgi. Reproduced with the permission of the publishers The Random House Group Ltd

Ian McEwan and Florence Parry Heide: surreal fantasy

In his book *The Daydreamer* Ian McEwan introduces us to Peter Fortune, a young boy whom others, particularly grown-ups, find rather strange. There are seven chapters, or rather interlinked stories, in which Peter becomes, amongst other things, a cat and a baby. Or does he? Are these happenings all in his imagination perhaps? The book certainly intrigues its readers and makes them puzzle and think. There is a dark side to McEwan's imagination and there are some Roald Dahl moments. Children might sometimes wish their family would disappear but Peter disposes of his by using vanishing cream. Teachers find many older primary children love hearing this original book read aloud and lively discussion nearly always follows the reading of each chapter. This is also an example of a perfectly matched author and illustrator: Anthony Browne's black and white drawings capture brilliantly the uneasy mood of the story.

Parry Heide's Treehorn books, beginning with *The Shrinking of Treehorn*, also tell of the life of a child who is distanced psychologically from his family and so they connect with what many children experience, for some of their growing up time at any rate. Treehorn endures his predicament – instead of growing bigger like other children he finds himself shrinking – with considerable courage. Unsettling as the stories are, children I have read them to enjoy the humour of Treehorn's bizarre experiences.

BOX 11.2 *THE AMAZING ADVENTURES OF CURD THE LION (AND US!) IN THE LAND OF THE BACK OF BEYOND* BY ALAN GILLILAND (RAVEN'S QUILL LTD)

Four soft toys go off on a journey to find a stolen brooch. Sounds cosy? It is not. In fact this is an exciting addition to fantasy novels for children from about age seven years, although it is also a most engrossing adventure story. The pencil drawings by the author fit the written text perfectly and add atmosphere and often energy to the story.

It is not surprising that this story has been compared to the work of Lewis Carroll and Edward Lear: riddles and word play, mysteries and surprises are wonderfully interwoven. The play on names is superb: for example, the four animals are called Curd the Lion, Pilgrim Crow, Sweenie the Heenie (a hyena) and O'Flattery the Snake.

Dialogue is convincing too. When the mother of Henry and Henrietta, the two children in the story, wrongly accuses them of losing her brooch she threatens that if they do not find it soon she will cancel their birthday party. Worst of all she will give their beloved toy animals to the charity shop for Children in Need, adding, 'You don't care about them. Look at the way you were treating Curd the Lion just now. Beating him to rags!'

Chapter 12

Building reading stamina for children of differing abilities and attitudes to reading

INTRODUCTION

How do we help children develop the powers of concentration, the sheer stamina, to read the longer stories and children's novels which have been the subject of these last few chapters? There follows a consideration of some of the books that appeal to children with different needs. The issues are discussed further in the next chapter, on using books in the classroom.

CHOOSING TEXTS FOR THE CLASSROOM AND SCHOOL COLLECTIONS: SOME THINGS TO CONSIDER

Teachers have long read books aloud so that all the children in a class can benefit from a story they might not yet manage to read independently. This at the very least shows children the rich experiences and enjoyment stories can give. To ring the changes, teachers and parents take advantage of the greater availability and quality of books on CD. Of course we have to evaluate these as carefully as we would a print book. We look for storytellers who know about the subtle timing and pace that sensitivity to the nuances of a book make possible. Ability to create different voices for different characters is also important. Stephen Fry's audiobook readings for the BBC Cover to Cover series show this ability to an extraordinary degree (Rowling and Fry, 2004).

In her article 'Listening to a Good Book' Angela Macpherson points out that teachers and parents often find that 'audio books have helped children change from being uninterested in books to being voracious readers' (Macpherson, 2004: 13). Children are free from any distraction from becoming absorbed in the story and this is a good way of increasing vocabulary too. Reviews of stories on CD are available on websites and in both *Books for Keeps* and *The School Librarian*.

Reading print books of an intermediate length and challenge, between illustrated books with little written text and a long story, also helps build robust readers. Children who can read but are reluctant to do so and children less forward on their journey to full reading independence often favour fast-moving adventure stories.

For some modern children it is graphic novels, with their affinity with comics and copious illustrations instead of daunting blocks of text, which make them see something in print books. These are considered in Chapter 6.

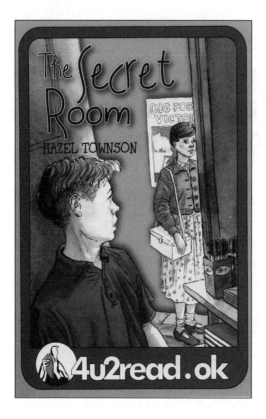

Above all, reading stamina can be nourished by books by the great authors of children's fiction, sometimes by beginning with their shorter stories and even picturebook versions. And so I have suggested some of these in Figure 12.2, which has suggestions for drawing in reluctant young readers either because their progress is slower or because they have not yet been persuaded that print books can be worthwhile and enjoyable. Figure 12.3 has further suggestions to challenge and interest avid and forward readers towards the end of the primary school years.

- *The Secret Room* by Hazel Townson and Martin Salisbury (illus.) (Barrington Stoke)
  This title is a 4u2read.ok book for young learners aged eight to thirteen whose reading age is just over eight. This page-turning mystery has some features thought to help: cream pages, clear print, copious illustrations.

- *Wartman* by Michael Morpurgo (Barrington Stoke)
  A 4u2read.ok book for reading age under eight and an interest age of eight to twelve. A funny and inviting first-person narrative.

Figure 12.2 *Books to build reading stamina: exciting reads for less forward or reluctant readers over age eight years*

- *Project X* by Tony Bradman and others (Oxford University Press)
  This guided reading scheme to motivate reluctant boy readers (but also interesting to girls) uses digital artwork, contemporary characters and quick moving adventures in the print books and video-clips, pictures and sound in related CD-ROMs.

- *War Game* by Michael Foreman (Puffin)
  A fictionalized story based on an actual event – a historic game of football between the two opposing sides one Christmas Day during the First World War – this book is compelling.

- *War Boy* by Michael Foreman (Pavilion Books)
  This personal, illustrated story drawing on facts and memories brings alive what it was like for a young child to live through the Second World War. The illustrations are a very important part of the book and make the memories coherent.

- *Beastly Things in the Barn* by Sandra Gover (Educational Printing Services Ltd.)
  For reading age eight and interest age eight to twelve, this book has clear well-spaced text and amusing cartoon-like illustrations by Derry Dillon. Mark's family have rented out their barn for the summer and he is rather looking forward to meeting the new neighbours – until he actually meets them and endures a series of catastrophes involving parrots and strange visitors.

- *The Adventures of Captain Underpants: An Epic Novel* by Dav Pilkey (Scholastic)
  This is the first of a substantial series about George and Harold and their bizarre superhero, Captain Underpants. The humour and wonderfully dynamic comic-like illustrations give the book pace and energy, which appeals to many primary-aged children, even to some ten-year-olds who do not usually like reading print books.

- *How to Train Your Dragon* by Cressida Cowell (Hodder Children's Books)
  This entertaining and original tale about an unlikely Viking hero and his dragon, Toothless, is becoming a favourite across the primary years – as are Cressida Cowell's other books. Teachers report that reluctant ten-year-olds like the amusing scribbly drawings and the humorous notes and maps.

- *Football Stories* by James Riordan (ed.) (Oxford University Press)
  Gripping stories by well-known authors like Michael Rosen, Barry Hines and Robert Swindells. In the latter's 'Going Up' Terry's Dad has lost his half-day off work two days before the match. Who will take Terry to the game?

- *Harry Potter and the Philosopher's Stone* by J.K. Rowling (Bloomsbury)
  (Children's edition.) Book 1 in this seven-book saga has a good plot, interesting characters and a sympathetic hero. There are mixed views on the quality of the writing, but there is no doubt that many young readers, not normally enthusiastic about print books, have been captured by this first story and the others that have followed.

Figure 12.2 continued

- *Flour Babies* by Anne Fine (Puffin)
  When the annual school science fair comes around, the children in Mr Cartright's class get six 1 lb bags of flour to care for as if they were babies.

- *Blood Fever* by Charles Higson (Puffin)
  One of a series of Young James Bond adventures. Is the secret society at school connected with the disappearance of a young girl in the Mediterranean? The books in this series are exciting, but be aware that violent events are sometimes described.

- *Treasure Island* by R.L. Stevenson (Templar Publishing)
  Edition in which the illustrations by Robert Ingpen add to the reader's enjoyment and understanding.

- *A Stitch in Time* by Penelope Lively (Mammoth)
  Maria, a lonely child, sees a girl from Victorian times reflected in the glass framing of an old sampler. The sampler is unfinished . . . Maria's search for what happened to the girl leads her to think about why things happen as they do and – a favourite theme of Lively's – how time changes us.

- *The Daydreamer* by Ian McEwan and Anthony Browne (illus.) (Red Fox)
  Are the extraordinary things that happen in ten-year-old Peter Fortune's life 'real' or only in his imagination?

- *The Stones Are Hatching* by Geraldine McCaughrean (Oxford University Press)
  Phelim strives to save the world from monsters that threaten the countryside.

- *The Vortex: Code Red* by Chris Ryan (Red Fox)
  This thrilling adventure story set on the Northumbrian moors begins when Ben and his cousin, Annie, try to spot the rare hen harrier birds. To their dismay they see one of the birds shot dead. Someone does not want the visitors that the birds attract . . .

- *The Earthsea Quartet* by Ursula Le Guin (Penguin)
  A Wizard of Earthsea is the first story of a trilogy about a young wizard and has complex themes and language which might interest and appeal to a forward reader of age ten.

- *Homeless Bird* by Gloria Whelan (Frances Lincoln)
  Koly, a girl of thirteen growing up in India, faces the prospect of leaving her family for an arranged marriage. The book tells us through a series of events of Koly's courage in taking some control over her own fate in spite of the powerful traditions of her culture.

- *The Subtle Knife* by Philip Pullman (Scholastic)
  The Subtle Knife is the second novel in Pullman's His Dark Materials trilogy and will stretch forward readers who have read the first of the trilogy. The battle between good and evil intensifies.

Figure 12.3 *Books to challenge forward readers nearing eleven*

- *Letters from Alain* by Enrique Perez Diaz and Francisco Solé (illus.) (Aurora Metro)
  A young boy's friend has set off to America with his family in a small boat. Nothing has been heard from them since they began their journey. Has the boat been lost at sea? Only the family dog returns. Unable to face up to the possibility of tragedy, the boy writes himself letters from his friend. Eventually he sets off in a small boat himself, almost meeting the same fate as his friend.

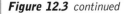 **Figure 12.3** *continued*

SUMMARY OF CHAPTERS 7 TO 12 ON SELECTING LONGER STORIES AND CHILDREN'S NOVELS

- 'Longer stories and children's novels' is a large category which is divided here into four main groupings: animal, realistic, historical and fantasy.
- The best-liked nearly always have page-turning narratives which help build up reading stamina.
- Other qualities to look for when selecting books for home or school include the communication of a strong sense of place or setting, the creation of interesting and convincing characters, the use of vivid language (including strong dialogue) and emotional power which draws empathy from young readers.
- Not all these qualities will be present in any one book and children may build up stamina by reading less than wholly memorable books on the way to becoming wide and reflective readers.
- Animal stories can be realistic, sticking to what is known through observation of real creatures and scientific facts or they can include anthropomorphic features.
- Realism is an amorphous category including animal, school and family (or domestic) stories. All stay within the framework of events that do not contradict the laws of nature.
- The historical novel is one of the genres that link fiction and non-fiction and can be considered under sub-categories like time-slips and war stories. The best achieve a good balance between 'the facts' and the artistic requirements of telling an absorbing story capturing young readers' hearts and minds.
- Fantasy stories, which go beyond the natural laws of our world, cover a wide range from the page-turning adventure stories with fantasy elements that are dominant in bookshops to works of great imagination and power.
- Teachers keep in mind the interests, abilities and attitudes of the children in their class when choosing, constantly seeking books to inspire the less forward or reluctant and books to challenge more advanced young readers.

Chapter 13

Using longer stories and novels

INTRODUCTION

For some children, just the provision of a wide range of books and the space and time to read them is enough. The books themselves can help readers grow as they take up authors' invitations – to be amused, sad, shocked or relieved and to pick up all those nuances that help us 'read between the lines'.

The challenge for the classroom teacher is to find ways of helping children not only to become absorbed by stories, but also to appreciate and respond to the subtle insights and messages. The wisest, best-chosen activities that precede, go alongside or follow reading fiction can help children find these deeper meanings and extra enjoyment from books. But it is possible to do too much and to 'spoil' enjoyment of a book.

Children fortunate enough to have been in classrooms where reading is valued and part of the weft and warp of daily experience – where books are displayed, read aloud, discussed and written about – are likely by the end of the primary years to be well on the way to becoming such critical readers. But critical reading best starts early. Even the smallest children have preferences and, by age five or six, are able to articulate these, giving reasons. We should encourage this, not least because part of becoming a critical reader involves a recognition of the subjectivity of the individual reading experience. Reading widely makes us become aware that people have different experiences and view those experiences differently.

When a young reader, some way on the journey towards becoming a reflective reader, responds to a story there are two aspects. There is the response a reader feels to the literary merits of the book – noting perhaps the skilful way David Almond describes the angel in *Skellig* or the way Philip Pullman uses images to do with fire in *The Firework-Maker's Daughter*. But alongside this are the more spontaneous, personal feelings evoked by the best fiction. Such feelings are often awakened when young readers are towards the end of *Tom's Midnight Garden* when Tom meets the old lady at the top of the house and realizes it is his friend Hattie grown old – quite an epiphany. As Nikki Gamble points out, 'While students might talk confidently about point of view, narrative structure or cohesion, this is to no purpose if they are not moved, excited, delighted, challenged or changed by what they read' (Gamble in Hunt, 2004: 755). And so spontaneous response, often involving the feelings, and learning to analyse need to be balanced. Sometimes reading and reflecting are enough. But quite often, especially when working with longer stories and children's novels, teachers seek ways of extending children's response, helping to stretch their imaginations and to nudge them forward on the journey towards critical and reflective reading. The creation of a reading environment where children feel part of a community of talkers, listeners, readers and writers is covered in Chapter 3. Here I consider how reading aloud, talk, improvisation and drama and writing can help deepen enjoyment and response.

READING ALOUD

Teacher reading to the class

Reading aloud to the whole class is one of the best ways of helping children enjoy and think about a longer story or novel. It is a rich, shared experience that helps make the class a community of young readers. I have never found this better put than by Aidan Chambers:

> One of the most obvious but most notable aspects of reading aloud is its socially binding effect. Those who read together feel they belong together as a community, for nothing unites more than the sharing of their imaginary experiences; and they feel together physically, for reading aloud is essentially a domestic, a family-sized activity.
>
> (Chambers, 1991: 57)

As children move through the primary years they develop as independent readers, but by reading aloud, the teacher can make it possible for them to appreciate more challenging plots and more subtle characterization. This is partly because the children can concentrate on listening. As a more experienced reader the teacher will vary pace and expression in line with the mood of the story and bring out the drama of the narrative. Facial expression, eye contact and gesture all help the teacher connect with the listening children. Many teachers are gifted at reading dialogue and making the characters in the book 'come alive' by creating different voices for them. But students and beginning teachers should be assured that this is a skill that can be developed by practice.

Some of the best audio CDs allow children to hear stories read by gifted actors and the changes can be rung by having these in the classroom. But this should not be instead of the teacher reading to the class because teachers can, unlike a CD storyteller, make eye contact and use gestures. The whole experience is much more personal because teachers know their class – what they like, what they will find amusing and what will move and affect them. Less forward and reluctant readers and young learners acquiring English as an additional language who might have difficulty in reading a long book on their own will benefit hugely from all this, but it is valuable for able young readers too.

The emphasis when reading aloud should be on enjoyment and sharing responses rather than there being any sense of children being tested on what they have heard. Above all, the point of making reading aloud a priority is to show children what books can offer – how the best stories can reach into our minds and hearts.

139

BOX 13.1 SOME THINGS TO CONSIDER WHEN SHARING A CLASS STORY OVER A NUMBER OF WEEKS

- Does anything need explanation at the first reading? If it is a story about a journey, a special place or event some introduction, using perhaps a picture or map, might be helpful.
- How can children's interest and attention be captured at an early stage? Some preparatory thought about the atmosphere you want to achieve and the contribution of dialogue is helpful.
- Are some activities helpful after reading the first few chapters? Some stories lend themselves to early exploration through improvisation. This encourages active, involved listening. For example role play about arriving in the countryside from the city as evacuees is often introduced early in reading *Goodnight Mister Tom.*
- Bringing in writing early on helps integrate it into the reading experience. Writing in role appeals to children not normally keen writers and often follows drama.
- Visual representation is, for some children, an important way of exploring a story. I have seen children build understanding by drawing Stig's dump or portraying characters from a book.
- How can children's listening stamina be developed and maintained? Recapping and a little discussion are helpful at the start of each reading.
- How much discussion is best? It depends on the book and the class. Experienced teachers develop a sense of when it is a good place to pause.
- Personal response deserves encouragement and children gain confidence if they are shown how to support their opinions with reference to the text.
- How can the changes be rung so that we are not always asking children direct questions? Teachers sometimes admit to having had a change of mind about a character or event, helping nudge young readers and listeners towards a speculative, reflective approach.
- Imaginative, well-thought-out activities can increase children's enjoyment of the story. But sometimes just reading a book and discussing key events is enough.

BOX 13.2 CHILDREN'S COMMENTS ON THE EXPERIENCE OF THE TEACHER READING ALOUD

I only like reading books on facts but my best lesson is when Mrs G. reads a story to the class because she does all the voices and sometimes we all laugh.

(nine-year-old Jack talking about the class teacher reading Gene Kemp's book
The Turbulent Term of Tyke Tiler)

My best book is *The Ghost of Thomas Kempe* – it is exciting and you never know what the ghost is going to do next.

(ten-year-old Tracy commenting on the head teacher's reading of Penelope Lively's book about the haunting of young James by an apothecary from Tudor times)

Children reading aloud

Children can also be helped to hone their skills in holding an audience when they read aloud. Good contexts for this kind of support occur when children prepare to read to the class from story or poetry books or from their own writing. They can be helped with diction and to vary pitch and pace to keep up the interest of the listeners. Advice about what might be emphasized to aid understanding or create dramatic tension is also helpful.

These reading aloud experiences and skills may well transfer to drama work. There is more about this in Chapter 14.

I have found, too, that children's sense of audience in their writing is energized by the experience of reading aloud. The reactions of their listeners show the sort of review comments that make an impact. Snippets of dialogue from the book being reviewed, a strong opinion and perhaps some questions on the lines of 'I am still wondering if . . . what do you think?' all help bind readers and listeners.

TALK AS A WAY OF EXPRESSING AND DEVELOPING RESPONSE

Talking about texts is one of the most educative and life enhancing activities that takes place in a classroom and is a unique way of entering the world of a book. There has been a welcome move away from comprehension-type questions following class or independent reading towards a genuine conversation between children and the teacher.

The teacher, children's author and critic Aidan Chambers has articulated what has been called 'booktalk' clearly and inspirationally. In *Tell Me* he identifies the three sharings – sharing enthusiasms, sharing puzzles and sharing connections – which have so much helped teachers and children get far beyond the superficial in their book discussions (Chambers, 1993: 16–18). It is when they start to look for patterns that children's thinking and talk move up a notch. It means that they need to gain some control over a metalanguage to refer to 'characters', 'plot', 'dialogue', 'symbol', 'personification' and so on. But, as Nikki Gamble points out, analysis using these terms is fine as long as it is linked to an approach that values 'psychological and emotional engagement' (Gamble in Hunt, 2004: 755).

As a mature reader the teacher can help get this balance between spontaneous response and analysis right. Here is a case where Vygotsky's concept of the 'zone of proximal development' is helpful to our understanding: what you can manage with some help now you will be able to manage alone in the future because you have internalized the maturer person's thought processes (Vygotsky, 1986: 187). One of the things teachers do, when they take up the book they have been reading with the class, is to give the gist of the tale so far. But children can also learn much from talking to each other and this is why many teachers include 'response partners' in their planning and teaching. This helps children rehearse their thoughts and ideas before contributing them to class discussion. At the class discussion stage, the teacher can help focus the conversation, perhaps making notes using the interactive whiteboard or flip chart. Responses of all kinds should be welcome, but children need to support their opinions with evidence from the text.

IMPROVISATION, DRAMA AND MOVING IMAGE TEXTS

Drama in all its forms is an excellent way of involving children deeply in the themes, characters and actions in a story. Nothing else puts children so firmly in the shoes of a character in a story. It gives rise to much talk, discussion and analysis to plan and create the drama and evaluate it afterwards. It can also be a spur to many kinds of writing – writing in role (including letters and diary entries), scriptwriting and writing alternative endings to stories. For an exploration of the connections between drama and writing, see the article by Teresa Cremin *et al*. 'Connecting Drama and Writing: Seizing the Moment to Write' (Cremin *et al*., 2006: 273–91).

Children are increasingly being helped to work with film and televisual texts as well as with print. The British Film Institute have produced a comprehensive teaching guide on using film and television with children – *Look Again! A Teaching Guide to Using Film and Television with Three- to Eleven-Year Olds* (BFI, 2003). It is organized around eight teaching techniques for the study in school of film and television and includes a wealth of practical ideas which help take children beyond a superficial response. Details of their latest publications are available on the BFI website (www.bfi.org.uk/education). Most significant novels for children have been made into films, often for television and seeing and understanding the differences between the experience of reading a print text and watching a film is an important part of children's experience of narrative and story in different media.

Children's work with drama and film is also discussed and analysed in Chapter 14. Here are some drama activities to help extend children's response to longer stories and children's novels:

- Improvisation: acting out events from a key chapter.
- Scriptwriting: this can be done when an improvisation stabilizes.
- Hot seating: a technique which involves children answering questions in the role of a character and actually thinking and reflecting 'in role'.
- Monologues, a variation on 'hot seating': children take on a role and present a monologue of the character's thoughts at a particular point in the story.
- Critics programme: children are helped to make a radio programme with presenter and critics in role.
- Freeze-frame: a well-known technique which involves children in making a tableau of characters in a particular scene from a book. Some teachers act as narrator or appoint a child in this role to explain the significance of the scene; or the 'actors' can say their thoughts and feelings aloud.
- Comparing print and film version of a novel.

ART AND CRAFT

Art and craft activities around a book – including painting and storyboxes – deserve the same encouragement, enrichment and discussion at each stage as writing and drama. Some children like to create their own illustrations for the books they are reading. Are children's artistic interpretations best done *before* they look at different illustrators' work of the different editions of the same book or *after* some examination, discussion and analysis? Perhaps children are more likely to produce their own artistic response if they have not looked at too much of the published artwork for a book first? In any case, how illustrators, including child illustrators, emphasize a particular aspect or 'reading' of the story is a good discussion point and can lead to interesting annotated displays of children's work. The pictures by children, and by published illustrators, can be shown on the interactive whiteboard and the child can explain which aspect of the novel they believe their artwork highlights, the teacher and other children then making constructive comments.

For detailed and inspiring suggestions for extending response to the books of Philip Pullman, including artistic responses to *Clockwork*, *The Firework-Maker's Daughter* and *Northern Lights*, see the CLPE publication *Book Power* (Bunting *et al.*, 2006). Pullman is a visual writer and uses imagery and language to pull on our visual imaginations and these authors share good ideas about representing through artwork the different characters with their daemons; children are also invited to draw what they think their own daemon would look like.

WRITING ALONGSIDE AND AFTER READING LONGER STORIES AND CHILDREN'S NOVELS

Being exposed to language by the best writers expands vocabulary and exposes children to more involved and subtle syntax. Even more importantly, searching for meaning in books also develops thinking and sympathetic insight into the themes and characters. The benefits work the other way too. The very act of writing, the organization of ideas and insights, enhances understanding of and response to books. But these benefits can only be realized if children themselves see writing in this positive light. Writing involves effort and hard work and so children have to see the point. The writing tasks we invite have to be interesting and imaginative too. If you would like to go deeper into this link between the study of literature and writing development, you cannot do better than seek out *The Reader in the Writer* by Myra Barrs and Valerie Cork (Barrs and Cork, 2001). This study draws on a year's research into the reading and related writing of pupils in a Year 5 classroom. We see how children grow as both readers and writers.

Here I look at some of the ways teachers bring writing into older primary children's literature work, including reviews and reading journals, writing in role and author studies.

Reviews and reading journals

Reviews

Asking children to write reviews of the books they have been reading, listening to as a class or reading in guided or independent reading groups has a place, but if overused can be counter productive and, in a favourite word of many children, 'boring'! Giving children some choice about which books they choose to review is one obvious way to help secure a more than superficial response. Jack's class were asked to write a review of their favourite book by Roald Dahl. He enters into the humour of Dahl's book, producing cartoon-like pictures with annotation. The influence of Quentin Blake's illustrations is evident in Jack's drawings. But he brings his own touches to his pictures. This is an exuberant and well-sustained review.

143

Two insights which show a move towards deeper more critical reading are his noting that ugly thoughts might be reflected in a person's face and that someone's self-perception might be very different from how others see them. Writing of Mr Twit, he observes: 'But he thinks he looks terrifically wise and grand!' Later in the review he produces a good summary of the whole book: 'Mr and Mrs Twit got worse and worse with their nastiness until others took their revenge!'

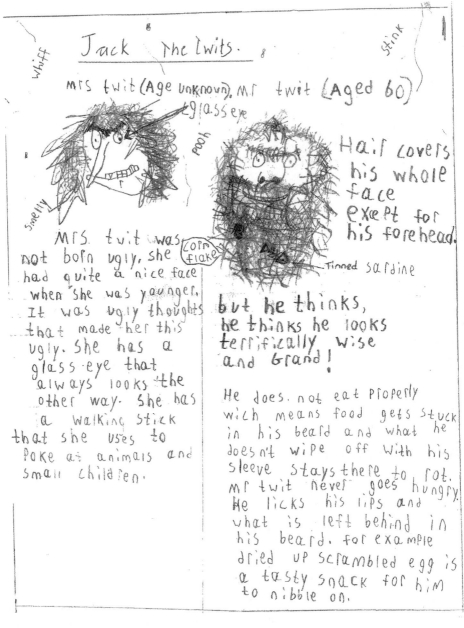

Figure 13.1 Review of The Twits *by nine-year-old Jack*

Reading logs/journals

The reviews children write can be part of their reading logs or reading journals. Keeping a written, word-processed or online record of what they read is a well-established way of developing children's critical reading and writing. But these can become routine and keeping them a chore. How can they be made an interesting and useful part of the children's work? Here are some ideas:

- Involve the children in the design and format. Something like the following is usually agreed:

  - Title of book, author, publisher
  - Kind of book – school story, realistic story, adventure story, fantasy, etc.
  - Comment (in longer reviews would include something on the setting, character, plot, language and imagery).

Some teachers make copies of these ideas on format, content and some guiding questions and stick them to the inside cover of the children's reading logs for reference.

- A list of questions could include:

Setting

- Where does the story take place?
- Does the writer make you really 'see' the place?
- Can you quote a snippet to show this?
- Can you sketch a scene?

Characters

- Are the characters convincing? Is what they say important as well as what they do? Quote from the book here.
- What do other characters say about the main character?
- How does the main character behave towards others?
- Write a short character sketch of your favourite and least favourite characters, giving reasons for how you feel about them. You might also like to sketch them.

Plot

- Does the book start well and make you want to read on?
- Does it have a satisfying ending?
- What would you say was the climax of the book?

Language

- Does the author draw you into the book with a conversational sort of language?
- Is the dialogue good, making you almost hear the character talking?
- Are there some images in the book that make it memorable? (For example, if the story is set in a very hot or very cold country can you find some words and images that the author uses to tell us this.)

General comment

- How many stars would you give this book? Explain why.
- Would you seek out another book by this author?
- Would you recommend it to a friend?

145

- Make the logs interactive by putting teacher comments at the end of some reviews.
- Children often like to have a system of stars to assess each book. The criteria for each rating can be discussed and agreed by the class. The *Books for Keeps* star format is:

*****	Unmissable
****	Very good
***	Good
**	Fair
*	Poor

- Make it clear that a long review is not expected for every book they read. Sometimes just brief bibliographic details and a succinct comment – 'Good story but disappointing ending' or 'Excellent if you like school stories. I don't!'
- Agree that everyone will write at least two longish reviews during each term.
- Encourage some extended writing, but allow the children to develop their own style – for example, welcome drawings, annotated diagrams and comic strips.
- With advance warning, ask children to read their reviews and comments on books aloud and encourage constructive comment from the other children. Children's drawings and comic strips can be shown on the whiteboard.
- Reassure them that they do not have to like every book or every aspect of a particular book – but just writing 'boring' is not enough. Reasons have to be given, with reference to the text.

Writing in role

Perhaps, like me, you have sometimes been disappointed with the results from this sort of task. How do we avoid a superficial response? My students and I have found that children sometimes write more insightfully if they have heard an absorbing book read aloud. This shared experience nearly always involves discussion at key points in the book where the actions of characters are significant. How does each character think, speak and act?, we might ask the children. Is there sometimes a mismatch between what characters say and what they do? Can we infer things about the characters that are not made fully explicit? Improvising key parts of the book also helps children 'get inside' the characters' skins. So intent listening, enthusiastic talk and thoughtful improvisation can all be helpful preliminary activities before starting to write. Emailing can provide another means of writing in role (Safford *et al.*, 2004: 72).

Keeping journals

The provision of journals in which children can draw and write alongside reading stories can help even reluctant young writers to find fiction satisfying. This strategy was successfully tried by a team of teachers of children in years 4 and 5 and researchers from the Centre for Literacy in Education. The mini-books in which the children explored their response to Louis Sacher's *There's a Boy in the Girls' Bathroom* had just the right amount of guidance in the form of prompts for particular kinds of writing and illustrating, including writing in role, making lists and designing annotated diagrams (Safford *et al.*, 2004).

CASE STUDY 13.1 NINE-YEAR-OLDS WRITING IN ROLE AS TOM OAKLEY FROM *GOODNIGHT MISTER TOM* BY MICHELLE MAGORIAN (PUFFIN)

History and English were combined in a unit on the Second World War, and it was in this context that nine-year-olds wrote letters in role. The teacher considered that reading the class *Goodnight Mister Tom* would inform and enrich their understanding of what it felt like to be an evacuee or one of the people who took in a young person. Orla manages rather well to take on the attitudes and manner of speaking of Tom Oakley in her letter.

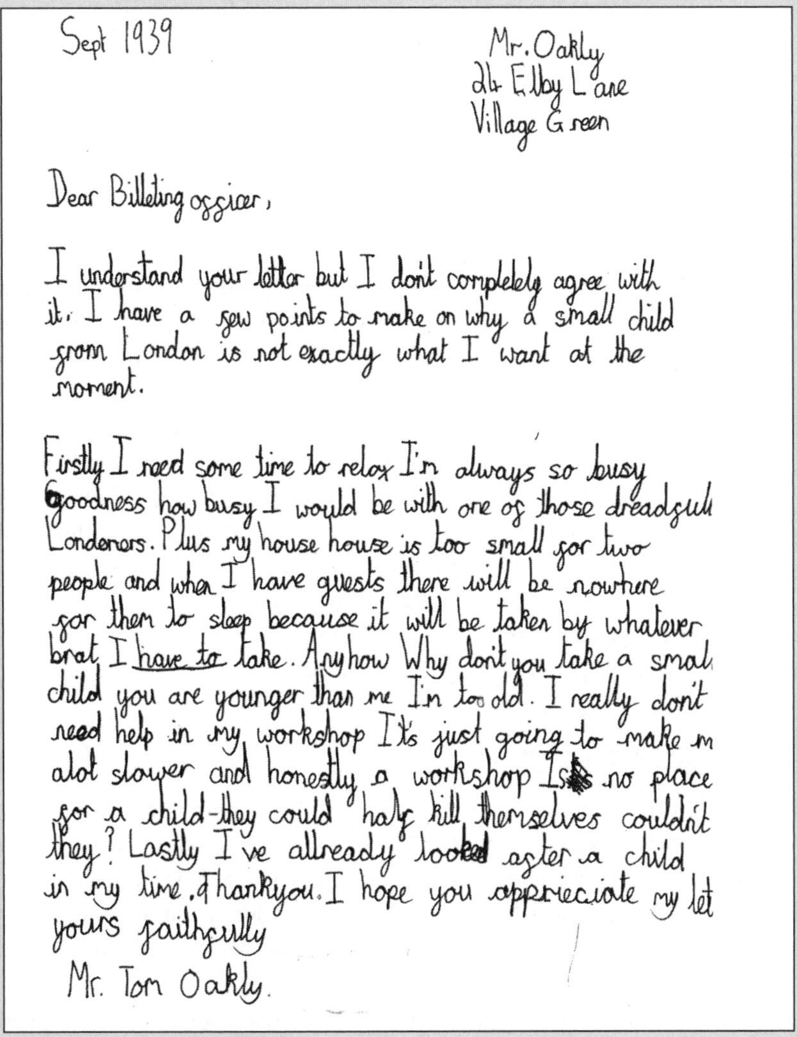

Sept 1939

Mr. Oakly
26 Elby Lane
Village Green

Dear Billeting officer,

I understand your letter but I don't completely agree with it. I have a few points to make on why a small child from London is not exactly what I want at the moment.

Firstly I need some time to relax I'm always so busy Goodness how busy I would be with one of those dreadful Londoners. Plus my house house is too small for two people and when I have guests there will be nowhere for them to sleep because it will be taken by whatever brat I have to take. Anyhow Why don't you take a small child you are younger than me I'm too old. I really don't need help in my workshop It's just going to make m alot slower and honestly a workshop Is no place for a child-they could half kill themselves couldn't they? Lastly I've already looked after a child in my time. Thankyou. I hope you apprieciate my let yours faithfully
Mr. Tom Oakly.

Figure 13.2 Orla's letter in the role of Tom Oakley, the main character in Michelle Magorian's book Goodnight Mister Tom

Writing scripts

Another favourite way of helping children to get deeper into stories is to ask them to write a key part of a chapter as a script. This is sometimes called 'genre exchange' and involves some preliminary discussion about the differences between a story and a playscript, including the need for what the characters say to carry the story in playscripts and the use of stage directions to help. There is an example of script writing arising from Dahl's book *James and the Giant Peach* in Chapter 14.

Making a book

Where children have been deeply involved in reading and responding to a children's novel over a number of weeks, they are enthusiastic about making a book about their work, with the teacher as editor with an editorial team. These books are often structured by photographs of children's activities – discussion, drama, scriptwriting and so on – and sometimes find their way into the class or school library to inspire others.

Author studies

Authors chosen have usually written significant longer stories or children's novels and include David Almond, Cressida Cowell, Roald Dahl, Anne Fine, C.S. Lewis, Penelope Lively, Michael Morpurgo, E. Nesbit, Philippa Pearce, Philip Pullman and Jacqueline Wilson. Author study activities usually run over several weeks and work may include class- and group-based sessions and some independent contributions. Opportunities are created for research, discussion, drama and writing and for presentations and displays at the end of the work. A main outcome for each pupil is usually an author study folder arranged in sections with writing and illustrations. This can draw on notes made during the course of the work in reading diaries, which could include diagrams and drawings – including some in comic strip with speech bubbles – as well as writing. The important thing is to try to make the writing tasks as exciting as the discussion and drama activities. Inviting children to read extracts from their folders to the class and to display the studies for others to peruse helps keep up interest.

Some other things to keep in mind

I have found four things helpful to keep in mind when developing this kind of work. First I think it is usually best not to give the project too big a scope. A close look at two or three of the author's books is more likely to lead to a deeper study than trying to cover a larger number.

Second, I find sustained work of this sort gains energy if children help to plan the tasks and activities right from the beginning of the work, rather than being given a list of things to do.

Third, children are entitled to have negative as well as positive opinions about particular authors and should be able to express these as long as opinions can be backed up. Towards the end of the project teachers often ask whether anyone has changed their mind about the books.

The fourth thing has to do with finding information to support the study. The internet has become a hugely useful resource for children's work in every lesson. There are some splendid sites to help with author studies. Nearly every author has an exciting website with details about their books, interviews and suggestions for interesting activities. The children's laureates have particularly good, and therefore well-visited, websites. The Booktrust website has good features about children's authors from time to time. Authors recently featured on the site include Michael Morpurgo, Katie Cleminson, Ed Vere and Anthony Browne. If your school is not near enough to the Seven Stories Centre for Children's Books to visit, their website provides much information about authors, books and their special events. But children need some guidance when researching on the Internet. To avoid copying chunks of information teachers can encourage children to take some of their own questions to their quest for information. This is an issue which comes up constantly in Part II of this book, particularly in Chapter 34, which covers library research.

Chris Powling's *Tell Me About: Roald Dahl* praises the author's originality, humour and sheer success, but does not hide his eccentricity and capacity to upset other people. A book which selects some intriguing incidents is Geoff Fox's *Dear Mr Morpurgo: Inside the World of Michael Morpurgo*. This starts with a true and dramatic story – a story that will invite young readers in. When Michael was a baby, his pram somehow got attached to a stationary car. When the car started, the pram was pulled along at a great speed. Fortunately Michael was tipped out and only bruised – otherwise we might have missed out on his riveting books. If children are asked to prepare presentation on a particular author, ask them to try to find something particularly interesting like the 'pram' incident to start off.

Most author projects include some of the following:

- research to gain biographical information: where the author was born, school days, how they got started as a writer;
- class and group discussion of settings, plots, characters, themes and use of language and illustration;
- experience of the narratives in some different media – audio CD or film as well as print;
- improvisation on themes from the books;
- taking on roles of key characters and answering questions;
- answering questions in the role of the author;
- recording or filming a group of children who take up the role of critics, speaking about the books on a pretend radio programme;
- final outcomes – a short film, a web page, an annotated display, a PowerPoint presentation or a written report for others to read.

ASSESSING AND RECORDING PROGRESS

Building up the stamina to enjoy and respond personally to longer stories is in itself an achievement. Then, particularly when children approach the end of the primary years, the enjoyment can be accompanied by some analysis and we would expect them to be able to talk about a book's 'plot', 'characters' and 'setting' and the 'patterns' referred to in Aidan

Chambers' book *Tell Me: Children, Reading and Talk*. Longer books have, of course, more potential than shorter ones for plot and character development. We also look for a developing capacity to use inference to get at an author's more subtle meanings and intentions. Having preferences and opinions that you can defend with reference to the text is part of becoming a critical reader. Other promising signs include a developing ability to share insights with an audience – the teacher and the other children – and to listen thoughtfully to the views and contributions of others.

A formative approach, like that developed for the Primary Language Record by the team at the Centre for Literacy in Primary Education, has the advantage of keeping assessment and record keeping within the cycle of planning and learning. Rather than merely assess what a child can do at the present time, such an approach also shows the way to further progress. This record has been expanded to include four five-point scales, two in reading and two in writing. The two reading scales present a continuum along which a young reader's progress can be plotted. Details of the Centre's publications giving guidance about all this are available on their website (www.clpe.co.uk, accessed 5 February 2009).

Teachers and children have many demands on their energy and time and a good assessment and record system needs to take this into account. Only some of the following suggestions for what to include in the child's English, language and literacy folder need be taken up, and some assessment activities, for example interviewing a child about their progress, will only happen from time to time:

- extracts from children's reading logs;
- teachers' records of what children have read with dates and brief annotation;
- short transcripts of children's group talk around books (which might, for instance, show how far a child was able to use inference in getting meaning from text and illustration);
- film of children working with stories;
- samples of related writing with dates and annotation: reviews, writing in role, author appreciations, scriptwriting and children's own attempts to write a story in chapters;
- photographs of author displays;
- photographs of improvisation around themes in fiction;
- comments from parents on child's home reading – very much in the spirit of the Primary Language Record approach;
- transcript/notes of interview with child about their reading preferences and their own perception of their progress – could include some 'next step' agreements.

SUMMARY

- Creating a classroom where reading and discussion about books are part of the daily routine makes for a classroom where they are valued.
- Activities before, during and after reading or listening to longer stories and novels can, if well-chosen, take young learners deeper into themes and situations.

- Reading aloud makes enjoying a book a shared experience. It helps less forward young readers to benefit from a sustained story and to become involved with plot and characters and to ideas of some sophistication and subtlety. Further, it exposes them to more varied vocabulary and syntax.
- Talk – in the class context and in groups – makes learning collaborative and encourages children to listen to the views of others as well as communicating their own, thus helping them towards critical reading.
- Improvised drama is a way of exploring story themes and characters and playing with possibilities.
- Children can also be helped to explore stories in different media – film, television as well as print.
- Writing parts of a story as a script helps point up differences between reading and watching a story in play form.
- Writing in role helps children get inside a character's mind and grasp understanding of their thoughts and feelings.
- As well as reading a range of novels by different authors, older primary children also benefit from reading several books by the same author and preparing an author study.
- A formative approach to assessing and recording children's progress in becoming reflective and critical readers of longer stories and novels gives a fuller and richer picture than sticking to a summative record alone.

Chapter 14

Playscripts

INTRODUCTION

In this chapter the emphasis is on performance and on playscripts as texts, those playscripts children read and perform and those they write and perform. Plays, like stories, have a strong narrative drive and appeal partly because we want to know what is going to happen next. The plays children study can, like the stories and novels they enjoy, be based on ancient myth and legend from different cultures and traditions or be concerned with modern themes and dilemmas. There have always been primary school teachers, including the present writer, who have introduced young children to Shakespeare as part of a literature programme. And so this chapter includes a section on how Shakespeare can be studied and presented for different age groups. There is also a section on film making now that the digital camera has made it much easier to make short films in school.

Working together on a play project develops many skills and I have often found that children not so keen on reading come to appreciate the power of story through acting it out. I believe, too, that the skills and abilities to do with creating, editing, performing, evaluating, improving, learning to articulate your opinion – developed through what is both practical and creative – will be useful to children in may other contexts, even beyond school days.

FEATURES OF PLAYSCRIPTS

Playscripts are texts in prose or in verse written for performance. As plays introduce characters and set out events (usually chronologically, although there may be flashbacks) they have some things in common with storytelling and story writing. So 'story grammars' which are ways of conceiving of the shape of a story or novel can also be used to structure and comment on a play. These story and play 'shapes' generally include the following elements: introductory scene setting, sometimes called 'orientation'; people or 'characters' moving through time; a series of events and often a conflict or a problem that needs solving; some sort of resolution. It is often the middle part of a play or story, when events and conflicts and the reactions of characters are complex and sometimes exciting or alarming, that entertains and 'holds' readers or listeners.

Playscripts differ from stories most obviously in that dialogue must carry the meaning, and in their inclusion of stage directions and sometimes notes about props and costume. While stories for children, at any rate the longer ones, are organized in chapters, young readers will learn that plays are divided into big shapes, acts, and within acts there may be shorter discrete episodes called scenes. Playscripts for children often have only one act with a number of scenes. When plays are performed the audience sees the whole work of art unfold during an afternoon or evening, while we can leave a book at the end of a chapter or page for days or even months. In this sense, the reader has more control over the pacing of reading a book than viewing a play. Stories and novels provide background information about why things have come about and why people are as they seem in the story. Plays, on the other hand, show character traits and responses to events only through dialogue, facial expression and gesture. So we learn about what happens through what is said and done. Sometimes devices are used to help here; a narrator may be included or a soliloquy allowing characters to confide their deepest thoughts or most devious intentions directly to the audience. Costume, scenery, props and sound effects and music all help communicate atmosphere and mood.

When it comes to the language features of plays, these are extremely diverse. It depends on when the play was written and the background and circumstances of the characters. We find lyrical language in some plays – as in some of Shakespeare's dialogue – and the use of devices used in other literature, devices that help make lines memorable, including imagery, metonymy and personification. Modern plays may use language that is down-to-earth and colloquial. Whatever the style of the language used, it makes us reflect on the meaning of what is written as well as on the language used to communicate it. When we write dialogue, we re-read and consider what we have written and how it might be revised to achieve our purpose.

CHOOSING PLAYSCRIPTS

The stories on which published playscripts for children are based come from many sources; some draw on familiar traditional tales while others come from the work of recent writers. Most playwrights waive their rights and allow their plays to be performed in the classroom and in school for parents. They are often prepared also to allow teachers to photocopy parts of the play so that children can take their parts home to learn.

Then there are collections of plays where children are the intended audience but the expectation is that the performers will be professional actors belonging to a children's theatre group. Some of the plays in these collections are suitable for performance by older primary children in school and, again, copyright is usually waived if these are performed by children in school.

Pre-school and nursery, 3–5-year-olds

We think of improvised drama and role play as being the right kind of playful acting experience for the very young. But there are helpful ways of introducing them in a more focused way to plot and character. Storyboards, both those on the market and those teachers and classroom assistants make, are a way of extending children's experience of story, plot and character.

Picturebooks often link with drama and sometimes include a pull-out 'stage' and cut-outs to re-enact the story. Julia Donaldson's Gruffalo stories, with their universal themes about being frightened, brave and then safe, appeal strongly to this age group. One of the more recent Gruffalo publications, *The Gruffalo Pop-Up Book*, is a big novelty book which tells the complete story of a little mouse's adventure and also provides a pop-up stage. Young children can use the character cut-outs, placing them on the 'stage' to tell the story or make up their own tale. There is a playscript and a cast of characters to introduce very young children to some of the features of plays. Axel Scheffler's distinctive illustrations and Nick Denchfield's ingenious paper engineering add much enjoyment to the reading experience.

Another way teachers and parents help young children to act out stories is by using puppets. Sets of finger puppets based on well-known stories, for example *The Gingerbread Man Puppet Set*, are available from the Puppet Company. For age three and above, Deb Darling Designs have interactive toys, for example *Three Billy Goats Finger Puppet Story Set* and a six puppet *Nursery Rhyme Puppet Set*.

Is working with a playscript ever appropriate for these very young children? There is no doubt they like to put on a performance for parents at the end of term. Some nursery teams create their own presentation of poems, songs and plays but others welcome some help from a published playscript. When it comes to Christmas plays for the very young, many find Vicki Howie's plays for Barnabus Press a good resource. Her board book about the Nativity – *Knock! Knock! Who's There?* – serves as a forerunner to simple scripts. Children can speak out as each flap is lifted, preparing them for an encounter with scripted dialogue later on. For teachers working with mixed age groups her plays in *Easy Ways to Christmas Plays: Three Complete Plays* ('Come to My Party'; 'The Star Who Could Not Twinkle'; 'Shine Your Lights') have the advantage of keeping all the children on stage throughout and thus avoiding lots of entrances and exits. There are speaking parts for the older ones in the nursery class. The text starts with a summary of the story of each play so that children are well prepared when they come to the script. This provides early experience of how a story in one medium is adapted for another. Those teachers less experienced in producing plays will welcome the stage plan and advice about simple props and costume. Brian Ogden has also written three easy to perform plays in *Nursery Rhyme Nativities*. There are suggestions for props and costumes.

5–8-year-olds

This is the age group during which children particularly enjoy listening to and reading traditional tales and so it is not surprising that many of the best playscripts for Key Stage 1 are based on fairy and folk tales. Vivian French has written two appealing plays, based on favourite stories, *The Gingerbread Boy* and *The Three Billy Goats Gruff*, for Walker's Story Play series. In big as well as small book format, these playscripts cater for different reading abilities, red being for less and blue for more experienced readers; the text also has different colours for each of the four parts so that children know quickly when their character speaks. The four parts can be spoken by one or several young readers. Children at the beginning of this age range or even younger enjoy the Meg and Mog series about the loveable witch and her faithful cat who get in an entertaining muddle with her spells. David Wood has adapted some of these stories by Jan Pienkowsky and Helen Nicoll as playscripts: 'Meg and the Stegasaurus', 'Meg and Sir George', 'Meg on the Moon' and 'Meg at the Zoo' in *Meg and Mog: Four Plays for Children*. The plays can be read aloud in the classroom or performed for another class or to the whole school and parents. There is a cast list, plan of the stage and some imaginative advice about props like the cuckoo clock and the cauldron.

Puppet plays also help children learn about staging a play. Shyer children who might be reluctant to take a part in a conventional play are often prepared to speak the words for a puppet. Look out for Diane Stanley's *Mozart the Wonder Child: A Puppet Play in Three Acts*.

Children at the older end of this age group and the beginning of Key Stage 2 would learn, from reading and acting Brenda Parkes' playscript *Yeh Shen and the Magic Fish*, that some stories seem to tap into universal fears and longings. Yeh Shen lives in ancient China and has an unkind stepmother who makes her work very hard at heavy tasks. Just as Cinderella meets the Prince and marries him, so does Yeh Shen meet and marry the King. Robin Kingsland's *Porky Pies* is an entertaining play about three wolves accused of villainy who end up in a court room with nursery rhyme characters. Another collection of lively playscripts, including 'The Legend of Persephone' and 'Three Billy Goats Gruff', is Julia Donaldson's *Play Time!: A Selection of Plays by the Best Selling Author of The Gruffalo*.

Roderick Hunt, Jacquie Buttris and Ann Callander have adapted Oxford Reading Tree's Magpies storybooks into scripts and these include tales of magic and fantasy – for example *The Rainbow Machine* and *The Magic Carpet*. These plays, which have four to six characters, are intended for group reading. They help children become familiar with the conventions of scripts, with their staging annotations and suggestions for sound effects. It is worth making time for the children to stage the plays and discuss simple costumes, props and adding music and sound effects as indicated in the scripts.

David Wood has adapted some of Roald Dahl's stories as playscripts for children in his 'Plays for Children' series for Puffin. They would suit children who are towards the end of Key Stage 1 or early Key Stage 2. Included are *The BFG* – the Big Friendly Giant – and *The Twits* – about a comically unpleasant elderly couple. Like others in the series this has clear,

Figure 14.1
Front cover of Three Plays for Children: The Devoted Friend, The Happy Prince, The Selfish Giant *by Oscar Wilde*
Adapted for the stage by Phil Clark, published by Oberon Books and reproduced with the permission of the illustrator John Angus

155

useful suggestions about staging, props and characters. The pictures that usually illustrate children's playscripts can be a good guide to appropriate costumes. David Wood recommends teacher and children study Quentin Blake's illustrations of the playscripts based on Roald Dahl's stories. When it comes to modern realistic themes for playscripts, publishers like, for example, Oxford University Press (in their Oxford Reading Tree programme) have published plays adapted from their story series, for example *Dad's Grand Plan* by Alex Brychta from Oxford Owls.

8–11-year-olds

If children have worked with playscripts in the earlier primary years they will be sufficiently familiar with the form and its conventions to take on plays with more challenging plots, characterization and language.

For the younger end of this age range Oxford University Press have produced some playscripts with lively plots and interesting characters in their Literacy Web Guided Reading series. Titles include *Thor's Thunder*, *The Golden Arrow* and *The Magic Pot* and are all adapted for staging by David Calcutt. There are a number of plays based on legends and traditional tales for older primary children. Ted Hughes brings his strong and lyrical voice to the six plays in *Collected Plays for Children*, in which 'Orpheus' and the Nativity story – 'The Coming of the Kings' – are included. Teachers and children seeking a play based on a Greek myth, perhaps those following an Ancient Greece history unit, would find David Orme and Wendy Body's *Theseus and the Minotaur* a coherent telling of the story. This coherence comes partly through the role of the narrator, who keeps up the momentum of the action and imparts helpful information. Different fonts and colours are used so that children can see quickly when a character is speaking (in green print), when the narrator is speaking (ordinary type) and when there is live action dialogue (in bold). A&C Black have brought out plays adapted from a range of traditional tales in their Curtain Up series, which, in addition to a playscript, include background notes about plot, characterization and staging. Each play takes about forty-five minutes to read or act and can be photocopied for classroom use. Titles include Diane Redmond's *The Odyssey*, Hiawyn Oram's *The Good-Time Boys* (based on an African folk tale and with some actors functioning as part of the scenery as in African theatrical tradition) and two fairy-tale adaptations – *Beauty and the Beast* by Jacqueline Wilson and *Sleeping Beauty* by Kaye Umansky. *Beauty and the Beast* has a modern slant and the beast is a huge slug! Umansky's *Sleeping Beauty*, with Dame and Principal Boy, gives children a chance to act within the pantomime tradition. This makes an entertaining end of term production.

Some playscripts can enrich lessons across the curriculum and this is particularly true of history. Two plays in A&C Black's White Wolves series are set in Tudor London, and would contribute something to children's understanding of the period as well as developing their knowledge of how plays work. It is wise not to claim too much here, as both plays aim to entertain rather than to inform. *Let's Go to London* by Kaye Umansky follows the adventures of a group of different Tudor people – an actor, a cook, a kitchen maid and a doctor. *Time Switch* by Steve Barlow and Steve Skidmore asks young readers and performers to imagine what it might be like to go to the Globe in present day London for an audition and then find yourself transported to a plague-ravaged London in 1600.

BOX 14.1 *TIME SWITCH* BY STEVE BARLOW AND STEVE SKIDMORE AND SUE MASON (ILLUS.) (A&C BLACK)

The five acts are more like scenes in length but the play is well structured. The print is beautifully clear, with the names of characters in bold and stage directions in italic. Sue Mason's black and white illustrations are full of wit and energy and also give some help with ideas for costume and stage props. The play begins atmospherically when the three children enter a cold, dark theatre with only torchlight to guide their steps. Then a quotation from *A Midsummer Night's Dream*, 'Now you shall but slumber here, while these visions do appear', seems to bring about the switch to Tudor times. Barlow and Skidmore know about children's sense of humour and this play would be fun to perform. This is a factor in our choices – after all, we want to turn children on to plays and not off them! When one of the child characters, Tim, describes the details of the symptoms of the plague – victims would develop pus-filled pustules, a dreadful rash and so on – Bev says, in the modern way, 'Too much information, Tim!'

Figure 14.2
Front cover of Time Switch *by Steve Barlow and Steve Skidmore and Sue Mason (illus.)*
Reproduced with the permission of the publishers A&C Black Ltd. Copyright 2007

Another involving play – *The Golden Goose* by James Mason and Wendy Body – would be helpful in tuning children into a history unit on Ancient Egypt. There are parts for ten characters plus some extra priests. Children are also taken into the past in David Calcutt's *Fool's Gold*, which is loosely based on the theme of lost wealth in Shakespeare's *The Tempest*.

Teachers looking for packs with six copies of the same playscript for classroom reading would find helpful TreeTops Playscripts, which are adapted for different reading stages from the vast number of stories in Oxford's TreeTops fiction series. In my experience, while children like to read and discuss playscripts in groups, it is when they are invited to stage the plays – for the class, for another class or for the school – that most enthusiasm is generated.

We would expect older, abler primary children to encounter dramatized versions of the classics. Shakespeare in the primary years is covered in a later section. Evans' Star series includes adaptations of classic plays suitable for children not yet of secondary age. Charles Dickens' *Oliver Twist* is dramatized by Keith West and illustrated with some style by George Cruikshank, whose black and white drawings show wonderfully expressive faces and, of course, the appalling conditions of the time. Stage directions are clear and helpful and often link text and illustrations. On page 20 the text is annotated with: 'Upstairs, the room is dirty and black. Oliver notices an old man dressed in a flannel gown.'

Modern classics with strong stories often make good plays. Berlie Doherty's novel *Street Child*, about Jim Jarvis, the first Barnardo boy, has considerable appeal for older primary children. It has been dramatized for children in Collins Educational Plays Plus series as *Street Child: Playscript*. Reading the story in novel form leads to much of educational value – not least discussion and a range of writing and illustrating. But where they study it as a playscript for performance, children also involve themselves in how they can get the incidents and their significance over to an audience. How will they use their voices, gestures, staging, costume and sound to interest and move those who watch?

Short stories can become classics as well as novels and the writer that comes to mind here is Oscar Wilde. His stories, which take children into imagined worlds about giants, princes and animals, transform into strong playscripts. Phil Clark has adapted three of Wilde's stories for performance and these playscripts are published in *Three Plays for Children*. These adaptations were commissioned by the Sherman Theatre Company for performance, by professional actors at the Sherman Theatre in Cardiff, for children between ages three and eight. The playscripts, based on *The Devoted Friend*, *The Happy Prince* and *The Selfish Giant*, can be read in the classroom by older primary children. But I also think that an ambitious and imaginative Year 6 teacher could help the children to perform the plays for the younger children in the school.

The Christmas play

A good resource to draw on at Christmas time is Gaby Morgan's *The Big Book of Christmas: Carols, Plays, Songs and Poems for Christmas*.

Teachers often seek a traditional telling of the Christmas story, but within a modern setting. *Have You Seen Christmas?* is one of three plays in Vicki Howie's collection *Story Plays for Christmas*. Luke is a homeless boy who has a much loved dog called Christmas. On Christmas Eve the dog goes missing. As well as finding the dog, Luke and his friends find the true spirit of Christmas.

If you are looking for a play involving the whole of an older primary class it would be worth considering Lucy Moore's *Topsy Turvy Christmas: A Musical Play for Children*. The playscript comes with carols on an audio CD and some ideas for staging and costumes. It begins with two angels discussing God's plan for Jesus' birth and then follows the traditional story.

- *Meg and Mog: Four Plays for Children* adapted by David Wood (Puffin)
  Based on Jan Pienkowski's series.

- *The Gruffalo Pop-Up Theatre Book* by Julia Donaldson and Axel Scheffler (Walker)
  Package includes a pop-up theatre, the story and a playscript.

- *The Magic Pot* adapted by David Calcutt (Oxford Literacy Web)
  An ancient Indian tale about greed.

- *Porky Pies* by Robin Kingsland (A&C Black)
  Bo Peep, Mary, Mary, etc. versus three wolf villains – full of humour.

- *Beauty and the Beast* by Jacqueline Wilson (A&C Black)
  Based on the traditional tale but with a surprising beast.

- *The BFG: Plays for Children* adapted by David Wood (Puffin)
  Appealing adaptation of the tale about Dahl's friendly giant.

- *Time Switch* by Steve Barlow and Steve Skidmore (A&C Black)
  A humorous time-slip play which starts with an audition at the Globe . . .

- *Oliver Twist* adapted by K. West (Evans)
  Fast-moving adaptation of Dickens' story.

- *The Selfish Giant* by Oscar Wilde, adapted by Phil Clark (Oberon Books)
  Written for performers of children's theatre, but Year 6 might be able to present it to younger children in the school.

- *Street Child: Playscript* by Berlie Doherty with resource material by Stephen Cockett (Collins)
  Based on Doherty's novel about the first Barnardo boy.

- *The Play of Room 13* adapted by Joe Standerline (Heinemann)
  Based on Robert Swindells' story about a school trip to Whitby which begins a series of ghostly events.

Figure 14.3 *Playscripts, roughly in order of challenge*

USING PLAYSCRIPTS

Playscripts can be used in a variety of ways and for different audiences and as the section on 'Choosing playscripts' shows, the texts lend themselves to particular activities. (Having a chorus, for example, would suggest that a class or group reading would be appropriate.) While whole-school productions for parents and friends of the school involve rich activity, satisfying collaboration and can provide a dynamic end to the term or school year, there are also valuable but less formal ways of involving children with plays. Sometimes group readings are satisfying and may lead to an attempt at performance later on. We can also work with extracts instead of whole plays, choosing a key event to enact. This often happens when teachers introduce children to Shakespeare's plays. A narrator can help contextualize an extract and the young actors' increasing ability to use voice, pause, space and facial expression can help bring briefer pieces to life.

When it comes to different audiences, the class itself is often a good sounding board for a performance by a group and, in this context, we often find that children themselves have ideas about how they interpret and understand play texts. Constructive peer evaluation thrives here too – in a relatively unthreatening environment. Sometimes another class can be invited in to see a performance and more polished pieces might be shown in assembly.

Not all performances have to be based on published playscripts of course. Sometimes improvisations stabilize and children want to commit them to paper as scripts. Children, with encouragement, will write scripts as a writing choice and I find that reading published plays and writing your own, perhaps in a group, can be a richly interactive process. When it comes to writing their own playscripts, children often find duologues a good place to start.

Pre-school and nursery, 3–5-year-olds

Activities which increase children's enjoyment of stories and prepare the way for plays and playscripts include:

- Saying or singing action rhymes which have an 'acting' element, even if it just involves pointing to parts of the body like 'eyes', 'nose', 'fingers', 'toes'.
- Role playing with dolls, teddies and toy cars, during which children may accompany the activity with a monologue or a playful conversation with an adult or another child.
- Role playing in the home corner, which may be set up as a café, baby clinic or shop.
- Dressing up, which adds to the enjoyment of role play. Just putting out some costumes and props – perhaps a crown, a table and chair, a shawl, a walking stick, a wooden box or a jewel – encourages imaginative story and play making. Sometimes teachers will develop the role play by taking a role themselves.
- Improvising puppet plays seem to help children to feel confident enough to take risks as the attention is on the puppets (Whitehead, 2004: 102).
- Doing the actions while interactive picturebooks are read aloud; examples include: *We're Going on a Bear Hunt* by Michael Rosen; *The Farmyard Jamboree* by Margaret Read Macdonald; *Who's That Scratching at My Door?* by Amanda Leslie; *One Duck Stuck* by Phyllis Root.
- Scribing children's first attempts at 'conversation poems', which are structured around dialogue between two characters.
- Extending interest in character by encouraging children's annotated drawings of people from stories they have listened to.

5–8-year-olds

Reading and discussing plays

Is it helpful for children in this age group to have their attention drawn to plot, character, setting and so on? Well, of course, it depends how it is done but I prefer a light touch myself.

Figure 14.4
Front cover of Meg and Mog: Four Plays for Children *by Helen Nicoll, David Wood and Jan Pienkowski (illus.)* Reproduced with the permission of the publishers The Penguin Group

If a class were reading the plays in, for example, *Meg and Mog: Four Plays for Children,* I think they would be able and happy to chat about things like: what the play told us about Meg, what was their favourite bit of the play (reading it from the text) and whether anything in it puzzled them. And, of course, children want to be involved in discussions about how to perform a play for a particular audience.

Using storyboxes

Storyboxes are boxes which are adapted by teachers, classroom assistants and children to make a scene from a story or play. Art and craft materials are used to make the scene – meadow, beach or townscape – and the characters may be cardboard cut-outs or Playmobil figures. Helen Bromley, who has adapted the storybox for young children, comments: 'The story may turn out to be a play, with clear lines assigned to each character and animal, with or without a narrator. In the latter case, the script can even be written down for other children to re-enact' (Bromley, 2004: 12). Older children's stories and plays using the storybox approach will be longer and more complex. Readers might like to turn to Helen's book *50 Exciting Ideas for Storyboxes,* which shows the creative potential of this approach.

Into writing

Talking about the characters they meet in both books and plays is important for this age group. A class of six-year-olds had been talking about their favourite storybook characters, saying what it is they like about them and what they get up to. Georgia took this thinking into her writing and shows she understands that the 'naughty' characters are often the most interesting (see Figure 14.5). By age eight, children might begin script writing with duologues. Often based on parts of stories or poems they have been reading, creating dialogue for just two speakers is a good forerunner to writing scenes for plays where there are likely to be a number of characters. Sometimes part of a story lends itself to children's speculation in talk and then in a written duologue. I have used as an inspiration for duologues Philippa Pearce's *A Dog So Small*; the point in the book when Ben realizes that he is not going to get the promised dog for his birthday after all often spurs children's writing.

Name: Georgia
Year: 1

My favourite character is ...Goldilocks....

from the story....Goldilocks....and the three Bears

I've chosen this character becuse she's nuty. (naughty).
She is bad.
The other characters say to her "get out of my house!"
She's important becuse she gose to the Bears house.
If I meet her I wod say "wod you like to come to my house?"
She is brave and so are the Bears.

8–11-year-olds

Reading, discussing and performing playscripts

By the later primary years children have read many stories and children's novels and are acquiring a more sophisticated grasp on plot and on character. Even if a playscript is just read in a group and never performed for an audience, the children are still involved in performance to some extent and their activity is certainly collaborative. Somehow reading aloud in character brings working with others to a more active level than discussion. The complexity of the characters becomes apparent too and children grow beyond simple notions of those that are good and those that are bad. They are becoming able, also, to use their voices to suggest characters' qualities and so are moving towards performance.

It is the discussion and sharing of ideas that makes working on a playscript so absorbing and valuable, even for young learners not usually keen on reading. Taking *The Play of Room 13* as an example, and drawing on the notes included with the play, a series of discussions would usefully include considering:

- How the atmosphere and suspense important in a ghost story plot might be achieved.
- Making a short film or some stills showing a bleak landscape and a grim building to start the play (as suggested in the notes with the playscript). Made by teacher and children using a digital camera, this could be shown on a screen at the back of the stage.
- Music or sound effects to accompany the poetic speech of the narrator at the beginning of the story.
- Music and sound effects at other points in the play to keep up the tension. Even if the play is read in the classroom rather than made into a production, music and sound effects would make the experience more satisfying.
- The role of the narrator/voice over and of asides as devices to make the play clearly understood and cohesive.
- How the poetic language of the voice over – 'A lonely house in haunting mist/To chill a dragon's breath . . .' – contrasts with the everyday conversational language of the pupils and the dramatic effect of this contrast.

(For further ideas, see the notes accompanying *The Play of Room 13* adapted by J. Standerline from the novel by J. Swindells.)

CHILDREN WRITING THEIR OWN PLAYSCRIPTS

The opportunity for children to write playscripts for performance sometimes arises from improvised drama in English and in lessons across the curriculum. I have had children actually ask if they could write down the play they had improvised. I remember such an occasions when I was working with nine-year-olds acting out the situation of plague victims in Tudor times in a series of history lessons. In English, stories often provide the starting point for playscripts; nine-year-old Bonnie attempted to write some scenes after the teacher had read

163

Narrator: James has been sent to Australia by the unkind aunts and finds himself on a ship with a giant peach and some insects – a ladybird, an earthworm and a centipede.

Centipede: Poor earthworm, he's blind you know.

James: Poor earthworm, I feel sorry for him.

Earthworm: What are you talking about?

James: Is it true that you are blind?

Earthworm: I'm only blind in one eye, you know.

Narrator: They decide to eat the peach.

Ladybird: Come on everybody – let's eat.

(After a while there are bits of peach everywhere.)

James: Look. Sharks in the water!

Ladybird: Distract the sharks. Throw some of the peach into the water.

Figure 14.6 Extracts from a two-page script by nine-year-old Bonnie based on the characters in Roald Dahl's story James and the Giant Peach

CASE STUDY 14.1 TEN-YEAR-OLDS CREATE A SCRIPT WITH A STUDENT TEACHER'S EDITING HELP AND PRESENT THEIR OWN VERSION OF 'BABOUSHKA' TO THE SCHOOL

After reading picturebook and story versions of 'Baboushka', the children created a script to guide their performance. In this Russian folk tale, which is inspired by the Nativity story, the three kings are lost in the snow in Russia as they follow the star guiding them to the new-born child. They ask an old peasant lady, Baboushka, if she will help them find their way. She says she will go with them, but asks them to stay overnight at her cottage while she completes some household tasks. But they do not want to miss the birth and are quickly on their way while Baboushka fusses over her chores. Next day she regrets not going with her strangely compelling visitors and sets off with toys for the new child. But the snow is deeper than ever so that she too cannot find her way. Her sack grows heavy and so she drops off gifts for the children she meets. According to legend, each Christmas Baboushka travels across the land in search of the kings and the new baby, dropping off presents to children.

The children noted two things that they wanted to emphasize in their presentation: some things are too important to be delayed and wise people learn to recognize what these are; and the joy of giving, particularly to those in need.

to the class Roald Dahl's *James and the Giant Peach*. She uses the device of a narrator so that her scenes will be understandable in performance.

Not all children's stories lend themselves well to being transformed into plays. There has to be a strong storyline with some dramatic events and the characters need to be interesting and appealing. An example of a story with these qualities is the tale of Baboushka.

Steps in creating a script

There are different ways of proceeding. Here is one:

- Improvise a story, part of a story or explore an issue or situation.
- Use techniques of improvisation – hot seating, freeze framing etc.
- Reflect on the drama: has it got pace and interest? Are the characters interacting well?
- Use writing journals to make notes on characters, props and costumes and sketch stage and scenery.
- Divide the improvisation into sections which may become scenes.
- Identify key moments.
- Decide what would appeal to the intended audience.
- Write the improvisation as a script.
- Read the script aloud.
- Act out the script.
- Discuss what worked well; amend the script where necessary.

USING SHAKESPEARE'S PLAYS

Primary school teachers have always drawn on Shakespeare's work for literature and drama lessons. This is for a number of reasons. First, many of the stories around which the plays are built are exceptionally engaging for any age group – people shipwrecked on an enchanted island, a king giving away his kingdom and lovers and fairies in confusion in an enchanted wood. Shakespeare usually got the basic stories for the plays from other sources but developed the characters and situations to produce works that come wonderfully alive when they are performed. Second, Shakespeare's mastery of language, in both prose and poetry, is unsurpassed and somehow taps into our deepest feelings and understandings about human life in all its complexity.

There are, of course, some implications for the subject knowledge of teachers and student teachers wishing to include Shakespeare's work in the children's literature programme. Collections of Shakespeare's plays usually include valuable background information, illustrations and helpful introductions by the editors. I will mention two: *The RSC Shakespeare: The Complete Works*, edited by Jonathan Bate and Eric Rasmussen, and Oxford's *William Shakespeare: The Complete Works*, edited by the Shakespeare scholar Stanley Wells. There are a number of books about Shakespeare's times and his plays that give useful background. *Shakespeare: His Work and His World*, by Michael Rosen and illustrated by Robert Ingpen, covers the ground well. If you are looking for a concise account with a touch of humour, Bill Bryson's *Shakespeare: The World as a Stage* might suit. For a quick and entertaining introduction to all

165

the plays you might consider reading *Shakespeare in a Nutshell: A Rhyming Guide to all the Plays* by James Muirden. Nothing beats seeing the plays performed at the Globe, in Regent's Park, at the Stratford theatres and at local theatres. This will help build the knowledge and enthusiasm needed to inspire children. Teachers' background knowledge will help them to select for their classes the extracts and scenes they are most likely to enjoy and connect with.

Books telling Shakespeare's stories

There are a number of books which tell the stories of Shakespeare's plays. The best of these are valuable in their own right, but also help prepare children for reading the plays and performing scenes from them. *Mr William Shakespeare's Plays*, written and illustrated cartoon style by Marcia Williams, tells the stories of seven of the plays, including *Macbeth*, *The Tempest* and *A Midsummer Night's Dream*. Young readers are asked to imagine they are on a visit to a performance at the original Globe Theatre and so it also teaches a lot about Elizabethan theatre. A challenging but favourite collection is Leon Garfield's *Shakespeare Stories*, which has twelve narratives which capture the essence of the plays and which include much of Shakespeare's dialogue. For fast-moving colourful retellings of ten of the plays, including favourites like *A Midsummer Night's Dream*, *Twelfth Night*, *King Lear* and *Hamlet*, you could not do better than offer the children Geraldine McCaughrean's *Stories from Shakespeare*. The stories are rich with quotations so that children are introduced to Shakespeare's language.

The Best-Loved Plays by Shakespeare, by Jennifer Mulherin and Abigail Frost, provides the background helpful in appreciating the plays. The chapter on *King Lear* is divided into sections – 'Words of love', 'A wicked son', ' Kent's loyalty', 'The Fool', 'Edmund's plot', 'Lear dispossessed', 'The blasted heath' and so on. The illustrations are modern in conception and I found I needed to get used to them to appreciate them.

The first collection many of us think of when we have Shakespeare's stories in mind is Charles and Mary Lamb's classic book *Tales from Shakespeare*. These stories stay in print because they are told in a lively and vivid way, taking on some complicated twists and turns in the tales and making then understandable by children. The Everyman Library edition is enhanced by the atmospheric pen and ink drawings of Arthur Rackham. For the colourful and striking modern illustrations by Joelle Jolivit, you need to track down the luxury edition from Harry N. Abrams.

Audio CDs provide a different kind of experience, exposing children to narration often by an established classical actor. *Shakespeare's Stories*, by David Timson and narrated by Juliet Stevenson, tells thirteen of the stories and uses a number of passages from the plays so that children can hear the cadences of Shakespeare's language. Some children aged ten and over may be drawn into the version of the tales in Ian Pollock's *Illustrated King Lear*, with its bleak, disturbing cartoon illustrations echoing grim themes.

Reading and performing extracts from the plays

The teacher's challenge in using Shakespeare's work is to find ways of helping children make some connection with the plays' themes and with the motivations, emotions and feelings of the characters. In a very interesting article, 'Introducing Play Worlds', Janet Bottoms recommends a practical and playful approach. First you choose the extract from the play you are working with, then you think of an imaginative way into the setting and the story. Generous space helps – whether in the school hall or in the classroom. Let me give an example of Janet Bottoms' approach by referring to her work with children on *The Tempest*.

The first scene of this play takes us into a storm and so the children could form the shape of a ship. Bottoms suggests the teacher asks them how they could create the sounds of a storm at sea. Then separate groups of children could concentrate on one sound, some on the wind, some on the beating waves and some on the beating rain – building up to a crescendo. Then the ship crashes on to a rock. What might the sailors say to each other? The children improvise the comments and are then helped to appreciate Shakespeare's words (Bottoms, 2005: 10–21).

The workshop approach to involving children of primary school age with Shakespeare's work is favoured in the education department at the Globe Theatre. Workshops for children above eight years on a play of your choice to help them with characterization are available and there are also guided tours of the theatre for children above seven years (www.shakespeares-globe.org/globeeducation, accessed 1 December 2008). The Royal Shakespeare Company reach out to teachers and children working with Shakespeare's plays and poetry at all levels in the school system, urging us to encourage children to 'do it on their feet' and 'see it live'. They also suggest we should start Shakespeare as early as possible (www.rsc.org.uk.education, accessed 24 November 2008).

There are different views about which of the plays are suitable for primary aged children to explore. Janet Bottoms, for example, wonders about the suitability for young children of *Hamlet*, with its theme of revenge and unsettling quick remarriage (Bottoms, 2005: 21). So it is interesting to reflect on the case study 'Developing Empathy: Hamlet with Years 3 and 4' described on the RSC site, which shows teacher and children taking up a reflective and active approach to this particular Shakespeare play.

Becoming engrossed in reading and acting Shakespeare's plays can lead to children's own writing. A helpful and inspiring book here is *Shakespeare and the Young Writer* by Fred Sedgwick. He argues passionately that once children are 'in the grip' of Shakespeare's words through reading and acting scenes from the plays they can move on to enthusiastic writing on the themes (Sedgwick, 1999: Introduction).

Drawing on children's experience of 'popular culture' texts to link with the worlds to be found in Shakespeare's plays

Reading and performing plays requires children to enter imaginatively into the world of the play; above, I draw on the insights of Janet Bottoms in showing how teachers can help by setting up what she calls 'play worlds'. However, what children bring to texts, including literary texts like Shakespeare's plays, is important. What they bring will include their life experiences and insights from the books and films they have seen. Sometimes teachers will find it helpful to make explicit links between 'popular culture' texts and experience and the situations in a play. I find Morag Styles' work, way back in the late 1980s, in tackling *A Midsummer Night's Dream* with nine- to eleven-year-olds a powerful example of how careful use of 'popular culture' texts, including television soaps, can contribute to children's developing understanding of characters and themes (Styles *et al.*, 1992).

USING FILM VERSIONS OF CHILDREN'S STORIES AND NOVELS

Researchers and teachers contribute constantly to the continuing debate about how to respond to the experience of and familiarity with film, electronic games, the internet and television programmes which children bring to the classroom. Marsh and Millard's book *Literacy and Popular Culture: Using Children's Culture in the Classroom* provides a good starting point for our thinking here (Marsh and Millard, 2000). For quite some time now primary school teachers have combined study of stories and novels with study of their filmed versions. This leads to interesting discussion about how narrative is presented in different media and, of course, makes an important contribution to children's developing literacy in a 'moving image' age. *Charlotte's Web* and *The Sheep-Pig* are favourite texts in book and film form for younger primary school children, while older ones often study *Tom's Midnight Garden* and *Goodnight Mister Tom*.

Annette Johnson found that reading *Charlotte's Web* and showing extracts from the film helped a Year 3 class understand something about how scripts are developed from stories. Her lessons were part of a joint action research project by the British Film Institute and the Centre for Literacy in Primary Education and explored, amongst other things, the inspiration that film can be to children's talk and writing about stories. *Charlotte's Web* was read aloud and then the children were shown extracts from the film. The interesting thing was that when children started to write about the story they included dialogue directly from the film. And, as Johnson observes, 'they also started to include the sound effects heard on the film soundtrack, including words like "sniff, sniff", "cry, cry", "sob, sob"' (Johnson, 2000: 22). This 'action research' approach can be used by teachers to explore for themselves the benefits of engaging children with stories presented in different media. Drawing on Johnson's work, these might include:

- building on children's experience of narrative in different media outside school and thus linking school and home literacies in a motivating way;
- encouraging comparison of stories in more than one media can raise the intellectual level of discussion;
- showing how film can enrich children's understanding of character and personality, understanding begun by reading the print text;
- exposing children to dialogue in film and thus making a contribution to growing competence in script writing;
- developing a set of terms to talk about stories in print – 'dialogue', 'character', 'plot' and adding for film – 'close-up', 'frame' and 'high angle shot'.

WRITING SCRIPTS FOR FILMS

Making their own short films is likely to make children more informed and critical audiences for the film and television programmes they watch. For help with all moving image media in school, visit the British Film Institute website (www.bfi.org.uk/education). A common approach is to begin by involving the whole class in some planning and evaluating, and then for groups of six to eight to work together to film short sequences. The timeline of processes might be something like this:

- Select an extract from a familiar story or poem.
- Talk about the setting, characters and meanings in groups and then bring insights to a whole-class discussion.
- Talk about how the main storyline, characterization and meanings can be shown through the medium of film, combining sound and vision.
- Make a 'first draft' of dialogue.
- Select simple scenery, costume, props, sound effects and atmospheric music.
- Create a shooting script – on the interactive whiteboard or flipchart.
- Return to groups and make a film script with actors' dialogue to use alongside the shooting script.
- Film key sequences, using the shooting script and actors' dialogue script.
- Each group shows their film sequence to the class for comment, reflection and possible re-shooting.
- Edit the moving images to make a coherent screen telling of the story.
- Add titles and narration.
- View the film and make final cuts.
- Add a sound track to match the film images.
- Evaluate the project.
- Show the film to other classes.

ASSESSING AND RECORDING PROGRESS

When it comes to literary texts one of the abilities looked for is the capacity to infer meaning beyond the literal. In a playscript, a character who seems to be giving one view through what they say may be revealing very different feelings and motivations when you consider their actions. It is becoming able to pick up on such mismatches and to understand more challenging plots that shows a young reader's progress.

Records kept in an English, language and literacy portfolio might include:

- details of contributions to classroom play readings and short films;
- lists of contributions to performances for others in the class, for another class or for an audience like the whole school and parents and visitors, together with photographs and sketches of scenery and costumes;
- extracts from any duologue or play a pupil has contributed to writing;
- extracts from writing diaries, if these have been used, showing the development of script writing and a child's own awareness of progress; photocopies of a sequence of entries would be evidence of developing skill;
- copies of writing and drawing about favourite characters, plays, sets or films;
- child's comments about their enjoyment and progress in this kind of reading, writing and performing.

169

Close-ups – film taken at close range.

Editing – putting shots together as sequences or a series of scenes.

Filter – a glass or plastic cover that changes the colour of the shot, perhaps giving the impression of a fiery sky or a grey sea.

Footage – the amount of film shot.

Frame – a single image or piece of film.

High angle – film taken from a high position looking downwards.

Low angle – film taken from a low position looking upwards.

Mixing – combining sound and music in making a film, and adjusting, for example, volume.

Sequence – a series of shots.

Shooting script – written instructions to the person operating a camera to make a film.

Storyboard – drawing used by some directors to plan and visualize film sequences.

Voice over – an unseen commentating voice during a film or a television programme.

Figure 14.7 Glossary: terms to do with film making

SUMMARY

- We seek commercial playscripts which tell a strong story, appeal to children's sense of humour and which use dialogue and action powerfully and skilfully.
- When improvised drama stabilizes, children can transform it into a playscript.
- Working with Shakespeare's plays introduces children to some of the most exciting plots, the most powerful language and the most interesting characters in the English language.
- There are ways of making some of Shakespeare's plays, or extracts from them, accessible to children by making links with popular culture texts.
- However, it should also be kept in mind that plays, like stories, create fictional worlds which are at a distance from children's everyday experience. Entering into the spirit of the play's world in its own terms imaginatively, thoughtfully and sometimes playfully is of great value.
- The availability of digital video makes it easier to help children make short films which give an opportunity to combine moving images with sound and music.
- Whether children are working with print playscripts or using 'shooting scripts' to create moving image films this 'story in action' kind of activity is amongst the most exciting, innovative and creative that teachers and children can share.
- Records of progress in playscript reading and writing have a valued place in a child's English, language and literacy portfolio.

Chapter 15

Poetry
An introduction

WHY IS POETRY IMPORTANT?

For some thoughts, feelings, observations and ideas poetry, with its appeal to the feelings and imagination, is the perfect medium. Poetry also makes a special contribution to children's language development as poets use distinctive kinds of language and patterning. Hearing poems read aloud and looking at them on the page leads to an increasing understanding of form. Vocabulary is enriched too, often by the images that are the essence of poetic language. Some words and phrases have a special poetic value because they evoke so powerfully situations, moods, memories, wishes and regrets. The linguistically playful side of some kinds of poetry, nursery rhymes and nonsense verse for example, make it possible for children to find sheer pleasure in manipulating sounds and images. So poetry's contribution has a lot to do with its appeal to the mind and senses through combining sound, rhythm and images.

Above all poetry develops the ability to reflect on lived experience – incidents, conversations and feelings. So our experience from the world enriches our reading of the text; critics call this *world-to-text*. Conversely the incidents and characters in the text can help us reflect more deeply on lived experience – *text-to-world*. On the occasion of his inauguration as Children's Laureate in June 2007, Michael Rosen urged teachers to help children connect with the experiences that poets write about rather than ask them to 'spot similes'. Other kinds of literature can do this, but perhaps poetry is particularly powerful in awakening memories and allowing them to be resavoured and even, sometimes, reinterpreted.

THE ORAL TRADITION

The oral heritage of playground rhymes have been a part of a school child's experience for centuries and now there are new influences at work; children draw on the jingles of television advertisements and other influences from popular culture in their language games. The work of Peter and Iona Opie showed children's creativity and ability to rework traditional rhymes (Opie and Opie, 1959). Teachers and publishers helping to compile the collection may have tended to omit cruder rhymes. Perceptions of what is acceptable constantly change; if the Opies were collecting today, some rhymes might be rejected because of their violent or politically incorrect themes. Should we use playground rhymes for teaching purposes? While 'popular culture' texts have a place in the classroom, we must remember that they often reflect children's genuine preferences and pleasures and they may well wish to keep some of these to enjoy with their peers. The subversiveness of some of the cheekier current rhymes and raps means they will be kept well away from adults and educational contexts and this, after all, may be their very point.

TYPES OF POETRY: THE ORGANIZATION OF THE POETRY CHAPTERS

Poems can be grouped in different ways. Here I have arranged them in five chapters, in a way that I hope will be helpful to students and teachers: 'Poetry: an introduction'; 'Poems playing with language: nursery rhymes and action rhymes, nonsense verse and limericks, riddles and proverbs and rhyming stories'; 'Poems with distinctive forms, rhythms and/or rhyming patterns: rhyming poems, haiku, cinquain, kenning, tanka, shape poems, thin poems and acrostics'; 'Story or narrative poems, classic poems and poems from other cultures and traditions'; 'Poems with freer, less traditional forms and patterns: free verse, conversation poems, blank verse and rap'. There is bound to be some overlap of course. The rhyming stories for younger children in Chapter 17, for example, are the forerunners of story poems for older ones in Chapter 18, and limericks could be placed as confidently with 'poems with distinctive forms' as where I have placed them here, with 'poems playing with language'. All poems communicate meaning through form as well as content, but I have chosen to group together the distinctive forms that we call haiku, cinquains and so on.

FEATURES OF POETRY AND TEACHERS' KNOWLEDGE

There are a number of books which help teachers, as part of their subject knowledge, to know about the rich variety of poetic forms encountered in the classroom. Recommended further reading includes: Morag Style's thoughts on 'Out of the Garden into the Street' which puts the work of Ted Hughes, Charles Causley, Roger McGough, Kit Wright, Wendy Cope, Carol Ann Duffy and Michael Rosen in a helpful context (Styles in Hunt, 2004: Chap. 30); John Rowe Townsend's lively analysis 'Writers in Rhyme' (Townsend, 1990/1995: 103–11); Angela Wilson's comment on Kit Wright's poem 'The Frozen Man' (Wilson, 2001: 109–13); Annie Fisher's exploration of such poems as Zaro Weil's 'From My Window' and Michael Rosen's 'Here is the News from Space' (Fisher, 2008: 14–18).

The introductions to poetry collections can also help and inspire. Anne Fine in her trilogy of collected poems for different age groups, *A Shame to Miss*, addresses young readers directly. With a light touch she helps with vocabulary, historical contexts and sometimes gives suggestions for children's own writing using a poem as a starting point.

We do, of course, have to distinguish between what a teacher needs to know about categories and terminology to do with poetry and what children would find helpful to know at a particular stage. Pressing technical terms and notions on young children before they are ready is contrary to the spirit of enjoying poetry which we want to encourage and could put them off. Progress is not only about controlling forms and structures, although this is part of it as children become older; progress is mainly about becoming able to find in poetry a way of exploring our experience of the world we inhabit and the inner world of the imagination. We will have succeeded if children leave primary school having seen how reading and writing poetry can connect with their own lives and preoccupations.

CHOOSING POETRY FOR ENGLISH LESSONS

As in other parts of the book I have indicated which age groups particular texts might appeal to. But I am on dangerous ground here. John Rowe Townsend reminds us that 'children can grasp imaginatively a great deal that in literal terms they cannot understand' (Townsend, 1995: 103). And poets themselves, Ted Hughes for example, are inclined to doubt that children need a special kind of poetry. By this I think he means that poets need not conceal from even the youngest readers the dark side of life, including the harshness of the natural world. Nevertheless in *Ted Hughes: Collected Poems for Children*, Faber & Faber's publication bringing together all Hughes' poems for children, the poems are arranged in volumes, with those for younger readers first.

An anthology with much of interest for teachers of children at the younger end of the Early and Primary Years age groups is *The Poetry Book for Primary Schools* edited by Anthony Wilson and Sian Hughes. Published by the Poetry Society, this book has a wealth of poems and games and also provides ideas for interesting activities to extend children's response. If you press me for advice on another poetry resource with something for each age group in the early and primary school years – a resource that could be usefully on the teachers' bookshelf in the staffroom – I would mention Alison Sage's *The Hutchinson Treasury of Children's Poetry*. There are sections on nursery rhymes and first poems, rhythm and rhyme for the young, poems for older children and a final section on classic poems by poets of the stature of Shelley, Yeats and Coleridge. *The Oxford Book of Poetry*, selected by Michael Harrison and Christopher Stuart-Clark, is also a strong contender as it has poems of every kind – narrative, free verse, classic poetry, as well as 'conversation' and playful poetry like limericks and riddles. It leans towards young readers in the middle and later primary years.

CHOOSING POETRY ACROSS THE CURRICULUM

Imaginative teachers have long used poems to enhance learning in every kind of lesson. Some poems give a tremendous sense of place that might not be communicated so well through prose. The poems in Shirley Hughes' *Out and About* invites pre-school and nursery children to join a little girl and her baby brother on a journey through the seasons. We visit the seaside in summer and see the bonfire on Guy Fawkes night – the fire is 'like a dangerous dragon'.

For the over sevens, I have found many of the poems in Agard and Nichols' anthology *A Caribbean Dozen* good material for conveying the nature of a distinctive landscape, its oceans and its weather conditions. For this purpose, I particularly like 'River' and 'Hurricane', both by Dionne Brand.

Poems about Earth, compiled by Andrew Fusek Peters, includes poems which tune into the ethical and emotional aspects of geography; there are good thoughtful poems on rainforests, deserts and earthquakes. If you want to bring a touch of wit along with information to a study of the human body in science lessons you might like to use some of the poems from Alan Wolf's anthology *The Blood-Hungry Spleen and Other Poems about Our Parts*. Big anthologies of children's poems are good hunting grounds for poems to illuminate particular lessons. *One Hundred Years of Poetry for Children* includes sections on Animals, War and History. For light-hearted poems on history I recommend Brian Moses' *Romans: Hysterical Historical Poems*, which includes poems about Hadrian's Wall, Roman baths and Julius Caesar.

173

ILLUSTRATIONS IN POETRY BOOKS

Poets and artists have long worked together on anthologies for children: Arthur Hughes illustrated the poems of Christina Rossetti, Leonard Baskin Ted Hughes' poems and Ernest Shepard is forever linked in our minds with the poetry of A.A. Milne. More recently Posy Simmond's artwork has adorned Kit Wright's work and Neal Layton's pictures with a light scribbly line are just right for the unusual poems in Roger McGough's *Wicked Poems*. We enjoy the sheer exuberance of Satoshi Kitamura's illustrations. Those in *The Carnival of the Animals: Poems Inspired by Saint-Saens' Music* keep up the pace of the poems (by James Berry, Kit Wright, Wendy Cope and Charles Causley, amongst others) and home in on the characteristics of the different animals. The print book is accompanied by a CD and poems, pictures and music create a harmonious experience for young readers and listeners. And in *Ted Hughes: Collected Poems for Children*, mentioned already, Raymond Briggs illustrates the entire book with great sensitivity. He uses a line that varies from firm to soft to reveal the nature of the animals which are the subject of so many of the poems. The illustrations seem to nestle amongst the words. It is good news for all who savour outstandingly good illustrations to accompany poetry that Oxford University Press have brought out new editions of some of Charles Keeping's work. For example, we have the evocative black and white illustrations of a bleak countryside through which the horseman rides for a doomed meeting with his lover, Bess, in this new edition of *The Highwayman* by Alfred Noyes.

A recent anthology of poems gaining their power and atmosphere from haunting pictures as well as words is *The Moon Has Written You a Poem: Poems to Read on a Moonlit Night* by Jose Jorge Letria and Anre Letria, translated from Portuguese to English by Maurice Riodan. The images, some of which nudge surrealism, linger in the memory. On one page there is a huge picture of the moon with a mildly disturbing fantasy face and the front cover shows a blue empty armchair with a rather solid blue crescent moon sitting upright on a small table. This most original poetry picturebook shows children how poem and picture can work powerfully together to make for a fascinating reading experience. With some encouragement children might be inspired to create their own poetry picturebook.

Cathie Felstead's colourful and inventive paintings fit wonderfully well with the poems in *A Caribbean Dozen: Poems from Caribbean Poets*, reissued by Walker in 2007. Another illustrator who gives us a strong sense of place in her illustrations of books and poems is Caroline Binch. Her watercolour paintings for Grace Hallworth's large format *Down By the River: Afro-Caribbean Rhymes, Games and Songs for Children* capture the spirit of the poems, in which lively children sing, play, laugh and dress up in a sunny setting.

Charlotte Voake's gentle black and white illustrations enhance *Allan Ahlberg's Collected Poems*, an anthology that brings together some of the best from *Please Mrs Butler*, *Heard It in the Playground*, *Friendly Matches*, *The Mighty Slide* and *The Mysteries of Zigomar*.

But one of the greatest modern illustrators of children's poetry, especially the playful kind, is Quentin Blake, whose name comes up frequently in the following chapters. He uses his sketchy but dynamic drawings, often set against colourful washes, to show exuberance, sadness and, above all, humour.

CREATING A POETRY FRIENDLY CLASSROOM

Changing displays of poems, poetry anthologies, reviews and children's own poems and pictures awaken interest. A 'poetry time' when children can read aloud their favourite poems and say why they have chosen them is also helpful and need not take up a lot of time – ten or fifteen minutes would suffice. I know several teachers who write poetry for their classes and many more who manage to convey their own enjoyment of poetry and to get across the notion that we are all entitled to have preferences and favourites. Making books or audio CDs of favourite poetry and their own poems of a certain kind or genre or on a particular theme is another well-established way of giving poetry a value.

HOW DO WE BEST HELP EXTEND CHILDREN'S RESPONSE TO AND ENJOYMENT OF POETRY?

There are different viewpoints about how we can best help children refine and develop their response to a particular poem. Some believe that just reading or listening to it read aloud is enough and this, I feel sure, is sometimes true. Others are inclined to think that a rigorous analysis of form and meaning moves children forward. I doubt it; particularly if done in ways more appropriate to the needs of secondary school pupils. There are ways, though, of helping understanding and appreciation that do more than just require attentive listening and yet do not bring in 'practical criticism' approaches too soon. So in the following chapters, as in the rest of the whole book, I keep in mind three things that I think make for good practice across the age ranges. First, children learn actively and so encounters with poetry should be spirited and interactive. Second, children learn well collaboratively and I notice that in the liveliest classrooms there are many opportunities in poetry lessons to listen and share. Third, there is the important role of the teacher who intervenes to make poetry work rich and enjoyable.

PERFORMANCE AND PRESENTATION

Children love to present poems they have liked, not least those they have written themselves. One benefit here is that children find themselves thinking about the needs of a particular audience, whether parents and friends of the school or a class of younger children. I have found that presenting a poem in assembly or to another class, with sound effects and a few props, is in the spirit of an energetic approach that augurs well for children's participation and enjoyment. After all, poetry can be 'chanted, sung, yelled, whispered, read quietly to yourself, mimed, illustrated, danced, filmed or accompanied by sounds that charm the ear' (Michael Rosen, inaugural lecture as Children's Laureate, 7 June 2007).

INSPIRING YOUNG POETRY WRITERS

The issue of whether children should concentrate on the communication of meaning and feeling or on the technical requirements of particular forms arises here. Some have felt that Sandy Brownjohn leans rather far to the 'teaching form and structure' end of things. But she would, I think, say that once in control of some of the forms poetry takes, children have a choice about

175

Acrostic – a poem in which the first letters of each line spell out the topic or theme of the poem.

Alliteration – repetition of the same consonant or phoneme.

Assonance – the repeated use of a vowel phoneme for aesthetic impact.

Blank verse – poetry which has rhythm and metre but not rhyme. Often it is iambic pentameter – lines of ten syllables with an unstressed/stressed syllable pattern.

Cinquain – five line poem of American origin with 22 syllables in a 2, 4, 6, 8, 2 arrangement. The last line sometimes relates in an interesting way to the title or the first line.

Couplet – two lines that rhyme and whose rhythm matches.

Free verse – poetry free in the sense that it need not adhere to a regular metrical pattern and rhyming system.

Haiku – three line poem of Japanese origin with 17 syllables in a 5, 7, 5 arrangement.

Image – a comparison in the form of a metaphor or simile, in which the poet's aim is to make it fresh, original, even startling, rather than familiar and banal.

Kenning – two word phrases which name something indirectly. So a priest might be a 'soul saver' and a mother a 'life giver'.

Limerick – a teasing short five line rhyme with a syllable pattern of 8, 8, 6, 6, 8 and a rhyme scheme of A, A, B, B, A.

Metaphor – the qualities of the first thing mentioned carry over to the second thing. So we might have some friends who call the matchmaking one 'the Cupid of our group'.

Narrative poem – ballad or story poem which tells a tale of romance or of heroic deeds.

Nonsense verse – amusing verse which uses sound, image, rhythm and rhyme.

Nursery rhyme – traditional rhyming song or story which often creates a subversion of the normal rules of the real world.

Onomatopoeia – language which echoes sense – 'squelch', 'buzz' or 'boom'.

Personification – a device which links human beings metaphorically with the non-human world of animals or objects.

Rap – a performance poem or popular song with a strong rhythm and quick pace.

Rhyme – a literary term to refer to words which are the same or similar in sound.

Rhythm – the beat of a poem giving it form and pattern and contributing to the meaning by enhancing mood and 'colour'.

Shape poem – has words in a layout that echoes the shape of the subject.

Simile – a comparison often using 'like' or 'as'.

Sonnet – a poem with fourteen lines and a regular rhythm and rhyming pattern.

Stanza – another name for a verse in a poem.

Syllable – part of a word which is pronounced in one beat: 'object' has two syllables, 'ob' and 'ject'.

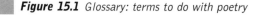

Figure 15.1 Glossary: terms to do with poetry

Tanka – a poem like a haiku with two more lines. The syllable form is 5, 7, 5, 7, 7.

Thin poem – this is presented in very short lines, and is sometimes a sort of list. (Similarly there are 'fat', 'square' poems, etc.)

Tongue twister – a rhyme or phrase using copious alliteration and therefore a challenge to say fast.

Figure 15.1 continued

how to communicate their meanings. And, after all, the form of a poem contributes to the expressions of emotions and feelings. She shares some ideas for activities and games to support poetry writing for nine- to eleven-year-olds in *To Rhyme or Not to Rhyme?* which is an omnibus edition of three of her poetry books with some new material (1994). But if there is one book that will help with the 'meaning versus form' dilemma, it is Ted Hughes' *Poetry in the Making*. This book, first published way back in 1967 to accompany a series on poetry on a BBC Schools programme, is written as if the author is talking directly to young readers (Hughes, 1967). Hughes makes the case for regarding poetry, both what we read and what we write, as a way of making sense of lived experience and the thoughts and feelings that are part of it.

ASSESSING AND RECORDING PROGRESS

Some teachers feel less confident about this than they do about assessing children's progress as readers and writers of other literary forms. And yet young learners appreciate and need the right sort of feedback here as well. One thing to grasp is that there is a strong link between good poetry teaching and the sound and imaginative evaluation of children's progress.

Reading

The more poems you read and listen to, the more chance you have to develop preferences and to give reasons for these preferences. The ability to infer something not made entirely explicit leads to the appreciation that poems (along with picturebooks and novels) can have several layers of meaning. Given rich and appropriate opportunities to read, talk about and enjoy poems, children start to look for more than the literal surface meaning. Do you know the poem by Robert Frost called 'The Road Not Taken'? With some help, older primary children would be able to understand that although the poet seems to be writing about two pathways – 'Two roads diverged in a yellow wood' – at a deeper level he is thinking about the choices we make on the journey through life. Teachers could usefully observe and note these 'critical moments' in a child's progress as a reader of poetry.

In the case of older children, teachers look for an ability to notice patterns of rhyme, rhythm and the arrangement of the words on the page and the effect these have on the ear and mind. There are also patterns in meaning to be detected, communicated by the careful choices of word and phrase. A language and literacy folder or portfolio might helpfully include:

- Teachers' dated notes on critical moments: a child's personal response, mentioning enthusiasms, appreciation of 'puzzles' and recognition of patterns in relation to particular poems or groups of poems.
- Dated notes on a developing ability to infer and to see deeper meanings in a poem. Teachers become aware of these achievements if they have regular discussions with the children and observe them talking in groups.
- Audio recordings of children reading aloud during a poetry presentation or of small group discussion could be stored within a print portfolio.
- Shorter pieces of writing might include dated annotations of displays of the work of a particular poet, short pieces about particular poems photocopied from a child's reading log, a comparison between poems with different approaches to a topic or a piece on 'why _____ is my favourite poem/poet'.
- All or part of a favourite poem written in an aesthetic script set against an atmospheric illustration.

Writing

How does a teacher best intervene to help move a young poetry writer forward? Opening up a dialogue about their poems is a constructive approach and this can start at the drafting stage, when the feedback is likely to be oral. There is some evidence that teachers' feedback on traditional poems is more helpful than that offered on poems with freer forms (Ofsted, 2007: 27). Some teachers may be less comfortable with poems which have no conventional rhythm and rhyme. But comments on vocabulary choice, originality of imagery and success in conveying meaning would all be relevant and helpful. Conversational poems can be praised if they have what we might call an 'honesty to experience' about them. Constructive advice about how to help children improve their work is a main theme in Sue Dymoke's book *Drafting and Assessing Poetry: A Guide for Teachers* (Dymoke, 2003: 155). Although mainly about the secondary school stage this has helpful general things to say, for example about how the peer group can comment helpfully on each other's poems at the drafting stage. Children do need advice, of course, about how to comment constructively.

Suggestions for portfolio items include:

- Examples of a child's poems selected by child and teacher, with date, context and some annotation. Comments might be to do with the child's choice of words and phrases, use of imagery, control over a form of poetry. Above all, we are looking for signs of developing creativity and originality.
- In some cases, it might be helpful to have earlier drafts clipped to the final copy. Drafting on screen tends to produce less permanent drafts as changes can be made so swiftly and easily.
- Computers have enhanced choices about how children present their work and sample poems are likely to include those with innovative visual patterns and illustrations.
- Include examples of newer forms like text message poetry. Text message poetry can have rhythm and rhyme and, like haiku, involves the discipline of condensation.
- An example of collaborative poetry writing, made more possible by an interactive whiteboard.

Chapter 16

Poems playing with language
Nursery rhymes and action rhymes, nonsense verse and limericks, riddles and proverbs and rhyming stories

INTRODUCTION

Children play with sounds from the early months of life. They do this for the sheer pleasure and fun of experimenting and of course it prepares the way for speech. Marian Whitehead observes how babies and their carers 'blow "raspberries", gurgle, squeal and babble' for the fun and delight of doing it (Whitehead, 2004: 90). This playing with sound happens when the child is alone too, and at night before they settle to sleep. Ruth Weir recorded and analysed the pre-sleep monologues of her own child, Antony, and noted that he sometimes made up nonsense sequences like 'Bink, let Bobo bink' (Weir, 1962: 105). Later research studies in the 1980s and early 1990s suggested that children's attempts at rhyming and using alliteration in their babbling may help with learning to read later on (Goswami and Bryant, 1990). This love of sound continues in older children and finds expression in their delight in nonsense verse and other verse that uses alliteration in witty and lively ways.

However, the appeal of nursery and nonsense rhymes is rooted not just in playful sound patterns but also in taking imaginative liberties with meaning. We find such absurdities as, for example, a cow jumping over the moon and a dish running away with a spoon in a nursery rhyme. This prepares the way for older children to appreciate the humour in the nonsense songs and poems in the work of Lewis Carroll, Edward Lear, Hilaire Belloc and Spike Milligan. It also links with the creative use of language by children so evident in their playground and street games. Why do children find these things so amusing? Chukovsky, a Russian writer about children's early language development, argued long ago that children need to introduce some nonsense into their 'small but ordered world'. He calls these teasing inversions of meaning 'topsy turvies' and believes that once children have a grip on what is 'normal', they can enjoy playful absurdities. The very ability to find the bizarre amusing strengthens children's grip on what is true and real (Chukovsky, 1963: 96).

Peter and Iona Opie spent many years researching children's poems, stories and playgound rhymes and their collections are stored in the Bodleian Library. *Oxford Dictionary of Nursery Rhymes* presents five hundred rhymes in alphabetical order. It is worth tracking down the 1997 edition as it includes a new essay on the singing tradition in children's experience of nursery rhymes by Cecily Raysor Hancock. The illustrations, many from some of the earliest nursery rhyme books, are of great interest. Puzzles still remain – not least which rhymes were based on real people and actual events. The Opies try to shed light on this in a book which is unrivalled as the standard work on the development of nursery rhymes over the past two hundred years. The other nursery rhyme book by the Opies, *The Oxford Nursery Rhyme book*, is organized as an anthology and includes eight hundred nursery rhymes, arranged as lullabies, dandling rhymes, alphabets and baby games. Again, the illustrations add to the book's value. Many are eighteenth- and nineteenth-century illustrations, woodcuts (some by Thomas Bewick) and engravings from illustrated toy books and chapbooks. It may be helpful to mention that there is a website, Nursery Rhymes (www.rhymes.org.uk), which gives historical details about a large number of rhymes (accessed 8 August 2009).

FEATURES OF POEMS PLAYING WITH LANGUAGE

Nursery rhymes and action rhymes

Nursery rhyme or 'Mother Goose' collections include a large number of forms: lullabies and songs, counting and alphabet rhymes, clapping, bouncing and dancing games, riddles, proverbs and nonsense rhymes. Then there is the huge and exciting body of action rhymes which invite little children to clap, point, bounce and dance.

Nursery rhymes are sometimes instructive ('One two buckle my shoe'), amusing ('Diddle diddle dumpling'), intriguing ('Little Miss Muffet'), upsetting ('Three Blind Mice') or jolly ('Here we go round the mulberry bush'). What do they all have in common? An important feature of nursery rhymes is their brevity, which makes them manageable units of language that can be enjoyed, remembered and resavoured by the youngest age group. Further, they have the sort of rhyme and rhythm which make them good to read aloud and to dance and move to. The rhythm, rhyme and repetition help us remember them and the alliteration of 'Simple Simon' and 'Jack and Jill' makes them catchy and appealing.

Nonsense verse and limericks

While nursery rhymes are for very young children, nonsense poems have something to interest older children with their more elaborate themes to do with the fantastic and the imaginary. The vocabulary is often unusual, novel and amusing. They share with nursery rhymes features of alliteration and assonance as well as rhyme and rhythm. Nonsense rhymes are full of strange, eccentric folk and wonderful creatures with strange names – Lear's 'jumblies' and 'popple', for example. But however fanciful and startling the situations and however inventive the vocabulary, writers of nonsense poems stick to conventional structures and syntax. The poem often used to demonstrate this is Lewis Carroll's 'Jabberwocky'. In the first line, ' 'Twas brillig, and the slithy toves', we use our intuitive knowledge of grammar to sense that 'slithy' is an adjective and 'toves' a noun. The language play beguiles the ear and the humour teases and tickles our minds.

A limerick is a special kind of nonsense poem which follows a traditional form with five anapaestic lines. Lines 1, 2 and 5 have between 7 and 10 syllables and rhyme. Line 3 rhymes with line 4 and these lines have between 5 and 7 syllables. This kind of verse goes back into the Middle Ages, when the content and themes were cruder and they were often said or sung in taverns and public houses. The limerick gained new life and status when *Edward Lear's Book of Nonsense* was published by Thomas McLean in 1846. Lear's ideas are imaginative and amusing and his rhymes most inventive.

It is worth remembering that rhymes, songs and nonsense verses continue to be created today, partly in the form of the rhymes, songs and jingles children hear on radio and television and which become integrated into playground games. So children develop a cumulative store of playful verse.

Riddles and proverbs

Riddles and proverbs are short, pithy language forms. Riddles are often in rhyming question and answer form. Children use riddles in the street and playground but often call them jokes. They often involve puns and conundrums. Proverbs are wise sayings giving advice or warnings, often using rhythm, rhyme and alliteration to make them easy to memorize.

Rhyming stories

These illustrated books for young children use rhyme to drive the story along. There may be an iambic rhyming form or a series of rhyming couplets.

CRITERIA FOR CHOOSING NURSERY RHYMES AND ACTION RHYMES, NONSENSE VERSES AND LIMERICKS, RIDDLES AND PROVERBS, AND RHYMING STORIES

Many of these forms are presented in collections, with an editor or selector and an illustrator. The quality of collections of nursery rhymes and nonsense poems is to do with how well the design, coverage, language and illustration work together to make for a coherent volume. Writing about nursery rhyme collections, Brian Alderson discriminates between the good and less good collections by suggesting that the best 'play in Mother Goose's melody but with their own key signature giving a distinctiveness'. In less praiseworthy collections 'words and pictures are strung together any old way' (Alderson, 2004: 27). Very often this coherence, or lack of it, is apparent the moment we open a book.

Choosing nursery rhymes and action rhymes

The many formats that nursery rhyme books take include board and cloth books for the very young, picturebooks devoted to one rhyme and big books with collections of rhymes. There is also a choice between print and audio collections.

Which we choose depends not only on how we judge their quality, but on how we are going to use them. Children aged three and under, sharing a book with an adult, tend to prefer brightly coloured illustrations with a bold line. The more subtle watercolour washes are appreciated later. I also find that at this age enjoying one nursery rhyme can be enough for a child's concentration span. So the ten-page board books edited by Ronne Randall and

181

illustrated by Emma Dodd in Touch and Feel format are likely to appeal. Look out for *Jack and Jill* and *Sing a Song of Sixpence*. Annie Kubler's bright and lively board book *Head, Shoulders, Knees and Toes* shows energetic children from different ethnic groups acting out the song and there are some dual-language versions, for example English and Somali.

I find the youngest children like books with holes, pull-outs and lift-the-flap features. Dan Adams has illustrated a board book telling the classic rhyming tale *There Was an Old Lady Who Swallowed a Fly*. The holes reveal the things the old lady has eaten and, together with the repetition in the rhyme, draw the young reader or listener through the story. But we must remember that even the youngest children can respond strongly to a poem or image. One of my children was found throwing a nursery rhyme book out of the window because she was frightened by the picture accompanying one of the rhymes; it showed Wee Willie Winkie going into a child's bedroom and she feared he might come to visit her to check whether she had gone to sleep. *Lucy Cousins' Big Book of Nursery Rhymes* is big enough to make sharing easy and the bold simple line and colourfulness of the illustrations make it just right for the age group. The illustrations are of great importance when choosing from the huge array of nursery rhyme books on the market. Axel Scheffler, illustrator of Julia Donaldson's fine Gruffalo books, is the artist for *Mother Goose's Nursery Rhymes and How She Came to Tell Them*, a collection of eighty-eight rhymes selected by Alison Green. Each clutch of rhymes is preceded by Mother Goose telling a story to her goslings, Boo, Lucy and Small. The pictures are bright, entertaining and likely to appeal to young children. I would have liked more than just the first verse of some of the rhymes, of 'Twinkle Twinkle Little Star' for example. *Michael Foreman's Nursery Rhymes* links the settings visually: The Grand Old Duke of York marches his men up one side of a hill, and on the next page we see Jack and Jill tumbling down the other side.

When it comes to nursery rhyme collections, old favourites are worth considering as well as those hot off the press. *The Orchard Book of Nursery Rhymes*, selected by Zena Sutherland, offers a good choice of rhymes with classics like 'Humpty Dumpty', 'Baby Bunting' and 'Rock a Bye Baby'. The illustrations by Faith Jacques are small but very bright and appealing; the rhymes are set in the eighteenth century, with small girls in aprons and boys in velvet suits. Another classic collection with rhymes set in idyllic countryside scenes, Kate Greenaway's *Apple Pie and Traditional Nursery Rhymes*, is still in print. Two big book collections which will be useful in the nursery class are *The Macmillan Treasury of Nursery Rhymes* and Kathleen Lines' *Lavender's Blue*, illustrated by Harold Jones and including old favourites and the work of contemporary poets like Charles Causley and Grace Nichols.

CDs of nursery rhymes are popular because young children love responding to rhythmic music by dancing, clapping and singing. It is best to select a CD that also has a print book in the package, or at least a leaflet with the words of the rhymes so that adults can join in with the singing. *Oxford Baby Nursery Rhymes CD* provides eighteen 'well-known rhymes with a twist'. So we have such classics as 'Polly Put the Kettle On', 'Pop Goes the Weasel' and 'Ring a Ring of Roses', but with an interesting range of musical style, with some jazz and reggae interpretations. *Playtime Rhymes*, edited by Sally Gardner *et al.*, consists of thirty-six rhymes set out in a lively, colourful book and an accompanying CD with the rhymes put to music.

Choosing nonsense verse and limericks

It is particularly difficult to assign nonsense poetry to age groups and so in this section I simply refer to younger and older readers. There are two giants here: Edward Lear and Lewis Carroll. Younger children as well as older ones can enjoy some of their nonsense poems, for example Edward Lear's 'The Owl and the Pussycat' and Lewis Carroll's 'Jabberwocky'. But some of Lewis Carroll's story poems, embedded in his books *Alice's Adventures in Wonderland* and *Through the Looking Glass*, are rather grim. 'The Walrus and the Carpenter', for example, is darkly absurd and probably best appreciated in the later primary school years. Also for older children are some of Hilaire Belloc's cautionary tales; in 'Matilda' a child who recklessly lies ends up burnt to death when her house catches fire. Of course, as the work of more modern poets – that of Roger McGough for example – shows, it is part of the understood nature of the nonsense genre that things that would be dreadful in reality can be coped with when distanced by a poem. Children learn what to expect of this genre surprisingly early. The impact of the horrific ends suffered by Hilaire Belloc's children in his cautionary tales is softened by his solemn tongue-in-cheek tone, which delights children. He is of course poking fun at the moral tales for children well known in Victorian times.

Why is the nonsense poetry of Carroll, Lear and Belloc so enduring? It is partly to do with their ability to create imaginative and entertaining alternative worlds, but also because of their ingenuity in language play and in achieving witty, unusual and memorable rhymes. We have in 'Jabberwocky' things and ideas that are imaginatively rich, while the rhyming lines show a mastery of a conventional form – 'slithy toves' and 'borogroves'. Lear has some ingenious internal rhymes; in 'The Owl and the Pussycat' the creatures take on the journey with 'some honey and plenty of money . . . .'. Belloc's work is full of inventive rhymes – for example 'Matilda' and 'killed her'.

Milligan and Dahl follow on from Carroll, Lear and Belloc. Roald Dahl poems often give comic twists to nursery rhymes and fairy stories. In *Revolting Rhymes* he gives reign to the excess that children like. We have Goldilocks breaking up the bears' furniture as well as eating their porridge. Lear's 'The Owl and the Pussycat', Carroll's 'Jabberwocky', Ahlberg's 'Dog in the Playground', Dahl's 'Revolting Rhymes' and Milligan's 'On the Ning Nang Nong' are all in Ofsted's list of the ten most commonly taught poems in the primary years (Ofsted, 2007).

Ogden Nash's nonsense poetry is anthologized in *Candy is Dandy: The Best of Ogden Nash* edited by Linell Smith. His poems play with words and meaning in quite a sophisticated way. Older primary children would like some of the animal poems, for example 'The Platypus', which begins 'I like the duck-billed platypus / Because it is anomalous'. Other contemporary poets who include nonsense and playful verse for children in their repertoire include: Brian Patten, Roald Dahl, Margaret Mahy, Spike Milligan, Tony Mitton, Robert McGough, Michael Rosen and Benjamin Zephaniah. There are also gifted illustrators to help bring out the humour of playful poetry: Quentin Blake, Herve Tullet, Edward Gorey and Satoshi Kitamura. Sometimes the character of the illustrations suggests an age group that would particularly appreciate the book. The playful world Michael Rosen creates in his *Alphabet Poem: An Imaginative and Hilarious Look at the Letters We Love*, illustrated perfectly and playfully by Herve Tullet, would appeal to readers of any age.

Margaret Mahy's poems are often about magic and mystery, but also about the humorous side of everyday life. Her *Wonderful Me! Stories and Poems* includes nonsense poems and is illustrated by Peter Bailey.

The over sevens will appreciate Roger McGough's poems about mischievous cats in *Bad, Bad Cats*. This is also available in audio form in Penguin Children's Audiobooks series. If you want a comprehensive selection of both classic and contemporary nonsense verse from which you can select poems you judge your class will like, a simply excellent resource is Quentin Blake's *The Penguin Book of Nonsense Verse*. The book is nicely arranged in sections with names like 'The World Turned Upside Down' and 'Chortling and Galumping'. Most of the nonsense poetry a teacher would want to use in the primary years is conveniently available here.

For any age, Colin West's *The Big Book of Nonsense Poems to Make You Laugh Out Loud* is hugely amusing. It has sections including ones on 'Curious Creatures', 'Tongue Twisters' and 'Dottie Ditties'. This is the sort of book teachers like to have handy – to read in an odd moment to reinforce the idea that poetry can be for sheer delight and amusement.

Tongue twisters like 'Peter Piper' and nonsense poems like 'Rub a Dub Dub' and 'Pop Goes the Weasel' can be tracked down in the many big anthologies of rhymes and verses. *The Macmillan Treasury of Nursery Rhymes and Poems: 300 Poems for Reading Aloud*, already mentioned in the previous section as an excellent source of nursery rhymes, is also a good source of nonsense poems. If you are a parent or teacher with mixed age groups to contend with, you would find that *The Hutchinson's Treasury of Children's Literature*, compiled by Alison Sage and with a foreword by Quentin Blake, has a good selection of poems for different age ranges.

If you are teaching about limericks, you will find sections including these in most of the big poetry anthologies for the primary years. Of course a particularly good hunting ground are the poetry volumes on nonsense verse. Quentin Blake's *The Puffin Book of Nonsense Verse* includes limericks by Edward Lear, Edward Gorey and Ogden Nash. The illustrations are perfect for the spirit of the limericks and a good talking point. For examples of less well-known limericks it is worth tracking down John Foster's *My First Book of Nonsense Poems*. There you will find, for example, Colin West's 'A Wisp of a Wasp Stung the King', Frank Richard's 'A Wasp on Nettle said: "Coo!"' and Willard Espy's 'My TV Came Down with a Chill'. A source of limericks for older primary children is Bill Person's anthology *Limericks for Children and Other Special Folks: Poems to Capture the Imagination*.

There are also some good collections of nonsense verse in the form of audiobook CDs. Alan Bennett reads some of the work of Edward Lear and others on *The Owl and the Pussycat and Other Nonsense Rhymes* in the BBC's Cover to Cover cassettes series. This selection has poems likely to appeal to the five to eight age group as well as older children – 'The Quangle Wangle's Hat' and 'The Jumblies', for example. Another well-liked audio CD is *Alice in Wonderland & Nonsense Verse and Prose* from Oxford Storypods, with the unabridged version of Carroll's work. Children who might not sustain concentration to read the print version may be drawn in when hearing the narration by a cast of actors. The nonsense poems are presented as songs, for example 'Jabberwocky' and 'The Mock Turtle's Song', and the CD can be downloaded onto an iPod.

Choosing riddles and proverbs

Riddles and proverbs are part of a country's oral history and folklore and they often pop up in nursery and playground rhymes and sometimes in fairy and folk tales. A riddle is a puzzle we are invited to solve, while a proverb is a wise or pithy saying, usually in one short sentence. Both are often presented as rhymes as this aids memory in what was originally an oral tradition.

Young children often get a sense of what riddles are by coming across them in stories There are lots in fairy and folk tales and in more everyday tales too. *Katie Morag and the Riddles* by Mairi Hedderwick is about a little girl striving to solve the riddles presented to the class by the teacher.

For children aged about seven and upwards there is a riddle book that is entertaining but also thought-provoking. It is called *I Spy Spooky Night: A Book of Picture Riddles* and written by Jean Marzollo. The illustrations are beautiful, atmospheric photographs in mysterious purples, greys and blues by Walter Wick. The pictures and rhyming text take the reader on a journey through a dark, strange house and give clues about the objects shown and described. The invitation at the beginning is:

> Use your mind, use your eye.
> Read the riddles – play I SPY!

A rich source of riddles (for example, Sally Angell's 'What Am I?') and other teasing poems playing with punctuation is John Foster's *Crack Another Yolk. A Children's Book of Tongue Twisters, Poems and Riddles from A-Z*, by David Marango and with illustrations by Jenny Marango, is a well-organized book suitable for the over nines. Finally, a good resource for the teacher of older primary children is *A World Treasury of Riddles* by Phil Cousineau.

Proverbs give advice and warnings often in rhyme and nearly always have some other poetic qualities like assonance and alliteration. They also condense meaning, often using metaphors to do so. A universal idea can be given local impact in proverbs like 'carrying coals to Newcastle', which in Greece becomes 'sending owls to Athens' (McArthur, 1992: 818). In my selection, I have avoided the more indoctrinatory collections which aim to bring children and young people in line with a particular belief system.

Shirley Hughes understands how to draw in young readers and listeners. Her collection of proverbs with clear explanations and appealing illustrations, *Make Hay While the Sun Shines: Book of Proverbs*, would be liked by children aged about six onwards.

Intended for age five upwards but enjoyed by some people in every age group is *Pooh's Little Instruction Book*, which has advice about how to live a good life 'Pooh style'. *My First Book of Proverbs* by Ralfka Gonzalez, and with an introduction by Sandra Cisneros, would appeal particularly to children in the five to eight age range, but would also be appreciated by younger and older age groups. The bilingual edition is in Spanish and English. The vibrant, jewel-like illustrations by Ana Ruiz, which bring alive a dry, sun-drenched landscape, are reminiscent of early Mexican painting. To entertain and challenge the eights and over I recommend Axel Scheffler's large book *The Silent Beetle Eats the Seeds: Proverbs from Far and Wide*. Organized in seventeen chapters on, for example, luck, wisdom, friendship and injustice, there is information about the countries from which particular proverbs seem to have originated.

185

Choosing rhyming stories

Writers choose to use rhyme when they judge that this is the best form for the story they want to tell. Often the rhyme drives the narrative on keeping up the young reader or listener's interest. For children at the pre-school and nursery stage you cannot do better than read the lively rhyming stories of Janet and Allan Ahlberg, for example *Each Peach Pear Plum* and *Peepo!*

Some of the best rhyming stories and songs use word play, rhythm and rhyme in adventurous ways. Cathy MacLennan's *Chicky Chicky Chook Chook* uses language play to show the joyful aspects of the natural world in summer. The dynamic pictures show bees, ducks and other creatures scurrying across the double spreads. Quentin Blake's exuberant book *Mister Magnolia*, first published in 1980, has a line to each wittily illustrated page and every line rhymes with 'boot'. The reissue in 2000 of Macgregor and Perring's *Bunnikin's Picnic Party,* allows a new generation to enjoy the sort of illustrations that are detailed enough to encourage lively talk.

Rhyming couplets are the perfect form for John Vernon's *The Giant Jam Sandwich* because they give momentum to the story and help children remember it. Villagers find swarms of wasps have arrived and decide to make a giant jam sandwich to tempt the insects and carry them away. But where can they put the huge sandwich? 'The gentlemen cheered, the ladies squealed, and Farmer Smith said "use my field"'. The large-scale bread making, the flying

---

BOX 16.1 *WRIGGLE PIGGY TOES* **BY JOHN AGARD AND JENNY BENT (ILLUS.) (FRANCES LINCOLN)**

John Agard uses rhyme in *Wriggle Piggy Toes* to take young listeners through a baby's day from 'wakey light' to 'moon-ball bright'. It includes all the things babies and their carers do, right through to a bath and a cuddle at night time. The rhymes and the affecting and colourful illustrations by Jenny Bent show the loving relationship between baby and mother.

Meena's plan was really quite clever
The crocodile ate its way to the river!

Figure 16.1
Image and text from page 40 of Catch that Crocodile! *by Anushka Ravishankar and Pulak Biswas (illus.)*
Reproduced with the permission of the publishers TARA Books. Copyright TARA Books 1999

machine and of course the wasps are just the right ingredients to appeal to children from about age five to eight. As well as the print book there is an audio CD 'read along' version with music and sound effects. The Ahlbergs' classic Jolly Postman books have enduring appeal for this same age group. The first one, *The Jolly Postman or Other People's Letters*, was boundary-breaking when it first came out in 1986. The Ahlbergs' books are the forerunners of other modern picturebooks which are intertextual, making semiotic links with other texts.

The folk tales of Anushka Ravishankar, with illustrations by Pulak Biswas, use an engaging rhythmic verse to tell lively stories, for example *Tiger on a Tree* and *Catch that Crocodile!* In these books a fantastical world is created. *Catch that Crocodile!* communicates realistically but comically the frantic efforts of some frightened townspeople to catch a crocodile found in a ditch.

The story rhymes in picturebooks are important because of the sheer delight young readers and listeners experience. But they also link strongly with learning to read as the rhymes are likely to strengthen children's ability to predict what comes next. Partly for this reason, Jill Bennett urges us to read young children linguistically powerful picturebooks which include rhythm, rhyme and alliterative phrases (Bennett, 2008: 5). There is a good summary of the research indicating that rhyming texts have a role in the process of learning to read by Ursula Goswami (Goswami, 1995).

USING POEMS PLAYING WITH LANGUAGE

Pre-school and nursery: an active approach

- Very young children love hearing nursery rhymes and songs read out by an adult or on a CD, and joining in the actions. Annie Kubler's dual-language board book *Head, Shoulders, Knees and Toes*, Grace Hallworth and Caroline Binch's *Down by the River* and Brita Granström's *Ring-a-Ring o' Roses* are just a few of the many quality books available.
- The dressing-up and props box can be an inspiration for saying and acting out the rhymes. Marian Whitehead suggests these 'symbolic props' indicate children's growing ability to represent ideas with words and objects. Something like a stick might be a kind of metaphor – named 'horse' but the child knows it is a stick (Whitehead in Beard, 1995: 49).

5–8s need to be actively involved too

- Five- to eight-year-olds add nonsense poems to their 'reading aloud' repertoire. There are a number of collections containing old favourites like Carroll's 'Jabberwocky' and Lear's 'The Owl and the Pussycat', and newer collections containing rhyming poems like 'Beware of the Sheep' from Sandy Brownjohn's *In and Out of the Shadows*. This jolly rhyming poem is about sheep who do absolutely everything except jump over a fence so you can count them. They somersault, dive, bang on drums and ski.
- Younger children would enjoy the short poems in Ernest Henry's *Poems to Shout Out Loud* – the alliterative 'The Busy Bee' poem, for example, while older ones could meet the challenge of the longer ones like 'The Dark Side of the Moon'.

Collaborative approaches and the teacher's role

Discussion and sharing lead to involvement and enjoyment and the teacher's role is important in creating a sympathetic classroom climate.

* Children will like reading their favourite lines from nonsense poetry aloud.
* When it comes to riddles and proverbs teachers often suggest that children make their own collections and illustrate them.
* In pairs or groups, children can seek out proverbs that seem to contradict each other – 'Look before you leap' and 'He who hesitates is lost' – and then decide in which situations each proverb would be most appropriate to guide action.
* For over nines, making acrostic poems and designing crosswords can be absorbing activities and they can be read out and shared.
* Older children who appreciate Hilaire Belloc's cautionary tales might like to read modern tales as a starting point for their own attempts at writing. Ian McMillan's 'Cautionary Playground Rhymes' in *The Very Best of Ian McMillan* provides a simple structure which would help get them started.

Helping children use pattern and rhyme in their own poems

* When it comes to children's own attempts we must remember that writing poetry that rhymes, scans and which does not sink to the trite or banal at a meaning level is difficult. Sandy Brownjohn has developed games to help older children control rhyme (Brownjohn in Beard, 1995: 80–95).
* One of Brownjohn's games is the demanding 'I'd rather . . . than . . .' game. The teacher might provide the first line, each child in the group then supplying a line where the end word rhymes. So we might begin with: 'I'd rather eat crisps than a stew'. This exercise obliges us to run through the alphabet putting different consonants in front of 'stew'.
* The over sevens usually like creating their own riddles along the lines of 'My first is in . . . but not in . . .' and getting their partner and then the class to solve them.
* For further advice on ways of helping children use their minds and imagination within a supportive framework, see Brownjohn's *To Rhyme or Not to Rhyme?* (1994).

Presenting poems

* Children of every age group enjoy presenting programmes of poetry for another class, in assembly or for parents and friends of the school on open day. Musical accompaniment and sound effects and a few props help make it satisfying.
* More informally, children in pairs or in groups might work on poems to present to the rest of the class. This can be followed by constructive comments on the performances.
* Choral speaking seems to be coming back as a life enhancing collaborative effort – this makes learning poems by heart worthwhile. Rhythm and rhyme make playful poems easier to learn. See John Foster's collection *I've Got a Poem for You: Poems to Perform*.

SUMMARY

- Nursery rhymes are often of ancient origin but appeared in print as Mother Goose Rhymes in the eighteenth and nineteenth centuries.
- The best collections of nursery rhymes and other poems in the 'playful' language and meaning category have a coherence and individuality in organization and illustration that make them a pleasure to read.
- When it comes to extending response to rhyming and nonsense verse, it is helpful to remember that children in the early and primary years are active creatures who enjoy drama, role play and discussion.
- Teachers can help by encouraging children in the different age groups to share their enthusiasms, their puzzles and to search out patterns and connections.
- Sharing poems by reading them aloud to others is enjoyable and helps reinforce what children have been learning.

Chapter 17

Poems with distinctive forms, rhythms and/or rhyming patterns

Rhyming poems, haiku, cinquain, kenning, tanka, shape poems, thin poems and acrostics

INTRODUCTION

All poems have distinctive patterns and forms. Here I gather together short poems often discussed together and in which the structure is dominant. Some patterning works best orally but other kinds are visual and need to be seen on the page. Shape and thin poems, for example, have to be seen on the page or screen to be appreciated; they can amuse, surprise and encourage children to experiment with their own poetry writing.

FEATURES OF POEMS WITH DISTINCTIVE PATTERNS AND FORMS

Rhyming poems

With these we help move children on to something more challenging than the familiar nursery rhyme. They often have an abab rhyming pattern or sometimes are organized in rhyming couplets – aabbcc and so on. They have rhythm as well as rhyme, giving them appeal and helping the memory if a poem is being learnt by heart.

Haiku

This is a poetry form with three lines and 17 syllables: line 1 – 5 syllables; line 2 – 7 syllables; line 3 – 5 syllables.

This ancient Japanese form was originally rather rigid and stylized. But it had new life breathed into it by Basno, a traveller and Zen Buddhist, living in the second half of the seventeenth century. Basno kept to two principles when writing his haiku poetry: lightness of touch and oneness with nature. The best poems in this form celebrate the small triumphs and beauties of nature – a flower opening, a blade of grass waving in the wind or a cloud reshaping. Modern poets who have used this form bring humour and a wider range of themes from contemporary life and when translated from the Japanese there can be some flexibility in the patterning. (In his anthology *The Very Best of Ian McMillan*, Ian McMillan teases with a witty parody of the haiku in his 'Three Wilsons'.)

Cinquain

Like haiku, these short poems do not rhyme and have a fixed form. Cinquains have 22 syllables arranged in 5 lines as follows: line 1 – 2 syllables; line 2 – 4 syllables; line 3 – 6 syllables; line 4 – 8 syllables; line 5 – 2 syllables. This form was developed by Adelaide Craprey in America in 1911. The themes of the poems are reminiscent of Japanese poems and include nature and the seasons, times of day, special events and festivals like Diwali and Christmas.

> Moonlight
> Brown mouse scurries
> Across the midnight fields.
> Owl swoops, scoops up, rides high, drops prey.
> Escape.

Kenning

This is a compound word used by a writer to name something as an alternative to the conventional noun. So an owl might be called a 'mouse-eater' or a burglar a 'goods-stealer'. A 'kenning' poem uses a succession of kennings. This device was a feature of Anglo Saxon poetry but modern poets also use imaginatively constructed compound words in their work.

Tanka

This is a Japanese poem, similar in its form and themes to haiku. A tanka has 31 syllables arranged in five lines as follows: line 1 – 5 syllables; line 2 – 7 syllables; line 3 – 5 syllables; line 4 – 7 syllables; line 5 – 7 syllables.

Shape poems

Here the words themselves may be woven to form a pattern like dance steps or a snail's journey along a path. Or the words may be fitted into an outlined shape like a box, a leaf or a house. In both cases, the structure echoes or extends the meaning of the poem.

Thin poems (including list poems)

These poems, as the name suggests, are thin and look like a list on the page, with just one word or a very few words in each line.

Acrostics

These are poems where the first letter of each line, read sequentially down the page, spells out a word or phrase. In a double acrostic, the writer has met the challenge of making the first and last letters of each line spell out a word or phrase.

CHOOSING DISTINCTIVELY PATTERNED POEMS FOR DIFFERENT AGE GROUPS

Rhyming poems

Children aged about six years and over are ready to experience the huge treasure store of rhyming poetry, and poetry with a lyrical rhythmic quality, available in single collections and anthologies. In her introduction to *The Puffin Book of Fantastic First Poems*, June Crebbin describes her collection 'as a stepping stone from nursery rhymes to poetry'. It contains poems that I know from experience children enjoy. They laugh out loud at Alfred Noyes' poem 'Daddy Fell into the Pond'. A not very interesting day with grey skies and lots of grumbling is transformed by the sheer hilarity of the event.

Another anthology rich in rhyming poems, which young children like, is John Foster's *My First Oxford Book of Poems* which is nicely divided into sections with titles like 'Out and About', 'Creatures' and 'From Dawn to Dusk'. The 'Creatures' section has such tried and tested delights as Kenneth Grahame's 'Duck's Ditty' and 'The Caterpillar' by Christina Rossetti, which has cadences reminiscent of Shakespeare's spells and songs:

> May no hound spy you
> May the little birds pass by you.

Others in this section of Foster's collection would appeal to the over eights as well as to younger children. Although for practical purposes we have to have some notion of what might appeal to children at a certain age or stage, poems should not be assigned too rigidly to an age group. A poem's memorable images can give it universal appeal: 'The Mouse in the Wainscot' by Ian Serraillier communicates the shyness and lightness of the creature in the line 'Hush, Suzanna, the falling of a feather' and 'A Dragonfly' by Eleanor Farjeon likens the creature's wings to 'spun glass'.

Another series with a good representation of rhyming poems – some with appeal for younger readers and others with enough challenge for the over eights – is Anne Fine's *A Shame to Miss*. In Book 1 we find Emily Dickinson's enigmatic poem 'Morning' and 'Windy Nights' by Robert Louis Stevenson – that poem with such a pull on the imagination that we 'see' the ghostly horseman and, with the poet, ask, 'Why does he gallop and gallop about?' John Betjeman's superficially jolly poem 'Hunter Trials' has some stinging lines and turns up in Book 2. This book has a number of poems that call for several readings to unpick and appreciate and, as Aidan Chambers might say, a sharing of puzzles. In Hilaire Belloc's poem 'Tarantella' which begins 'Do you remember an Inn, Miranda?', we have to work out that 'Miranda' is not a woman but Captain Miranda. And you need to know that a tarantella is a fast dance. Coleridge's 'Kubla Khan' is also full of mysteries. The rhythm and rhyme in all these poems helps create their distinctive character and makes them both memorable and easily memorized.

Haiku, cinquain, kenning and tanka

These short poetic forms are included in many anthologies for children, for example in Paul Cookson's *The Works*, John Foster's *The Poetry Chest* and Brian Patten's *Puffin Book of Utterly Brilliant Poetry*.

For the under eights there are a number of collections of haiku type poems. Keisuke Nishimoto's *Haiku Picturebook for Children*, illustrated by Koso Shimizu and Jack Prelutsky, and Ted Rand's *If Not the Cat* show how these short poems can create the essence of an animal.

Older primary children would be able to appreciate the sophisticated poems in Gerald Bensons' anthology *This Poem Doesn't Rhyme*. There are three witty haiku poems by Eric Finnery, a cinquain by Gerald Benson and another poem by Benson which is a teasing sort of poem, a parody of the rhyming dilemma 'Problems'. There are some sophisticated modern haikus, including 'Scottish Summer Haiku' and 'Hiker' in *The Very Best of Ian McMillan*. The *Puffin Book of Utterly Brilliant Poetry*, compiled by Brian Patten, and *The Poetry Chest*, both edited and written by John Foster, are good sources of these forms.

Shape poems, thin poems and acrostics

Shape poems can, like other poems, communicate deep ideas or strong feelings. John Agard's poem 'I'd Like to Squeeze', fitted into a globe shape, ends with the wish to squeeze the world until 'everyone had an equal share'.

Thin poems can be like lists and younger children find the form familiar and enjoy the simpler ones. 'The A–Z of Bopping Poems' by James Carter (in Jennifer Curry's *Animal Poems*) is a jaunty list of the movements birds make: 'ravens shuffle and twist' and 'vultures waltz'. The over eights would be amused by 'I Want a Sandwich' by Remy Charlie (in Michael Rosen's collection *A World of Poetry*).

Acrostics are often included in general collections of poetry for children. With some exceptions, I have found children begin to appreciate acrostics from about age eight. There are some interesting ones gathered together in a section of John Foster's *The Poetry Treasury Chest*. There is also a good selection in Paul Cookson's *The Works*; his own poem makes a play on words, calling an 'acrostic' 'a cross stick'. Also included here is John Hegley's entertaining acrostic making the words 'My Glasses'.

USING POEMS WITH DISTINCTIVE FORMS

Reading poems

- Poems with rhythm and rhyme come alive when children listen to them read, or read them aloud themselves. Poems lending themselves to 'performance' by children around age six or seven include Alfed Noyes' 'Daddy Fell into the Pond', Kenneth Grahame's 'Duck's Ditty' and Christina Rossetti's 'The Caterpillar'.
- Rhythm and rhyme are an aid to memory and learning poems by heart gives a resource for life.
- By their nature acrostics, shape and thin poems are best appreciated in print or on screen.
- From about age eight children appreciate the elegance of condensed forms like haiku and cinquain.

Writing poems

- Sustaining rhyme and rhythm can be difficult for children. The important thing is to make sure that children appreciate that there is no point in struggling with this just for the sake of it. A good reason for using rhythm and rhyme is that they can add to the mood of the poem.
- I find that while children can often control rhyme and rhythm for a while, they find it hard to sustain it in longer poems. Sometimes a few lines will suffice. Six-year-old Amy attempts to use rhyme in her vibrantly illustrated poem (Figure 17.1).
- Nine-year-old Casey manages to keep rhythm and rhyme going in her poem while communicating her meaning in a lively way (Figure 17.2).
- The more visual kinds of patterned poetry – acrostic and shape poetry for example – lend themselves to inspiring children's own writing.
- I find that some children, perhaps particularly boys, feel secure when they write within the constraints of a form. Ten-year-old Josh wrote a well-sustained acrostic which spelled out 'The Wild Area' (Figure 17.3).
- A list poem that makes a thin column is another way of giving children a form to work within without the restricting restraints of rhythm and rhyme.
- Shape poems can be placed within a shape – a leaf, dog or ship perhaps – to echo the subject or theme. Or the words of the poem could follow the movement of something – a snail's slithery journey across the page or a climb up a hill. There are other ideas for shape poems on the BBC Arts site (www.bbc.co.uk/arts/poetry).
- Older children enjoy trying their hand at haiku and limericks. You can be a bit more permissive of slight deviations and, of course, the range of topics deemed suitable has increased in modern times.
- Children of all ages like collecting their poems in a book, print or electronic, illustrating it and sharing it with other classes. The teacher is likely to be the editor if the children are young, but a small team of older children can often find this task satisfying.

Sing Bird Sing
By Amy

The bird sings
It has a curly tail.
The eggs are brown
And it has a crown
On its head.

Figure 17.1
'Sing, Bird, Sing' by six-year-old Amy

Trees and leaves are all
    around.
Listen to that blue-tit's
    sound!
In the rain or in the snow
A place for everyone to go.

Figure 17.2
'Wild Area' by nine-year-old
Casey

Acrostic

Together the army of ants search for grub
Helping one another to live.
Each one does their job.

Wandering squirrels scamper around.
I love the smell of colourful flowers.
Lots of different shades of brown and green,
Destroyed leaves that have been trampled on.

A lovely texture of bark and wood.
Riots of squirrels trying to find food from the feeders.
Earthworms hide under the rich mud.
A woodland I'd like to visit every day.

Figure 17.3 'The Wild Area' by ten-year-old Josh

SUMMARY

- Poems having 'distinctive forms' range from the rhyming poems that children begin to enjoy after the nursery rhyme stage to shape poems and to firmly patterned forms like haiku and acrostic.
- Poems of all these kinds can be tracked down in large collections for children and in single author volumes.
- When choosing anthologies containing these forms, as indeed in choosing anthologies generally, teachers look for imaginative editing, lively content, appealing design and sympathetic and exciting illustration.
- Relatively short rhythmic, rhyming poems lend themselves to learning by heart and to spoken presentations by small groups or by the whole class.
- When it comes to children's own attempts at writing, shape and thin poems are sympathetic forms for the younger children to experiment with; the challenge of poems where syllable counting is necessary, like haiku and cinquain, is usually best kept for older children.

Chapter 18

Story or narrative poems, classic poems and poems from other cultures and traditions

INTRODUCTION

Story or narrative poems, and ballads too, appeal to the over eights because of their drama, pace and rhythm. Classic poems and poems from other cultures also have a well-deserved place in the primary school collection. Both of these were mentioned in a recent Ofsted report, *Poetry in Schools*, as being underrepresented in the primary English classroom and it is hoped the analysis and suggestions here will be helpful. (Ofsted, 2007). Just as Chapter 16 leant towards the under eights, so this chapter is particularly relevant to those who teach the eights and over. The length and complexity of some story and classic poems make them more appropriate for the older primary classes. However, neither Chapter 16 nor this chapter homes in on one age group exclusively.

FEATURES OF STORY OR NARRATIVE POEMS AND BALLADS

The most ancient kind of story or narrative poem is the ballad of old, which usually tells its tale in short rhyming verses and was sometimes accompanied by music. The strong beat or rhythm keeps up the pace of the tale and helped with memorizing at a time when stories were passed from generation to generation orally. The ballad pattern can take many forms, but traditionally a ballad stanza is a quatrain.

Older ballads which have come down to us tell of heroic deeds and momentous events in a community. Then from the sixteenth century onwards printed poems called 'broadside ballads' about events in the kingdom and local area circulated and became popular in England. The 'popular culture' themes of the broadside ballads coexisted with the heroic stories of the old ballads and the folk songs passed down orally in rural communities. The roots of modern narrative poems – by Michael Rosen and Charles Causley, for example – lie here.

Another kind of ballad has survived well – the 'literary' ballad, which is a narrative poem written by a well-regarded poet. These poems, associated with the Romantic period, include Coleridge's 'The Ancient Mariner', Scott's 'Proud Maisie' and Keats' haunting 'La Belle Dame Sans Merci'. We find some of the pattern of the old ballads here and recognize some of their energy.

More recent ballads often use language to amuse, intrigue and chasten us. Effective, sometimes emotional, dialogue is often as big a feature of modern story poems as it was of the old ballads. Like the old ballads too, modern story poems lend themselves to learning by heart and performance and so their features of pace and conversation reflect this.

CHOOSING STORY POEMS

Rhyming stories for pre-school children and under eights are discussed in Chapter 16. Children's preferences do not always follow an expected path and some flexibility should be shown, leaving young readers to select what they like. But very generally I am looking here at poems often appreciated by children aged eight years or older, poems including classic ballads, 'literary' ballads and less structured, more modern narrative poems. *The Oxford Book of Story Poems*, compiled by Michael Harrison and Christopher Stuart-Clark, is a treasure chest of narrative poems of all kinds – some sad, some lively and some mysterious. There are sixty poems, including high ballads like 'Sir Patrick Spens', literary narrative poems like 'La Belle Dame Sans Merci' and more recently written story poems like Michael Rosen's 'Here is the News' and Alan Bold's 'The Malfeasance'. Bold's is a rather moving poem about how a beast responded not to aggression on the part of fearful people, but to kind consideration. Imaginative illustrators of the poems in this collection include Charles Keeping, Tudor Humphries and Valerie McBride. It is well worth having several copies of this excellent resource in the classroom and to have one on display for children to browse through. Another anthology which includes some modern story poems is Paul Cookson's *The Works*. This does not have the aesthetic qualities of *The Oxford Book of Story Poems* but it is good value, with a very useful collection of all kinds of poetry. The narrative poems include Michael Rosen's 'Me and My Brother', with its hilarious dialogue which reveals so much about the relationship between parents and children. Michael Rosen's special contribution is to show children that they can use story poems to explore the happiness, puzzles and sadness of their everyday lives. Another story poem in the list, Vernon Scannell's 'The Apple-Raid', always moves me with its tale of daring apple scrumping and the final revelation that one of the gang now lies cold, buried 'in an orchard in France beneath apple trees'. The story in this poem could help older primary children, exposed as they may be today to violence and death in the media and in their computer games, to reflect on the death of someone who had seemed so alive. Two of the poems in the list, 'What Has Happened to Lulu?' and 'Lucy Gray; or, Solitude', tell tales of lost girls, but they are enigmatic and leave what happened uncertain. I find both haunting.

There are some less usual poems for older primary and younger secondary children in Michael Rosen's anthology *A World of Poetry*; those in the ballad section include 'Dick Turpin and the Lawyer' and some of Bob Dylan's ballads.

USING STORY POEMS

Keeping poetry lessons active and collaborative

- Reading story poems aloud gets a lesson off to a dynamic start. In poems with a lot of dialogue the teacher might read the narrative, while children, with some warning and preparation, take the individual parts.

197

(All are reproduced in *The Oxford Book of Story Poems* by Michael Harrison and Christopher Stuart-Clark (eds) except where credited elsewhere.)

- 'The Listeners' by Walter de la Mare

- 'The Highwayman' by Alfred Noyes

- 'The Pied Piper of Hamelin' by Robert Browning

- 'Sir Patrick Spens' by Anon.

- 'What Has Happened to Lulu?' by Charles Causley

- 'The Lady of Shalott' by Alfred Lord Tennyson

- 'The Malfeasance' by Alan Bold

- 'Kubla Khan' by Samuel Taylor Coleridge
  (*A Shame to Miss, 2*, Anne Fine, ed.)

- 'Lucy Gray; or, Solitude' by William Wordsworth
  (*A Shame to Miss, 2*, Anne Fine, ed.)

- 'Me and My Brother' by Michael Rosen
  (*The Works*, Paul Cookson, ed.)

- 'The Apple-Raid' by Vernon Scannell
  (*The Works*, Paul Cookson, ed.)

Figure 18.1 *Story poems and ballads*

- Later, children who have been immersed in a story poem can give a choral performance, perhaps with costume, music and some props.
- These activities are often interspersed with discussion, about what children particularly like and what intrigues and puzzles them. The interactive whiteboard makes such joint attention to the text of the poem to share thoughts and ideas much easier.
- Children become involved in talking about poems with a mystery like Wordsworth's 'Lucy Gray' and Charles Causley's 'What Has Happened to Lulu?'. This could lead to dramatic exploration of the different possible courses of events.
- Illustrators of story poems and ballads bring their own particular imaginative insight and personal style to their task. Talking about the merits of a pictorial interpretation and sharing opinions and observations about it can help children reach deeper into the poem's meanings.
- Children might compare the illustrators of Robert Browning's 'Pied Piper of Hamelin', which include Kate Greenaway, who showed a piper surrounded by children in pinafores and breeches (Everyman); Sylvia Mears, who painted an elegant piper in a red and yellow checked coat (Quercus); and Andre Amstatz, whose picturebook piper is shown in vibrant hues (Orchard).

The teacher's role: into writing

- The structures of rhyme and rhythm make writing a ballad a challenge for children.
- Children may find the task less forbidding if they have a response partner and more fun if they work collaboratively in a group around a screen or flipchart.
- Teachers' constructive comments and suggestions at the drafting stage will encourage children to persevere.

CASE STUDY 18.1 A STORY POEM IS USED IN THE CONTEXT OF RICH WORK ACROSS THE CURRICULUM: 'MARKET SQUARE' BY A.A. MILNE

A teacher of a Year 2 class provided the children with a classroom pet: a small rabbit. Their observations of the creature fed into the science programme on living things and enriched art and English lessons. At one point the teacher read aloud A.A. Milne's 'Market Square', about a child searching the market for a pet. She commented: 'The poem seemed to tap into some children's longing for a pet of their own and discussion was deep and detailed about this. And it led to improvised drama and their own writing.' This glimpse into a classroom shows how one learning opportunity can flow into another, taking children from the scientific to the affective.

CASE STUDY 18.2 YEAR 4 AND YEAR 5 CLASSES EXPLORE 'WHAT HAS HAPPENED TO LULU?' BY CHARLES CAUSLEY: A CLPE PROJECT

'What has happened to Lulu, mother?' It is the repetition of questions that give the poem its anxious tone. The poet indicates the events leading up to the girl's disappearance: in the night voices were heard and the sound of a car engine. Children in several Year 4 and Year 5 classes discussed what might have been written in the note found and the nature of the relationship between the characters. In their analysis, the CLPE team and the teachers were interested to find that the children used what they knew from television about people disappearing to interpret the poem. Theories about kidnapping, adoption, drug abuse and cruel step-parents came up. The more 'taboo' topics seemed to be the ones the boys, in particular, found fascinating and motivating.

Improvisation, talk and writing and ICT were used in innovative and exciting ways. There was available interactive software with a printable writing prompt and an email address for the children to write to Lulu. Even normally reluctant readers responded enthusiastically to the poem and the activities convincing the teachers and research team that boys are capable of appreciating poems that call for some emotional insight; one boy commented that he liked the poem and the work because it was 'like real life'.

(*Boys on the Margin: Promoting Boy's Literacy Learning at Key Stage 2* by Kimberley Safford, Olivia O'Sullivan and Myra Barrs, pp. 40–50)

- The free verse form of many modern story or narrative poems might be a more sympathetic form.
- Teachers can help children use modern media like texting and email to explore themes.
- Some children might like to illustrate the ballads or story poems they have written themselves or to illustrate the work of others. They will need to focus on the words and mood of the poem to extract its meaning so that their illustrations will complement or enhance the written text.

FEATURES OF CLASSIC POEMS

A 'classic' poem is one whose qualities have been recognized and appreciated over more than one generation. In other words, it has stood the test of time and this means that it is likely to contain some universal truths about human experience that young readers can connect with. Some poems written relatively recently promise this universality and also have the vitality, originality and appropriateness of language and imagery that are the mark of classic poems. These poems are prime candidates for classic status in the future. Classic poems, reflecting the time when they were written, tend to be systematic and conventional in their use of rhythm and rhyme and, to some extent, in their themes. But they have lasted because they use language in a way that perfectly describes a scene or feeling so that the rest of us who do not claim to be poets recognize and resavour common human experiences. It is also the ability of these poems to excite and surprise that appeals. The complexity and subtlety of the ideas and feelings expressed may make several readings necessary. And teachers can help by giving the poem's context and explaining any vocabulary that has fallen out of use.

Children deserve to be introduced to classic poems because of their inherent worth and because they are part of their heritage. It is likely, too, that during their education they will encounter texts that make reference to these classic poems.

CHOOSING CLASSIC POEMS

If asked to choose classic poems for primary aged children, informed people would tend to come up with a remarkably similar core list. So I do not claim any special originality in my choices in Figure 18.2. The first poems in the list are likely to be enjoyed by younger as well as older children. Those that follow lean towards the later primary and early secondary years in theme and language. Favourite themes include animals and the natural world, adventure and the world of magic and make believe.

Poems about nature in my list include Frost's 'Stopping by Woods on a Snowy Evening'. The lines: 'the woods are lovely, dark and deep, But I have promises to keep . . .' have stayed with me over many years. Adventure poems are often story poems as well as having classic status, see previous section. Coleridge's 'Kubla Khan' draws young readers in with its mesmerizing rhythm and wonderful images. Experience suggests that we cannot always predict what children will like. 'Ozymandias' may seem a poem likely to appeal to secondary school children. However, it was used most successfully with a Year 4 class in the north of England along with some other poems as preparation for a visit to the Angel of the North, a visit which led to children's own writing (Mallett, 2007).

- 'Chanticleer' by Anon.
  (*My First Oxford Book of Animal Poems*, J. Foster, ed.)

- 'Choosing a Name' by Charles and Mary Lamb
  (*A Shame to Miss, 1*, Anne Fine, ed.)

- 'Stopping by Woods on a Snowy Evening' by Robert Frost
  (*The Poetry of Robert Frost*, E.C. Lathem, ed.)

- 'Cargoes' by John Masefield
  (*A Shame to Miss, 1*, Anne Fine, ed.)

- 'A Smuggler's Song' by Rudyard Kipling
  (*The Works of Rudyard Kipling*, Wordsworth Poetry Library)

- 'Tartary' by Walter de la Mare
  (*A Shame to Miss, 2*, Anne Fine, ed.)

- 'The Way through the Woods' by Rudyard Kipling
  (*The Oxford Book of Twentieth-Century Verse*, Philip Larkin, ed.)

- 'Meg Merrilies' by John Keats
  (*One Hundred Best Poems for Children*, Roger McGough, ed.)

- 'Upon Westminster Bridge' by William Wordsworth
  (*Poems about Earth*, Andrew Fusek Peters, ed.)

- 'Ariel's Song', *The Tempest*, Act 1, Scene ii by William Shakespeare
  (*William Shakespeare: The Complete Works*, Stanley Wells, ed.)

- 'Ozymandias' by Percy Bysshe Shelley
  (*A Shame to Miss, 3*, Anne Fine, ed.)

Figure 18.2 *Classic poems*

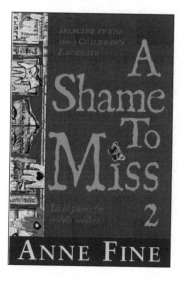

Figure 18.3
Front cover of A Shame to Miss, 2 *by Anne Fine (ed.)*

Borders and decorations by Vanessa Card. Reproduced with the permission of the publishers The Random House Group Ltd. Copyright 2003

USING CLASSIC POEMS

Active learning

- Hearing poems read aloud by poets helps bring out the nuances of meaning in classic poems. The audio CD version of Brian Moses' *Poems Out Loud* includes some readings of classic poems, for example Blake's 'The Tyger' read by John Agard and with atmospheric background music.
- Children can be helped to get more out of a poem by talking about the story, language and imagery. Several readings and much discussion may be needed for children to create the meanings in the poem for themselves.
- The literary devices used by the poet are not the place to start. Easing into the poem by thinking of your own experiences that seem to link with the poet's is a more sympathetic way in. On reading 'The Listeners' sharing anecdotes about times when you have come across a mystery might be fruitful.
- A classic poem can be rinsed with new energy if children work towards a choral reading. Thinking about what the different characters are like has new point and interest if the poem is to be presented to an audience.

The teacher's role

- Children sometimes need some help with contextualizing classic poems, for example some input on the sort of names families chose when Charles and Mary Lamb wrote their poem 'Choosing a Name'.
- 'Ozymandias' calls out for some explanation about the kind of ruler the king was and how wealth and power are empty of meaning if kindness and justice have been absent. These are excellent discussion points.

CASE STUDY 18.3 WHAT IS A BONG TREE? MICHAEL ROSEN'S INAUGURAL LECTURE AS CHILDREN'S LAUREATE, 2007–9

The audience at Michael Rosen's inaugural lecture was asked to experience two approaches to 'The Listeners' with Rosen as 'teacher'. First he read the poem and asked some questions – on the lines of 'Who do you think the listeners are?', 'What sort of poem do you think this is?' and so on. Verdict? Dull, dull, dull!

So he started on a second approach, reading the poem to us again, and this time he suggested we take a response partner, the person next to us, and each tell the other what we responded most to in the poem. Did it connect with some real life experiences of our own? Soon everyone was chatting animatedly – about times where they had come upon the unexpected, times when they had been disturbed or even frightened by something. This was a much more dynamic, interactive approach than the first and one which could be adapted for any age group.

Visit Rosen's website and look at the video-clips, which offer copious ideas for helping children respond to and write their own poetry (www.childrenslaureate.org.uk).

- Children are often fascinated to learn why Coleridge managed only to write a third of the poem 'Kubla Khan' as he was interrupted by 'the person from Porlock'.
- The teacher can help with all these things, not least by showing what a mature reader of poetry does – the questions they ask, their willingness to consider the ideas of others and their tolerance of puzzles.

CHOOSING POEMS FROM OTHER CULTURES AND TRADITIONS

Children deserve to be introduced to the best poetry from across the globe. One limitation on our ability to select freely is that not a great deal of children's poetry from other countries has been translated into English. Creative and sensitive translators who can capture the nuances and subtle meanings in each language are needed. Poets from other countries have particular kinds of knowledge and experience to share. For example, their poems can bring alive the history, landscapes and customs of the places where they grew up. Such poems have a place in lessons across the curriculum as well as in English.

Poets who have spent their childhood in one culture and their later years in another are in a good position to make comparisons between different experiences of childhood and growing up. They can show us some of the differences, but also the universality of some human experiences and feelings.

Where does the teacher turn to find the best poems from other cultures? There are some single poet volumes but large anthologies are also a source of these poems likely to appeal to children in the primary years.

The work of poets whose roots are in the Caribbean islands is well established in poetry collections in the UK and brings alive the vibrant environments and experiences of their childhoods. The rhythmic poems by Valerie Bloom and the energetic, colourful illustrations by David Axtell in *Fruits* would appeal to the nursery and pre-school age group. This is a counting book which also introduces the names of some Jamaican fruits.

Older primary children would enjoy the variety of poems in *A Caribbean Dozen* edited by John Agard and Grace Nichols. In the introduction to the collection, the editors comment that the poets now live in Britain, Canada and the USA but 'their formative meeting with the magic of the word happened under tropical skies where fireflies were shooting stars and English nursery rhymes and fairy tales mingle with the tricky doings of Anancy spiderman and ghost stories about duppies and jumbies with turned back feet'.

A number of these poems speak eloquently of a sunny climate – Marc Matthews' 'Boat' and Grace Nichols' 'For Forest', for example. But Dionne Brand's 'Hurricane' reminds us that the weather can turn enemy and, like the other poems creating the Caribbean environment so powerfully, this one could inform a geography lesson. What better way to learn about the sheer terror of the great wind on the mountain than this poem?

Benjamin Zephaniah is a major 'voice' whose work appears in many collections – Paul Cookson's *The Works*, Michael Rosen's *The World of Poetry* and Debjani Chatterjee and Bashabi Frazer's *Rainbow World* for example. His single authored anthologies, which include *Talking Turkeys* and *Funky Chicken*, contain lively 'street poetry' and exuberant and humorous poems often about animals. But he uses some of his poems to reflect deeply on social problems and green issues. Older primary children will find depth and challenge in his poem 'For Words' in *Funky Chicken*. It is about the power, variety and richness of human language. Different sizes and orientations of print help communicate his message and give the poem visual appeal. Words can, he tells us, 'explain', 'burn like fire' and can 'set me free'.

There have been a number of good translators of Japanese poetry and, for a comparatively long time, children have found in a number of poetry collections examples of haiku and tanka (see Chapter 17).

There are still relatively few collections for children which include the work of poets whose roots are in India and South East Asia. One poet, born in India, whose first language is Bengali but who also enjoys writing poems in English is Debjani Chatterjee. Her themes have a truly global perspective and resonance as she has lived in Japan, Bangladesh, Hong Kong and Egypt as well as the UK at different times in her life. Teachers of young children are likely to know her delightful poem 'My Sari' in which she says her fine orange coloured garment 'wraps round her like sunshine'. You will find this poem in Paul Cookson's collection *Unzip Your Lips: 100 Poems to Read Aloud* or in Anne Fine's *A Shame to Miss, 1*.

Chatterjee is the compiler, with Bashabi Frazer, of *Rainbow World: Poems from Many Cultures*, showing her commitment to ensuring that children have the opportunity to read and enjoy poetry from as many different pens and places as possible. The sections include poems on families, animals, food, festivals and school; by including the work of Valerie Bloom, Tao Lang Pee, Benjamin Zephaniah and Bashabi Frazer as well as some of her own poems she goes far beyond western traditions.

Probably it is the older primary school readers who will appreciate 'Hungry Ghost', Chatterjee's poem about going shopping in an Indian market with her father.

Thinking still of older primary aged children, they would find the poems in Michael Rosen's *A World of Poetry* interesting, challenging and not easy to find elsewhere. 'Clowns' by Miroslav Holub is written as a series of questions by a child to his mother, ending with the devastating last question:

> What do clowns do when nobody,
> Just nobody laughs
> Any more
> Mummy?

I came across this poem for the first time while I was reflecting on what to recommend in this section and the lines have often returned to me. I think it is one of many poems that show the best poetry transcends time, space and culture and speaks directly to human feeling.

BOX 18.1 'HUNGRY GHOST' BY DEBJANI CHATTERJEE

This poem moves between past and present and deals with change. Since she went to the same market as a child with her grandfather 'the market is bigger. I have grown too'. Just a few telling images evoke the atmosphere: 'smelling the spicy scents' and hearing 'the shouts'. This poem is in her collection entitled *Albino Gecko*.

- 'Fruits' by Valerie Bloom
  (*Fruits* by Valerie Bloom, David Axtell, illus.)

- 'I Like to Stay Up' by Grace Nichols
  (*Come into My Tropical Garden*, Grace Nichols, ed.)

- 'Clowns' by Miroslav Holub
  (*A World of Poetry*, Michael Rosen, ed.)

- 'My Sari' by Debjani Chatterjee
  (*Unzip Your Lips: 100 Poems to Say Aloud*, Paul Cookson, ed.)

- 'The Spider' by James Berry
  (*A Caribbean Dozen*, John Agard and Grace Nichols, eds)

- 'Hurricane' by Dionne Brand
  (*A Caribbean Dozen*, John Agard and Grace Nichols, eds)

- 'Cinquains' by Gus Grenfell
  (*The Works*, Paul Cookson, ed.)

- 'Chicken Dinner' by Valerie Bloom
  (*A Caribbean Dozen*, John Agard and Grace Nichols, eds)

- 'Paper Boats' by Rabindranath Tagore
  (*Black Poetry*, Grace Nichols, ed.)

- 'Sea Timeless Song' by Grace Nichols
  (*A Shame to Miss, 1*, Anne Fine, ed.)

- 'For Word' by Benjamin Zephaniah
  (*Funky Chicken*, Benjamin Zephaniah)

Figure 18.4 *Poems from different cultures*

USING POEMS FROM OTHER CULTURES AND TRADITIONS

The suggestions in Figure 18.4 are just a few examples out of a potential treasure store, but even this short list indicates how rich and varied poems from other cultural traditions are. These poems deserve to be read, shared and discussed like any other quality poem. Sometimes they are a fruitful starting point for children's own poetry writing. Here are some further suggestions:

- Reading some of these poems, including those that describe an historical event, brings an interesting perspective to lessons across the curriculum.
- Poems which powerfully create the physical world would find a place in geography as well as English. Dionne Brand's 'Hurricane', for example, gives children a sense of the drama of a destructive wind and its impact on human beings.

- Some of the poems in the list above might inspire children's painting and drawing – Valerie Bloom's 'Fruits' and Debjani Chatterjee's 'My Sari', for example.
- The energetic rhyme and rhythm of many of the poems mentioned makes them good to read aloud. The audio CD version of Brian Moses selection *Poems Out Loud* has forty poems read by poets, including those from different cultures and traditions: John Agard, Valerie Bloom and Debjani Chatterjee. Hearing the work of these poets is likely to enrich children's own reading of poems and would give ideas for sound effects and music.
- But some of the poems also have a visual impact and need to be seen on the page or screen. 'Hurricane', 'Sea Timeless Sea' and 'For Word' come into this category.

SUMMARY

- Story, or narrative poetry, includes the classic ballads of old, 'literary' ballads of the Romantic period, broadsheet ballads and more modern narrative poetry.
- What all these have in common is that they tell a tale, using devices of form and language to do so in an inviting and memorable (and memorizable) manner.
- One collection stands out as a magnificent resource for any primary school classroom: *The Oxford Book of Story Poems* edited by Michael Harrison and Christopher Stuart-Clark.
- Because their roots are in an oral tradition, story poems lend themselves to being memorized and read aloud to a class or the school in assembly.
- Classic poems are those that have stood the test of time and have been enjoyed by more than one generation. They have appeal to universal human concerns and are written in memorable language. Their lyrical qualities make them enjoyable to learn by heart and to read aloud, perhaps in dramatized choral speech.
- Poems by poets from different cultures and traditions remind children that although there are different environments, customs and situations in different parts of the world, some themes have universal interest and concern. Those that describe a particular, historical event, climate or environmental feature may be helpful in lessons across the curriculum.

Chapter 19

Poems with freer, less traditional forms and patterns

Free verse, conversation poems, blank verse and rap

INTRODUCTION

Freer poetic forms have helped breathe new life into reading and writing poetry in the classroom. Modern poets choosing this approach are released from unforgiving patterns of rhythm and rhyme and there is much potential to create meaning, mood and atmosphere. The conversational cadences of some of this poetry appeal to children of all ages and help them to understand that poetry can be about everyday incidents, preoccupations and ideas. This, together with a freer form, opens up opportunities for children as writers of poetry, and encourages them to find their own 'voice' to express meaning and feeling about their own lives and experiences.

FEATURES OF POEMS WITH FREER FORMS AND PATTERNS

How might we explain to children that poems that do not conform to traditional and familiar rhythm and rhyming patterns of verse nevertheless qualify as poetry rather than prose? A child on first encountering free verse might wonder whether it is simply a piece of prose, sliced up into lines to arrange on the page. Having this conversation allows us to talk about all the things a poet can do to engage the listener or reader's attention. You could start with something visual. Some freer poems are imaginatively patterned on the page, making interesting use of space and of print size, font type and orientation. The layout of Kit Wright's poem 'The Frozen Man' gives a visual impression of the stranger's journey from the frozen countryside to the warmth of a dwelling. Unrhymed poems can still use poetic devices like imagery, alliteration, repetition and condensed language. The careful use of word and phrase is a distinguishing mark of poetry: just the right lyrical language can capture a scene or feeling. Anne Wilkinson's free-verse poem 'Once Upon a Great Holiday', in John Foster's anthology *Let's Celebrate*, has some attractive alliterative phases – 'swarms of stars' for example. This tells us how thickly starred the sky is, with its reminder of how insects can crowd a space. The lyrical line 'my father whistled and my mother sang' speaks of the family harmony which is an important part of the poet's memory of this particular holiday. The condensation that is so much a feature of poetry is well achieved here, giving us in one line an impression of the emotional climate of the remembered holiday.

'Conversation' poems, as the name suggests, are structured around a dialogue, which gives them an everyday flavour. Harold Monroe's 'Overheard on a Saltmarsh', a duologue between

207

a goblin eager to have some green glass beads and a water nymph who does not want to give them up, has the kind of drama and pace children like.

Blank verse has a rhythmic pattern of ten syllables in each line, five of them being stressed, but it is not usually constrained by rhyme. Older children can see an example of this – an extract from Alfred Lord Tennyson's 'The Passing of Arthur' – in Gerald Benson's anthology *This Poem Doesn't Rhyme*.

Rap is thought of as a form of poetry or song that is freer and more conversational than traditional forms. However, some raps have a rhyming pattern and all have to conform to the discipline of a strong rhythm. There is a lively and useful selection of raps in Paul Cookson's anthology *The Works*.

CHOOSING POEMS WITH FREER FORMS AND PATTERNS

Pre-school and nursery, 3–5-year-olds

Anthologies and collections for this age tend to favour nursery rhymes and short poems with traditional rhymes. But there are interesting free verse poems for young children to enjoy if you look for them. Jennifer Curry's *Animal Poems* is a good hunting ground. 'Have You Ever Seen?' by K. Lampard describes a bat, a cat, a spider, a pheasant and a deer, using compound words to bring each creature 'alive'; a fox is 'bushy-tailed, sly-thinking' and 'ever hungry'. Other unrhyming poems in this collection include 'Bats Are Beautiful', a very short poem by Patricia Leighton, and Brian Moses' poem 'A Protest about Cabbage', about some militant guinea pigs who want grass and not cabbage: 'Grass to a guinea pig is Angel Delight, strawberries and cream . . .' There is also a remarkable poem by five-year-old Vorakit Boonchareon, 'The Tiger', who is angry on the animal's behalf – they put traps to kill him and 'take his coat for rich ladies to wear'.

Large anthologies such as John Foster's *My First Oxford Book of Poems* usually have some poems with a freer form that would appeal to the very young. In this collection, 'The Sea', a short non-rhyming poem by Lilith Norman, is full of colour and texture, with phrases like 'deep glass-green sea'. It ends with a lovely image of 'little waves nibbling at sand'.

5–8-year-olds

'List' poems appeal to this age range (and younger) because they can provide a structure without imposing a rhyming pattern. *The Very Best of Ian McMillan* includes two favourite list poems. 'Ten Things Found in a Wizard's Pocket' begins every line but one with 'A' and includes 'A bucket full of stars and planets' and 'A bag of mints you could suck for ever'. The other, 'Ten Things Found in a Shipwrecked Sailor's Pocket', selects 'a gold coin' and 'a letter from a mermaid'.

Conversation poems echoing the rhythm of the human voice also offer a sympathetic form. Harold Monroe's 'Overheard on a Saltmarsh', a haunting conversation poem, has already been mentioned. There are some more recent witty conversation poems. Michael Rosen's collection *The Hypnotiser* includes 'The Car Trip', in which children nag their mother, as children do, while she is trying to drive. The poem builds momentum as the children ask for crisps, drinks and so on until the exasperated mother threatens to stop the car because their moaning and shouting are spoiling her concentration. The pattern of the print on the page and the occasional large font for emphasis help convey the feelings of frustration on both sides. Not only does Rosen show that rhyme is not needed to give a poem a pattern, he also shows that everyday but deeply significant things can be the subjects of poems: parent–child relationships, quarrels with friends, feelings about school life and all the hope and fears involved.

Others who produce good work on these lines include Allan Ahlberg, Kit Wright, Roger McGough, Brian Patten and Wes Magee. In 'At the End of a School Day' (reproduced in Paul Cookson's *The Works*) Wes Magee begins the poem with children shouting and running as they leave school at the end of the day. Then, suddenly, they come across a small hedgehog on the tarmac. Here, where the creature is likened to 'an old frayed cricket ball', the mood of the poem changes from exuberance to concern for a small creature. Berlie Doherty's short unrhyming poem 'Grandpa' is also full of memorable imagery. Grandpa's hands are 'rough as garden sacks' and the skin around his eyes is 'crushed paper wrapping up their secrets'. 'Little Bird', by Charlotte Zolotow, provides in just six short unrhyming lines the essence of a little hurt bird's fear – 'your heart beats like the pound of the sea' – when held in a human hand. This poem, which you can track down in *The Puffin Book of Fantastic First Verse*, edited by June Crebbin, is a small masterpiece of condensation and is all the more powerful because the poet addresses the bird directly.

BOX 19.1 'MY NEIGHBOURS' RABBIT' BY BRIAN PATTEN

Neighbours have gone away leaving their pet rabbit to fend for itself, providing only some dry food and water. Appalled by their callousness the poet comments: 'What they haven't left behind is love.' In the poem the heart is the symbol for caring and imagining. When he gives it some food and some kindness, the creature that has been shivering with cold comes alive like 'a furry volcano'. This is a poem in which young readers would find depths of meaning and therefore one they would want to return to.

8–11-year-olds

Entertaining poems are still liked by this age group. 'I'm Just Going Out for a Moment' is a delightful conversation poem in Michael Rosen's *Wouldn't You Like To Know* in which every other line begins with 'Why'. We have all had conversations like this when we have had to think of more and more ingenious reasons for doing what we simply feel like doing. Gerald Benson's substantial collection, entitled *This Poem Doesn't Rhyme*, also has some intriguing, teasing poems. Here we have poetry from different historical periods and different countries, including some not often encountered elsewhere. All, in Benson's words, 'flout the rules'. 'Freer' poetry can take up serious themes too. An anthologist who includes unusual, sometimes reflective poems in her collections is Anne Fine. She calls Neil Curry's unrhyming poem 'The Doll's House' 'sinister'. It is a first-person poem in which a doll invites the reader to 'open the doors' of the doll's house and look at all the rooms and their unsettling contents. It ends with the disturbing discovery that the doll has been stitched into her chair.

Release from traditional rhyme and rhythm sometimes undams a flood of powerful imagery. Berlie Doherty's line 'I think I can hear the stars being switched on' in her poem about settling to sleep, 'Night Sounds', is one of those images that stays in the memory. (This poem is reproduced in June Crebbin's *The Puffin Book of Fantastic First Poems*.) In 'Famous', a poem in her anthology *The Oldest Girl in the World*, Carol Ann Duffy creates visual images of the world of the rich and famous. We learn of such things as the 'pale pink eggs' they feast on for breakfast, the 'gold and silver clothes' they wear and the caviar they devour, which is 'scooped out with silver spoons' by menservants. 'Floating on a Plate' by Frank

- 'Little Bird' by Charlotte Zolotow
  (*The Puffin Book of Fantastic First Poems*, June Crebbin, ed.)

- 'Boys' by Allan Ahlberg
  (*Heard It in the Playground*, Puffin)

- 'Slow Reader' by Allan Ahlberg
  (*Please Mrs Butler*, Puffin)

- 'Sea Timeless Song' by Grace Nichols
  (*A Shame to Miss, 1*, Corgi)

- 'The Day of the Gulls' by Jennifer Curry
  (*Animal Poems*, Scholastic)

- 'My Neighbours' Rabbit' by Brian Patten
  (*Juggling with Gerbils*, Puffin)

- 'Floating on a Plate' by Frank Flynn
  (*The Hutchinson Treasury of Children's Poetry*, Alison Sage, ed.)

- 'I'm the Youngest in Our House' by Michael Rosen
  (*Wouldn't You Like to Know*, Puffin)

- 'A Small Dragon' by Brian Patten
  (*The Orchard Book of Poems*, Adrian Mitchell, ed.)

- 'The Famous' by Carol Ann Duffy
  (*The Oldest Girl in the World*, Faber & Faber)

- 'The Frozen Man' by Kit Wright
  (*A Year Full of Poems*, Michael Harrison and Christopher Stuart-Clark, eds)

- 'Hunger' by Laurence Binyon
  (*Wicked Poems*, Roger McGough and Neal Layton, eds)

- 'What a Poem's Not' by John Hegley
  (www.bbc.co.uk/arts/poetry/)

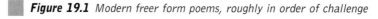 ***Figure 19.1*** *Modern freer form poems, roughly in order of challenge*

Flynn (selected by A. Sage for *The Hutchinson Treasury of Children's Poetry*) shows that free, unrhyming verse can be imaginatively rich. This poet finds inspiration even in the mundane task of washing up – the plates float 'across a Sargasso sea of spaghetti strands'. Another very different poem which affects us because of the power of the images it evokes is Robert Binyon's 'Hunger', written in 1921 and available in Roger McGough's anthology *Wicked Poems*. This is a dark poem in which the use of the first-person voice – the poem is written as if Hunger itself is talking – somehow makes the nature of hunger more appalling. It is its insidious nature and its slow but deadly acceleration that are apparent in images likening hunger to 'a silent tide' and 'a deepening frost'.

In Figure 19.2 I reproduce John Hegley's poem 'What a Poem's Not' and the image, one of a changing series, provided by RCA Animation students. By making this a still, I make what should be dynamic static, but the reproduction below gives some indication of how visual and oral poetry might work.

WHAT A POEM'S NOT
A poem is not an <u>Ant</u>
but it can be quite short.
A poem is not a <u>Banana</u>
but there may be something under its skin.
A poem is not a <u>Coat</u>
but it may have some warmth in it.
A poem is not a <u>Dog</u>
but it might be quite a friend.
A poem is not an <u>Endless</u> pair of trousers
but it can be quite long.
A poem is not a <u>Football</u> shaped like a cucumber.
A poem is not a <u>Great</u> number of things.
A poem is not a <u>Hedgehog</u>
but it might be hard to get hold of.
A poem is not an <u>Igloo</u>
but it can feel like home.
A poem is not a <u>Jumble</u> sale,
but it might contain some rubbish.
A poem is not a <u>Kite</u>
but it might enjoy the wind.
A poem is not a <u>Lightbulb</u>
but you can change it if you want to.
A poem is not a <u>Monkey</u>
but can be quite human.

Figure 19.2
'What a Poem's Not'
by John Hegley
Reproduced with the permission of John Hegley for the poem, and by Lewis Campbell and Tim Web of the Royal College of Art for the picture. More poems to watch and hear on John Hegley's website (www.johnhegley.co.uk)

USING POEMS WITH FREER FORMS AND PATTERNS

Reading freer forms of poetry: an active and collaborative approach

- Young children enjoy listening to freer forms on themes they connect with, particularly those with a pattern, for example beginning with the same line or having a lot of assonance or alliteration.
- Some images stay in the memory long after we have heard or read or listened to them. As with other kinds of poetry, young children are able to share 'enthusiasms', which often include these images, and also to discuss 'puzzles' in class and group discussion.
- Five- to eight-year-olds can enjoy longer 'free' poems, including 'conversation' poems which, like Monroe's 'Overheard on a Saltmarsh', lend themselves to lively duologues and drama.

CASE STUDY 19.1 A WHOLE-SCHOOL POETRY PROJECT

Teachers and governors worked together to encourage children's poetry writing.

It so happened that an exciting wild area had recently been created in the school grounds where children could observe nature and draw, paint and write. So this was the chosen topic for the children's poems.

A selection of the poems was read out by the children, who had the opportunity to practice, at an assembly and the other children were able to comment. The children greatly enjoyed hearing each other's work. It is, of course, quite a different experience to hear poems read aloud rather than to read them from a written display. Children chose many different forms for their poems; ten-year-old Casey wrote a long, reflective poem in free verse. When she read her work aloud children of different ages remarked on one particular image:

In the middle of the spongy path
Is a solitary bluebell helpless and confused.

Comments were: 'Some flowers grow in the wrong place'; 'I like the way she says the bluebell was "helpless and confused"'; 'someone might stand on it – it's in the wrong place . . . might not see it till too late'.

- The over eights are able to read and discuss more sophisticated poems, including teasing poems like Gerald Benson's 'Problems', which makes an amusing comment about the challenge of rhyming lines (see Benson's anthology *This Poem Doesn't Rhyme*).
- Some free verse poems help develop older children's ability to 'infer', to glean things that are not spelt out. Poems in this category include Brian Patten's 'A Small Dragon' (in Adrian Mitchell's collection *The Orchard Book of Poems*).
- Freer kinds of poetry have a place in poetry readings and dramatic presentations by all age groups and can also lead to making an audio tape or DVD.
- Part of the slow resavouring of a poem can sometimes come from learning by heart.

The teacher's role: encouraging children's writing

Finding a theme

- Teachers of nursery-aged children through to Year 1 find that 'colours' or 'the senses' – themes which link with everyday experience – are good starting points for children's 'free' poetry writing. Using a whiteboard or flipchart, teacher and children can create a shared poem on one of these themes. (Some of the poems in *The Very Best of Wes Magee* – 'What Is the Sun', for example – seem to awaken children's imaginations.)
- Contemporary poets give workshops in school which encourage children to view their everyday encounters and conversations as a rich source of material for their poems. Children often jot down what people actually say or do and then share these lists – perhaps with response partners.

Figure 19.3
'Sun Rising' by Charlie

Sun rising, fly buzzing
Eggs hatching, people hiding
Birds flying, squirrel climbing
Grass growing, spider webbing
Beetles cutting, ants crawling
Moon blinking.

NB Charlie was helped with achieving consistency in the punctuation of his poem at the drafting stage.

- Like mature poets, children need to choose a form for their poems as well as a theme.
- Seven-year-old Charlie has produced a poem with rhythm but not rhyme (Figure 19.3); it is full of life and energy, with images made dynamic by the use of the continuous present throughout. The poem has a pleasing symmetry beginning with 'sun rising' and ending with 'moon blinking'. When Charlie read his poem aloud to the class, another child commented on the 'good beginning and ending'. Several children liked the use of the word 'webbing', commenting that it was 'original'.

Other starting points

- Poems by others that can be a starting point for children's writing include: 'Ten Things Found in a Wizard's Pocket' by Ian McMillan from *The Very Best of Ian McMillan*; 'Things I Have Been Doing Lately' by Allan Ahlberg from *Heard It in the Playground*; 'Night Sounds' by Berlie Doherty from June Crebbin's collection *The Puffin Book of Fantastic Poems*; and 'I'm Just Going Out for a Moment' by Michael Rosen from *Wouldn't You Like to Know*. (Children might choose a different title – for example 'Why I Cannot Do My Homework Now' or 'I Cannot Clean Out the Rabbit Hutch Today').
- Poems by other children can also inspire young writers. Gemma Hearn's *A Pocketful of Rhyme* is one title in a splendid series of anthologies of poetry written by seven- to eleven-year-olds.
- Other starting points teachers use, adapting them for particular age groups, include: newspaper articles on an issue; photographs, paintings and pictures on postcards; objects like small ornaments, old carved boxes or jewellery; music or CDs of evocative sounds. Of course teachers will have reasons for selecting particular starting points, reasons to do with other things children are involved in, and will be wary of overuse of one approach which might lead to only superficial responses. The important thing is to encourage an experimental approach to finding a poetry writing 'voice'.

Drafting poems

- 'Poetry frame' may suggest a mechanistic approach, but some young children gain confidence by using a simple structure, like a list perhaps. For example, each line or verse could begin with 'I like . . . because'.

CASE STUDY 19.2 YEAR 5 WRITE POEMS FOR CAMBODIA DAY

Children in a Kent primary school were moved and inspired by a talk from a drama teacher who had worked with young people who had been wounded by landmines in Cambodia. In preparation for the drama teacher's return visit, on Cambodia Day, each class worked on an aspect of Cambodian culture – art, dancing and theatre – to make a display. Year 5 wrote poems after researching the problem of landmines left behind at the end of the war. By using the first person, and spare lines, Craig gives in his poem an immediacy to the events, taking us into the shocking suddenness of landmine injury (see Figure 19.4). The freedom to focus on meaning rather than rhythm and rhyme has certainly helped him. In the later part of the poem, the use of the continuous present gives the texture of the aftermath of the event powerfully and very much from a child's point of view.

I touched a green thing
I tasted my own red blood.
　Landmines are scary.

　I'm very worried
Because I could be dying.
　My Mum is shouting.

　I'm in hospital.
Some of my fingers are gone.
　I can't go to school.

　Nurses keep chatting.

Two years on, I now go to school
　Grateful to be alive.

Figure 19.4
'An Atrocious Cambodian Tale' by Craig

- To encourage drafting of the freer kinds of poetry, ask children first to play with language around a theme in their notebooks or on screen, and then to begin shaping the best ideas into a poem.
- Try out a version of Ted Hughes' 'intense concentration' approach. Children may be inside the classroom or in the school garden or grounds or on a visit away from the school premises. Ask them to concentrate on an object of their choice – a stone, beetle, twig; encourage them to jot down all they see and think of in relation to the object; suggest they refine their lists and carve out a poem that, for them, expresses the essence of that object; read the poems aloud (see Ted Hughes' *Poetry in the Making*).
- It is at the drafting stage that the teacher or 'response partner' can give constructive advice.

SUMMARY

- Freer forms of poetry writing tend not to adhere to conventional metre or to have rhymes at the end of the line.
- But some features of poetry are evident, sometimes in the shape of the poems on the page and the presence of devices like imagery, alliteration, cadence, assonance and repetition. Free verse may have the rhythmic pattern of everyday conversation.
- There are a number of modern poets writing for children in these freer forms; those mentioned in this chapter include: Paul Cookson, Berlie Doherty, Frank Flynn, John Foster, Brian Patten, Michael Rosen, Wes Magee and Kit Wright. These poets show children some of the other ways of giving their poems a structure than conventional pattern, rhythm and rhyme.
- Children of all ages respond best to approaches which emphasize active participation: discussion, choral speaking and dramatic presentation.
- Experimenting as writers with freer forms often helps children to say what they mean and feel in their poems without what can be inhibiting strictures of conventional rhythm and rhyme.
- Starting points for young writers of poetry can include poems by others, pictures, music and interesting objects. Above all, a child's own experiences, including incidents and conversations, provide the inspiration and content for their poems.
- When it comes to drafting, an experimental and sometime collaborative approach seems helpful; constructive comments on first drafts from both 'response partners' and the teacher are of great help.

Part II

Children's non-fiction literature

Chapter 20

Introduction to Part II

Children's non-fiction literature has not always enjoyed the same critical attention given to fiction and yet has great potential to inspire children's learning across the whole curriculum. Part II of this book sets out to convince you that the best information texts are interesting, exciting, challenging and sometimes boundary-breaking. For some young readers they are the principle gateway to enjoyable and critical reading. There can be adventures in the real world (Davies, 2005) and the best non-fiction texts can help start the process of reflecting and wondering, with 'the ever present possibility of being unsettled' (Meek, 1996: 12).

In the United Kingdom, teachers have been working with six non-fiction text types for some time: recount, instruction, report, explanation, discussion and persuasion. I have treated 'explanation' as a kind of 'report' and 'reference' as another category. One challenge for teachers is that the mature versions of these text types mismatch somewhat with the texts children actually use and enjoy. They tend to be, particularly for younger children, 'transitional genres', having some but not all of the features of the adult texts they relate to. So we might have a book or CD-ROM using some of the devices of fiction to explain facts and ideas or a favourite character from a book or a television programme to inform and explain. The younger the intended readers, the more conversational the style is likely to be.

So, the term 'information texts' or 'non-fiction' includes texts which differ widely in format, in mode and in media. There is, however, one principal aim: an information text informs or instructs about a subject, an event or a set of ideas. Of course information texts can amuse and entertain, but their main, indeed their defining, purpose is to inform and to extend knowledge. They are, therefore, an enormously important resource in the school years. In this book we are concerned not with the text and course books that steer older post-primary pupils through a topic or body of information, but with children's information texts and the kinds of non-fiction used in the nursery and primary school years.

Early experience of non-fiction comes with adult and child sharing the bath, cloth and board books which label objects and introduce the alphabet and concepts like number, shape and colour in playful ways. At home they see print on food packages, labels, newspapers and on the letters, flyers and circulars that pour through our letterboxes. Outside they see print on shop fronts, on notices and on the large poster-size advertisements on buildings and hoardings.

Many families now have computers and use email and the internet for a multitude of purposes: children see the new technology used to buy food and other items, for visiting interactive sites and to seek information on travel, medical matters and all manner of other things.

Once children begin nursery or main school they encounter a huge array of print and electronic texts. They read from living books, CD-ROMs and a variety of software programmes as well as from print material. It is now to the internet that children most often turn when researching topics across the curriculum. New kinds of texts have come into being to meet the needs born of societal change and made possible by new technology, and they bring the need for new kinds of literacy. They affect the way children think, learn and imagine and have implications for the achievement of 'critical literacy'. The new texts which support new literacies need to be carefully evaluated with an eye on the purpose and audience for which they are intended. Print texts are changing and developing too. We give much more status now to multimodal texts, those books that combine design, writing and illustration in new and interesting ways. We are still learning about how to evaluate these and the multimodal texts children create themselves (Bearne in Evans, 2004: 16).

Most publishers of reading programmes have non-fiction titles in print and electronic format. Note has been taken of the old criticisms of reading schemes – unvaried vocabulary, unwelcome stereotyping, unexciting text. The notion that any writer can produce a worthwhile children's information text with a bit of swotting and some library pictures has been challenged and publishers often seek out distinguished authors for their non-fiction titles. It used to be remarked that while teachers could reel off the names of good writers of fiction for children they could remember the names of very few non-fiction writers. This is no longer true. My 'first thought' list would include: Aliki, Laurence Anholt, Stephen Biesty, Ruth Brown, Nicola Davies, Vivian French, Meredith Hooper, Brita Granström, Claire Llewellyn, David Macaulay, Jennie Maizels, Mick Manning, Lucy Micklethwait, Jacqueline Mitton, Ifeoma Onyefulu, Kate Petty, Richard Platt, Sally Purkis, Jo Readman, Karen Wallace, Angela Wilkes and Gillian Wolfe. Then there are authors of exciting, boundary-breaking books like Nicholas Allen's *Where Willy Went*, Sara Fanelli's *My Map Book* and the titles in Terry Deary's Horrible Histories series. Just type their names into a search engine and their titles will come up. Oxford's Oxford Reading Tree was an early pioneer in producing quality non-fiction strands and the TreeTops Non-Fiction titles have such distinguished authors as Jacqueline Mitton, Errol Lloyd and Michael Rosen. In fact it is generally a welcome trend that publishers are seeking out quality authors of imagination and expertise. Collins Big Cats non-fiction reading materials are written by well-known writers, including Claire Llewellyn, Clare Gittings and Nic Bishop.

The illustrations in non-fiction texts describe, inform and sometimes persuade as much as does the written text. They also help identify a text with a particular genre. Much less is written about illustrations in and illustrators of children's non-fiction texts than fiction. At a talk on this topic at the May 2008 Write Away conference on non-fiction, 'Non-Fiction: More than Information', Martin Salisbury, who is Course Director for the MA in Children's Book Illustration at APU Cambridge, remarked that his students nearly all wanted to become illustrators of fiction, not least picturebooks. Nevertheless there are many fine illustrators of children's information books. Some topics deserve lyrical illustrators like those of the Read and Wonder and Wonderwise series, for example: Mick Manning, Brita Granström, Mike Bostock, Jane Chapman and Sarah Fox-Davies. These illustrators use sketches and watercolours to show the sheer poetry of some landscapes and phenomena. Other illustrators use 'popular culture' approaches like cartoons – for example Martin Brown, illustrator of some of the titles in Deary's Horrible Histories series, and Marcia Williams, who uses cartoon strip to great effect as a communicator of information in her non-fiction books like *Archie's War*. The illustrations in children's early non-fiction books on everyday experiences are most important. These may be photographs, drawings or water-colours. Stars here are Sarah Garland, Richard Scarry, Fiona Pragoff and the Ahlbergs (I am thinking of their non-fiction book of lists, *The Baby's Catalogue*).

Some illustrators of non-fiction, David Macaulay for example, have a background in architecture which informs their meticulous drawings showing how structure is related to function. Information about engineering and architecture is also shown in the magnificent cross-sections of Stephen Biesty. We see in his work the 'big shapes' of, for example, ocean liners, Greek temples and the Colosseum of Ancient Rome, but also revealed is the interesting detail of the lives of individuals. And we must not forget the paper engineers who, for some decades now, have used ingenious pull-outs, pop-ups and cutaways to enhance and explain – and also to delight young readers of non-fiction. Neal Layton and Jenny Maizels stand out here.

Quite a number of non-fiction books use the work of fine photographers. Fiona Pragoff structures her books around colourful photographs of children's experiences at nursery school and their early science activities. Others use the camera to show particular landscapes and environments: Ifeoma Onyefulu uses vibrant photographic images to bring alive on the page the daily experiences of people living in African villages; the illustrators of Frances Lincoln's A Child's Day series, based on the original idea of author and photographer Prodeepta Das, shows children experiencing the environments, people and customs in countries where their family's roots lie. A large proportion of texts for older primary school children are illustrated by photographs, often using the latest technology. Dorling Kindersley's Eyewitness series uses photographs alongside diagrams and drawings, using the gifts of photographers like, for example, Vassili Papastavrou. The work of illustrators of non-fiction print texts and of those who produce digital images and create moving images for the screen permeate the whole of Part II of this book.

Interestingly, at a time when electronic texts are expanding and improving, print children's books confront us in many places apart from the traditional bookshop and library. All manner of books appear in supermarkets, in chemist shops and newsagents, in museum and art gallery shops and on websites. Many print information books now link with websites or are part of a package which includes a disc or CD-ROM. Television programmes have long been a source of information for young learners, particularly children's news and wildlife programmes. The Barnaby Bear BBC programmes, for example, link television programmes with print resources. So this second part of the book aims to celebrate the exciting and varied non-fiction resources that teachers and children now choose from. But it is also concerned to suggest how teachers may become good critics of these resources, able to select wisely and use successfully. There is always passionate debate about how subject-centred a primary curriculum should be. Here I have discussed texts under the familiar headings – science, history and so on – but my analysis is relevant to a cross-curricular approach as well.

Chapter 21

Children's non-fiction literature in the twenty-first century

INTRODUCTION

We now have a larger repertoire of information texts than ever before. Material with an informational function reflects cultural needs and social change just as much as fiction does. The global markets for information texts and the rise of popular culture affect what is produced and published. A study by the NFER (National Foundation for Educational Research) on the state of reading as we begin to move through the twenty-first century found, as we might expect, that children's reading has to take its place alongside other activities like texting, emailing, surfing the web, watching television or films or playing interactive games. Visual literacy is increasingly valued and many children respond enthusiastically to images and graphics, both print and electronic (Twist *et al.*, 2006). There follow some comments on the main non-fiction media which children now encounter.

PRINT BOOKS AND RESOURCES

Print information books have to compete with electronic and multimedia texts, with the internet and with all the other activities, hobbies and interests of children. The main publishers of non-fiction for children – Dorling Kindersley, Usborne, Kingfisher, Heinemann, Franklin Watts, Oxford University Press, Evans Brothers, A&C Black and Collins – acknowledge that books must be pleasing in both design and illustration and provide good coverage of the topic for the age and interests of the intended readers.

A trend has been to combine print and electronic resources to promote children's learning. Therefore we find packages containing a print book, a related CD-ROM and directions to websites which will carry children's research further into the topic.

Reference and information books

In the recent past there have been two main strands of development. One is the colourfully illustrated book, often using high-quality photographs and clear text which is sometimes in rather short blocks. The best books in this category are discussed and evaluated in Chapter 29 and Chapter 33. 'Star' books include the encyclopedias of Dorling Kindersley and Usborne and titles in DK's Eyewitness series. One concern many have is that teachers, parents and children might assume that these texts represent the 'model' for information books. Although they may have many good qualities and should be represented in the school collection, we do not want young readers to be locked into formulaic structures. So this brings me to the second main strand of print books and to the individual 'voice' in novelty and lyrical non-fiction.

Novelty books and lyrical non-fiction

Novelty non-fiction books include those with pull-outs, 'lift-the-flap' devices and objects like magnifying glasses. Of course we need to be convinced that the novelty features serve a purpose in communicating information and concepts. We do not want miscellaneous objects popping up just for effect. So the best are not only increasingly inventive as paper engineering advances but also imaginative and informative. The fine work of Kate Petty and Jenny Maizels and others is covered in Chapters 29, 30 and 33.

Lyrical non-fiction uses some of the devices of fiction to capture young learners' imaginations. Walker's pioneering Read and Wonder series brought feelings and imaginative power to non-fiction topics by using language and illustration with a poetic quality. Another distinctive feature of books like Karen Wallace's *Think of an Eel* and Vivian French's *Spider Watching* was the use of two kinds of text: large standard print for the main narrative and conventional information in italic (Mallett, 2006). Lyrical books remain an important element in the non-fiction collection and are discussed in Chapter 26.

ELECTRONIC RESOURCES

These complement rather than replace print texts, but they offer important kinds of reading experiences children need to acquire in an electronic world. The changing skills young readers need in interpreting moving text, colour and sound and the use of interactive whiteboards in helping to achieve this are clearly explained in *Reading on Screen* (Bearne *et al.*, 2007).

Electronic texts have the potential to be interactive and users can reply, post comments and borrow. They are also multimodal and while print texts can also offer multimodality – combining design, illustration and writing in interesting and useful ways – electronic texts are also multimedia, and thus offer, in some ways, a richer experience. Words, sentences and paragraphs dominate most print texts; digital texts also use symbols, layout and hyperlinks to make meaning. The linear nature of reading and writing paths in print texts does not apply to reading and writing on screen. So in some ways working with digital texts is a freer and more complex experience as the text is not confined to the pages of a book. And of course there are some practical advantages of electronic systems. Two important facilities are the capacity to store large amounts of information on databases and the potential to update and change texts easily.

An important 'voice' to help us think clearly about using multimedia texts and on the influence of television is David Buckingham's. In his article 'Superhighway or Road to Nowhere?' (Buckingham, 1999: 3–12) he covers computer games, citing evidence that these can be a collaborative activity and lead to other activities like talking with family and friends, watching related TV programmes and reading magazines, all of which might have positive implications for literacy.

A number of studies make the point that children need to be active in their use of ICT texts and to be helped to produce moving image texts as well as simply accessing them. The benefits of encouraging children's digital writing in English and across the curriculum are assessed in a study by the Social Science Research Unit entitled *A Systematic Review of the Impact of ICT on the Learning of Literacies Associated with Moving Image Texts in English, 5–15* (Burn and Leach, 2004).

In an interesting chapter, 'ICTs and Multimedia', in their book *Teaching English, Language and Literacy*, Wyse and Jones emphasize the continuing importance of the teacher's role. Their advice is as follows: 'You should view ICTs as useful tools which, with the appropriate pedagogy, can enhance learning and teaching' (Wyse and Jones, 2008: 238).

Before moving on to consider the different kinds of electronic texts, I would like to recommend a useful site that offers teacher evaluations of packages to support children's work in every lesson: Teachers Evaluate Educational Multimedia (TEEM, www.teem.org.uk/).

CD-ROM, software and multimedia texts

CD-ROMs are discs which are read by a computer system and usually combine text, sound and video-film. 'Hot-links' allow the user to move from one piece of text to another by clicking on a word. They have not replaced print texts, however, and need to be evaluated before purchase just as rigorously as print texts should be. Criteria for choosing CD-ROMs and software would include looking for those that match with the needs of the age group, balance entertainment and information, make imaginative use of the technology, are the right medium for the subject, provide quality search systems and bookmarks, offer quality content – i.e. accuracy and comprehensiveness, appeal to children's creativity and interest and provide quality images and audio experiences.

CD-ROMs have greatly assisted children's research across the curriculum. Information that might become cumbersome in print encyclopedias can be easily stored electronically. There are some exciting electronic resources now. Dorling Kindersley (DK) has produced user-friendly interactive encyclopedias, including the 'World Explorer' series. And Oxford University Press have published *Dictosaurus*, a splendid resource to support young writers from about age eight years. DK's CD-ROM *Eyewitness Encyclopedia of Space and the Universe* shows the huge amounts of information that can be made available to the young learner. The interactive areas are exciting and users can, for example, prepare a rocket for launching or visit the Star Dome to explore the night sky in any place on any date.

CD-ROMs and software involve a different sort of reading approach to reading print; for one thing reading them is not linear. They often include snippets of film and so processes like a machine working or the digestive and blood systems of the human or animal body can be shown, dynamically indicating how structure and function relate. A print diagram would have to use colour or devices like arrows to try to achieve what the moving image does so easily. The speech, sound and music which can be included also make using them a more motivating experience for some young learners than using print.

The internet

The internet is an unrivalled source of information about every possible subject we could imagine. Indeed its impact has often been compared to that of the invention of the printing press in the fourteenth century. This huge 'library' is of great help to practitioners as it offers a treasure store of teaching resources. Interactive whiteboards and computers in classrooms, libraries and in designated computer rooms are now commonplace in primary schools and access to the internet is built in to all this activity.

I have said a primary school teacher needs to be an expert on all kinds of text for children. There is no doubt that the internet is unbeatable when it comes to finding information from the hundreds of sites about children's literature, both fiction and non-fiction, print and electronic. Organizations publishing print journals about children's books nearly always combine this with a website. *Books for Keeps* has been granted an Arts Council award to develop the archive of children's books and to create interactive areas of the site allowing teachers and researchers to debate issues about children's literature and resources (www.booksforkeeps. co.uk). Other strong websites to help busy teachers become informed about the latest publications, research, books and resources for children include the English Association (www.le.ac.uk/engassoc), Booktrust (www.booktrustchildrensbooks.org.uk), the School Library Association (www.sla.org.uk), *Times Educational Supplement* (www.tes.co.uk/ reviews-and-resources), the Seven Stories Centre for Children's Books (www.sevenstories. org.uk/home/) and CLPE (www.clpe.co.uk). Teachers can help children access web-pages linking them with museums and all the visual material these provide, with art galleries and sites about particular children's authors. The websites of the children's laureates – past and present – invite children to review books and sometimes to interact with other young readers, sharing opinion and recommendations. There are quizzes and competitions and children are able to have a voice in judging texts of all kinds (www.childrenslaureate.org.uk).

This global network of linked computers that we call the internet is constantly being expanded and developed. Quite young children become computer and internet literate and find new independence in some of their learning. But its strength is also its potential weakness. On the one hand it gives anyone who can use it access to huge stores of information from all over the world. On the other hand it is anarchic and uncontrollable – extremely difficult to regulate. Nowhere is this more obvious than in the educational and medical information found on some sites. Internet encyclopedias are also problematic as we do not know how reliable the information is. Wikipedia, for instance, is collaboratively written by its readers. Those editing entries are asked to provide references, but it seems unlikely that it will be scrutinized as rigorously as the quality print encyclopedias for inaccuracies and for opinion masquerading as 'the facts'. There is also room for improvement. Some websites are dull and unimaginative and difficult for children to learn from.

MOVING IMAGE MEDIA: DVD, FILM AND TELEVISION

There have been a number of studies and analyses which point to the positive effects moving image media can have on children's developing literacy. Naima Brown carried out research on the viewing experiences of young children and notes how actively they respond to their favourite television programmes, often dancing, singing and talking about the events and characters. This positive response suggests that televisual texts need not reduce children to passivity, as many parents and teachers have suspected they might, but can be the starting point for role play, storytelling and, later on, writing (Brown, 1999). Of course it all depends on how actively and successfully we support the viewing experiences of children, how we discuss these experiences with them and how, in school, we can encourage linked drama and writing. In their book, *Literacy and Popular Culture* (2000), Jackie Marsh and Elaine Millard argue that dramatic technological changes have expanded the ways in which meanings are carried. Children's visual literacy can be supported in new and exciting ways. 'It is these new literacies that we need to develop in the primary classroom alongside print literacy if we want children to be flexible thinkers in a technological culture' (Mallett, 2008: 326). At home children often see television films based on children's picturebooks and novels and non-fiction programmes about space, wildlife and history. They will certainly see advertisements and, in the school context, these can be analysed in English lessons as part of a study of persuasive kinds of language. Thus one of the most important reasons for using moving image media is the fact that it is motivating for children to study and learn through a medium so central in our culture. It is also the case that for some children, perhaps boys and children for whom English is an additional language, film can be an inspiration and support to writing. Another plus is the useful tie-ups between books and video-film or DVD. These are more commonly found in fiction, but non-fiction books are often published alongside a wildlife or travel programme on television.

The new emphasis on televisual texts from mainstream television in school may change parents' perception of television to more positive ones. When it comes to non-fiction, teachers and children are more likely to view pre-recorded programmes either from school programmes or from mainstream television. This makes for considerable flexibility over when and how the input is used.

In English, moving image advertisements are often used in English to tune children into persuasive kinds of materials. Even very young children can be helped to see how such an advertisement is constructed to influence the viewer. Carolyn White's chapter in *Visual Images* by Jon Callow shows how five-year-olds were able to view some advertisements aimed at children and to discuss the colours used, describe the music and the characters and to record who speaks and what is said. The teacher then asked them the reasons for these decisions and they showed signs of understanding – in the words of one child – that 'Somebody made a choice' (White in Callow, 1999: 48).

One of the most successful resources for five- to seven-year-olds which links print, film and television programmes is the Barnaby Bear material to support children's lessons in geography and citizenship. *Barnaby Bear in Brazil* uses video-film to take young viewers into the lives of a rainforest family so that they can see how their lives differ from those of others. For details of the resources visit the BBC Schools website (www.bbc.co.uk/schools/).

3D VIRTUAL WORLDS

The virtual worlds which advanced technology can now create have an increasingly important role in the classroom. These 3D 'worlds' can make a valuable contribution to children's development of digital kinds of literacy (Merchant, 2007: 3). They are highly motivating for many pupils as they are both visual and interactive. Organizations, for example Virtual Learning, design 3D environments for educational and business purposes (www.virtual learning.org.uk). If you would like to read a case study about teachers and children using this approach, I recommend an article by Guy Merchant, 'Out of the Classroom and into the World' (Merchant, 2008: 12–14). This project, called 'Barnsborough' – an imaginary town – involved ten Year 5 classes who were able to 'visit' the maze of the town's streets and were able to chat to the people. Rather suddenly, most of the inhabitants of the town left and the children had the intriguing task of trying to discover why. As Merchant points out, this kind of approach draws on Gee's insights about how children's experience of video-games can be used to promote thinking and literacy (Gee, 2004). Further, the work of the teachers and children in this case study and others like it shows how paper literacies can be linked to what are often called 'the new literacies'. For example, the 'Barnsborough' children read print texts to try to solve the mystery and wrote newspaper reports. This kind of link between print and digital texts is explored in a book called *New Literacies: Everyday Practices and Classroom Learning* (Lankshear and Knobel, 2007).

Exciting as this kind of work using virtual worlds and other innovative texts and technologies can be, the resources used and the learning achieved have to be evaluated over the long term, as is the case with any other approach and resource. So a welcome development is the establishment of the Cambridge/Homerton Research and Teaching Centre for Children's Literature whose first director, Professor Maria Nikolajeva, aims to include moving image texts and video-games as well as more traditional children's books and resources in the work of her team (www.educ.cam.ac.uk/centres/childrensliterature).

Chapter 22

Models of non-fiction kinds of learning and some guiding principles

INTRODUCTION

Crucial though texts are, and important as it is for teachers to make informed choices about them, we use non-fiction texts above all to support children's learning in all its variety. So this chapter first considers three models of non-fiction learning: the skills model, the EXIT model and the language and learning model. All contribute to our understanding of non-fiction learning. The chapter continues with some guiding principles which underpin the 'language and learning' approach that I believe best brings non-fiction into all the tasks and activities of the classroom, grounding all that is argued in an approach that embeds use of texts in the bigger shapes of lessons and activities.

MODELS OF NON-FICTION KINDS OF LEARNING

I consider here three models. Each has strengths and they are worth reflecting on because they help us think critically and creatively about how children learn and how we can best use non-fiction texts to help that learning.

The skills model

Until comparatively recently the 'skills' model of reading and writing non-fiction held sway in schools. It was thought that the acquisition of study and library skills was, in the main, what was needed to become able to learn from secondary sources. Of course these skills have an important place and need to be taught. You will find a detailed consideration of the role of the school library and the acquisition of both library and study skills in Chapter 34. Library skills include learning how to use the modified Dewey system most primary school libraries have in place and how to find the print and electronic sources of the information children need. Once they have tracked these down, children need to be competent in using retrieval devices we find in texts, like contents pages and indexes. They need to see how chapter and section headings organize a text and help the reader. Most children also require support in learning how to take useful notes to inform their writing. This, as Chapter 34 explains, involves much more than what we tend to mean by 'a skill' and has to do with reaching a level of intellectual development which makes it possible for a young learner to deal with hierarchies of meaning.

Too great an emphasis on 'skills' can lead to a mechanistic approach and deny children the help they need to be active in integrating knowledge coming from both first-hand and secondary sources. So we want more than the skills model can offer if children are to become mature readers. By 'mature' I mean the ability to read flexibly, becoming able to 'skim' to get the gist of a passage, to 'scan' to find a date or place name and, where appropriate, to read more carefully, critically and reflectively.

The EXIT model: Extending Interactions with Text

The importance of interaction, evaluation and communication in non-fiction kinds of reading and writing, which goes far beyond a 'skills' model, was recognized in the EXIT model; this was an outcome of the Nuffield funded Extending Literacy research project undertaken in the 1990s by David Wray and Maureen Lewis. The project was classroom-based and has generated a large number of publications, some suggesting devices like writing frames to help children structure non-fiction writing. Perhaps the fullest account of their work is in their book *Extending Literacy: Children Reading and Writing Non-Fiction* and here you will find the EXIT model (Wray and Lewis, 1997). The model describes ten 'process' stages in coming to new learning and texts to support it. The researchers regard these stages not as linear, but recursive. They are:

1   Activation of previous knowledge
2   Establishing purposes
3   Locating information
4   Adopting an appropriate strategy
5   Interacting with text
6   Monitoring understanding
7   Making a record
8   Evaluating information
9   Assisting memory
10 Communicating information.

The model also suggests the question a child might helpfully ask at each stage. So, for example, the question suggested for process stage 1, 'Activation of previous knowledge' is 'What do I already know about this subject?' This takes us well beyond a narrow skills model but, as I detail below, there is no very clear indication of how practical activity and first-hand experience mesh with learning from texts.

The language and learning model

My own smaller-scale research, also carried out in the 1990s, gave greater emphasis than did the EXIT model to the kinds of experience that precede, go alongside and sometimes follow reading and writing (see stage 2 in the list below) (Mallett, 1992: 61; 2003: 11). I am thinking here of the practical work children do: cooking and science experiments, role play and the outings and visits which give life to their talking and writing and which also make them more active in their reading. This 1990s version of my model had six stages and, apart from stage 2, was not unlike the EXIT model:

1   Organizing prior experience
2   Offering new experience
3   Formulating questions
4   Discussion and planning
5   Study skills and retrieval devices
6   Summarizing, reformulating and reflecting.

Commenting on stage 2, Riley and Reedy emphasize the importance of 'offering new experience' to awaken children's curiosity. 'Once this is done, the question 'What do I need to find out?' becomes an imperative and the desire to seek out that information and develop understanding is kindled' (Riley and Reedy, 2000: 145).

In their analysis of both the EXIT model and my 'language and learning' model, Riley and Reedy go on to reflect on the problems that arise when models set out stages in a linear way. This tends to make processes seem more clear cut and tidy than they actually are in the rich, even sometimes creatively chaotic, environment of the typical primary classroom. I agree, and Figure 22.1 shows my most recent attempt to make the original model more dynamic, indicating that the different stages can occur in different orders. This version of the model indicates that the stages may come in any order and that activities like 'questioning' can be to do with a whole stance towards the research, rather than being confined to one stage. As Riley and Reedy also point out, different lessons and projects will demand different amounts of time are spent on each stage.

Figure 22.1
Revised language and learning model
Based on the model in Mallett, 2007: 6

SOME GUIDING PRINCIPLES

Are there some principles that underpin non-fiction kinds of literacy and learning if we adopt what I have termed a 'language and learning' model of non-fiction? I believe that there are and that they are the same three very general guiding principles which inhabit all good primary school practice: children learn actively; learning is social and collaborative; the teacher's role is central. These principles, or something very like them, will be familiar to informed practitioners but they have not always been applied to children's learning from non-fiction. In the chapters that follow the suggestions for work around texts and the case studies are in the spirit of these principles.

Children learn actively

Non-fiction texts are best placed in the context of other things that young children are doing – their experiences, encounters and activities. Piaget's adaptive model of learning seems to me to be a powerful explanation of how a child organizes new learning (Piaget, 1952). This 'new learning' will include making sense of unfamiliar objects and new situations. Later on it will be a matter of combining learning and understanding from first-hand experience with that from secondary sources. Food begins a process of assimilation, mixing with gastric juices to make it absorbable by the body. And, at the same time, the body's digestive organs modify to accept the new input. So, says Piaget, it is with learning; we take in new knowledge and change it so it is compatible with what we already know, and as we do so we adjust the existing frameworks of knowledge to take in the new. Further, and this is very important in informational kinds of learning, Piaget argues that we have a self-regulatory mechanism which he calls 'equilibrium'. When children become curious about some aspect of the world this mechanism kicks in, causing them to feel excited, even unsettled. These puzzles and concerns upset their feeling of equilibrium and make them eager to find things out. Even babies seem to feel this need to find solutions to everyday challenges. In *How Babies Think* young children are compared to scientists in their persistent need to find answers to challenges that come up in everyday situations (Gopnik *et al.*, 1999). Piaget's work helps us less when it comes to the social context of learning and particularly the role of language in finding out. Here teachers have turned to the work of Vygotsky on the role of language in organizing thinking and communicating (Vygotsky, 1986). This leads us to the kind of practice that places early literacy development in play situations and role play. Thus early years teachers bring texts into role play: notices for the 'doctor's surgery', menus in 'the café' and labels and prices in 'the shop'. Outside the classroom, children can be helped to prepare bills and receipts in 'the garage', make signs to help motorists next to 'road works' and write lists of items for sale on chalkboards in 'the market garden'. Children then see that written language makes their role play more real. Now is the time to read information stories, by authors like Sarah Garland, about everyday experiences; these books show children that non-fiction can relate strongly to their everyday interests, activities and preoccupations (Larkin-Lieffers, 2010).

As children become older they are increasingly able to learn independently from secondary sources and to control the written forms needed and valued by society. But they still need and benefit from continued practical work and activity. Experiments in science, field trips in geography, outings and museum visits to enliven history and English all help sustain and deepen interest, and all nourish learning from texts. Drama across the curriculum continues to be a good way of exploring real, and sometimes unsettling, issues to do with the environment, the media, poverty and conflict. The deeply involving effect of drama often helps link lessons across the curriculum, leading to interesting kinds of reading, writing and illustrating. The more than superficial investment of interest in drama and role play and discussion and debate makes it more likely that children will muster the mind-stretching concentration and commitment needed for the kind of reading and writing tasks that demand some control over difficult concepts and ideas. To paraphrase James Britton, we cannot make difficult things easy, but we can help make the effort of young learners worthwhile (Britton, 1970).

Learning is social and collaborative

It is often said that becoming able to learn from secondary sources allows children to learn independently. This is true and yet there is a paradox here. It is discussion and collaboration that often makes independent learning fruitful and mature and which breathes life into the notes made from books or the internet. The constructive comments, questions and puzzles of others about a topic stimulate a child's developing understanding of how to go about research and what to ask of texts. Talk also helps a group or class of children to make those crucial links between what they learn first hand and what they find in secondary sources. I remember the comments of a group of eight-year-olds who were looking after snails in a classroom vivarium as part of their work on living things. The student teacher had provided a small shelf of books about snails. The children read in one of the books that 'snails nearly always prefer green food stuffs'. But, as one child pointed out, their snails – given a choice – 'went for carrot tops'. The activity and the talk brought home to the children that texts often included what people had seen and done, and that some texts were better than others. Becoming a critical reader depends on this insight and having reasons for finding some texts better for a particular purpose than others. This group of children gained the confidence to write and illustrate their own book on snails drawing on their daily observations. There was further talk and interaction when they read out their book to the rest of the class and answered their questions. Rich and varied talk opportunities help make new learning deeper and more likely to be knitted into our ways of thinking and conceiving of something. Social, oral and interactive approaches, as in the 'snail' example, seem to appeal to all young learners, not least reluctant male learners (Safford et al., 2004; Bearne et al., 2005).

Then there is talk to share and explore children's increasing textual knowledge of the different genres of the non-fiction texts they are using. This helps them move forward in understanding the implications of the different modes and the different media through which information can be communicated.

The teacher's role is central

The effective practitioner of every age group needs considerable knowledge and expertise to help transform children's developing knowledge in every lesson into understanding.

Subject knowledge in the primary curriculum areas is essential and this is particularly demanding for teachers of older primary children. Whatever guiding framework is required or advised, it is the teacher who understands how each individual in their class of children learns and who plans lively lessons and activities and creates appropriate and interesting opportunities for talk, drama and writing. Not only are effective teachers knowledgeable about areas of learning, pedagogy and child development, they also know about the different modes and media through which informational knowledge and understanding is communicated. And, of course, they need themselves to be good models of researchers. Part of becoming a competent young researcher involves acquiring library and study skills. In my experience a programme for teaching these skills and abilities, from the nursery stage right through to Year 6, is best created collaboratively. Discussion with colleagues on these matters is often led by the English, language and literacy manager. Study skills are not an end in themselves and so they are best taught in the context of lessons and activities where children see them as meeting particular needs and purposes. Children also need to combine what they learn from primary and from secondary sources. Chapter 34 explores how we support children as they learn about all those strategies that help them find out and record information.

Teachers show their concern for children's progress by commenting on spoken contributions and written work in a constructive way and recording their observations and assessments. I find children respond positively when they sense genuine concern for their progress.

SUMMARY

- Learning from non-fiction texts involves more than the acquisition of study and library skills and so a narrow 'skills' model does not suffice.
- Non-fiction reading and writing help children to learn and often involve integrating what is learnt from texts with what is learnt from first-hand experience.
- The EXIT model brings a welcome emphasis on genuine interaction with texts and communication of what has been learnt.
- A language and learning approach, in addition, brings a more explicit embedding of text learning in the bigger shapes of lessons and activities. Children then have interest and knowledge from experience to bring to learning from secondary sources.
- Three main principles which helpfully inform all teaching and learning in the early and primary years have the potential to inform good practice in non-fiction kinds of thinking and learning. These are: children learn actively; learning is social and interactive; the teacher's role is central.
- A 'language and learning' approach helps make the encounters of very young children with non-fiction part of their everyday experience of the world in and out of the classroom.
- The learning from non-fiction texts of older children continues to benefit from being explicitly connected with wider purposes and relevant first-hand experience be it practical work in science, geographical field-work, visits to museums or role play and drama.

Chapter 23

Non-fiction and classroom organization, gender issues and assessment

INTRODUCTION

Whatever the statutory and guidance requirements at a particular time, and these requirements are constantly changed and modified in the UK, there are three main ways of organizing groupings in the classroom. Teaching and learning can be class-based, carried out in groups or pairs, or take place on a one-to-one basis. There has been a movement towards more flexibility in how the curriculum is organized, including in literacy time, but schools are likely still to use some of the routines and terminology associated with the frameworks. This chapter begins with a look at how teachers organize non-fiction kinds of learning in literacy time and in other lessons across the curriculum. It goes on to look at gender differences in children's reading of informational kinds of material. Finally I address how non-fiction reading and writing can be assessed and progress recorded.

CLASSROOM ORGANIZATION AND NON-FICTION

Non-fiction in literacy time

The National Curriculum English orders have historically had a genre-based approach to texts, as did the non-statutory Literacy Frameworks of 1998 and 2006. This led to children being taught systematically about the features of different text types. In the case of non-fiction these have been: recount, instruction, report, explanation, persuasion and discussion. In this book I have added 'reference' to this list because these texts have distinctive roles and purposes in the classroom and deserve separate attention. There is more about how non-fiction texts might be classified in the next chapter. There has been a loosening of the rather tight week-by-week guidance in the Framework and teachers are more likely to refer to 'literacy' or 'literacy time' than to the 'literacy hour', with its strict division into times for shared and group reading. Even before the 1998 Framework, English and literacy lessons were organized so that there was shared reading (class-based reading and writing) and group reading and writing of two kinds – guided and independent. And teachers have always made time for hearing individual children read aloud to them. The changes and modifications made to statutory requirement and guidance materials is available on government sites (see for example www.standards.dfes.gov.uk).

Class-based reading (shared reading and writing)

Shared reading can mean a teacher and a pupil reading together and talking together about a book, as in Campbell's approach (Campbell, 1995). But the UK National Literacy Strategy in its 1998 and 2006 versions saw 'shared reading' and 'shared writing' as a whole-class, teacher-led, activity. The shared text may be a big book, pages enlarged on an interactive whiteboard or reading material on screen. The same text can be used in literacy time – to show its features – and in another lesson across the curriculum as a source of information to inform the topic being studied. So, to give just one example, in geography children might be using an annotated diagram to find out how the water cycle works and then use this same text in literacy time to explore the features of an explanation text.

Children, particularly those in the younger age groups, benefit from shared readings of whole non-fiction texts. Favourites, such as information stories like *Think of an Eel* by Karen Wallace and *Where the Forest Meets the Sea* by Jeannie Baker, can be enjoyed in their big book form and be a basis for learning. Short biographies can also be read in their entirety in a 'shared reading' context.

One-to-one reading

The benefits of a child reading regularly to the teacher or parent are well understood. Apart from allowing the teacher to observe and record progress, this is an opportunity to talk about a book and to develop and maintain some social interaction with one child. Of course stories have been the traditional material for the initial teaching of reading, but for some children reading non-fiction is equally motivating and interesting.

The emphasis on class and group contexts for reading (and writing) in the Literacy Frameworks put this sort of quality time for one-to-one reading in school at risk. I join with those teachers who hope that the more flexible approach we are moving towards will mean a return to hearing individual children read as a regular feature of the school day.

Group reading (and writing)

Teachers organized children's literacy tasks and other activities in groups long before the National Curriculum and the Literacy Frameworks arrived and will do so when these are modified or abandoned.

Guided reading (and writing)

Here each child in a small group of children of similar ability has a copy of the same text. After some preliminary discussion the children are supported by the teacher while they read independently. At Key Stage 1 children will need help in reading the text, while the support for older children will be in coming to understand the features of the text and responding to its content. One good outcome of the 2006 Literacy Framework and its predecessor was that they formalized the place of non-fiction kinds of literacy in the classroom. Reading aloud helps children become familiar with the rhythm and vocabulary of the different non-fiction genres.

Publishers have responded to the need for books in sets for guided reading and these now include non-fiction titles. Oxford University Press was one of the first to include non-fiction in packs for guided reading. Their Firefly series is for age seven years and younger, while their TreeTops series is for the seven to eleven age range and is explicitly linked with lessons across the curriculum. Ticktock's guided reading packs have the same title available at three different levels of text. Their I Love Reading series includes a pack of twenty books for five- to seven-year-olds, many on science and nature study themes. The Heinemann, Rigby and Ginn publishing group have produced guided reading programmes and packs with the potential for cross-curricular links. ICT activities are built into the Rigby Star Guided Reading Programme. Packs of books in the reference category include Heinemann's *The Heinemann First Atlas* for older primary children, which sets out the skills needed for map work. Usborne have put some of their existing non-fiction titles into guided reading packs. These include *Anne Frank*, a biography, and *Pompeii*, which retells the story of a catastrophe. Evans Start-Up series covers history, geography and science, and the visual strength of the series with its varied illustrations – diagrams, photographs and colourful artwork –makes it helpful to young readers with English as an additional language.

Ladybird's non-fiction titles in the Ladybird Learning to Read series are good value. (Individual copies of *Mad About Pirates* are only £1.99.) Reading on screen now goes alongside reading print books. For children in the Key Stage 2 years Collins have brought out a CD-ROM pack with an accompanying booklet for guided reading called Virtual History. It links literacy and history teaching and provides the sort of information and activities that help children think like young historians. The London Institute of Education has published two books which describe and evaluate the main series for guided reading. These are *Book Bands for Guided Reading at Foundation and Key Stage 1* by Shirley Bickler *et al.*, 2007 and *Bridging Bands for Guided Reading: Resourcing for Diversity, Key Stage 2* by Angela Hobsbaum *et al.*, 2004.

Books in reading programmes are often by respected authors and the old criticisms of uninspiring language and dull pictures apply much less. If a guided reading pack is of good quality, good value and will suit your class there is every reason to purchase it, but some teachers prefer to organize their own packs by purchasing trade books that are not part of a reading programme. Individual trade books and series of books can help make for a varied and interesting non-fiction experience for young learners – Tony Mitton's books on machines for Kingfisher, *Flashing Fire Engine* and *Dazzling Digger*, for example. The titles in Franklin Watts' Wonderwise series are also written for the sevens and under in a lively way and are well illustrated. Some of the books in the Cat in the Hat's Learning Library are worth considering for the five to eight age range. Tish Rabe's jolly rhyming text propels young readers along as well as helping with anticipation. *Inside Your Outside!* informs young readers about all the organs of the body in an entertaining way. Children in the Key Stage 2 years would enjoy Manning and Granström's titles in Frances Lincoln's Fly on the Wall series.

Independent group reading (and writing)

This was a key element of the Literacy Frameworks but there is more flexibility now about when and how independent reading and writing fall into the language and literacy programme. It is practical good sense to have some children working independently so that guided groups can benefit from the teacher's help.

Individual reading and writing

Teachers have long held to the principle of making available times for children's silent reading. And there is no reason why the reading material should not sometimes be a non-fiction text like a biography or an information story rather than a novel or short story. Why should we provide time for silent reading in a busy school day? Reading has to compete with so many other activities that just making this quality time available suggests to children that this is a worthwhile and valued activity. It is also an opportunity for children to make the transition from reading aloud to reading silently or 'in your head'. Children of all ages need time and space in which to savour a book and to read at their own pace. Often just a nudge to try 'reading in your head' is all that is needed but children need peace and quiet to achieve this (Graham and Kelly, 2007: 61). For me the most passionate argument for individual reading time in school is made by Aidan Chambers in *The Reading Environment*, in which he reminds us that this sacrosanct period 'is one of those rituals that condition our set of mind' (Chambers, 1991:38). A teacher who can help a child find the will to enjoy sustained reading will have done more than anything else to make that child a committed reader for life.

In the same way, making time for individual sustained writing, perhaps when it comes to non-fiction – writing an autobiography or journal – can help a young learner find a writing 'voice'.

NON-FICTION IN LESSONS ACROSS THE CURRICULUM

A positive contribution made by the Literacy Frameworks was their emphasis on the direct teaching of non-fiction text types. However, this direct teaching sometimes risked removing the texts from the very contexts which give them point and meaning – the lessons across the curriculum. Teachers now try to make links between using non-fiction texts in lessons across the curriculum and looking at these same texts as examples of a genre. So, for example, if children are writing recounts in history or geography, the features of this text type can be explored in literacy time. Likewise, when looking at ethical aspects of science – issues to do with endangered species and global warming perhaps – there is an opportunity to link up with thinking about discussion and persuasion texts types in literacy time. If children are using cross-sections to understand the Earth's layers in geography it makes sense for them to look at explanatory diagrams in literacy. Thoughtful teachers have of course always made these connections.

When it comes to classroom organization of lessons across the curriculum, the work will of course include class-based, group-based and one-to-one contexts. The previous chapter, on models of non-fiction kinds of learning, argues that planning and organization can usefully be based on three principles. The first, that children learn actively, emphasizes the importance of linking secondary sources with first-hand and practical experience whenever appropriate. The second, that learning is social and collaborative, leads to the kind of practice where children talk in class, group and one-to-one contexts both about new ideas and concepts to do with lesson topics and about the features and quality of the texts and materials they are using. The third principle recognizes the important, indeed central, role of the teacher as planner of lessons and activities, selector of resources, organizer and manager of the classroom and assessor and record keeper of progress. In the chapters that follow you will find that the teacher's role as supporter and inspirer of children's non-fiction talk and writing is given a prominent place.

GENDER AND NON-FICTION READING (AND WRITING)

Are boys more interested in non-fiction than in imaginative literature? Do girls mainly read stories if given a choice? These have been commonly held views, but the picture is more complex. The research on gender and literacy based at the Centre for Literacy in Education, in London, has made a considerable contribution to our understanding not only of the issues, but also of how we achieve good practice in the classroom. Their publication *Boys and Writing* identified some of the main factors to keep in mind to support boys' developing literacy. They recommend – and this comes from classroom-based research – that we provide: opportunities to reflect and talk about topics and books; a strong role for ICT; opportunities to work with graphic forms – drawing on mapping in planning writing (Barrs and Pidgeon, 2002: Foreword). Let me now say a little about each of these.

While the CLPE studies found evidence that reinforcing boys' interest in non-fiction texts helped their confidence in reading and writing, it was also noted that given the chance to talk and reflect many boys responded enthusiastically to powerful and involving fiction. The importance of interactive ICT as a motivating force has led to teachers using software and film to promote boys' literacy learning. The Education department of the British Film Institute is able to help with moving image texts (www.bfi.org.uk/education). There are details of all the CLPE research studies on their website (www.clpe.co.uk).

There has been a surge of interest in visual kinds of literacy now that the value of graphic forms is accepted. Pahl has researched in nursery classrooms and concludes that we should regard children's diagrams as texts to be read and valued just as we value written texts (Pahl, 1999). Boys are particularly likely to illustrate their very first writing, often completely integrating word and image in early list making. The work of Eve Bearne on multimodal print texts which combine design, illustrations and written text to make meaning shows the motivating effect of reinforcing boys' efforts here (Bearne, 2002).

But what about girls' literacy and particularly their competence in reading and writing non-fiction? Some of my readers will not remember the emphasis on girls' literacy prevalent in the 1970s and 1980s. At this time the results of studies and teachers' classroom observation suggested girls were often dominated by boys in mixed group discussions, sometimes with the teacher's unwitting connivance. The article to track down if you want to know more about this is 'Gender Inequalities in Classroom Talk' by Swann and Graddol (1988: 48–65). This concern fell away somewhat when the introduction of SATs in the 1990s in the UK revealed that, in general, boys lagged behind girls in reading and writing: not unreasonably, much research attention was drawn to this, as we have seen above. However, some girls have continuing needs, including: encouragement to talk confidently in mixed groups; help in using the computer and multimedia tools and texts; and support in learning from non-fiction. Here I am particularly interested in the last of these. Myers and Burnett find that girls can be tempted into non-fiction by offering them narrative non-fiction – life cycles, journeys and 'day in the life of' texts (Myers and Burnett, 2004). I think this is true, but I find both boys and girls benefit from the 'information story' approach in the early years. Purely based on my own classroom observations, I would say that girls also connect with books on controversial subjects like endangered species and other 'green' issues. They are often also comfortable with non-fiction that values feelings and responses as well as 'the facts'. Apart from recognizing that girls and boys need to be able to use non-fiction texts of all kinds to make progress across the whole curriculum and operate in the world on a day-to-day basis, there is another reason why girls in particular need to become critical readers of non-fiction. By the later primary years many girls show an interest in relationships and this is exploited by certain sections of the mass media. There are articles about diet, make-up and relationships with boys, and magazines are also peppered with advertisements for beauty products and fashion items. So it is important that girls develop a critical approach so that they are less likely to be manipulated by this kind of reading material.

The advice on how to promote all kinds of literacy and competence in language use in both boys and girls is well worth noting. But we should remember that children are individuals with their own preferences, strengths and interests. Boys' relative difficulty in writing does not mean that some boys cannot be fine young writers. And we all know of girls who are very comfortable with non-fiction kinds of reading and writing. Above all I warm to those researchers and writers about gender and literacy who are concerned that we should not approach gender issues in a competitive way but regard them as different aspects of the same social and educational questions (Judith Baxter, 2001; Elaine Millard, 2001; Eve Bearne, 2002). (For summaries of the work of these and other scholars interested in literacy and gender differences, see pp. 35–7 and pp. 142–4 in Mallett, 2008.)

ASSESSING AND RECORDING PROGRESS

There are sections more specific to assessing and recording progress in particular kinds of non-fiction reading and writing at the end of most chapters.

Non-fiction reading

Children's abilities in informational kinds of reading have been tested formally in the UK SATs in Year 6, which have included non-fiction reading and comprehension tasks, but we also need some richer ways of assessing and recording children's progress.

Reading diary kept by the teacher for each child

A good way of recording progress in reading both fiction and non-fiction is for the teacher to keep a reading diary for each child with dated entries which are based on hearing the child reading to the teacher one-to-one and on observation. Some teachers prefer to have the diary in an electronic form, others find written notes more user-friendly as they move around the classroom or library. The diary is a good focus for talking to the child and parents about progress. Teachers may send the diary home from time to time so that parents can add something about home reading. When it comes to non-fiction kinds of literacy, observation of developing study and library skills and abilities is important. The English Subject Manager and colleagues will have a programme for teaching these to different age groups, keeping in mind statutory requirements and guidance. We would expect children to learn how to use the Dewey system to find books in the library and to show progress in using retrieval devices like contents pages and indexes. Observing children using texts and resources in the library gives teachers the opportunity to note progress in 'skimming' to get the gist of a passage or 'scanning' for a name or date. In Chapter 34 there is a detailed account suggesting how to support note-taking.

Children's reading logs or journals

Another tried and tested way of recording children's progress in reading all kinds of books is to help them keep their own reading log or reading journal. This could be dated and have bibliographic details of books read, including non-fiction books, and book reviews. Children need some help in deciding on a format but enjoy the freedom to decorate and illustrate their log. I find it best not to request a review for every book read, but to allow children to review a book they have found helpful or interesting. Led by a keen boy, one class liked the idea of awarding each text a star grading from 1 – weak to 5 – excellent. This made for interesting discussion when children read their entries to the class and found readers had awarded different star ratings for the same book.

Formal assessment of reading

The formal assessments of reading in the UK take place in Year 2 and Year 6. Year 6 children sitting the SATs for reading are given a booklet which, in recent years, has contained some non-fiction writing and illustrating, followed by some comprehension-type questions to glean what they have understood. Some questions require short answers or multiple choice selection, while a few tap deeper into understanding by requiring inference. The existence of the SATs means that children are prepared for the tests throughout their time in school and this can have a narrowing effect on the curriculum.

Non-fiction writing

Like reading, writing is formally assessed by timed SATs in Year 6 but progress is assessed and recorded in a number of other ways during the early and primary years. Here, of course, the emphasis is on non-fiction kinds of literacy.

Portfolios of writing samples

Teachers, with some input from children, select examples of writing for a portfolio. Practitioners date these examples, give the context and add a brief evaluative comment: 'Lucy wrote this list of ingredients with only a little help', 'his best piece so far showing awareness of audience'.

At the nursery stage the non-fiction contribution to this might be a drawing showing an activity the child has taken part in – a nature walk or painting; the child's name and a title for the drawing could be added. Lists and labels from home corner role play about the 'café' or 'baby clinic' and photographs of notices and price lists for 'market gardens' and 'garages' used to extend outdoor play can be included.

As children move through the Key Stage 1 years some of the following might be added to the portfolio to show what has been achieved in non-fiction kinds of writing: simple labelled diagrams; lists of ingredients for cooking; instructions for a recipe; science writing; recounts; short illustrated reports; an example of texting from role play; notices, labels and lists; writing on the computer; photocopies of illustrated pages from class books on pets, people who help us or caring for our teeth.

Children in the Key Stage 2 years in the UK will have examples of extended writing across all the text types, including challenging genres like persuasion, discussion and report, added to their portfolios. Much more value for all age groups is now attached to multimodal productions which combine design, illustrations and writing and these would be a welcome addition to the portfolio for any age group.

Formal assessment of writing

The details of the SATs requirements have changed from time to time. But the writing SATs have, for some years, involved a short and a longer writing task. The shorter task is marked first with reference to sentence structure, punctuation and text organization and second for composition and effect. Third, there are marks for spelling.

Non-fiction writing is included, and the tasks are often rather interesting with a clear sense of purpose and audience built in. For example, in 2006, children were asked, in the shorter writing task, to write a page on the Tonga Lizard in an information book about endangered creatures. This task drew on their understanding of 'report', a text type that is organized not chronologically but according to the logic of the topic.

The longer task is marked under the same sort of criteria with the addition of marks for handwriting. The results of these tests are used to assess a child's National Curriculum level for writing; level 4 is the average for children at the end of Key Stage 2. As Wyse and Jones point out, the qualities of writing being 'interesting' and 'imaginative', terms which are evident in the level descriptions, are not part of the framework for assessing the writing SATs (Wyse and Jones, 2008: 173). I agree with Wyse and Jones when they point out that being able to write in an interesting way is crucial in becoming a competent writer and that this omission in the assessment matters.

There are a number of websites to help children tune into the requirements of the tests. The revision exercises tend to be multiple choice in format and help children build up a text typical of a genre, for example a recount or a flyer. One limitation of those I looked at is that they tend to involve children not in actually producing and organizing text themselves, but rather in choosing from a number of options the sentences that are most appropriate. An example of a site which has some entertaining tasks and good visual input is the BBC's Bitesize Revisions for Key Stage 2, which guides children in building up a text that might be a newspaper report or an advertisement (www.bbc.co.uk/schools/ks2bitesize/english).

The results of the writing SATs are usually given separately and children are assigned a level of achievement. Like progress in reading, summaries of what has been achieved in writing can be added to a format like the CLPE Language and Reading Record (Barrs et al., 1998).

These notes will summarize observations and the sampling of children's work. They will also take account of children's comments about their writing and add parents' contributions.

Talk about non-fiction texts

Work around informational themes offers rich opportunities for speaking and listening. Children and teacher will organize prior knowledge about a topic through talk before turning to activities and texts. So, very young children learning about frogs would pool their experiences of finding frogspawn and tadpoles and their understanding of the stages from frogspawn to the mature frog. And then they would be invited to say what they wanted to find out from pond visits and from books. Older children starting on a science unit on forces would talk with the teacher about everyday experiences of forces like pulling and pushing.

It is important that children are given support in becoming critical readers of non-fiction and, with this in mind, teachers encourage talk about the books and resources used. It is a good idea to encourage children to add some of the non-fiction texts they have been using to their reading log, jotting down the reasons they found them useful. Most teachers give children the opportunity of a more comprehensive evaluation through discussion at the end of a body of work.

How might we structure this? Although Aidan Chambers had mainly fiction in mind when he developed his approach to book talk, I find it works well also with group talk around non-fiction texts. In a nutshell, this sort of talk invites three 'sharings': children share enthusiasms, saying what they liked about a text; they share 'puzzles' – things that they find difficult; and then they share the 'patterns', which, in the case of information books, might mean commenting on the global structure and the way each page was organized, with headings, text and illustrations. Of course children may not talk about the 'sharings' in any particular order and they may revisit different 'sharings' during their conversation (Chambers, 1993: 16–20).

A ten-year-old who was part of a group researching Tudor food for rich and poor was asked to report to the class on the texts used. Interestingly, she covered the three elements mentioned by Chambers. Asked which text she had liked most, she said that the more general books and websites on the Tudors tended to have only brief accounts about food and most 'gave similar information'. She had found a book devoted entirely to Tudor food and this gave her group the detail needed. The 'puzzle' she noted was to do with the vagueness of some of the recipes, which did not give precise amounts of ingredients or cooking times. When it came to 'patterns' she praised the organization of the book – in chapters with sub-sections – and said the group had benefited from the user-friendly retrieval devices. She also noticed and liked the way Tudor menus and anecdotes were peppered across the book.

When it comes to children's writing, talk to plan and organize the piece and to evaluate it later is most helpful and shows the young learner the importance of the process as well as the merit of the final draft.

Finally, the evidence from the reading diary, the child's reading log, the writing portfolio, the notes on observations and talk around texts and the results of SATs can all be summarized from time to time and added to a format the staff have designed on the lines of that provided by the CLPE Language and Reading Record (Barrs *et al.*, 1988).

SUMMARY

- Teaching about non-fiction text types was formalized in recent statutory requirements in the UK.
- The modification of the National Curriculum and the abandonment of the Literacy Frameworks for guidance promise to lead to schools deciding on their own approaches and to more flexible teaching.
- Efforts to link teaching about text types with the contexts that give them purpose and meaning in lessons across the curriculum are to be welcomed.
- Although children are individuals there has been helpful classroom research which shows some general differences in attitudes and abilities in the reading and writing of boys and girls. This work can be used to help teachers adopt helpful strategies.
- Children's reading and writing have in recent years been assessed in England at the end of Key Stage 1 and by timed SATs at the end of Key Stage 2. Progress can also be assessed and recorded through talk, observation, reading diaries, children's reading logs and recorded in portfolios with examples of children's writing.

Chapter 24

Classifying non-fiction text types and thoughts towards a critical approach

INTRODUCTION

Part I of this book showed the central role of fiction as a way of coming to understand the world and the place of the individual in it, of developing literacy and nurturing the inner world of the imagination. All this is very much what comes to mind when we think of what is learnt in English lessons. In this second part of the book I turn to the contribution that non-fiction texts make in English and across the whole primary curriculum. Non-fiction, by definition, helps us understand about the world and its complexity and it certainly makes a huge contribution to children's developing literacy. While the best non-fiction can be imagination stretching, it tends to be directed towards the world around us. However entertaining and imaginative a non-fiction text may be, its primary purpose – as we might expect – is to inform, describe or argue a case.

Information or non-fiction texts are important resources in every subject and have a key role in enriching and extending learning. Quality texts not only present information and ideas, but also provide models for children's own writing. Young readers are introduced to a rich general, and sometimes specialized, vocabulary in context and encounter a range of syntactic structures. The illustrations in non-fiction include diagrams, cross-sections, illustrated charts, photographs, line drawing and paintings and these help us link a text with a particular genre or text type. The recognition that non-fiction can play an important part in learning to read is evident in the UK in its inclusion in statutory expectations and in the presence of non-fiction strands in most commercial reading programmes or schemes. Oxford University Press' Oxford Reading Tree was one of those at the forefront of this development.

CLASSIFYING NON-FICTION

Information texts can be classified under different genres or text types. Of course these genres are not static, but change just as needs in society change. One of the best books about the different genres children encounter as they make their way through the primary years, and covering both fiction and non-fiction, is Alison Littlefair's clearly written *Reading All Kinds of Writing* (Littlefair, 1991). In Chapter 4, Littlefair explains that each text type has a 'register' and varies according to the situation in which it is used. Three things come into 'register': what is written about (field), who is being addressed (mode) and how the message is given (tenor). In the UK teachers have for some time used six text types as a framework for teaching non-fiction kinds of literacy. These are recount, procedure (instruction), report, explanation, persuasion and discussion.

The genre theorists

We can trace these categories to the work in the 1980s of the Australian genre theorists – John Martin, Frances Christie and Joan Rothery, for example. These researchers noted, during their forays into primary school classrooms, that narrative and story were the main genres used to develop children's reading and writing. They considered that this approach was unbalanced and that children were being denied systematic help to control some of the text types most valued by society and most linked to eventual job opportunities. These tended to be the non-narrative forms that we call 'report', 'explanation' and 'persuasion'. If you want to read their argument in more detail you might start with a well-known book by I. Reid, *The Place of Genre in Learning*, which contains an exciting collection of articles. Some contributors, sympathetic to the genre theorists, passionately advocate a systematic teaching programme around what they consider to be the main genres. One of the best known of these articles, defending their position and responding to their critics, is by John Martin, Frances Christie and Joan Rothery, and is entitled 'Social Processes in Education: A Reply to Sawyer and Watson (and Others)' (1987).

Some responses to genre theory

So what did the critics of genre theory argue in some of the other articles? They pointed out that once you set out a classification of genres, somehow you give them a status that seems permanent. In fact, new ways of making meaning come up all the time in response to societal need. Digital technologies and popular culture bring into being new and creative combinations of semiotic material. New kinds of text cohesion, including spatial cohesion in children's multimodal texts and how we might assess them, are discussed in *More than Words* by Eve Bearne and her colleagues (Bearne *et al.*, 2004). Perhaps we have not always placed enough value on the multimodal texts children have always created, which combine design, illustration and writing in interesting ways that do not always fit with existing genre categories. And so critics of a genre approach in its more extreme form have felt that young writers should be free to develop their own ways of making sense of information and ideas, often using the 'expressive', exploratory kind of talk and writing recommended by James Britton and others (Britton, 1970: 138). Pressing mature forms of the genre categories on young children could give too much emphasis to writing structures and too little to the opportunity to make sense for themselves and to use language for learning.

This view is eloquently argued by Myra Barrs in her article 'Mapping the World' in *English in Education* (Barrs, 1987). She suggests that since children's first attempts to write non-narrative texts are efforts to organize an aspect of the world and reveal a certain stage of thinking, forcing mature forms on them is unlikely to be helpful. So, the issues around genre remain alive today. In the UK, the National Curriculum is genre-based and this continues into the guidance in the 2006 *Framework for Literacy and Mathematics*. Children are required to have made some headway in controlling non-fiction genres by the time they reach the end of the primary years. Perhaps it is best for teachers to find ways of both helping children to meet the expectations here while accepting that early writing is likely to be transitional in a move from the 'expressive' to the more structured non-fiction forms. In Chapter 29, the usefulness of 'writing frames' is discussed. Wray and Lewis take on some of the insights from the genre theorists in organizing headings in their writing frames but insist that the frames should not be used directly to teach genre (Wray and Lewis, 1996: 53). For an extended account of the issues, see also Wyse and Jones' *Teaching English, Language and Literacy* (2007: 121–31).

In this part of the book I have organized the text types into two main groups: chronological and non-chronological. So Chapters 26 and 27 are about recounts and instruction texts, while the later chapters cover report, explanation, discussion and persuasion. As they are so helpful in lessons in English and across the curriculum, I have also devoted a chapter to reference texts – to dictionaries, thesauri, atlases, study guides and encyclopedias.

I think the more genre-based kinds of reading and writing tasks should be used flexibly with younger children. By Year 6 I think it is reasonable to expect children to be able to appreciate the structures of the main text types, and to have made some headway in controlling them as confident readers and writers. The chapters in this part of the book explore ways of achieving this. But we must be open to new ways of making meaning – and recognize the importance of the popular culture texts which are likely to motivate and inspire young learners. We also aim to help children to become critical readers, able to evaluate the texts and resources they have been using.

EVALUATING NON-FICTION: TOWARDS CRITICAL ATTENTION AND THE INCREASING STATUS OF CHILDREN'S NON-FICTION

While children's fiction has received critical attention for some time, there has been less interest in developing a way of evaluating information texts. Those who review non-fiction cope not only with changing perceptions of childhood, which also impact on reviewers of children's fiction, but in addition with an overwhelming and continuing augmentation in the range of information texts both print and electronic. Indeed being able to comment helpfully on both print and electronic texts makes considerable demands on a reviewer's knowledge and experience. Victor Watson puts it rather starkly: 'in Britain, at least, information books still suffer from a lack of a sustained, critical reading by interested and well-informed adults, such as have influenced other areas of children's literature' (Watson, 2001: 368).

While taking Watson's point, I think things are improving. There have been recent inspiring conferences devoted entirely to children's non-fiction with speakers, amongst them teachers, children's authors and writers and illustrators of children's non-fiction, speaking passionately about informational kinds of reading and how we appraise the best texts.

In October 2005, Nicola Davies, well-known for her dedication to communicating bio-logical science to young readers, organized a conference called ' Adventures in the Real World' in Swansea which brought together a large number of teachers, publishers, and writers and illustrators of non-fiction. Then there was the Write Away conference in May 2008 – 'Non-Fiction: More than Information' – organized by Nikki Gamble and attended by those who wanted to find the best in non-fiction for children, covering, among many other important topics, what we look for in biography and autobiography, in lyrical information books and in information picturebooks, including those which explore true stories of children battling for something resembling a proper childhood in war situations. The consensus at this conference was that there was a wide range of discourses, both narrative and non-narrative, which children can not only learn from, but also enjoy.

Another promising development is the increasing number of journals and newspapers which include reviews of non-fiction texts. *Books for Keeps* has a long record of according reviews of information books the space and consideration they deserve, not least because, at one time, they had a dedicated non-fiction editor, Eleanor Von Schweinitz. *The School Librarian* also has strong review sections on non-fiction and a special new section on ICT texts. *English 4–11*, the primary school journal of the English Association, not only reviews non-fiction but also awards prizes annually, giving children's fiction and non-fiction illustrated books equal status. Thinking of awards, for many years the TES had a 'junior information book award' that attracted much interest and brought before a wide readership quality books like Manning and Granström's *What's Under the Bed* and the television programme *Blue Peter* has an award category called 'the best book with facts' each year. I have noticed that reviewers of children's literature in the quality newspapers – Nicolette Jones of *The Times* for example – have turned attention to non-fiction, writing particularly insightfully about what to look for in reference books and about lyrical kinds of non-fiction. All this contributes to a developing expertise in pinpointing what makes an information book 'good' – here I am thinking of the 'connoisseurship' of which Margaret Meek writes (Meek, 1996: 109).

In this book I have kept in mind three elements in the texts I mention: the quality of their design, the appropriateness of the coverage and the effectiveness of the language and illustration. But it is not a matter of ticking boxes on a checklist and the reason why a book appeals may be beyond these elements. Some authors know just how much detail to include for their intended readership and achieve an 'authorial voice' that invites young readers to share in their expertize on a topic. Enthusiasm is infectious and, above all, a questioning, speculative approach which admits that there are some things about which we only have incomplete knowledge will appeal to young readers.

SPECIALIST REVIEWERS AND CHILDREN AS REVIEWERS

Specialist reviewers

When it comes to coverage and accuracy one issue that arises particularly for teachers of older primary school children is how to judge books in areas where you are not a specialist. In the United Kingdom, teachers have at least one primary curriculum subject as a specialism, and are expected to have subject knowledge in the core subjects and to be competent to teach and resource the other primary subjects.

As a specialist in primary English, I have had to work hard to feel reasonably competent to judge the more challenging books on science and geography for the over nines. I have found it useful to read book reviews by specialists in these subjects. For example, *Books for Keeps* has amongst its reviewers Felix Pirani, Emeritus Professor of Rational Mechanics at the University of London. He contributes enormously to helping us assess the worth of science encyclopedias and science books. He is a stickler for accuracy and has harsh words for authors and publishers who fall short, particularly where errors mislead over important matters. One encyclopedia, from a major publishing house, drew from him a fierce review pointing out errors that would confuse young scientists. The list of inaccuracies was so long that the publisher sought his help in bringing the book up to standard. This led to the following comment by the editor of *Books for Keeps*: 'this incident underlines the importance of the reviewing of children's non-fiction by subject specialists whenever possible' (Stones, 2002, 'News Briefing').

Felix Pirani is extremely thorough, pointing out small errors and inconsistencies even in books he broadly likes. He praised Dorling Kindersley's *Space Encyclopedia* for its overall accuracy, clarity and sound cross-referencing, but even here, he spotted 'some assertions not universally accepted by astronomers' and which therefore needed revision when the book was reprinted (reviewed in *Books for Keeps* 121, March 2000). There are an increasing number of reviewers with expert knowledge who are helping us towards a literacy criticism of the discourses that make up the body of children's non-fiction.

Books for Keeps draws on the expertise, for example, of Martin Salisbury, an illustrator and expert on children's book illustration in both information books and fiction, of Sue Unstead, who was an editor of children's non-fiction for many years, and of Ted Percy, who spent his working life as a children's librarian. *The School Librarian* also draws on a wide range of reviewing expertise, and on reviewers who are specialists on books and resources for particular age groups covering the whole of the school years. Then there are their experts on particular kinds of text; they draw on the knowledge and wisdom of Prue Goodwin, a specialist in children's picturebooks, both information stories and fiction. All of these people, as well as many others, bring reviewing to the level of an art. I am always drawn to Ted Percy's reviews: they are so entertaining as well as useful. Some are titillatingly stinging. If we do not want bland books neither do we want anaemic reviews. Listen to this from a review by Percy of a book about bees: 'the pictures – you couldn't call them illustrations – are dreadful: un-bee-like bees, slug-like birds and the most grotesquely distorted hives, smokers, extractors and beekeepers imaginable, all suggestive of the clumsiness that is the anathema of the capable beekeeper' (Percy, 2008: 19). He always writes honestly and entertainingly and, where appropriate, with the great enthusiasm of a good reviewer. He also constantly has the intended reader in mind. Here is a snippet from his review of *How to Turn Your Parents Green* by James Russell: 'It's all good basic stuff – the words are most attractive, and utterly accessible, illustrations are not to my taste, but for all I know may be the acme of contemporary cool' (Percy, 2008: 19).

However, authors can strike back. I received an acerbic response from a well-regarded author following my review of what I took to be an information picturebook about a cave boy. In my *Books for Keeps* review I suggested that young readers might be misled by seeing a dinosaur alongside a mammoth in a representation of a prehistoric cave painting. The author complained that his book was a story and therefore he was entitled to improvise on reality. What do you think? Should 'information stories' stick to scientific truths?

248

Children as reviewers

One challenge for reviewers of children's books is that they are commenting on texts for another age group to their own. What insight and knowledge do they draw on? All of us probably use our memories of the sort of books we enjoyed when young and what we particularly liked about them. Teachers and parents can also draw on their observations of what children enjoy and note their preferences. But there is another source of help: the opinions on and experiences with texts expressed by the children themselves. At the end of a series of lessons, teachers often encourage children to talk about the resources they have been using. I have sometimes tried out with groups of children books that I have been sent to review. Sometimes this has led me to tear up my draft and to try again in the light of the children's comments. Children, given encouragement and time, can be most insightful about texts. I provided a basket of information books for some volunteers from a Year 5 class to look at. They spoke eloquently about *Erika's Story* by Ruth Vander Zee, illustrated by Roberto Innocenti; both boys and girls remarked on the comfort afforded in a sad story by 'the small pink bundle of hope', by which they meant the illustrations showing a tiny baby thrown to safety from a train making its way to a concentration camp. One child thought the writer and illustrator had worked together to tell this true story so that the reader felt 'a mixture of hope and sadness'.

A boy in this group particularly liked some history books I had provided which were presented like newspapers: 'you get the information but the book makes you laugh as well'. I was interested that the group thought that this kind of 'popular newspaper' format was a device that made you 'more able to remember things'. In the context of this kind of talk children can express reasons for their opinions and learn that some books do a job better than do others.

SUMMARY

- There have been attempts to classify children's non-fiction text types into categories, but we must remember such classifications need to be sensitive to changing societal needs.
- The Australian genre theorists believed that children needed to be directly taught how to control the non-narrative kinds of text considered important in our society.
- The work of the genre theorists influenced researchers in the UK and, through them, the statutory requirements and guidance given to teachers of primary school children.
- The present book organizes non-fiction into chronological or narrative forms and non-chronological or non-narrative forms.
- It is argued that genre classifications are dynamic not static and that new ways of making meaning are being produced all the time. Thus we need to take account of new literacies and the popular culture texts which appeal to young learners.
- While older primary children are expected to have made headway in controlling some of the main non-fiction text types as readers and writers, younger children are not intellectually equipped to take on mature structures and need first to be encouraged to make meaning in their own way to make sense of the world.

- There are signs that non-fiction texts are becoming valued. Good signs here include the organization of conferences devoted to these texts and to non-fiction kinds of literacy and the emergence of specialist reviewers of non-fiction in journals and quality newspapers.
- All this contributes to the development of a critical approach to non-fiction texts.

Chapter 25

Introducing chronological text types
Recount and instruction

Look at any nursery or primary school collection and you will find a good number of non-fiction texts for children that are organized chronologically: life cycles, journeys and biographies, for example. Teachers know that children respond readily to chronological texts; after all we plan and live our lives in a time sequence, think and even dream in this way. Very young children are familiar with this kind of organization and their oral recounts of what they have been doing are narratives. The power of the chronological and the narrative as a way of relating to and organizing our world is explored in a well-known essay by Barbara Hardy entitled 'Narrative as a Primary Act of Mind' (Hardy, 1977).

Chronological non-fiction texts are often divided into two main categories. Here I have followed the terminology used in UK statutory and guidance documents, and refer to two chronological texts types, 'recount' and 'instruction'.

The 'recount' stable takes in a range of texts including accounts of events in the real world, diary and logbook writing and two more 'literary' forms – autobiography and biography. Children first organize their thinking through speaking and listening, and at the earliest stages they might do this by relating their 'news' to the class or smaller group. Then, later, they are helped to write down and illustrate these retellings. However, children come to know and understand their world not just through direct experience, but also through books and other resources. These secondary resources have a considerable role to play in encouraging children to talk and reflect about the real world.

As they move through the early and primary years children find that many topics of interest in lessons and activities fall naturally into a time sequence, not just journeys and life cycles but also historical events, lives of well-known people and 'day in the life of' accounts. While by definition narrative is the primary principle of organization, recounts often include opinion, comment and analysis. We find, for example, evaluative comments in children's own recounts of sports day, outings and holidays. It is also true that what is broadly a recount text in a time sequence may include other kinds of writing, for example explanation. A good example of this is the detailed and carefully annotated explanatory diagram of a skeleton included in *Dinomummy* by Phillip Lars Manning, which tells the story of the unearthing of a mummified dinosaur.

The 'instruction' stable houses those texts which set out procedures, often using numbers, letters or bullet points to help structure a sequence. This kind of thinking finds expression in the discussions between teacher and children: how to care for the classroom tadpoles or

251

Autobiography – a first-person, usually chronologically organized, account written by the subject that may seek to justify, explain or excuse as well as to inform; we get one person's version of the things that happened and how they felt about them.

Biography – the life story of an individual, written in the third person.

Discourse – a term referring in a general way to a conversation, dialogue, sermon or lecture. It is used by linguists to discuss any piece of spoken or written language longer than a sentence.

Expressive language – a term which was used by James Britton to refer to the fairly unstructured kind of speech and writing we adopt when we formulate action plans or new ways of construing experience. Children's first writing is often like 'written down speech' and more to do with their own immediate thoughts and preoccupations than the needs of an audience.

Faction – a term sometimes used for texts that combine features of both fiction and non-fiction. An example of such a text is Geoff Waring's *Oscar and the Frog: A Book About Growing*, which uses the device of talking animals to explain facts.

First-person writing – gives one person's viewpoint and response to experiences and can take the form of a letter, diary, factual narrative (recount) or a full-length autobiography.

Fonts – refers to the different sizes and kinds of print – large, small, bold, italic and coloured – in texts.

Format (of books) – refers to size and shape.

Genre – refers to the features that identify a text with a particular category. So, for example, the recount genre describes events chronologically.

Inference – refers to the ability to work something out from information you already have rather than information being made fully explicit.

Information stories – texts which follow a time sequence but which also impart information and ideas. Unlike a conventional story, an 'information story' may have a fact file, a glossary and an index.

Instruction – refers to those texts which tell us how to do something. Young children talk, read and write in this genre about, for example mixing paints, following a recipe or setting up a wormery.

Procedural (see **instruction**).

Recount – a chronologically ordered retelling of events.

Transitional genre – a term referring to texts, usually for children, which have some of the features of mature texts but which are modified to make them appealing and accessible to younger learners.

Voice – can mean one of three things: the 'voiced' sounds in phonetic (b d g z), the active or passive 'voice' in grammar, and the 'narrative voice' of a narrator or the character who 'speaks' in a story.

Figure 25.1 *Glossary: terms to do with chronological text types*

snails, how to clear up after painting and cooking, how to carry out science experiments and how to operate the computer or DVD recorder. The thinking patterns first encountered in talk are carried into children's first attempts at writing structured in this way. We turn to instruction texts to help refine children's understanding of a topic and the practical activities that are part of it; we also teach about how this understanding can be communicated and presented.

The best texts labelled as 'recount' or 'instruction' are enormously varied and show signs of the author's genuine concern about how children read, think and learn. Print texts for the early and primary years are nearly always multimodal, combining design, visual material – diagrams, photographs and drawings – in helpful and imaginative ways to get young readers thinking and learning. Multimedia resources can show processes in action – for example the metamorphosis of a caterpillar into a butterfly or the actual workings of a crane.

After defining the formal features of these two text types, both the following chapters suggest a range of texts and resources to help children think and learn. In line with the rest of the book, each is arranged in three age groups: pre-school and nursery, five- to eight-year-olds and eight- to eleven-year-olds. Then there are some suggestions about ways of using the texts in school and some examples of children's work.

Chapter 26

Recounts
Young researchers read and write chronologically ordered accounts

INTRODUCTION

Some of the first writing and drawing children do is 'recount', for example retellings of recent experiences in and out of the classroom. Early books and resources in this genre support and enrich children's understanding and writing and are useful in lessons across the curriculum. There are 'life cycles' for science, journeys and 'day in the life of' accounts for geography, and autobiography and biography for history and English lessons. As children get older the recounts they read and write become longer and more complex and the evaluation and analysis of people, incidents and ideas begun earlier on are now more evident and more sophisticated.

FEATURES OF NON-FICTION RECOUNTS

The main characteristic of a recount is its narrative organization. Events follow a time sequence, but this does not rule out opinion, analysis or the writer's response to all that is happening. Recounts usually begin by setting a scene, go on to record a series of events through time and then add a concluding statement. When it comes to language features, recounts are usually given in the past tense and time connectives – 'then', 'next', 'later' – help make the text cohesive. They are written in either the first or the third person. I now give some attention to the features of particular kinds of recount: information stories; logbooks, diaries, letters, autobiography and biography; and journalistic writing.

Information stories

Teachers and children often refer to texts which follow a time sequence but which also impart facts and ideas as 'information stories'. The life cycles of animals and plants, journeys and historical events all have an inherent chronology which is helpful to young readers and listeners familiar with the rhythms of story. Some information stories have features associated with non-narrative information books, for example fact pages, information boxes, labelled diagrams and a glossary or index. Others have a fantasy element – a talking animal asking questions perhaps – even though the function of the text is informational.

Logbooks, diaries, letters, autobiography and biography

Logbooks and diaries are the kind of recounts that provide a record and entries are usually dated and headed. Ships' logs provide an account of a voyage and are often a valuable historical source. School logbooks, required in the UK until the 1990s and still kept by some schools, record attendance, numbers on the roll and everyday school events of importance within the school walls. The appointment diary or calendar on the wall helps us manage our time. A 'diary' can be something more personal, a journal which can record the writer's actions, inner thoughts and preoccupations. Some information stories use the diary format as a device to help young readers understand the lives of people in history or those who live in different parts of the world. *Castle Diary: The Journal of Tobias Burgess, Page* by Richard Platt and Chris Riddell captures the day-to-day life of a medieval page and takes in feasting, jousting and hunting. Above all, we learn about the page's private opinion of those living and working alongside him. Using the diary device in a similar way in his book *Charles Darwin*, Alan Gibbons charts the events during Darwin's journey to collect scientific specimens through the eyes of a ship boy. To be clear about where factual information is accompanied by invention he writes in an author's note that: 'James and his pet are fictional characters that I have created. They were not on the *Beagle*'s voyage, but the people in James' diary did exist, and the events described are based on what actually happened.'

Autobiographies are more sustained first-person accounts, often drawing on diaries, telling of the events of a life from the subject's point of view. The writer may seek to justify, explain or excuse particular actions and attitudes. And of course the author is inevitably, and for their own reasons, selective about what is included, what is left out, what is skimmed over and what is emphasized. No reader whether child or adult is going to be entertained by the banal or self-promoting sort of autobiography. We want to be intrigued, puzzled perhaps or led to review our attitudes and opinions.

Authors of biographies usually write life stories in the third person. Over the last thirty years biographies written for children have become more varied and more care has been taken over accuracy. But when judging whether to bring a biography into the classroom, we consider more than how well 'the facts' are recorded. A good biography for children needs to encourage reflection and this is achieved partly by not hiding the puzzles and inconsistencies that are so often part of an honest account of someone's life. Margaret Meek comments that we look for 'an encounter with a life and ideas' (Meek, 1996: 60). In the UK, publishers have brought out quite a number of books, very often in series, about great lives with an eye on the English and history programmes of the National Curriculum. As is the case in autobiographies, many of these add interest by including remembered snippets of conversation, letters, diary entries, photographs, timelines, maps, posters and theatre programmes. Printed out email and text messages now join this list. Children can be helped to see all these as identifying features of the genre and will, with encouragement, learn to use them in their own attempts at biographical writing. Teachers and children will find television programmes and DVDs on famous lives helpful. Biographies in this medium can show location, historical context and dramatic recreations. For more recent figures children will be able to see and hear from the biographer's subject. It is worth checking what is available to complement print accounts. The motivational aspect of electronic biographies should not be underestimated.

But print biographies may also draw in children who are not normally avid readers. Linnea Hendrickson recommends for these young learners 'well-illustrated small biographies of sports heroes and entertainers' (Hendrickson in Watson, 2001: 83). Biographies (as well as autobiographies) can help young readers understand the choices a writer makes and these insights help when they attempt their own writing.

Journalistic writing

Some kinds of journalistic writing in newspapers, magazines and on the internet – on events in the UK or in other countries – are really recounts even though they are sometimes called 'reports'. Television 'reports' are also often recounts with some comment and analysis. CBBC's *Newsround* provides children with accounts of events in a time sequence with analysis. As with all texts, print and electronic, spoken and written, we need to make children aware of the possibility of bias – for example, who is presenting the piece and what might be their viewpoint.

SOME CRITERIA FOR CHOOSING

The non-fiction texts which are the subject of Part II of this book are evaluated in each chapter under three main elements: design, coverage, language and illustration. Here I consider how these 'big shapes' apply to recount texts.

Design

Good design, achieved through the skilful arrangement of print, graphics and illustration, will capture the interest of young readers and aid their learning. Further, it gives global cohesion to a text and thus plays a part in helping young readers get to grips with the topic. The younger the children, the less cluttered the pages should be: too intricate a collage of print and pictures can confuse the eye and mind. This is what I have always thought at any rate, but I comment about the danger of generalizations later on. Both print and electronic books now use different sizes and styles of print to flag the status of particular blocks of information. We associate indexes and glossaries with the typical non-narrative information book, but these can also be valuable retrieval devices in information stories and in autobiographies and biographies.

Anyone writing an autobiography or biography for children needs to think how to use design to draw their young readers in. I think imaginative decisions were made by Menno Metselaar and Ruud Van Der Rol in their biography for the over tens *The Life of Anne Frank*. First the format of the book is just right; it has the small square shape of many diaries. The authors wanted to include many photographs never before published but always contextualize, annotate and explain their significance. Chronology is often stressed as a defining feature of biography, but here the book begins with a large coloured photograph of the red and white checked diary Anne was given on her thirteenth birthday, together with an account of the events of that day. Only then do we move into a chronological account. The reasons for this decision and the impact of starting here, rather than with Anne's birth, would be an excellent discussion point for older primary children and their teacher.

Coverage

Good coverage of a topic is to do with providing the information needed to interest and inform a particular age and ability range. Experienced teachers are able to see quickly if the key things are covered in the right amount of detail. The publishers and authors of quality books and resources in the recount stable ensure that information is as accurate as possible given the state of knowledge at a particular time.

Judging coverage in autobiography and biography can be more problematic as the information is inevitably selective and the perception of the same events by different people can genuinely vary. But we can expect authors to take care of accuracy of dates, names and details of important events.

Language and illustration

Language needs to be appropriate to the topic and age range and to link well with the visual elements in the book. I believe a friendly but not banal tone is best, particularly for younger children on the lines of 'I have something interesting to share with you'. And there is no reason why fiction should grab all the best images. Analogy and imagery are important linguistic devices for the non-fiction writer. In that lyrical information story *Think of an Eel*, Karen Wallace tells us that the elver is 'like a willow leaf, clear as crystal' and with 'teeth like a saw blade'. Referring to secrets and puzzles is another good way of involving young readers in a more than superficial way. Karen Wallace writes: 'No-one has ever seen a wild eel lay eggs or an eel egg hatch'. A speculative tone, implying that knowledge is not static but develops through time and that our attitudes to that knowledge change too, helps children become reflective readers. If young learners want to read and research the topic further after finishing a book, it suggests that the author found the right way to explain things and create interest. Illustrations link a text with a genre and need to be appropriate, appealing and helpful in extending children's understanding. In 'life cycle' books the illustrations contribute to the narrative drive and, in the best, the right weight is given to each event in the life of a plant or creature. The same point is applicable to texts about journeys and 'day in the life of' books. Diagrams – cross-sections for instance – work best if they are helpfully annotated, closely linked to the written text and unambiguous. In some print texts the meaning of symbols and the significance of the orientation of arrows need to be explained to children encountering these devices for the first time. When a text is illustration rich, strong linking narrative is needed to maintain coherence.

The skilled non-fiction writer for young children knows how to use just the right amount of detail in language and illustration to satisfy and not confuse a young learner. Nicola Davies, speaking at a conference on non-fiction for children, shared her strategy in writing *Bat Loves the Night*. The concept of echolocation – the high pitched sounds a bat makes and which are bounced back from objects to reveal their location – was evoked by the words 'Bat shouts as she flies'. This is the sort of image that gets a child's brain into gear so that there is a basis for more advanced science input later on (Davies, Write Away conference, 22 May 2008).

Autobiography and biography are amongst the most literary kinds of non-fiction. Insightful writers of these genres for children use language and illustration not just to give a chronology, but also to provide insight into the subject's experiences, feelings, ideas and motivations.

Generalizations sometimes create difficulties. I once suggested to a group of students that we should look for uncluttered pages in the information texts we offered to primary aged children. In general this is true if fairly obvious. But someone pointed out such a criterion would rule out some of the work of excellent and exciting writers of children's non-fiction – not least Marcia Williams, Richard Scarry and Stephen Biesty, all of whom produce richly detailed illustrated books.

When I was talking about this very point with a group of children, ten-year-old Robert commented helpfully: 'I think you can have a lot on a page sometimes as long as it is all connected.' So although the pages of the authors mentioned above may look 'busy' at first glance, we find that each picture and block of writing builds to a harmonious web of meaning. Every text we select should justify its place in the classroom or central library. But we also need to look to the variety and completeness of the collection as a whole.

CHOOSING RECOUNTS FOR DIFFERENT AGE GROUPS

Texts organized as informational narratives often include other text types, particularly instruction or explanation text and illustration. The narrative form can help convey a lot of information in a strong and interesting context. Although the non-narrative kind of information text becomes more prevalent in the collection as children get older, the best recounts remain a powerful and sympathetic form to help children learn in lessons across the curriculum.

Pre-school and nursery, 3–5-year-olds

One of the most prevalent recount texts for this age group is the 'information story'. The best of these help children to respond imaginatively to experiences in the real world. For the very young there are many books about the daily experiences that people a young child's world. Children enjoy Eric Hill's Spot books, for example *Spot's Touch and Feel Book*, which is illustrated with textured materials to simulate rough grass, a smooth ball and knobbly steps – all encountered during a walk on a sunny day. There is no doubt that the Spot series is liked by young children at home and in the nursery classroom. When it comes to picturebooks of this kind, I do think that the sharing adult needs to take children beyond mere recognition of objects towards comment and speculation.

There are a number of books on children's first experiences of school. *Victoria's Day* by Maria de Fatima Campos follows a child who happens to have special needs through a day filled with activity: painting, baking and playing games with friends. Skilled writers of this kind of book know how much detail to include. Sarah Garland seems to have got this just right in her classic information picturebooks about such everyday experiences as swimming, doing the garden, picnicking and going to playschool. Favourites include *Going Shopping* and *Coming to Tea*. In the latter we follow the preparations for a tea party explained in brisk lively writing: 'roll the biscuit, mix the cake'. But it is the illustrations, including those showing the down-to-earth clutter in the family kitchen, the wooden spoons sticking up from a pot, the iron and a tea towel hanging out of a drawer, that seem to get children talking. And it is this talking and reflecting that we want a book to inspire. So we look for books which do more than nudge children to point to and name objects. Rather we treasure those books that

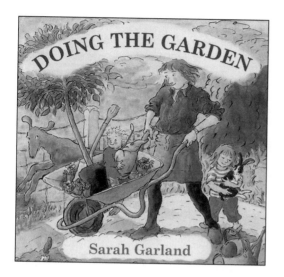

Figure 26.1
Front cover of Doing the Garden
by Sarah Garland
Reproduced with the permission of the
publishers Frances Lincoln Ltd.
Copyright 2006

encourage children's thoughtful comment, imaginative speculation and interesting questions. It is best not to be too taken with elaborate design features and bright pictures, seeking out rather those books that open up discussion.

It is often recount texts which provide a sympathetic introduction to the thinking associated with lessons across the curriculum (Mallett, 2003: 96). Those books on the natural world which recount the life cycle of a human being, an animal or plant have a natural narrative rhythm and help orient children towards scientific ways of construing the world. *Horse*, by Malachy Doyle and illustrated by Angelo Rinaldi, follows one foal's development as he begins to move on shaky legs and gradually gathers the strength to run and jump. My early years students and I have found *Baby's First Year* by Debbie MacKinnon and Anthea Sieveking a book that has enormous appeal for young children. It fits well with projects on growing as it features annotated photographs of a baby's progress each month. One mature student teacher obligingly brought in her own baby, at intervals, so that the children could compare his progress with the baby in the photographs.

Another information storybook which is often used in the context of themes and activities on growing is Ruth Brown's *Ten Seeds*, which relates the story of the growth of seeds planted by a young child. Case Study 26.2 allows us to join children reading about the dangers a seedling faces on its way to fruition.

An information story can sometimes create a strong sense of an environment or habitat through writing and illustration. Harriet Blackford's *Elephant's Story* tells a dramatic tale about the life of a young elephant calf on the vast African savannah. The landscapes are beautifully brought to life by illustrator Manja Stojic. Some of these early books help children begin to construe their experience in the world in a way that develops into scientific or geographical thinking. Included here are books about a day at the beach, wood or river which draw attention to the physical features of the world and those that explore what human beings have made — towns with parks and shops. Meredith Hooper's *River Story* uses simple written narrative and vivid paintings to show the river at different stages of its journey and provides a context for children's talk. This book would also be useful when children move into the five to eight age group.

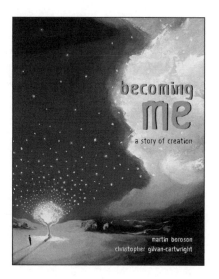

Figure 26.2
Front cover of Becoming Me: A Story of Creation *by Martin Boroson and Christopher Gilvan-Cartwright (illus.)*
Reproduced with the permission of the publishers Frances Lincoln Ltd. Copyright 2000

There are some books which are difficult to place in a category but deserve to be mentioned as they are among the most inspiring. *Becoming Me: A Story of Creation*, by Martin Boroson and illustrated by Christopher Gilvan-Cartwright, tells an intriguing story and is illustrated with colourful pictures with an aura of mystery. It tackles universal questions about how a human individual begins and about the meaning of life and so has appeal for any age group. I place it here as some people have found it helpful to refer to when responding to the questions of very young children about the universe and their place in it. This book was the winner of the Special Award in the *English 4–11* Awards for the Best Illustrated Book of 2000.

5–8-year-olds

This is the golden age of the recount text to support learning across the curriculum. Texts abound about life cycles, journeys and lives of historical figures and sporting personalities. The best are the result of careful reflection and effort on the part of authors and illustrators and inspire children to 'wonder' and to find out more.

Science and nature study

By now, children can usually manage to read 'life cycle' books independently, helped by the 'story through time' approach and the accompanying illustrations. Eric Carle's beautifully illustrated picturebook *The Tiny Seed* extends the message in Ruth Brown's *Ten Seeds* about nature's necessary prolificacy and shows young readers the complexity of the life history of plants. The tiny seed in the narrative is blown from the plant and lands on fertile soil. It grows until it produces hundreds of seeds itself, which begin the journey again. But the book makes clear that this seed is fortunate as so many never manage to embed themselves in earth of the right quality for germination and growth. It is this skill in showing us the way nature works that makes it worthwhile seeking out books of this quality.

Often recounts put children in touch with some of the conventions of non-fiction by including charts and information boxes. Angela Royston's *Life Cycle of a Frog* has an illustrated timeline on each page which charts the stages within the creature's life span. This text type can also explain challenging concepts. *From Caterpillar to Butterfly*, by Deborah Heiligman and illustrated by Bari Weissman, begins with the homely image of a caterpillar being brought into school in a jam jar, but manages to explain the process of metamorphosis skilfully. Some recounts, in the form of 'information stories', use devices from fiction, doing so to get information and concepts across to young readers. In *A Seed in Need: First Look at the Life Cycle of a Flower* it is the dialogue between an inquisitive ladybird and snail which makes the book special. Sam Godwin and Simone Abel use humour and lively text and pictures to make this an exhilarating read. This question and answer device is used skilfully by Vivian French in *T.REX*, a story about a young boy's visit to a dinosaur exhibition with his grandfather. The book is structured around the boy's questions and the grandfather's speculative answers.

BOX 26.1 *T.REX* BY VIVIAN FRENCH AND ALISON BARTLETT (ILLUS.) (WALKER)

'Did he hunt with his friends?
Did he hunt with his mate?'
'He probably hunted and ate alone,
But then again – we don't really know.
It was millions and millions of years ago . . .'

The young readers are given the fossil evidence we have so far to help answer the questions. So children learn from this book that scientific knowledge is a process – a series of ideas modified by new discoveries. They learn something about dinosaurs, but also something about scientific analysis and speculation.

Other science topics which can be tackled well in the recount form are to do with food chains and water cycles. *The Drop in My Drink* by Meredith Hooper tells the story of water on our planet. The book, as we would expect from this author, is invitingly written, presenting scientific concepts poetically; it shows so effectively the relationship between water and living things and is enhanced by Chris Coady's superb illustrations. It also provides a reading experience that may well enrich the writing of this age group and that of older children too.

Geography

The recount genre lends itself to introducing children to geographical concepts. Texts telling the story of a day, or week perhaps, in the life of a child growing up in a particular country across the world or of a visit made to relatives help young readers connect with the customs and lifestyles of other places. *Prita Goes to India* by Prodeepta Das and *Ikenna Goes to Nigeria* by Ifeoma Onyefulu are two titles in a series of photographic information books showing the events in each child's visit to meet members of their extended families. On the same lines are the titles in Frances Lincoln's A Child's Day series. These books make it possible for young readers to learn about the lives of children from many countries, including China, Russia, India, Vietnam, Lapland and Peru. *Enrique's Day: From Dawn to Dusk in a Peruvian City* by Sara Farjado begins with the young boy's visit to the local bakery to buy 'chaplas' for the family breakfast and goes on to tell how he gets a taxi to school and later we join him at a family meal in the evening. The books in these series, and similar books by other publishers, concentrate on the positive aspects of children's lives rather than on the problems of poverty, oppression and conflict that are encountered in some countries. There is an issue about how soon we can or should explain to children something about these issues. I offer this as something for all of us who believe in the power of reading for knowledge and understanding to reflect on. *Gervelie's Journey*, which is discussed on p. 270 for the eight to eleven age range, gets the balance right.

Before leaving geography books organized as recounts, Jo Readman's lively stories which introduce children to 'products' from around the world deserve a mention. *The World Came to My Place Today* begins with young George fearing he has a boring day at home ahead. But Grandpa arrives with a globe and the day is structured around finding out where the things we eat, like cereal and chocolate, come from and which countries provide the materials for everyday things like the rubber tyres on bicycles and the wood for toys. The book uses quirky drawings together with photographs and the reasons for the choice of each illustration would be a good talking point.

History

Reading about and understanding events in history demands, from the earliest stages, some concept of chronology. So the recount text type is a good vehicle for communicating historical information in story form and the best books appeal across the whole primary age range. A number of publishers have a large history collection, for example Evans Brothers, Heinemann Library, Oxford University Press and Franklin Watts. For the five to eights we seek history texts which draw children into the topic in an interesting way and which children can manage to read independently. You will find on the websites of these publishers details of the titles available. There are a number of books available on 'great historical events', partly because these feed directly into National Curriculum history topics. *The Great Fire of London* by Stewart Ross is a good example of a book written in an 'easy to read' way for these young learners and there is extra information in some concluding notes. The dramatic illustrations help encourage talk and informed speculation. Deborah Fox's book, also entitled *The Great Fire of London*, is a title in Heinemann's How Do We Know That? series. Like the other titles it helps children begin to distinguish between historical narrative and the presentation of historical evidence. Part 1 tells the story of the event and Part 2 examines the evidence on which the story is based.

Franklin Watts' Family Memories series also helps children to develop a concept of time passing by focusing on the memories of living people about the events of their youth. So *When Your Mum Was Little*, written by Jane Bidder and illustrated by Shelagh McNicholas, compares living now with how things were in the 1960s and 1970s based on real memories.

Autobiography and biography

These texts support and enrich both history and English themes from this age group onwards. Anecdotes shared in discussion draw on children's lives and a lot of the writing children do in English lessons is written in the first person. This kind of writing draws on personal experiences and real events and on their response to them and so children come to autobiographies tuned into this way of making sense of things. Many fictional narratives use first person writing as a device to create an involving story. But Anna Sewell's timeless classic *Black Beauty* nudges at the boundary between fact and fiction; the horse 'talks' to the young readers and listeners so that they become captivated and encouraged to take on the book's ethical message. It is a passionately written book because the author had a strong desire to let everyone know about the cruel treatment of horses in Victorian times. Only able readers from about eight or nine are likely to be able to read this book for themselves, but some younger children would appreciate listening to a reading. Teachers find the book leads to a lot of questions and are aware that some children find the cruel things that are done upsetting. Dorling Kindersley have brought out a book together with a tape with music and sound effects and narrated by Juliet Stevenson, the book illustrated by Victor Ambrus.

Another book which uses the 'first person' as a device to help young readers become involved is *The Brontës: Scenes from the Childhood of Charlotte, Branwell, Emily and Anne*, which is written and illustrated by Catherine Brighton. Readers learn about some of the episodes in the children's lives as if from Charlotte Brontë herself: 'we climb Papa's double cherry tree and as dusk creeps over Haworth we play bed plays in the cellar'. The illustrations are imagination stretching, both those that show the bleakness of the moors and those that show the children's domestic environment. Care has been taken to show period detail in the pictures of furniture, toys and ornaments.

Figure 26.3
Front cover of The Brontës *by Catherine Brighton*
Reproduced with the permission of the publishers Frances Lincoln Ltd.
Copyright 1994

There are more biographies written for this age group than autobiographies. Books in Oxford Reading Tree's True Stories series for up to about seven or eight are well written and visually alive. Each book tunes into what makes the subject interesting. In *The Life of Alex Brychta*, for example, young readers can connect with the subject by seeing the illustrator's insect drawings done when he was a child.

If you want to introduce children to some short, well-illustrated biographies you might find useful Evans Brothers' Tell Me About series, which includes biographies of writers for children such as Roger Hargreaves, Enid Blyton, Beatrix Potter and Roald Dahl. The author of the last of these, Chris Powling, does not hide the more eccentric aspects of Dahl's personality: 'he was an outsider – someone who never behaved as others expected him to'.

Children in this age group like to be able to read independently and would appreciate the large clear print, clearly expressed information and arresting black and white illustrations in Franklin Watts' Famous People, Famous Lives series. This includes subjects like King Alfred, Boudica, Mahatma Gandhi and John Lennon. In *Mary Seacole*, Harriet Castor and Lynne Willey raise the question: why do some people achieve fame easily while others who seem to have done as much for humanity have to wait a long time? (Recognition for her contribution to nursing came late in the day for Mary Seacole.)

One of the strongest titles in the Time for Kids series, about remarkable Americans, is *Harriet Tubman*. She began life as a slave, but the book starts with this sentence: 'Harriet Tubman was born a slave but she would not die a slave.' The way the author, Renee Skelton, describes Harriet's determination and courage as she makes her mark makes the book inspirational. This series is written in short chapters and demonstrates the usefulness of timelines to show chronology.

The titles in another series of biographies, Short Books, include *Who Was William the Conqueror?*, *Who Was Wolfgang Amadeus Mozart?* and *Who Was Boudica?*, and could be read independently by forward young readers in this age group and read aloud to others. They draw young readers and listeners in by quickly identifying some puzzles in the life of the person who is the subject of the book. In Charlotte Moore's *Who Was Florence Nightingale?*, for instance, we start with her parents and their rich person's lifestyle, and then are shown how Florence, their younger daughter, was quite different in her aspirations. She was not interested in parties but wanted to do something special with her life. The book also manages to convey how extraordinary it was for a girl from such a background to want to nurse soldiers wounded in the Crimean War.

If we need convincing that the nature of the design of a series has the power to draw in less eager young readers, ask children what they think of Brilliant Brits. The titles in this series entertain and inform by using colourful comic strip and speech bubbles to capture children's interest in such well-known historical characters as Shakespeare, Boudica, Queen Elizabeth I and Henry VIII. Subjects are also drawn from popular culture. Richard Brassey's *David Beckham* includes pictures of all the footballer's ever-changing hairstyles and *The Beatles*, by the same author, relates how each young musician travelled from boyhood to adulthood and fame. One Amazon UK piece of feedback tells how the 'easy to read' modern looking design by Orion Books meant that this was 'the first book my seven-year-old had ever read from cover to cover'. Again with an eye on those young learners who do not want to be faced by huge blocks of print, some of Stewart Ross' biography picturebooks in the Hodder

Wayland Stories from History series are worth considering. In *Clever Cleo: The Story of Queen Cleopatra* it is the illustrations that carry the detail and there are notes for teachers and parents at the end of the book.

8–11-year-olds

This is the age group where non-narrative texts and particularly 'report' become more dominant in supporting learning in many lessons. Nevertheless recounts still have a role to play in the reading and learning of this age group and are not only longer, but also more intellectually demanding; this is reflected in a richer general vocabulary, a more precise technical vocabulary and in more complex syntax. They also rely on children's increasing visual literacy as the illustrations are more detailed and complex.

Science and nature study

Perusal of the websites of the main publishers of children's non-fiction give details about the print and electronic texts to support science. These texts are usually a mixture of report, instruction and explanation writing and illustrating. But there are some books and resources which include recount. A good example of a text which is clearly in the recount genre and which makes considerable demands on the young reader while being an extremely satisfying and exciting 'read' is Phillip Lars Manning's *Dinomummy*. There are two related narratives. First we have an imaginative reconstruction of a dinosaur's last day. Then, more than 65 million years later, another story begins: the discovery by a young scientist of the mummy of the dinosaur in the first story, which was found on the flood plains of prehistoric North America. Here written text and illustrations, including photographs and annotated diagrams, show how palaeontologists unearth remains and the procedures they carry out to discover what the creature looked like in life, how it died and how its body was preserved. The book's problem-solving approach fits well with Key Stage 2 science. The excellent clear diagrams explaining the structure of the creature and relating it to functions like digesting, moving and mating show how explanation and recount texts can work together to energize children's learning.

The natural history books of Nicola Davies embed quite complex information in interesting accounts, often with a touch of humour. *What's Eating You? Parasites – the Inside Story* shows in fascinating detail how the amazingly adaptable creatures we call parasites invade the skin, hair and feathers of living creatures. Young readers learn about the life cycle of such parasites as the tape worm and about cell structures and the immunology of the host's body through powerful written explanation and through the lively illustration of Neal Layton.

Geography

Travel kinds of writing, including diaries about journeys, are geographical texts falling into the recount rather than the report genre. *Antarctic Journal: The Hidden Worlds of Antarctica's Animals* by Meredith Hooper and Lucia deLeiris makes a strong contribution to children's scientific understanding of how creatures are adapted to their habitats. But the authors'

BOX 26.2 *THE SECRET JOURNAL OF VICTOR FRANKENSTEIN: ON THE WORKINGS OF THE HUMAN BODY* BY DAVID STEWART (BOOK HOUSE)

This is one of those exciting but perplexing books that is extremely difficult to place neatly in a genre. The visual element is as important as the writing – so it has some claim to being a picturebook. It uses the conceit of the long-lost journal of a fictional scientist, Victor Frankenstein, to explore the human body in considerable detail. So there is a sort of time sequence which persuaded me to place it in this chapter. The frisson comes from the intriguing combination of fact and fiction, and particularly the allusion to the terrifying monster created by Dr Frankenstein in Mary Shelley's classic.

The book is visually interesting with vividly coloured body parts – muscles, heart, lungs and organs of digestion. There are huge skulls leering out of the pages and splashes of blood decorating the margins. The diagrams and charts, meticulously detailed and annotated, and the quality information drawing on more recent knowledge make the science trustworthy. Retrieval devices are comprehensive too. Contemporary newspaper cuttings, copious pull-outs (with articles from newspapers and magazines about grave robbing and murders) and pictures and paintings all make for a rich and original book. It appeals to older primary children, who have a taste for this kind of information and sometimes rather dark humour.

Antarctic trip in a sturdy ice-breaker ship is also an inspirational, powerfully written account which makes a contribution to geographical understanding. It communicates a strong sense of 'place', telling of distinctive landscapes – 'of a desert vast and frozen'. Children learn about 'the ice clenched mountains' of Antarctica and the 'huge wrinkled glaciers that slide slowly to the sea'. The drawings and paintings that illustrate the journal are atmospheric and have great imaginative appeal. *The Island that Moved* draws on the same series of research trips to Antarctica that led to *Antarctic Journey* and explains plate tectonics by telling the story of a remote island which was pushed up through the sea bed as the plates split millions of years ago. Can there be any more interesting and imaginative explanation of how the forces that shape the Earth work?

Another exciting travel book, *Marco Polo for Kids: His Marvellous Journey to China* by Janis Herbert, draws on much research to tell this true story and would interest able young readers in the final year of the primary school. We are taken on a journey to China from Venice along the thirteenth-century Silk Road, taking in the vast deserts and steep mountain ranges that the seventeen-year-old explorer would have passed on his travels by caravan. The insight into Venice at this time – with its busy wharves where traders brought ships laden with 'silks, spices, dyes, salt and wool' – makes the book of value too in history as well as geography lessons. It certainly encourages further research because of the vivid way in which it tells the story and because such a rich and varied treasure store of photographs, paintings and maps of people, places and objects is incorporated. There is some instruction writing here too: we learn how to put on a wayang-kulit (shadow puppet play), how to make yoghurt and how to produce paper. To help extend knowledge, as so many print information books do these days, the book directs young readers to relevant websites.

History

Two author/illustrators who show that the information story can be the vehicle for imparting much historical information are Mick Manning and Brita Granström. Their titles in the Fly on the Wall series, including *Roman Fort*, *Greek Hero* and *Viking Longship*, are all based on meticulous research and some collaboration with primary specialists. In *Viking Longship* we follow the life of a fine ninth-century vessel and hear the stories of the Vikings who sailed in her. The design of the book draws young readers in as the pages are alive with colour and fascinating information alongside the main story. Granström's distinctive hand lettering to annotate the diagrams and pictures seems to whisper secrets to young learners (Mallett, 2006).

For children who have reached the final primary school class, information stories can still help communicate detailed and sophisticated information – not least in history lessons. Anyone needing convincing of this should look at Stewart Ross and Stephen Biesty's fine cross-section books about Ancient civilizations – Egypt, Rome and Greece – which hang copious information in text and picture around a narrative and include scholarly annotations, indexes and glossaries. *Greece in Spectacular Cross-Section* tells the story of eleven-year-old Neleuo, who set off in 436 BC with his father and brother to see the great games at Olympia. The journey takes them to the port and streets of Athens, to the Acropolis and the oracle at Delphi. The sheer scale of the buildings is captured through the fine cross-sections and cutaways and detailed and well-researched annotations. This is a book for ten-year-olds and above, but the rich pictures and detailed text could be appreciated by younger readers if the book was shared with an individual or in a group.

Another fine book, organized chronologically and suitable for the tens and over, is Anne Millard's book *A Port through Time*, illustrated by Steve Noon. A title in the Through Time series, this book leads young readers through the 10,000 year story of a port. The panoramic, detailed pictures combine with a scholarly written text to reveal some of the 'big shapes' of history. Even older primary children will need the help of a teacher or parent to understand some of the more challenging ideas here about the impact of change on landscape and on people's lives.

Figure 26.4 *Text and illustration from page 25 of* Viking Longship *by Mick Manning and Brita Granström, showing a farmyard scene with a Viking woman in the foreground*
Reproduced with the permission of the publishers Frances Lincoln Ltd. Copyright 2006

Figure 26.5 *Front cover of* A Port through Time *by Anne Millard and Steve Noon (illus.)*
Reproduced with the permission of the publishers Dorling Kindersley. Copyright Dorling Kindersley 2005

267

Autobiography and biography

Autobiographical and biographical kinds of writing become more important for this age range in both history and English lessons and we find the same publishing houses mentioned in the previous section – Evans, Usborne, Heinemann, Franklin Watts and Oxford University Press and Frances Lincoln – remain dominant in this area. Well-known and less well-known individuals from every historical period are covered. The range of area of influence is also wide and you will be able to track down those whose contributions have been as leaders, to the arts or sciences or as explorers or humanitarians.

Sometimes biographies include autobiographical elements – letters, diary extracts and newspaper stories. All these are found in Stewart Ross' *Evacuation*, a title in the At Home in World War II series (Evans Brothers) and are gathered from the collection at the Imperial War Museum to tell the story of individual experiences. Ten-year-old Matthew remarked that autobiography gave you the feeling that 'someone is talking to you'. But although it can sound spontaneous like a conversation with the reader, in fact the author of an autobiography has made careful choices, highlighting some things and perhaps skimming over others. We see this in Marcia Williams' *Archie's War* – a boundary-breaking book telling about events at home and in the battlefields in the First World War through the eyes of a young boy. The selection of what is told is very much Archie's and children would find convincing examples of text and pictures which seem close to the likely preoccupations and interests of a boy living through this period; for example, we find Archie and his friends love their pets and their comics. The story is told through Archie's 'voice', often using comic strip. All kinds of writing – letters, diary extracts, notes, cartoon 'bubble' writing and notices – are used.

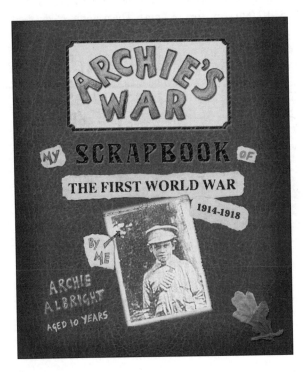

Figure 26.6
Front cover of Archie's War: My Scrapbook of the First World War *by Marcia Williams*
Reproduced with the permission of the publishers Walker Books Ltd. London SE11 5HJ

> **BOX 26.3** *TAIL-END CHARLIE* **BY MICK MANNING AND BRITA GRANSTRÖM (FRANCES LINCOLN)**
>
> Mick Manning listened to his father's tales about life as an RAF air gunner during the Second World War and decided to share these exciting, but terrifying, real experiences. After a great deal of research, the book was written as if Charlie were talking. The extremely dangerous nature of a tail-gunner's job is communicated through a lively written text and wonderfully atmospheric illustrations, which include some showing the plane and crew flying into the darkness and dodging the enemy planes. There are some powerful images here to help young readers imagine what it was really like to be doing such dangerous work. Gentler images are evoked too; for example, high over Belgium the fluffy clouds looked like 'mashed potato' and the patterns of the autumn fields 'were like an abstract painting or a patchwork quilt'. In spite of the beautiful view, Charlie remembers that his plane is on its way to bomb a bridge used by enemy troops. 'We were going to kill people and they were going to try to kill us.' The sheer sadness of war for all concerned comes through and this underpinning to all that happens makes the book moving.

The pages are visually exciting and there are wonderfully rich double spreads arranged like a scrapbook, with drawings, photographs, mementoes, jottings, diagrams and letters.

Marcia Williams has recently turned her attention to people's experiences in the Second World War; she has used the device of a diary to tell of the daily life of a nine-year-old girl in her book *My Secret War Diary by Flossie Albright*.

Another book with a tremendous sense of 'voice' is Mick Manning and Brita Granström's *Tail-End Charlie* (Box 26.3).

Two of the autobiographies most likely to be found on any upper primary school shelf are *Anne Frank's Diary* and Roald Dahl's *Boy: Tales of Childhood*. The contexts in which these two writers relate their stories are very different. What they have in common is a robust style and a willingness to include what is startling, confusing, intriguing or even upsetting. Bland autobiographies do not make for the kind of urgent need to read on that we want young readers to experience.

One of the most powerful accounts that I have used with children uses 'first-person' writing as a literary device to make a true story compelling. In the affecting book *Erika's Story*, Ruth Vander Zee relates the experiences of a woman who had given her an oral account of her life. So the book reads as if it is an autobiography although it is unlikely to be word for word exactly as the woman told it. The story begins with a desperate mother throwing her baby girl from a train taking Jewish people to a concentration camp. The spare text and detailed, often moving illustrations by Roberto Innocenti work well in this story of courage and survival.

Teachers are always on the lookout for truly exciting texts for their pupils and worthy of mention while thinking about biography is Vivian French's *Chocolate: The Bean that Conquered the World*, illustrated by Paul Howard. French herself spoke eloquently about the book at the Write Away conference on non-fiction in May 2008, and she certainly transformed my own understanding of what a biography could be like.

269

> **BOX 26.4 *CHOCOLATE: THE BEAN THAT CONQUERED THE WORLD* BY VIVIAN FRENCH AND PAUL HOWARD (ILLUS.) (WALKER)**
>
> This 'biography of chocolate' describes the changing use and significance of the chocolate bean from the Aztecs to modern times. Author and illustrator combine facts, recipes, speculations and memories in an imagination-stretching way bound to appeal to young readers. Even the cover is witty and original – giving the impression of being a bar of chocolate complete with wrapper depicting on a map the places where the chocolate bean grows.

The absolute honesty which is a quality in the best autobiographical writing is very apparent in a dramatic and moving account of a girl who escaped from the outbreak of fighting in the Congo in the late 1990s. *Gervelie's Journey: A Refugee Diary* by Antony Robinson and Annemarie Young tells the story of a courageous young girl. This true story is told in Gervelie's own voice and relates how the family was torn apart and the young girl and her father arrived in Britain, where they were granted asylum. There are ordeals and situations of physical danger, but it is often the smaller upsets that children will connect with. For example, Gervelie often has to move on quickly from one place to another – 'not time to say goodbye to our friends'. She finds her mother's behaviour puzzling sometimes, too; on her birthday Gervelie got no call or card from her – 'even though she knew where we were'. This is a book that will help develop a young reader's ability to read between the lines and to appreciate the complexity of the situations in which Gervelie finds herself.

> **BOX 26.5 *A TIME TRAVELLER'S FIELD NOTES AND OBSERVATIONS OF ANCIENT EGYPT BY H. GRAY* BY GORDON VOLKE AND ROBERT NICHOLLS (ILLUS.) AND NEIL REED (ILLUS.) (QUEST)**
>
> Since the discovery of my father's time machine, my brother Tom and I have secretly travelled back through the ages . . .
>
> This is the intriguing beginning to a fictional journal written by young Henrietta Gray in 1916, the year when she and her brother Tom travelled back to Ancient Egypt.
>
> The diary device works particularly well here. Young readers are introduced to every aspect of life in those ancient times, including the building of the pyramids, the procedures surrounding a pharaoh's burial and the landscapes, people, animals and customs. The author also manages to make Henrietta and Tom convincing as young people – with rounded personalities and the usual disputes and rivalries with other family members. The book makes historical information accessible through a variety of pictures and diagrams, while being written in the engaging style of a novel that will keep children gripped until the last page.

Autobiography has unrivalled immediacy and the best writing gives a sincere account of events and feelings about them. But it is bound to be selective and it is by definition written from one point of view. A biography is also usually written by a sole author, but the events are viewed in a somewhat less partial way as biographers distance themselves from the events and feelings related. In the 'biography' paragraphs of the previous section I noted that many publishers of non-fiction titles produce biographies, often in series, for different age groups. One series which pitches the biographies at the older primary school age group is Oxford's *What's Their Story*; titles include *Cleopatra*, *Thomas Edison*, *Roald Dahl* and *Shakespeare*. For the older, abler readers in this age group, there is a biography which serves well as a companion book to *Anne Frank's Diary*. It is called *The Life of Anne Frank* by Menno Metselaar and Ruud Van Der Rol, translated by A.J. Pomerans, and is chronologically organized in seven sections from 1925 to 1945 and after. It is rich with annotated photographs of Anne and her family during their time in Germany and later on when they settled in Holland.

- *Going Shopping* by Sarah Garland (Frances Lincoln)
  One of a series of information picturebooks with just the right amount of detail in text and illustrations.

- *Ten Seeds* by Ruth Brown (Andersen Press)
  A child plants ten seeds. How many survive to become a sunflower?

- *The World Came to My Place* by Jo Readman (Transworld Publishers)
  A child learns about products and places during a day with Grandfather.

- *Clever Cleo: The Story of Queen Cleopatra* by Steward Ross (Wayland)
  Older less forward readers respond to the detailed information in pictures as well as text.

- *Antarctic Journal: The Hidden Worlds of Antarctica's Animals* by Meredith Hooper and Lucia deLeiris (Frances Lincoln)
  Communicates a strong sense of a particular place in lyrical text and fine illustrations. A good model for children's own attempts at information journals.

- *Greek Hero* by Mick Manning and Brita Granström (Frances Lincoln)
  An exciting information story is the context for much information about an ancient culture.

- *My Secret War Diary by Flossie Albright* by Marcia Williams (Walker)
  Young readers learn about the Second World War through the eyes of a nine-year-old child. Uses different kinds of writing and illustrating to tell the story.

- *Castle Diary: The Journal of Tobias Burgess, Page* by Richard Platt and Chris Riddell (Candlewick Press)
  Witty and informative account from the viewpoint of the young page in training.

- *Dinomummy* by Philip Lars Manning (Kingfisher)
  A fascinating account of the unearthing of a mummified dinosaur.

Figure 26.7 Recount texts, roughly in order of challenge

Do we need a biography of Anne's life when her diary is such a powerful account? I think we do: this book gives the political and social background to the times in which Anne lived her short life. It also tells us about how things developed after the war and tries to illuminate some of the puzzles children often raise after reading the diary. For example, who are those suspected of betraying the existence of the secret annexe in Amsterdam?

USING RECOUNT TEXTS

Children are active learners: starting with first-hand experience

Children's experiences, in and out of the classroom, are the raw material first for their oral recounts and later for their written ones. Appropriate texts shared with the teacher help them reflect on their first-hand experiences. Here are some suggestions for linking texts with experiences and activities.

- Teachers of very young children base much of the day's work around practical activities: painting, cooking, role play and gardening. Books chosen to connect with children's activities and preoccupations inspire them to make comparisons between what they have been doing and the activities of the children in the book.
- Class visits to a farm, pond or museum can also be enriched by accounts in books read before, during or after the outing.
- Information stories can be inspiration for the home corner, which can become a 'café', 'baby clinic' or 'office' well-stocked with lists, menus, catalogues and letters.
- Outside play areas can become 'garages', 'gardening centres' and 'market stalls'. Vigorous play on bikes and with gardening equipment like buckets and pretend hoses can be linked with literacy through use of lists of materials, garage services and fruit and vegetables. Role play can enable children to live through events that they can retell later on.

CASE STUDY 26.1 SCIENCE: YEAR 6 RECORD PRACTICAL WORK ON FORCES IN AN ELECTRONIC BOOK OF ANNOTATED PHOTOGRAPHS

Using an interactive whiteboard the teacher explained what forces were and how their presence could be demonstrated. Then in groups, accompanied by a teaching assistant, the children went to the gym and carried out exercises like 'pulling', 'pressing' and 'pushing' to demonstrate the concept of forces. Photographs were taken with a digital camera to make an electronic book of photographs with annotation – a recount of the children's activities on the journey to understanding this topic in physics.

When the children turned to the collection of print information books and CD-ROMs and later on websites, they did so with a firm and helpful underpinning of first-hand experience.

- Practical activities and first-hand experience continue to be a desirable underpinning to learning from secondary sources in the later primary years. Class outings, including geography field trips, museum visits to support history and visits to art galleries, all provide variety and keep up interest.
- Older children also find drama and improvisation are great energizers of their thinking and learning. I have often watched a teacher, perhaps in costume, take on the role of a person from history – Samuel Pepys, a Tudor cook, a Greek slave and Florence Nightingale – and recount their memories of an event. This shows children how they too might tell of experiences and their response to those experiences 'in role'.
- Talks by visitors, for example by older people who have experienced evacuation during the war, give young learners another source of information to combine with what they glean from texts.

Learning is collaborative: speaking and listening

Becoming able to structure and share an oral recount with others is a very good start in controlling the genre and helps children become able to write as well as tell and read. Suggestions here include:

- 'Oral recount' is a rather grand name for something teachers and children in the early years have long made time for in the school day. I find that reading an information story and showing the pictures can inspire ideas that give children the confidence to tell their anecdote (see Case Study 26.2). If the teacher also contributes anecdotes, it makes it feel more like a conversation. Children learn form these discussions and 'sharings' that an oral recount informs but its purpose may also be to entertain. This brings us to awareness of audience – something else that is developed through speaking and listening in the class or group context.
- Listening to a teacher's true story strengthens children's ability to structure a recount. When I told seven-year-olds who were following a theme on 'Pets' about the day my guinea pigs were lost, a host of fascinating accounts of lost pets burst forth. But the liveliest response came from my reading of a book – an information story about a child who broke an arm – which told of the procedures which took place in hospital to put things right. Each anecdote was more dramatic than the last.
- As children move through the primary years they can be helped to extend their repertoire beyond personal oral recounts. Drawing on their reading of history texts, children can be invited to tell of an incident or event from the viewpoint of a particular historical figure.
- The teacher or a pupil might bring in a news story for discussion each week. Discussion and analysis would follow someone reading the recount aloud. Older children are ready to talk about issues of bias, about how knowing who is writing a recount helps us become aware of the promotion of a particular viewpoint.
- Children enjoy sharing events in their lives with others. Telling oral recounts helps reinforce their sense of purpose – to inform and sometimes to entertain; linked to this

is the support given to children's sense of audience. The teacher's contributions demonstrate how to go about telling a recount and strengthen children's understanding of the typical structure.

- Sometimes it is talk about events in their lives that helps children get a grip on their structure before they write. We think of news sharing as being for younger children, but the English lesson is a good context for sharing oral recounts of stories in the news. After recounting them there can be analysis. The teacher could bring newspaper recounts in perhaps once a week and read them out for discussion.

- Older children can be helped to make television-type reports, in the third person, on sporting events.

CASE STUDY 26.2 READING AND TALKING ABOUT *TEN SEEDS* BY RUTH BROWN (ANDERSEN PRESS)

Starting to read a book with a question in mind often awakens and sustains interest. A group of four- to five-year-olds who had been following themes on 'Colour' and 'Growing' looked at the front cover of *Ten Seeds* and the teacher wondered, 'How many of these seeds will grow into plants?' Some of the children assumed they would all flourish, but Tommy said, 'A cat might eat some of them'. We had to read the book to find out, the adult reading aloud and the children joining in. Only one seed survived to become a glorious sunflower.

Several things seemed to encourage the children to talk. The colourful pictures of the growing plants and their predators are drawn with a strong clear line and these linked with children's experiences in their own gardens. So they shared stories about cats, dogs and rabbits eating plants.

The language manages to be simple without being banal and works well with the pictures. So we have on the page where only two seeds have become buds: 'Two buds' and then, above the fading plant: 'too many greenfly'. Tuned into visual meanings as children are these days, this group soon saw why one plant had survived. They spotted a ladybird on the leaves of the healthy plant.

Ruth Brown uses humour, perfectly adapted to what is likely to amuse this age group, with great skill. The children chuckled over the visual humour – the predatory mouse putting its pink paw into the soil to scoop up a seed and the mole rising from the earth with a seedling on his head.

The book teaches about a plant's life cycle, about number and colour and also about the 'bigger shapes' of nature. 'You have to have a lot to start with to make sure you get some flowers', remarked one child. Yes, indeed: as so many seeds perish before they become plants, nature has to be extravagant so that a reasonable number manage to win through.

CASE STUDY 26.3 COMPARING BIOGRAPHY AND AUTOBIOGRAPHY: *BOY* BY ROALD DAHL (PUFFIN) AND *ROALD DAHL* BY CHRIS POWLING (PUFFIN)

A group of Year 6 children and a teacher read aloud from these books and talked about how they might learn from these writers about autobiographical and biographical writing.

They looked particularly at the advantages and possible disadvantages of first-person writing and third-person writing. To summarize, they felt that the first-person writing of autobiographies could provide:

- An immediacy that came from the direct recounting of the writer's experience. The best, like *Boy*, had a confiding tone.
- Detailed insight gained into one person's way of dealing with life events and people. Enough detail needs to be given to involve the reader. The children particularly appreciated the way the painful operation on the kitchen table was graphically described by Roald Dahl.
- Some insight into the views of other characters by, for example, including direct speech. In *Boy* Roald Dahl constantly evaluates his own behaviour as well as that of others.

The third-person writing of biographies could provide:

- A distancing from the subject that might make for a more balanced view.
- A less self-serving view of events and people's behaviour. Chris Powling writes that Roald Dahl, for all his gifts, was rather an odd character. The best pick out those events that make for an interesting 'read'. As Dahl himself warns in the introduction to *Boy*, accounts should avoid being 'full of all sorts of boring detail'. This applies to all writing, whether first or third person, of course.
- A more detached view than might be the case in an autobiography of the personalities and behaviour of people encountered by the subject.

The same sort of issues could be discussed by comparing *Anne Frank's Diary* with one of the biographies of her life, for example *Anne Frank* by Josephine Poole and illustrated by Angela Barrett.

The teacher's role is central: into writing

The examples of practice above show that when it comes to getting into the 'recount' kind of thinking, the teacher's role in setting up interesting and relevant lessons and activities and in providing strong contexts for speaking and listening is important. These accounts about events which may be recent or historical are likely to be the first sustained non-fiction writing children attempt. Teachers can help young writers to: get the events in the right sequence; select what is relevant and interesting; find effective ways of presenting the account with an eye on purpose and audience. Some suggestions follow:

- Drawing a series of pictures enables children to structure a recount, getting the sequence of events right.
- When preparing to write an historical account a time-line is helpful both to get the chronology right and to include in the fair copy. But children might be helped to understand that a more dynamic beginning might be to leave the chronology and start with a dramatic incident which had an impact on the subject's life.
- Books which contain facts within a narrative can inspire young writers to create their own illustrated accounts. A good book to use is Paul Geraghty's *Dinosaur in Danger*, which tells of a young dinosaur's plight when a volcanic eruption separates her from her pack. Powerful verbal and visual images tell how she can hear dinosaur calls. But are they the cries of her own pack? Geraghty consulted dinosaur experts at the National History Museum to get the details as correct as possible in the present state of knowledge about dinosaur life in the lower Cretaceous period.
- 'Writing journals' can be used to write about events and information and to share these by reading them aloud. There is evidence that attitudes towards writing improve through this kind of writing and sharing (Graham and Johnson, 2003). Children aged nine years and older would find inspiration for using a diary format as a device for biographical writing in Marcia Williams' book *My Secret War Diary By Flossie Albright*. Young writers following a Second World War history unit might draw on this book for writing in the role of an evacuee.
- Reading autobiographies and biographies helps children see how successful writers select the interesting or significant. I find that the websites of the children's laureates, current and previous, show how a writer goes about producing an interesting, short autobiography.
- As children become older the teacher can show them that even non-fiction stories are often shaped from a viewpoint. In their writing speculation is welcome but ways of communicating its status are sought, for example '. . . may have done this because . . .', or 'some people think . . .'. And of course much history writing is done with the benefit of hindsight. Part of becoming able to write good biography involves sensitivity to how issues and events were viewed in earlier eras. Children often find the way children were treated and criminals punished puzzling and upsetting.

CASE STUDY 26.4 NINE-YEAR-OLDS PRODUCE WAR SCRAPBOOKS, INSPIRED BY *ARCHIE'S WAR* BY MARCIA WILLIAMS (WALKER)

Nine-year-olds were following a history unit on the Second World War. Their teacher read them Marcia Williams' *Archie's War* which is of course about the First World War. It was suggested they try to make a scrapbook diary of a child living through the Second World War, adapting some of the ideas in the book. The children produced some powerful accounts in their scrapbooks which included letters, annotated pictures and advertisements, luggage labels – all used to tell a personal story.

- Older children would enjoy drawing on these accounts for an author study, transforming what is written as autobiography into biography perhaps and adding in information gleaned from a variety of sources and not just websites. Support for older primary children's biographical writing is available in Helen Bromley's book *Author Study Activities for Key Stage 2*.
- Writing sometimes for parents, sometimes for children younger than themselves and sometimes for their peer group helps children learn how to vary language to suit particular audiences. Children might try a recount in a history lesson about an event or in a geography lesson about a journey first for a friend their own age and then for a younger child. In my experience children greatly enjoy reading their writing aloud.
- Elaboration, for example adding extra details or opinions, can be guided by reminding children of the audience they are writing for. Direct speech, questions and including something entertaining can help make a recount lively for a young audience.
- A book can often be the inspiration for children's own research and writing. Following the approach in Vivian French's unusual biography entitled *Chocolate*, for example, children could choose a product and make a sunray diagram (see Figure 26.8) as a planning tool. The sunray annotations can then become headings to organize children's writing and guide further research. Children would enjoy adding pictures, photographs, quotations from people they know about the product and recipes. As Vivian French and her teacher colleague told us during their Write Away workshop in May 2008, this approach to children's writing of biography points up the flexibility and possibilities of the genre. Information books and the internet can still be used, but the children will be in the driving seat in their own writing and illustrating.
- The visual can be a good way into biographical kinds of writing. Old photographs, portraits and book illustrations can all help. One starting point could be a book in Laurence Anholt's Artist series so that children can see how illustrations can play a strong and interesting role in bringing a person's biography to life.
- Electronic books children make can use music, sound, film and photographs to good effect in biographical kinds of writing.
- Older children can be encouraged to write newspaper style accounts of events like school sports days.

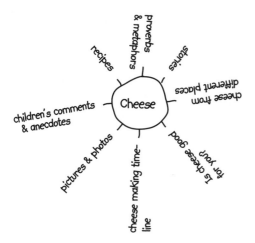

Figure 26.8
Example of a sunray plan

MAKING PROGRESS

Progression in reading and writing recounts is to do with increasing control over chronology and more refined use of connectives like 'first', 'then' and 'next'. The ability to respond to and evaluate the events and experiences related is also a sign of greater maturity. As children become older they are more able to keep in mind their 'audience' when writing. Where opportunities are created for reading their own work aloud to the class or a group children's sense of audience is likely to be encouraged. They learn how accounts can entertain as well as inform. (For an insightful account and case study of a child's progress in writing this text type see Liz Laycock's analysis and case study 'Monitoring and Assessing Writing' (Chapter 6, pp. 124–41 in Graham and Kelly, 2003).

The use of appropriate illustrations, including diagrams, is also evidence of progress in understanding the potential of the genre.

SUMMARY

- Recounts are events retold or written in a time sequence and are a major form which children read and use to make sense of and communicate experience and their response to that experience.
- The 'news' children share in early years classrooms, the anecdotes children contribute about what they have seen and done are oral recounts.
- Letters, diary entries, emails and text messages fall under the written recount umbrella.
- Alongside a chronology, the best recounts offer comment, opinion and some evaluation.
- Teachers look for quality of design, accuracy and appropriateness of language and illustration. A good question to ask is: How far do all these combine to make young readers learn, reflect and want to research further?
- Some topics fall naturally into a time sequence: life cycles, journeys and 'day in the life of . . .'.
- Autobiography and biography are examples of literary kinds of recount and are important texts in both English and history lessons; readers expect more than a bare chronology and look for insight into the person's ideas, attitudes and any puzzles and inconsistencies in their life.
- Children read, use, write and illustrate recount text in lessons across the curriculum – not least in science, history and geography.
- First-hand experience, speaking and listening and teacher support all play a part in children's increasing genre control as readers and writers.
- Progression is to do with becoming able to read and write recounts of greater complexity for particular purposes and audiences.

Chapter 27

Instruction texts

INTRODUCTION

Instruction or 'procedural' texts tell us how to do something. Their chronological step-by-step organization makes them a sympathetic genre for young children.

FEATURES OF INSTRUCTION TEXTS

Instruction texts usually begin with the statement of a general aim and then list materials or ingredients to be used. Then a sequence or steps are set out and these may be numbered, identified by a letter or presented in bullet points. Illustrations can help us identify the genre of a text. So in the case of an instruction text each step may be accompanied by a clarifying diagram or picture.

The simple present tense in the second person is often used, with steps set out in chronological order ('First you . . .') or the imperative tense ('Turn on the printer . . .'). Mature instruction text might be in the passive: '30 millilitres of water is added to the mixture'. For younger children the active form makes for a more interesting and involving set of instructions. 'Mix the sugar and margarine together, making a smooth paste' is more inviting than 'the sugar and margarine are mixed until a smooth paste is made'. Time connectives like 'when', 'then' and 'finally' help structure the writing and this text type tends to be succinct.

SOME CRITERIA FOR CHOOSING

As with other non-fiction texts quality can be considered under three headings, taking account of the age of the young learners.

Design

Clear global organization and well-organized pages will help make the instructions clear and easy to follow. Procedures are often numbered, bullet pointed or marked with letters of the alphabet.

Coverage

Accuracy and completeness are essential when instructions are given.

Language and illustration

Words and pictures should work well together in setting out each step of a procedure. The best texts avoid over-elaboration and keep tightly to the point. But there is room for humour, particularly in instruction texts for younger learners.

WHERE DO CHILDREN FIND INSTRUCTION TEXT?

Many information books, print and electronic, include more than one text type and instruction text is often found alongside report and explanation. Before looking at some promising texts for specific age ranges, I have some suggestions about where to find strong examples of instruction text which I hope will be helpful.

Non-book print

Non-book print is a rich hunting ground for information text, including instruction. Newspapers and magazines are a good source of recipes and gardening procedures. Then most homes will have instructions about games or using equipment. We have all experienced the terrors of a badly written instruction manual! Charts and posters for schools will also offer examples.

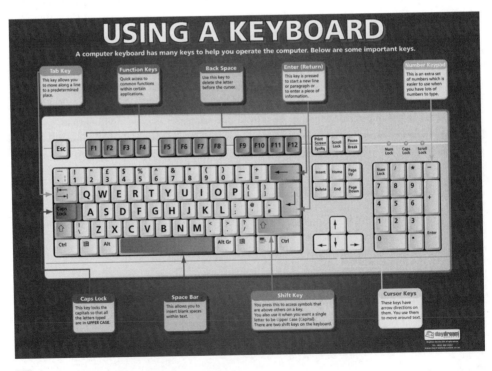

Figure 27.1 *Using a keyboard, ICT 009*
Chart reproduced with the permission of the publishers Daydream Education.
© Daydream Education 2003.

Books in series

Information books, print and electronic, often include different text types and instruction text is found alongside report and explanation. Publishers known for their reading schemes and programmes now include non-fiction titles, many published in a series. The quality of non-fiction titles has greatly improved, whether trade books or part of reading programmes; many respected writers and illustrators have been commissioned to research and write them. These books can support lessons across the curriculum and those for lessons in science, geography and design and technology are good sources of instructions for experiments and procedures. Publishers with strong and varied non-fiction titles include Oxford University Press, Usborne, Dorling Kindersley and Franklin Watts. Information about their titles is available on their websites. While books from non-fiction series and reading programmes now justify a place in the non-fiction collection, children deserve quality texts from many sources and should not be locked into one publisher's programme, however good.

Large format 'activity' books

Do you remember those large 'activity' books with titles like *Activities for a Rainy Day*? These were a treasure store of things to make and do. The modern 'activity' tome for children is a promising place to look for good models of instruction text. Amongst strong publishers here are Dorling Kindersley and Usborne: their 'activity' titles are packed with ideas and instructions for cooking and making all manner of things. They are nearly all attractive and user-friendly and worth having in the classroom collection. A good example is Angela Wilkes' *Activities for All Year Round*, which has instructions for planting seeds in spring, making strawberry trifle in summer, planting bulbs in autumn and making gifts in winter. Another general activity book useful across the curriculum is Ray Gibson's *Big Book of Things to Do* which is organized under the headings: 'What shall I cook, grow, draw, make?' It gives clear, numbered instructions for jolly recipes like that for chocolate octopuses. Here we have a splendid example of use of the imperative: '1. Mix the sugar and margarine until creamy. 2. Sift the flour and cocoa and add egg. 3. Mix to make dough.' And so on.

A large format book which would be handy for reference is *The Usborne Complete Book of Art Ideas* by Fiona Watts, which covers paper weaving, collage book covers, paper sculpture and mixing paints; all activities are clearly described and well illustrated.

New style 'activity' books

A new sort of big activity book has received a lot of publicity. I am thinking here of books like *The Dangerous Book for Boys* by Conn and Hal Iggulden which has caused some excitement amongst children, teachers, parents and reviewers; it had eighty-seven customer reviews when I visited the Amazon UK site on 12 March 2008. Like the version of the book for girls, *The Daring Book for Girls* by Andrea Buchanan and Miriam Peskowitz, it aims to get children to switch off the television and computer and to try instead some of the many activities and hobbies suggested. So there is a lot of well set-out and illustrated instruction text setting out step-by-step procedures. The chapters in the boys' book include 'Conkers', 'Astronomy', 'Making crystals' and so on. This is an old-fashioned sort of omnibus which might get families enjoying things together: making paper aeroplanes, constructing compasses and periscopes, planning a camping expedition. The girls' book is just as vigorous and challenging as the boys' book, with instructions about how to make and fly a kite, how to survive in the wild, how to cook over a fire in the open. Other publishers have taken up HarperCollins idea and there are now many rival books. You have to look carefully at some of these. The reviewer of one such book (not mentioned by name here) in *Books for Keeps* finds the instructions for making a tree house risky for the inexperienced. The book is compared unfavourably to the excellent encyclopedia by Arthur Mee entitled *Children's Encyclopedia* and published in 1926.

Websites, CD-ROMs and DVDs

A number of websites now give ideas for planning and resourcing lessons. Teachernet (www.teachernet.gov.uk/teachingandlearning) is a government site that has help for teachers following the National Curriculum. Using the plans and ideas of others too inflexibly can stop us from focusing on the interests, preoccupations and capabilities of the children in our classes. But drawing on ideas to serve our own carefully thought out purposes seems fine. The BBC Schools site (www.bbc.co.uk/schools) is a useful online resource for lessons across the curriculum. On the children's section there are non-fiction texts of all kinds. While I think that these are best embedded in the topics and themes of a lesson, the revision clips of the different kinds of non-fiction reading and writing are lively and will help secure their understanding of the different genres. Instruction text examples include making tea, feeding a pet and loading a CD-ROM. There are also clips from children's schools television programmes. For example, children in the upper primary years can follow step-by-step instructions on how to make a news film or a film drama.

Museums

Larger museums nearly always have an education department willing to help organize a group visit to explore a topic with a particular age group. Science and transport museums have much to offer in showing how things are constructed. The Science Museum in Kensington, London – slogan 'Bring science to life' (www.sciencemuseum.org.uk) – will send a team to your school if you are within reasonable distance, to carry out workshops. One of their themes for the eight to eleven age group is 'Get a Grip', about forces, and children follow instructions to make their own anti-friction hovercraft.

CHOOSING INSTRUCTION TEXTS FOR DIFFERENT AGE GROUPS

Pre-school and nursery, 3–5-year-olds

Very young children first come across this genre when they listen to oral instructions and then pass them on to others. They might do this when they are learning the rules and procedures of a new game or in role play involving listing and instructing. Early books – cloth, board and print – help children gain control of the format and organization of instruction text and pictures. The liveliest and best are close to children's experience and are visually alive. Two books that would encourage the sort of manipulative play that helps hand–eye co-ordination and, above all, the ability to concentrate are Gaby Goldsack and Jo Moon's highly interactive Play and learn books. *What's in the Fridge?* has a door that can be opened to reveal the food in the fridge and the cut-out items, made of cardboard, can be taken out and given to the people in the story. The front cover of *Are the Clothes Clean?* is a washing machine that can be opened to put clothes in and take them out. There is even a wheel which can be turned to show the clothes whizzing around.

A look in any children's section in a bookshop shows how young children like books about how things are pulled, pushed and pressed. Jakki Wood's book in large landscape format, *A Hole in the Road*, shows the steps taken to make the repair. Children see that some machines break up the old surface: backhoe loader, mini excavator and a digger, while others help fill in the hole: the tipper truck brings in crushed stones. Then the dump truck carries the hot asphalt to make the hard surface of the road. All the machines are large enough to encourage talk about how each one is designed to carry out its task. Young children like to grow things. Claire Llewellyn's *Make a Bottle Garden* is one of a number of books that set out instructions for getting things growing and then for looking after them.

Cooking is another favourite activity in the early years. There are a lot of cookery books called 'First Cookery . . .' but the under fives need help with them. A good one to start with is Felicity Brook's *First Picture Cookbook*. With practical laminated wipe-clean pages, it has a clear, illustrated recipe on each double spread, including cheesy shapes and chocolate cornflakes. Becky Johnson's *Baking with Tiny Tots* is another book which introduces a series of procedures in an enjoyable way.

Non-book print in the form of charts, posters and notices provides strong contextualized models of instruction. Sometimes teachers and classes create posters with bullet points about looking after the classroom tadpoles, mixing paints or planting seeds. Notices in some classrooms are procedural – for example, 'Please wash your hands after using the paints'.

5–8-year-olds

This is the age group that gains great satisfaction from developing their ability to make things and to look after pets. Activities where following instructions is strongly involved include making models, using machinery like computers and printers, gardening, creating their own books, cookery and experiments.

Science and nature study

There are a number of books about how to care for pets and most these days are clearly written and well illustrated. The RSPCA Pet Care series is written by animal experts and the books can be shared by child and adult to ensure kind and efficient care. *Caring for Your Rabbit* by C. Collins includes sections on housing, feeding, handling, grooming and even first aid. Older children would manage to read the text and learn from the photographs independently.

Instructions often come into books that are mainly organized as report. Clare Llewellyn's *My First Book of Time* is like this; it covers the main aspects of time but is also packed with instructions, for example on how to make a calendar, grow beans and make clocks. There is a splendid fold-out clock which helps with demonstration. Time telling skills are also shown and reinforced in Alice Proctor's book *My Day at School*.

Children need to learn about computers and how to control their many functions from a young age. A title from Usborne's Starting series, *Starting Computers* by Susan Meredith, could be used by six-year-olds, albeit with quite a lot of help. It describes the procedures for using some basic computer tools; for example, there are instructions on 'Dragging Shapes' showing how shapes and pictures can be dragged around the screen to make special effects. Other guidance on using computers is available in Franklin Watts' series Computer Wizards whose titles include *Internet Magic* and *Windows Magic*.

Books about plants and gardening often contain some elements of instruction. *Growing Plants: Leaves, Roots and Shoots* by Sally Hewitt is mainly in report genre, but has sections with instructions on how to plant and nurture. Children will like the step-by-step instructions on how to plant a miniature garden in *The Gardening Book* by Jane Bull.

Books on cooking provide children with good experience in following instructions. There are a great many for this age group and most are well designed and vibrantly and relevantly illustrated. My forays into classrooms and bookshops to track down the best of these left me feeling overwhelmed. Fiona Watt's *Cakes and Cookies* helps children to make their efforts match up to those in the photographs, but most five- to eight-year-olds would need help from an adult. Some children like savoury recipes. With this in mind I can recommend Angela Wilkes' *The Children's Step-by-Step Cook Book*. This is a very visual book with photographs of each step in the preparation and cooking procedures and pictures of cooking utensils and ingredients. An Amazon UK customer reviewer comments, 'it has real recipes along with the biscuits and little snacks which are the only things you find in most children's cookery books'.

Geography

Two books about soils which link science and geography and include instruction text are: Jen Green's *Rocks and Soil* (Our Earth series) and Sally Hewitt's *Rocks and Soil: Gems, Metals & Minerals*. These, like similar books, give instructions about how to sort rocks and how to make a rock collection.

One way to introduce important geographical concepts like climate and distance to this age range is through the planning of a holiday. As well as print books there are interactive websites for children, which they can use to help them build up instructions and lists. Usborne's quicklink site (www.usborne-quicklinks.com/uk/) takes the user to 'weather and climate'. Clicking on a holiday destination on a world map gives the local weather conditions and then the task is to select the appropriate clothes for a particular country from a moving carousel.

Design and technology

Book-making projects bring together design and technology with literacy. The design of a book made by children of any age – its size, shape, organization and the devices used to captivate the reader – all contribute to its power to communicate, entertain and inform. Paul Johnson has provided clear instructions about how to go about making every kind of book from picturebooks and stories to a variety of information books. His books make possible a creative sharing between teacher and pupils and I have seen them used throughout the early and primary years. *Making Books,* for example, is written to guide book-making from age four right through to age eleven years. Like his other publications, this book helps teachers and children exploit cross-curricular links and to tailor their writing for different audiences.

8–11-year-olds

As children move towards the upper primary years they become increasingly able to use and write instruction text of greater length and complexity.

Science and nature study

I have said above that instruction text is often part of books mainly written in another text type. But Usborne have brought out two big books devoted to procedures involved in science experiments. The first, for older less forward readers (or younger children), *100 Science Experiments* by Georgina Andrews and Kate Knighton, uses everyday things for the experiments. The second title, *The Usborne Big Book of Experiments*, is a step up and supports the Key Stage 2 science curriculum – covering, for example, 'electricity and magnetism', 'light and dark' and 'pushing and pulling' – and so would be a handy classroom resource. The author, Alastair Smith, has included a detailed index which would help take children forward in using retrieval devices.

Older primary children continue to enjoy cooking; Katherine Abbs' *Children's Cookbook* scores well on clarity of written text and helpful illustrations. A good example of an internet-linked cookery book is Angela Wilkes' *Children's World Cookbook*. There are forty recipes from all over the world and for all occasions. Cooking procedures like 'simmering', 'sifting' and 'folding' in are well explained and there is easy access to websites via Usborne's quicklink site (www.usborne-quicklinks.com/uk/).

Books on caring for pets and animals are often aimed at younger primary children. But the *Complete Book of Riding and Pony Care* by Gill Harvey and Rosie Dickins is a demanding book for this older age group which includes instructions for making cross-pole fences and mastering tricky jumps.

ICT

Anne Rooney, a well-known writer of children's non-fiction, has written an introductory ICT series – Let's Start – for age five plus: *Making Pictures*; *Making Charts*; *Starting with Words*; *Using Instructions*; *Sorting Information*; *Finding Facts*. She has extended the series, covering the same areas for the over sevens using more advanced material.

Photography

National Geographic Photography Guide for Kids by Neil Johnson is for forward young learners at the top end of this age range who want to know how to take good photographs using a

- *A Hole in the Road* by Jakki Wood (Frances Lincoln)
  Goes through all the procedures of repairing a hole in the road in a way that will appeal to young children. Pictures and text work wonderfully well.

- *First Picture Cookbook* by Felicity Brook (Usborne)
  As well as bright and helpful illustrations, this book has practical laminated pages and generous spacing of the recipes.

- *Baking with Tiny Tots* by Becky Johnson (Hamlyn)
  This attractive first cookbook helps young children learn to make things, with some adult supervision.

- *Making Books* by Paul Johnson (A&C Black)
  This is one of a number of fine books by this author which use clear step-by-step instructions and illustrations to help teachers and children make a variety of books in which to display their writing and pictures.

- *My First Book of Time* by Claire Llewellyn (Dorling Kindersley)
  An exceptionally useful and appealing book which both gives copious information and sets out instructions for making calendars and simple clocks.

- *Internet Magic* by Claire Pye and Ruth Cassidy (Franklin Watts)
  One of the titles in the Computer Wizards series, this book makes using the internet interesting, explaining that it is 'like a massive library, packed with information'.

- *100 Science Experiments* by Georgina Andrews and Kate Knighton (Usborne)
  Young children are guided through experiments using everyday materials.

- *Children's World Cookbook* by Angela Wilkes (Usborne)
  Usborne are one of the leaders in producing internet-linked books like this one; the aim is to combine use of each medium to promote children's research and learning. This book has clear instructions on how to 'simmer', 'sift' and 'fold' ingredients.

- *Complete Book of Riding and Pony Care* by Gill Harvey and Rosie Dickins (Usborne)
  Another of this publisher's internet-linked texts, this one explains how to do difficult jumps and to make cross-pole fences.

Figure 27.2 *Instruction texts, roughly in order of challenge*

digital camera and to send photographs to friends via the internet. Photographic concepts are taught through text, diagram and examples of successful photographs. Digital photography is used in primary schools to enhance work across the curriculum and this book is suitable for the teacher to share with the children who are able to use digital photography on classroom projects and are ready to work with mature instruction texts and diagrams.

Design and technology

For help with making things, Doug Stillinger has a number of instruction books, for age ten and over, on creating models of buildings and ships. *How to Build Castles* is a book and kit package with a set of study cards and 150 building cards to use in the construction. Book-making can contribute to many lessons but the new emphasis by publishers on design and on technical sophistication through devices like paper engineering demands the skills and abilities children acquire in D&T lessons. *Get Writing: Creative Book-Making Projects for Children* is Paul Johnson's follow-up book to his *Making Books*, discussed earlier. Children in this age group are encouraged to combine words, images and paper engineering by following the instructions in the book, while younger children may be able to do so with help.

USING INSTRUCTION TEXTS

The teacher's task is not only to do with choosing suitable texts, but also to do with helping children use them in the context of the tasks at the core of a lesson.

Children are active learners: starting with first-hand experience

Suggestions include:

*   In the early years classroom making lists and following procedures is built into the day's activities. Children like to be involved in what adults are doing and 'naturalistic' activities are better for some learning than formal teaching. Nursery teachers often make a list of the ingredients for a recipe, writing up the children's suggestions on a whiteboard.
*   Talk and writing come into science experiments, cooking, growing things and looking after classroom creatures like tadpoles or worms.
*   First-hand experience and practical work continue to be important in the science and design and technology lessons of older children and are a strong context for instructional kinds of talk and writing.

Learning is collaborative: speaking and listening

Talking through the instructions they are following helps children get their thinking into gear. They might usefully:

*   Give a response partner or group oral instructions – this helps the children judge what an audience needs to be told to understand the complexities of the task.
*   Be asked to explain to the class or group how they would plant a seed or play a game. This can lead on to younger children writing down the instructions, perhaps with annotated pictures. Such an approach – using oral presentation of instructions – can be adapted for older children.

The teacher's role is central: into writing

The first step in the creation of an instruction text is often a list. Listing is one of the earliest kinds of non-fiction writing children do. Myra Barrs calls listing 'mapping the world' and argues that it involves both thinking and planning (Barrs, 1987).

- Young children might list the items for the new baby in the home corner or the presents they want for their birthday. Texts to help here are Mothercare or Early Learning catalogues and the Ahlbergs' *The Baby's Catalogue.*
- When they move from the list to the instruction text itself, children will find it helpful to read out their first effort to a 'response partner' and to refine what they have written in the light of comments.

When children begin to structure a piece of instruction writing there are some things we can usefully remind them of:

- Write the procedures in a logical order.
- Number or bullet point each step.
- Keep numbered or bullet points short.
- Write in the present tense.
- Use pictures to make meanings clear.
- Choose a good title.

As children progress through the primary years they will be more able to:

- keep purpose and audience in mind, for example thinking about the needs of the reader;
- use adjectives and adverbs to hone precision – 'beat until creamy', 'stir gently';
- cope with longer more complicated sets of instructions.

The following case studies show children responding to challenging tasks like writing helped by the activities being placed in a purposeful and human context.

CASE STUDY 27.1 A NURSERY CLASS LEARN TO MAKE LISTS

Making lists is often part of an instruction text – ingredients for a recipe, for example. A nursery class and their teacher made the home area into a baby clinic as part of their 'Growing' theme. They used Mothercare catalogues and the Ahlbergs' *The Baby's Catalogue* to make their own lists for what is needed to feed, clean and amuse a baby.

Figure 27.3
Front cover of The Baby's Catalogue
by Janet and Allan Ahlberg
Reproduced with the permission of the publishers Viking. Copyright Janet and Allan Ahlberg 1982.

CASE STUDY 27.2 A YEAR 5 FOOD PROJECT

Nine-year-olds made project books based around the theme of 'Food I Like'. They made up their own recipes and researched on the internet for information about where the different ingredients come from to be able to write something about their origin and history. Orla's recipe for a prawn salad is shown in Figure 27.4 with photographs which show the steps to make the salad.

My recipe

Ingredients

Chopped coriander
Linseed croutons
Cucumber
Romaine lettuce
Tiger prawns (shelled)
Celery
Parmesan
Sliced apple
Carrot

Freshly squeezed lemon juice,
Extra virgin olive oil,
Curry powder
And Honey for a dressing

Figure 27.4 Ingredients for Orla's prawn salad

CASE STUDY 27.3 SIX- TO SEVEN-YEAR-OLDS CREATE INSTRUCTION TEXTS ARISING FROM THE CREATION OF MR TOGS THE TAILOR

A teacher in a primary school in Scotland created one of the most powerful contexts for encouraging children's writing I have encountered. Teacher and children created a shop run by 'Mr Togs the Tailor', a tailor's dummy. When it came to instruction writing the children wrote recipes for Mr Togs' favourite dishes and an instruction manual for a burglar alarm. The context the teacher had created made the writing purposeful and lively. I have seen many variations of this device with children up to about age eight years (Glen, 1987).

CASE STUDY 27.4 A YEAR 2 CLASS HELP WILLIAM UNDERSTAND INSTRUCTIONS

A student teacher wanted to encourage children's instruction writing. The classroom bear, William, needed to learn how the computer worked, how to make sweets with icing sugar and how to look after the tadpoles. He was a forgetful bear and needed to have instructions written down. So the children created annotated pictures of the procedures.

This basic idea – asking children to give instructions to creatures or people who need a lot of help – takes many forms. On the BBC Schools website (www.bbc.co.uk/schools), the idea is adapted for older children. Here we have the device of an alien from the planet Zog who needs very careful instructions on how to make tea, feed a pet or load a CD-ROM. He had a tendency to interpret language literally and so it is suggested that the children show their writing to each other to check that the procedures they have written are crystal clear.

Anything that makes a writing task more fun and interesting is worth considering.

SUMMARY

- Instruction is often found alongside other genres in children's books and resources and comes into lessons across the curriculum.
- It is a chronologically organized text giving, step-by-step, the stages in a procedure.
- The present tense is used and often the second person singular, sometimes in the imperative.
- Numbers, letters or bullet points help organize this kind of writing.
- Diagrams are used to clarify written instructions and some texts are presented as an annotated series of pictures.
- Listening and talking through instructions helpfully precedes reading and writing them.
- Teachers and children find instruction text in information books and non-book print like posters and leaflets, on CD-ROMs and DVDs and on websites.

290

- The best texts, taking into account the age range, are well designed, accurate, clearly written and illustrated.
- Talk about the procedures set out in the texts is crucial in getting children thinking and learning.
- When it comes to writing, teacher support includes help with planning, editing or, in the case of younger children, scribing.
- Some children may present their instructions in the form of a multimodal and/or multimedia text.
- Progression is to do with becoming able to use and write fuller and more complicated instructions.
- As children get older, they become more secure in holding on to purpose and they refine their concept of audience.

Chapter 28

Introducing non-narrative non-fiction texts
Report, explanation, discussion and persuasion and reference

If you browse through the children's section of a bookshop or in a school library you are unlikely to find many books with mature and relentless non-chronological or non-narrative text. There would be little point in producing books of the kind that children find difficult to understand and hard to enjoy. These text types can be found in books for children but in the form of transitional genres with only some of the features of mature text. Of course children need to encounter non-chronological text as they move towards the end of the primary school years and prepare themselves for the demands of the secondary years and beyond.

As the term implies, non-chronological texts are organized according to the inherent logic of a subject, with the hierarchical ordering this implies. So a non-chronological text about squirrels would have sections like 'kinds of', 'habitat', 'food' and 'predators' rather than having a 'day in a life' chronological or narrative form. Non-chronological texts fall into some broad categories: report and explanation, argument (discussion and persuasion) and reference. These are explored in the chapters that follow.

Powerful as it is, narrative is not the only way in which even the youngest children order and relate to experience. Books with recipes and books with instructions for making things are part of the early years collection. So I suggest books and resources to support children's developing ability to cope with non-chronological text; each chapter mentions what I think are some of the liveliest and most interesting of these, together with some suggestions for using them. Children of any age have to be interested in and care enough about their work to put in the effort needed to control the more difficult kinds of reading, writing and thinking. Teachers can help by embedding the use of the texts in lessons across the curriculum which throw up the questions and issues that create motivating contexts for learning. The case studies – examples of promising practice – included are intended to help here. One thing that stands out in these examples is the importance of talking about ideas, gleaned from reading, practical work and first-hand experience. The teacher's mediating role in helping children combine information from these different sources is a skilled and important one.

When it comes to children's own non-chronological writing, abilities develop over a number of years. The capacity to order information on hierarchical principles and the ability to integrate ideas and facts from different sources have a lot to do with general intellectual development and are difficult to force. When children first begin to write to describe or explain they will use an 'expressive' kind of language which helps them get minds around ideas. A sense of purpose and audience is crucial in the development of the abilities we want young writers to acquire. Recognition of the importance of these in children's progress as readers and writers stems, in particular, from the rich and wise thinking and research of James Britton set out in his classic book *Language and Learning*, which never goes out of print.

Analytic competence – a term used by Jerome Bruner to refer to the ability to learn from written texts (Bruner, 1967: 284). It has to do with becoming able to control and think about ideas and concepts which are relatively context free. Margaret Donaldson calls this 'disembedded thinking' (Donaldson, 1979).

Argument – a reasoned analysis for or against a proposition or point of view. Young children can begin to think in this way if their interest and concern are engaged.

Assimilation and accommodation – central processes in Piaget's adaptive model of learning: 'assimilation', which means the absorption into general schema of a specific piece of new learning, and 'accommodation', in which the internal cognitive structures modify to enable the new learning to take place. Piaget used the metaphor of the digestive system to explain these processes. Piaget believed we have a self-regulatory mechanism which he called 'equilibrium'. Children lose equilibrium when curiosity is aroused and return to a state of equilibrium when new knowledge which satisfies their need is incorporated into their understanding (Piaget, 1952). This dynamic view of a child constructing its world contrasted with the behaviourists' picture of the child as a relatively passive responder to stimuli. So writers of children's non-fiction do best when they think of young readers as active and questioning.

Bias – can mean unwelcome stereotyping in particular texts, for example of race, gender and class. It can also apply to an imbalance in the whole non-fiction collection, if one viewpoint and one kind of experience of the world is dominating.

'Big shapes' – a term referring to large textual structures which provide a framework for the reading process. These overarching textual structures are reflected in the 'rhythms and tunes' of the written text and identify it with a genre (Barrs and Thomas, 1991: 6). The term 'big shapes' is also used to refer more generally to larger hierarchies of ideas and concepts in bodies of knowledge like science and history. Information texts need to include enough interpretive writing to relate small events and details to the larger picture (Meek, 1996: 58).

Captions – titles or short annotations accompanying photographs, drawings and diagrams in texts or on displays.

Catalogue – a list, usually in the form of an illustrated booklet or available online, which sets out items for sale or mail order. Bibliographic catalogues indicate the contents of a library or libraries.

CD-ROM – stands for Compact Disc–Read Only Memory. These discs are read by a computer system and often combine a number of media – texts, video and sound.

Chart – a kind of diagram which usually has a numerical element.

Cohesion – helps create what linguists call 'textuality': the sense that we have a text, something continuous and linked, rather than a random group of sentences. Cohesive links or ties can be used at sentence level by using conjunctions ('and', 'but') and adverbs ('soon', 'there'). At text level, cohesion can be achieved by using pronouns such as 'he', 'she', 'they',

Figure 28.1 *Glossary: terms to do with non-narrative non-fiction*

which help a reader make referential connections to earlier parts of the text. There are a large number of connectives and cohesive ties which differ according to the particular kind of texts in which they appear. An instruction text, for example, might give numbered or bullet pointed steps in how a piece of machinery should be used to achieve cohesion.

Compositional aspects of writing – these include getting ideas, selecting vocabulary and grammar. Frank Smith in his book *Writing and the Writer* distinguished these more creative aspects of writing from the transcriptional or secretarial aspects (Smith, 1982).

Concept mapping – a way of accessing and organizing prior knowledge, particularly when a new topic is being introduced. A teacher might use a flipchart or interactive whiteboard to write down all the ideas children can think of about a certain topic.

Critical reading – reflecting on the information and ideas in a text and responding to them with heart and mind. Non-fiction kinds of reading can demand just as much work from the imagination as does fiction. We need, for example, as Bruner argues in *Actual Minds, Possible Worlds*, to be able to imagine the possible as well as the actual (Bruner, 1986).

Cross-sections – diagrams, usually labelled, showing the inside of a creature, the structure of a building or the workings of an object.

Diagrams – in children's non-fiction texts and resources, these show structures like parts of a machine or an animal or processes like the water cycle or the blood system.

Discussion text – sets out a viewpoint on a topic, usually alongside competing views, and is used in school to help children establish a coherent argument on a topic.

Email – a shortened version of 'electronic mail' and refers to messages and documents prepared on personal computers and delivered electronically, using fixed line or satellite communication links.

Explanation text – text explaining a structure like that of a plant or machine or a process like the digestive system or how a lever works.

Expressive language – the kind of unstructured speech and writing used when we formulate action plans or develop new ways of construing experience. James Britton applied this term to children's first attempts at writing, which he argued were very much like 'written down' speech and more directed towards their own interests and preoccupations than towards an audience. 'Expressive' touches in young children's writing should be welcomed as a sign that they are actively making sense of experience (Britton, 1970).

Field of discourse – a linguistic term to do with 'register' and refers to the topic or content of a spoken or written text. When teachers open up a new topic they often invite children's existing knowledge and ideas and make these into a concept map or web. In this way they are opening up a new 'field of discourse'.

Flow chart – a kind of diagram showing the stages involved and the options to choose from in various courses of action.

Fonts – different sizes and kinds of print (large, small, bold, italic and coloured) which help communicate the meaning and significance of information in a text in print or on the screen.

Figure 28.1 *Continued*

Genre exchange – a term meaning the reordering of information set out in one genre into another.

Global structure – the 'big shape' of a text which identifies it with a particular genre (Pappas, 1986).

Hypermedia – a computer text which includes words, pictures, video-film, animation and virtual reality.

Hypertext – a facility to jump from one page of text to another coming earlier or later.

Iconic representation – the representation of experience through images.

Impersonal language – a formal kind of language used in textbooks and official reports.

Knowledge telling/knowledge transforming – terms to differentiate between writing which depends simply on the recall of facts and that which transforms, rather than just repeats, information (Bereiter and Scardamalia, 1987).

Literal and inferential comprehension – terms to refer to the depth and subtlety of a person's reading of a text. Literal reading takes what is written at face value, while inferential comprehension requires more profound reflection on reading and the ability to infer things not actually stated.

Metacognition – an individual's awareness of how they came to know something and so it implies some consciousness of the learning strategies we use and how useful they are. Some implications of this are explored in Chapter 5 in Galton's *Learning and Teaching in the Primary Classroom* (Galton, 2007).

Metalanguage – language to think and talk about language.

Mode – a linguistic term which is part of 'register' and refers to how we adapt our language use to different situations. 'Mode' refers to both the pattern of a text and the medium in which the spoken or written text is given.

Multimedia – a term used to describe the many modes of representation and communication used in computer software and CD-ROM. Reading multimedia texts has given rise to new kinds of literacy and new opportunities and challenges.

Multimodal – texts that combine a number of different modes of communication. Paper multimodal texts use writing, design and images, while electronic multimodal texts may also include sound, speech and music (see Bearne *et al.*, 2005).

Page layout – important in making information books attractive to children. It is to do with how writing and illustrations are organized on each page.

Persuasion – a text which sets out an argument, with evidence, for a point of view.

Register – a linguistic term to refer to the way in which language varies according to the context in which it is used. The three aspects of 'register' are 'field' (the topic), 'mode' (the pattern of the text and medium used) and 'tenor' (the way a message is given – for example how personal or impersonal it is).

Figure 28.1 Continued

CHILDREN'S NON-FICTION LITERATURE

Report – a written form which is organized under aspects of a topic and not chronologically. The typical children's illustrated information book is written in 'report' on topics like 'Magnets', 'Volcanoes' and 'The Vikings'. (See also **global structure**.)

Retrieval devices – those parts of a text, the contents page and index, which help direct readers to the information they need.

Scan – to check through a text for a date or name.

Schema theory – concerns the prior knowledge and expectations children bring to their reading. So in this theory we have an active learner able to talk about their existing knowledge of a topic and to bring their own questions to reading texts.

Skim – the kind of reading we do to get the 'gist' or main sense of the meaning of a passage of written text.

Spiral curriculum – a term used by Jerome Bruner to challenge the view that learning occurs in a neat sequence. Rather, children once introduced to an idea or concept, revisit it on later occasions, as their knowledge and understanding develop and are refined.

Spontaneous and scientific concepts – terms first used by Piaget and then developed by Vygotsky in his book *Thought and Language* (Vygotsky, 1982 edition). 'Spontaneous' concepts are those that a child learns through everyday experience – 'cup', 'like' or 'sister'. 'Scientific' or 'non- spontaneous' concepts, for example 'catalyst', 'medieval' and 'hypotenuse', are learnt in more formal contexts like the classroom. The teacher's role is to help children make links between these two kinds of concept.

Structural guiders – headings and sub-headings which organize an information text.

Summary or précis – a shortened version of a longer text giving the most important points. Children's oral summaries of what they have read precede written ones.

Text cues in non-fiction books – common 'signal' words. They may flag cause and effect ('because' or 'since') or sequence ('before' or 'after'). The provision of these words is a feature of the writing frames designed by Wray and Lewis (1997).

Text organizer (see **retrieval devices**).

Transcriptional aspects of writing – sometimes called 'secretarial aspects', these include spelling, punctuation, legibility, capitalization and paragraphing.

Visual literacy – concerns 'reading' images of all kinds and seeing connections between picture and print.

Writing frames – headings around which children may structure their writing.

Zone of proximal development – a term associated with the writing of Vygotsky and refers to the area of a child's emerging abilities – to the gap between what a child can achieve on their own and what they can achieve with some help.

Figure 28.1 Continued

296

Chapter 29

Report texts
Choosing texts and resources

INTRODUCTION

As children move towards the later primary years and beyond, report texts are used increasingly to support lessons across the curriculum. Illustrated children's information texts on one topic like 'Rivers', 'Magnets' or 'The Vikings', organized non-chronologically, are what people often think of first when they hear the words 'non-fiction for children'. In spite of increasing use of the internet for children's research and the availability of CD-ROM and software, the print information book is still in evidence in primary school libraries and classrooms.

There is a trend towards grouping report and explanation together, as, for example, do Medwell *et al.* (2007: 191). This is because, rather than being the text type of a whole book, explanation text often pops up in children's fact and information books, particularly alongside report. Explanation texts use writing and very often annotated diagrams to show structures – such as of a plant or building and processes like the workings of the digestive system or a vacuum cleaner. A sub-category of report they may be, but I feel choosing explanation texts and resources deserves detailed and separate treatment and so I consider them in the next chapter. Here I consider the global and linguistic features of report and go on to look at some criteria for choosing texts. In a separate chapter, I discuss ways of using both report and explanation texts with different age groups.

Teachers need to know about the structures and linguistic features of particular text types. More controversial is how and when these are taught to children. Direct teaching and focused discussion are helpful, if done with a light touch, and there is increasing emphasis on these when it comes to the over nines. My own view is that teaching about genre is more likely to be successful if children have a grounding in using and enjoying texts as part of their learning across the curriculum.

FEATURES OF REPORT TEXTS

Report is a non-chronologically ordered account which is organized hierarchically according to the demands of a subject or topic. Texts in this genre, written for adults and secondary aged children, open with a general statement about the topic and a description of the phenomenon under study. They tend to be on generic subjects like the history of aviation, mammals or travelling in the East. Report texts to do with plants or animals will of course include life cycles, while texts on machines like cars, ships or vacuum cleaners will probably incorporate written and visual explanation text. Report is usually written in the present tense, in the third person and may use the passive voice. The language of report will describe and inform and often compare and contrast. Non-chronological information texts for children will have some of these features but those for younger children, in particular, will be transitional genres using devices which help connect with young readers.

One of the most helpful analyses of the global or overall structure of 'report', in its form as a children's information text, was presented by Christine Pappas at a conference in Texas at the annual meeting of the National Reading Conference. She identified what she believed were the obligatory elements of the genre; in other words, what will always be present in a children's information book. So a teacher should be able to open any information book that is non-chronologically ordered and find the elements Pappas identifies. These are 'topic representation', 'representation of attributes' and 'characteristic events'. There may be additional elements, but these three should always be present. She believes that the presence of these elements, and importantly in this order, build up children's expectations of what they will find in an information book and therefore how to read and understand it (Pappas, 1986). I happen to have by me as I write, a Dorling Kindersley information book for children of about age five to eight years called *Tree* written by Penelope Arlon. The first double spread begins: 'I know what a tree is! There are three main kinds of tree in the world: palm trees, coniferous trees, and deciduous trees.' This takes care of 'topic presentation'. Then it continues as follows: 'All trees have a trunk, leaves, branches and long roots that stretch out underground.' I think you will agree that this is a succinct statement of a tree's main attributes. The next main heading is 'The life of a tree' and through simple text and pictures we are taken from the beginning of a tree as a seed and its growth to a large tree, taking in typical changes through the seasons and something about the lives of the creatures that live in trees. Built into the structure of the book are large flaps that lift to show, for example, the creatures that live in trees and the inside of a tree trunk containing the sap.

Looking at the language of *Tree*, it has a less formal and altogether friendlier tone than mature report. There is an effort to explain new vocabulary in an appealing way. For example, the three kinds of tree are explained with accompanying pictures. There is also much effort to link what is written to children's likely experience and so we have the conversational sentence: 'Believe it or not, the maple syrup that you put on your pancakes is sap from the sugar maple tree!'

SOME CRITERIA FOR CHOOSING

As is the case with other information texts, teachers judge – bearing in mind the age, ability and interests within the class – non-chronological information texts under three main categories:

- *Design* that makes the book inviting and user-friendly.
- *Coverage* that is in sufficient depth for a particular age group and which is accurate and as free as possible from unwelcome bias.
- *Language and illustration* that work together to describe and explain in a way that draws young learners in, moves them forward in their understanding and encourages them to find out more.

But we also need to look at the whole collection of this kind of information text and check that we have not chosen books and CD-ROMs so similar in approach as to be formulaic and predictable. This can be the problem with series of non-fiction texts organized in the double spreads so much liked by publishers. Some of the books should go beyond describing and informing and provoke, challenge and even at times unsettle. So we want some books written and created by courageous authors and publishers. Knowledge is not static but changes and develops as more evidence is discovered. Understanding this is a sign of progress. A book that encourages young learners to see that scientific arguments and theories are linked to a particular time and a particular state of knowledge is Kathleen Kudlinski's *Boy, Were We Wrong about Dinosaurs!* This takes young readers through the ages and, with the help of entertaining pictures, shows how our theories about what dinosaurs looked like, how they cared for their young and why they died out have changed over time and continue to change. So this book introduces the 'big shapes' of scientific investigation as applied to the study of dinosaur remains and would appeal to many children from about age eight years.

We should also include books which embed information in a story. In these books the reader is helped by the two kinds of discourse being distinguished by print of different size and style. One of the earliest examples of books of this type was Walker's Read and Wonder series for children up to the age of about eight. Even books for older children mix information story with report and the best of these can capture children's interest.

Report is also discussed in Chapter 33 because it is a main kind of writing in reference books and particularly encyclopedias. Of course in reference books for children these days the writing is less formal and efforts are made to connect information with children's likely experience and understanding. Electronic texts, including CD-ROMs and software, also organize information in the form of report and when children visit websites, again report text types dominate. The core categories above are relevant to electronic as well as print texts. However, we are moving towards defining additional criteria to judge how successfully moving images are used and the quality of the on-screen spatial and visual effects.

Publishers and authors of print books know that they now have new competitors and have responded by using advanced technology to produce print books of considerable originality. They cannot show the moving image, but the best have considerable visual impact and sometimes create three-dimensional effects achieved through innovative paper engineering. But as Nicolette Jones reminded her audience in her presentation at the 2008 Write Away conference on non-fiction, devices like flaps, pull-outs and tools like magnifying glasses in science books have to justify their inclusion. Mere novelty will not be enough for the discerning purchaser.

Important as visual aspects of a print book are, we must make sure that we offer children some books which have continuous written text to build up deeper understanding of the information and to present a coherent and detailed argument. If in a classroom or library collection there are too many books which are organized around illustrations with short blocks of text, older primary school pupils will not benefit from the mind-stretching experience of reading sustained written text, which, if made interesting, will help develop reasoning power. A welcome trend is the linking of print resources with designated websites, creating a new kind of resource combining the advantages of print and electronics.

Pre-school and nursery, 3–5-year-olds

- *I'm Not Scary* by Rod Campbell (Campbell Books)
  Lift the flaps to find minibeasts. These are not scary but then a huge spider springs out with a speech bubble saying 'I am scary!'. Children and their parents/teachers either love it or loathe it.

- *The Very Funny Fish* by Jack Tickle (Little Tiger Press)
  Exciting lobsters and cuttlefish spring up from the pages flashing fearsome teeth and claws.

- *Amazing Colours* by Miriam Stoppard (Dorling Kindersley)
  A green apple becomes red when you pull a tag and a leaf changes from yellow to brown. Just the right amount of detail for young children.

- *Dog* by Matthew Van Street and Brian Stanton (photos) (Simon & Schuster)
  Tags to show movement and fluffy bits to stroke.

5–8-year-olds

- *Big Yellow Sunflower* by Frances Barry (Walker)
  A 'fold-out and find-out' novelty book in which the clever design shows how a seed becomes a sunflower. The pages form the complete flower at the end.

- *The Wonderful World Book* by Kate Petty and Jenny Maizels (Bodley Head)
  Moving parts give a dynamic explanation of landscape features like oceans, mountains, rivers and information about their inhabitants.

8–11-year-olds

- *Ships* by Robert Crowther and Paul Harrison (Walker)
  History of ships shown by a leading paper engineer.

- *The Story of Everything*: *From the Big Bang until Now in 11 Pop-Up Spreads* by Neal Layton and Corina Fletcher (Hodder Children's Books)
  Ingenious devices help young readers take on the big shapes of history including how the universe appeared and the end of the dinosaurs.

Figure 29.1 *Novelty information books with movable parts*

CHOOSING REPORT TEXTS FOR DIFFERENT AGE GROUPS

Pre-school and nursery, 3–5-year-olds

What are the forerunners of information organized as report for the very youngest children? A lot of early books are made of cloth, board or plastic rather than paper and take the form of alphabet and counting books which help young children to point to objects and to start to organize their world. Concept books on colour, shape and size are also embryonic forms of report and encourage an organized way of thinking to build on later. Some blur the distinction between book and toy, particularly early books on how things work and move; these are considered in Chapter 30.

A visit to the children's section in a bookshop, a nursery school bookshelf or, increasingly, in supermarkets and corner shops shows that a huge number of these early concept and fact books have been published. The best are thoughtfully designed, written and illustrated. Books to look out for include Lucy Micklethwait's titles in the A First Art Book series. *Colours*, for example, uses a succinct text and carefully chosen paintings in a particular colour palette to help children to compare, classify and to make connections. Classifying foods on account of colour or texture is achieved particularly successfully in Sally Smallwood's book *Cool as a Cucumber!* I read this with a nursery class whose theme was Colours and who were fascinated by how the book showed colours changing when foods are prepared for cooking. As one boy remarked: 'Potatoes are brown when they come out of the earth but they are nearly white when you cut them up for chips.'

Young children benefit from the chance to talk about the new information and ideas they meet in books and teachers are always on the lookout for texts that are large enough to share with a class or group. Two books from the highly regarded author/illustrators Mick Manning and Brita Granström are of a generous size. These authors know just how much detail to provide in text and illustration for the younger age group. *Yuck!* helps children to classify animals by their diet. The pictures of the baby creatures eating worms, rats and fish are highly appealing and the final page showing a human baby drinking its milk makes the point perfectly: what some like, others do not. *Snap!* by the same authors also informs through lively text and pictures and shows how each creature in the food chain is eaten up by an even bigger creature. 'Frog gobbled the fly that came buzzing by.'

Also big enough to share with a class or group is *Actual Size* by Steve Jenkins. This is an excellent starting point for lots of talk and questions and reflection on the implications of a

---

BOX 29.1 *FIRST THE EGG* BY LAURA VACCARO SEEGER (FRANCES LINCOLN)

How do you introduce the concept of growth and metamorphosis to very young children? This book succeeds magnificently through imaginative design, the choice of a vibrant palette and boldly executed illustrations. But what makes it exceptional is that it takes children from the notion of change in nature to their own capacity to create, whether with words or with paint.

It has a very brief written text with just a few words for each idea: 'First the egg, then the chicken, First the tadpole, then the frog.' Then it changes key: 'First the word, then the story' and 'First the paint, then the picture.' Children aged 3–5 years would respond to the use of colour and imaginative placing of die-cuts. The pattern is set in the first illustration. A snowy white egg against a burnt orange background is formed by using the whiteness of the chicken we discover on the next page. When the page is flipped over, the body of the newly hatched chick gets its colour from the yellow background to the egg. There is much to talk about and the book would be an inspiration for children's own creations.

creature's size for its lifestyle and habitat. Young learners see the Atlas moth — so big it is sometimes mistaken for a bird — and can contrast this with the tiny nine millimetre Dwarf Goby fish and wonder about how size affects their lives.

The choices teachers and parents make over early factual texts and resources are important in building positive attitudes: the best books combine facts, fun and an opportunity to chat, share and wonder.

5–8-year-olds

At this stage children want interesting details as well as some main facts; and so we seek inspiring information texts written and illustrated by those skilled enough to turn young readers on to this kind of reading and writing.

Science and nature study

First I want to mention the inviting kind of early nature study or science book which narrates an episode in a creature's life or follows a journey, but which also, in a different font, gives information in report style. *Ice Bear* by Nicola Davies is more than an information story as interesting facts in early report form thread through the book, mostly set against the cold blue and white landscapes and inky blue skies the bear inhabits but also against fiery sunsets and the green plants and yellow and purple flowers of the arctic Spring. Another book that in my experience always gets a positive response and sets off discussion is Nick Dowson's *Tracks of a Panda*. This shows the mother and baby panda in their mountain environment and gives a powerful sense of their daily lives. Again the factual strands of writing in 'report' style give an abundance of interesting and detailed information. How the animal's structure and physical characteristics relate to how it moves, climbs and eats comes over clearly. *The Emperor's Egg* by Martin Jenkins and Jane Chapman narrates the story of a male emperor penguin, adding extra factual information. Like other books of this kind, the different fonts and print sizes are used to show the status of the different kinds of information. Another appealing thing about all the books mentioned is that the illustrations are carefully drawn and often have a lyrical feel to them. For a consideration of the lyrical aspects of some early non-fiction, see Margaret Mallett's bookmark *The Lyrical Voice in Non-Fiction: Think of an Eel by Karen Wallace and Mike Bostock* (The English Association, 2006).

In Box 29.2 is some comment about *Woolly Mammoth*, a book which is lyrical in both its rhyming text and illustration, but which also involves young readers with some text approaching mature report.

The imaginative use of paper engineering is another way to capture the interest of young readers. *Sharks*, written by Phillip Clarke and illustrated by Peter Scott, uses the device of flaps which are pulled open to reveal different species. So children are shown the similarities and differences between great whites, tiger sharks, hammerheads and the strange goblin shark and learn about how to classify them.

Two cross-curricular packs are worth mentioning: Oxford University Press' *Cross Curricular Jackdaws* and the *Curiosity Kits* devised by Maureen Lewis and Ros Fisher when they were based at the University of Exeter Education Department. The Oxford materials are resources for science, history and PSHE; they typically contain an information story, a non-chronological

---

BOX 29.2 *WOOLLY MAMMOTH* **BY MICK MANNING AND BRITA GRANSTRÖM (FRANCES LINCOLN)**

This information picturebook has a rhyming text accompanying detailed pictures of great mammoths from youth to old age and places them in wonderfully atmospheric Ice Age landscapes. Scale is helpfully indicated by showing the huge mammoths next to other creatures like hyenas and reindeer. Writing on a strip down the side of each double spread adds extra information and takes children a step further towards coping with mature report. 'African elephants and musk oxen form circles for defence. Scientists think mammoths behaved in the same way.' There is helpful imagery to indicate how the creature moved: the mammoth 'used its tusks like snowploughs to find food: grass, moss, sedge, juniper and wild flowers'.

Mammoth bones have been found at the bottom of cliffs. Some scientific knowledge is provisional, so we then read: 'Were mammoths deliberately panicked over the edge? Or did humans scavenge the meat after a natural accident?' It is this speculative approach that helps make insightful young scientists.

---

report and, if helpful to the topic, an historic legend. *Curiosity Kits* are intended for less enthusiastic young readers, particularly boys, and typically include a book, a game and a toy for the young reader and a magazine on the topic to help the participating adult to encourage conversation. Teachers and parents can either use prepared kits or make up their own for the children in their classes (Lewis and Fisher, 2003).

I have tried to show that the print information book is still a core part of the non-fiction collection and offers a distinctive kind of reading experience. However, electronic books and CD-ROMs are now important resources in lessons from the earliest stages. They can develop children's ability to read in a non-linear way and to use interactive features, for example pop-up boxes and video-clips. Publishers who have long produced reading schemes and 'fact' book series are bringing out electronic versions of their non-fiction titles on science and nature study, indeed across the whole curriculum. The range of information books in print and electronic form can be seen on publishers' websites. Oxford Reading Tree was one of the first initiatives giving weight to non-fiction titles and there is now an electronic series based on them, for example e-Fireflies. We look for CD-ROMs and electronic texts that are not just print books transferred to the screen, but which exploit the strengths of the medium – its capacity to show the moving image and its non-linear structure.

Geography

In the best geography texts, interesting and relevant illustrations work alongside clear written text to help children to develop the sense of place so important in geography lessons. There are a lot of colourful fact books for this age group on the main geographical topics, often published in series. The titles in Hodder Wayland's Geography First series cover coast, islands, rivers, maps and symbols, mountains and volcanoes. Clear contents pages, indexes and glossaries, and annotated diagrams and large bright photographs identify the books of early report text type.

Ape, by Martin Jenkins and illustrated by Vicki White, explores conservation issues with much sensitivity. The increasingly rare orang-utan, chimp, bonobo and gorilla are shown in close up and their plight would inspire older children's thought and discussion.

Some imaginative resources on the market encourage and support geographical kinds of thinking. A package entitled *My World and Globe: A First Book of Geography* includes an illustrated book by Ira Wolfman and a 12-inch inflatable globe on which children can draw with washable marker pens. There are chapters on key areas – for example on maps and globes, physical features and people, places and things. Illustrations and maps are accompanied by a text that moves children towards the kind of thinking that underpins report writing, but does so skilfully; the material is organized under headings and sub-headings, and bullet points are used. The text is written invitingly in the second person, with the sort of questions children might ask popping up regularly. This is a 'worth seeking out' geography book that makes a good job of linking the new information to the child's likely existing knowledge and experience.

Thinking of imaginative approaches, the First Discovery series from Moonlight Publishing, is well worth investing in. This successful, small, independent publisher uses in its titles transparent overlays to transform pictures to show change and process. *The Desert*, illustrated

BOX 29.3 *BARNABY BEAR*, BBC AND THE GEOGRAPHICAL ASSOCIATION

These materials include print books, photographs, maps, letters, flyers and posters, videos of television programmes, DVDs and photographs. All are specially designed to make the crucial link between the familiar and the unfamiliar. Barnaby is a small bear who travels throughout the UK and to many countries on each continent. There are stories, poems and pictures, and many different kinds of writing on both print and electronic resources. This multimodal and multimedia material also has some report writing well embedded in interesting adventures, and a range of helpful visual materials. Although the materials are ideal for Key Stage 1, nursery age children would enjoy the video-film *The Seaside*. Older children at Key Stage 2 would find some of the materials interesting and relevant to their geography lessons. The series has its excellent website, constantly updated, with pupil and teacher sites showing photographs and maps, relating to the case studies in the materials. Many schools find the Barnaby Bear DVD is easy to use; it has the BBC's four programmes on Dublin, Brittany, English Seaside and Badger Watching (www.bbcactive.com/schoolshop) and Barnaby Bear at the Geographical Association (www.geography.org.uk/primary/barnabybear/).

Teachers often buy the Barnaby Bear hand puppet and display pictures of his many adventures to help make the link between the places children know and those that are new to them. On the website for teachers and pupils children learn that 'Barnaby loves getting letters' and many write to him at the Geographical Association in Sheffield telling him what they have found most interesting in his reports. The approach in the Barnaby Bear materials is to develop not only a sense of place, but also an understanding of values.

by Donald Grant, uses overlays to reveal how a landscape can be altered by changing weather conditions like wind and heat, and tells how people survive in this harsh climate.

More traditional information books but with a bright modern look are to be found in Franklin Watts' Making a Difference series on human geography. *Reusing Things* by Sue Barraclough introduces children to basic principles of ecology. It would contribute to lessons on rubbish recycling and is packed with ideas for follow-up work. You can tell when an author and illustrator have given real thought to how to introduce each section of a topic. Peter Kent's *Take a Flight* starts with the 'big shape' of an airport, with a wonderfully detailed picture showing the car park, terminal, runway and control tower.

When thinking about geography for the five to eights, one publishing initiative stands out: the Barnaby Bear materials (Box 29.3).

Early geography texts and resources are also discussed in Chapter 30 and Chapter 33.

History

History texts should not only relate a bald sequence of events; rather we want texts that help children to begin to understand the relationship between the events in terms of cause and effect. A wonderfully dramatic introduction to the 'big shapes' of history is Neil Layton's *The Story of Everything: From the Big Bang Until Now in 11 Pop-Up Spreads* (paper engineering is by Corina Fletcher). Using exciting paper engineering, the book starts with the moment that the universe appears, jumps to the end of the dinosaurs and moves on to the beginning of human history. One of the eleven double spreads shows an Icthyostegas climbing on to land and where it develops legs and in another there is a timeline showing houses from mud huts to modern apartments. Flaps on the mammal family tree can be lifted to show what each creature evolved from. And speaking of evolution, there is even a minibook attached entitled 'A Word about Evolution' by Mr C. Darwin. Of course this book blurs the lines between history, geography and science. It is certainly likely to encourage much questioning and wondering.

Still keeping to the 'big shapes' of history, *The Usborne Book of World History* by Anne Millard, Patricia Vanags and Jenny Tyler would be a good source of material on a wide range of historical topics. It is not designed to be used by individual pupils of this age on their own, but rather as a resource for the teacher to read aloud and help with their questions. The book is written in clear report: 'We find out about people in the past by looking at the remains they left behind them and by reading the things they wrote.' Individual chapters cover the role of archaeologists in finding historical evidence and different methods of dating objects — radio carbon and tree dating, for example. This scholarly book would be a good resource through the primary years.

When it comes to smaller topic areas there are lots of series of first history books, many of them well illustrated and written. The Usborne Beginners series includes titles on Celts, Romans and the Ancient Greeks which young readers could manage on their own. *Romans* by Katie Daynes, like others in the series, has dynamic pictures and a simple clear text which introduces children to non-chronologically ordered history books. The Heinemann Library People in the Past series is more demanding of young readers and uses primary sources to provide evidence of how things have changed through the centuries. The series on Victorian times includes *Victorian Schools*, *Victorian Homes* and *Victorian Children*. *Victorian Children* by

Brenda Williams examines how young people lived then, what we can learn from those times and how they have changed. Hodder Wayland's You Wouldn't Want to Be series has short bursts of simple report writing alongside small witty pictures, some of which are annotated diagrams. For example, *You Wouldn't Want to Be a Victorian Miner* by John Mallam has a labelled diagram of a mineshaft drawn by artist David Antram. These books about what it was like to live past lives, and how they are different from our own, show children that history is a subject that helps them understand what it is to be a human being. Here imagination as well as evidence has a role and knowing something of their own history will help the children to develop a sense of identity.

Books on painting often use 'report' to provide an historical perspective. Those on portraits, for example, will inform children about changes in who was painted and the setting in which they are portrayed. Art galleries often have an excellent collection of art books for children in their shops. One book to look out for is Clare Gittings' *What Are You Looking At?*; this is a lively examination of portraits in their historical context and shows what they can tell us. Most art galleries and museums have good websites these days so that children can look at works of art and objects from different historical periods even if they do not live near enough to a museum to visit. The Show Me site (www.show.me.uk, accessed 8 February 2009) always has new and exciting information on all manner of things; for example, it gives children quick access to all sorts of interesting artefacts and explains how and when they were used or worn.

English and PSHE

Some books increase children's emotional resilience by making it acceptable to have strong feelings. Much fiction can serve this purpose, but stories for children tend to resolve problems at the end. Some non-fiction books confront the reality of the sad and difficult things that happen to people and present no easy answers. *The Sad Book* by Michael Rosen, illustrated with great sensitivity by Quentin Blake, is suitable for children at any stage in the early or primary years. Rosen explains how sad feelings can sometimes overwhelm a person and make them feel helpless and unable to know what to do. He suggests family reunions, friends and birthday celebrations can help lift our mood.

Another book which helps children explore feelings, using flaps which show happy and sad faces to encourage discussion of the range of emotions human beings feel, is *All Kinds of Feelings* by Emma Brownjohn.

8–11-year-olds

After about age nine, we can introduce texts with demanding syntax, a more differentiated vocabulary and with a more formal written style. Content too will have moved up a notch, with more detailed accounts extending information and ideas. There is still room for the imaginative and original books that younger children enjoy and the best of these still require the concentration and perseverance we want to reinforce.

ICT resources – CD-ROMs, software and websites – have a well-established place and many use the report genre to get information across in a way that interests the iPod and digital generation. But these need to be evaluated as stringently as any other resource.

Children's newspapers – *First News*, for example – use all kinds of writing, including report in articles and the editorial (www.firstnews.co.uk). Some newspapers have an occasional section for young readers: *Young Times* provides interesting if challenging reports on topics of current interest (www.timesonline.co.uk/youngtimes).

Science and nature study

Too many dense pages of report writing can be off putting. There needs to be good, inviting design and a balance between written text and illustration even for children at the older end of this age group. Some children's authors and illustrators use comic strip to great effect. Marcia Williams' *Three Cheers for Inventors*, dedicated to Leonardo da Vinci, gives much information about the great inventors including Thomas Edison, James Watt and John Logie Baird. Here, what is technically 'report' runs alongside other kinds of writing – biography and explanation. It shows that we need to show some flexibility over assigning children's books to a particular genre. Another writer for children who knows just how to give quality information in an interesting way is Nicola Davies, well known for her books on the animal world. Her book *Extreme Animals: The Toughest Creatures on Earth*, with Neal Layton, is written in her usual engaging style but veers helpfully towards report when she informs the readers about the survival strategies of animals in the extreme temperatures of the Arctic and desert. Her other books, not least *Poo: A Natural History of the Unmentionable* and *What's Eating You? Parasites – the Inside Story* show how topics which at first might not sound riveting can be made fascinating while not compromising the quality or balance of the information. The best authors and illustrators of information books seem to achieve a rhythm in their books where design, written text and illustrations all combine successfully. Often, as in Davies' case, some wit and humour helps too.

As children near the secondary school years they need to have experienced some mature report writing. You will find this in Karen Dudley's Wild World series which gives scientific information on classifying animals, on their social activities, life cycle, habitats and food.

BOX 29.4 *ASK DR K. FISHER ABOUT MINIBEASTS* BY CLAIRE LLEWELLYN AND KATE SHEPPARD (ILLUS.) (KINGFISHER)

There is always room for a playful book that also communicates quality information. This one uses the 'agony uncle' device. The male hoverfly who thinks he is a 'messy eater', getting himself covered in pollen, is praised by Dr K. Fisher for pollinating flowers and 'helping new seeds to grow'.

A splendid double spread shows how the structure of minibeast bodies is adapted to help them function and survive. Children at the younger end of Key Stage 2 will enjoy this colourful information-packed and energetic book, while older ones will understand the more sophisticated jokes – like the one about the spider worried that she is 'wasting a lifetime on the web'.

Figure 29.2
Front cover of Can You Feel the Force? *by Richard Hammond*
Copyright Dorling Kindersley Ltd 2006. Foreword copyright Richard Hammond 2006

Titles in the series include *Giant Pandas* and *Alligators and Crocodiles*, and the fact that these books have gone into new editions indicates their popularity with young readers and school. The diagrams which typically accompany report are all here: maps to show where animals live, diagrams and photographs. Issues about the endangered status of some of the creatures will get young readers thinking and organizations and websites to help take their research further are provided.

Another text which combines a variety of visual ways of presenting information and also uses mature report writing is Robert Winston's *What Makes Me?* This book sets out information and ideas about the mind as well as the body and tackles such brain-stretching things as genetics in an interesting way.

There are a large number of science texts for all the primary stages, often in series, produced by publishers of non-fiction and sometimes part of reading programmes like Oxford Reading Tree, Usborne and Dorling Kindersley. These are usually well written and illustrated, but need to be checked before big purchases are made so that you can be sure they will suit the children you teach. A writer who knows how to make science accessible and interesting to children around eight or nine years old is Richard Hammond. In his exciting book, *Can You Feel the Force?*, he makes physics in general and forces in particular come alive for young learners by using everyday examples with explanatory illustrations to help understanding of the principles of physics. He explains how planes stay in the air, how we can ride a bike and even attempts to explain the concept of relativity for young minds.

Geography

There are, as children get older, an increasing number of texts to do with geography, physical and human, which are mainly written as report and include the visual material that helps identify them with the genre. Children encounter many texts which help their understanding of environmental issues and those for older primary children need to go beyond the superficial. These publications are likely to draw on the expertise of specialists and often include visual information obtained through the new technologies, including satellite photographs. A book that would stretch the ablest eleven-year-old but would be accessible for children over nine with some support is *The Future of the Earth: An Introduction to Sustainable Development for Children* by Yann Arthus-Bertrand *et al.* It has a strong visual impact and uses aerial photographs and maps to show, for example, population density and the distribution of water resources. *Earth Matters: An Encyclopedia of Ecology* by David de Rothschild is another books which presents 'in depth' knowledge about our world and our role in preserving it. First it looks at our world – its oceans, mountains and rainforests. Then it shows photographs from space that show all too well how our world is changing. Finally young readers are given help with doing something positive, from obvious things like recycling our waste to less obvious ones like helping to preserve special habitats.

If you want a most original and involving book exploring global aspects of geographical research and thinking, I recommend David Smith's *If the World Were a Village* (Box 29.5).

CD-ROMs and software have an important place alongside print resources and this is particularly true of geographical information. Collins Virtual Geography material for the over eights is interactive, enquiry-based and easy to use. As each topic is accessed, a voice gives information to accompany the pictures as they move across the screen. There is an excellent photo bank but, of course, it is the moving image which gives electronic material the edge over print resources. Take the material on rubbish disposal: we see a driver in a tipper truck dumping a huge amount of paper waste at a landfill site. As we watch the load being discharged the sheer amount of the waste becomes only too evident. Watching this

---

BOX 29.5 *IF THE WORLD WERE A VILLAGE* BY DAVID SMITH (A&C BLACK)

David Smith's hugely interesting and effective idea is to use a device, that of a village of just one hundred people, and then to look at such issues as availability of water and food, literacy, culture and customs and at concepts like the standard of living. I often look on Amazon UK and other sites with feedback on books and resources from teachers and pupils to see what others think of new and interesting texts. Feedback on Amazon by a teacher of a mixed Year 5 and 6 class on this book was that it 'stimulated good debates' and was the basis of a lively presentation to the school in assembly. The publishers have provided a website extending the information contained in the book; it suggests ways of using the book, with ideas for further research such as into the availability of water and food across the world (www.acblack.com/globalvillage).

together on a whiteboard, and perhaps also on their pupil screens, means that teacher and children can debate the spoken, written and visual information offered.

The best electronic resources have some of the merits of quality print books as well as the advantages of the moving image. Amongst the pollution materials the picture of a forlorn oiled bird on a deserted polluted beach is as powerful as the best print book photographs and of course it is easier to have a shared response where there is an interactive whiteboard and pupil screens.

History

Biographies of key historical figures for older primary children are often combined with contextualizing chapters written in the language of report. Good examples of this 'mixed text' approach are the titles in Book House's Graphic Non-Fiction series. These include *Spartacus: The Life of a Roman Gladiator* by Rob Shone and Anita Ganeri, with illustrations by Nick Spender. This book begins with some contextualizing chapters about gladiator training and information about the Roman Republic. Then we have the exciting story of the gladiator revolt, led by Spartacus who was angered by the treatment gladiators received from their masters. Cartoon strip with speech balloons prove a dynamic format for the dramatic tale.

We also get a mix of text types in the very successful series Horrible Histories by Terry Deary. In *The Terrible Tudors* there are 'recipes' and quizzes as well as report text about food, games and customs at this period in history. Scholastic have brought out audio cassettes with Terry Deary reading to complement the print versions of the histories.

Electronic resources and websites are very much part of the modern history collection, not least because the moving image can be used to simulate battles, feasts and dramatic scenes from the past. Christine Cooper and Alison Ewin's *Virtual History* resource is an interactive source for the over eights. We are shown, for example, how life might have been experienced on a Viking ship. There is a useful image bank, including pictures of artefacts from the British Museum, and there is both spoken and written text. So this resource is both multimodal and multimedia and this will appeal to many young learners, who benefit from visual as well as verbal input.

Some history books home in on one aspect of the past. *The History of the Steel Band*, by Verna Wilkins and Michael La Rose and illustrated by Lynne Willey, is an interesting and very detailed account about the history and growing popularity of the steel pan as a musical

'Grooving' the pan to separate the notes.

Figure 29.3
'"Grooving" the pan to separate the notes', an illustration by Lynne Willey on page 30 of The History of the Steel Band
Reproduced with the permission of Lynne Willey and the publishers Tamarind

- *Cool as a Cucumber* by Sally Smallwood (Zero to Ten)
  A vibrant book about foods, for children from about age three years, going beyond picturing and describing them to showing how they change – for example, cooking changes their texture and colour.

- *The Worst Children's Jobs in History* by Tony Robinson (Macmillan Children's Books)
  While communicating that children's jobs through history have been hard, unpleasant and sometimes dangerous, this book manages to use humour to show young readers how comparatively fortunate they are.

- *Three Cheers for Inventors!* by Marcia Williams (Walker)
  Children from about age eight learn about Edison, Watt, Baird and other inventors through a lively written text and engaging cartoon-like illustrations.

- *Poo: A Natural History of the Unmentionable* by Nicola Davies (Walker)
  An original take on the topic by an exceptionally fine writer of information texts.

- *Boy, Were We Wrong about the Dinosaurs!* by Kathleen Kudlinsky (Puffin)
  Lively pictures and an interesting written text show how scientific work has changed our understanding of the life, lifestyles and disappearance of these animals.

- *First News* (children's newspaper)
  This has clearly written and well-illustrated news reports and feature articles. See more about it on the website (www.firstnews.co.uk, accessed 7 February 2009).

- *Show Me* (website for children)
  www.showme.uk (accessed 8 February 2009). There is information about all manner of things including artefacts of all kinds. There is information about children's reading interests with book suggestions.

- *If the World Were a Village* by David Smith (A&C Black)
  By imagining the world as a village of 100 people, children enter the debate about all aspects of human life. Exciting follow-up activities are available on the website (www.acblack.com/globalvillage, accessed 8 February 2009).

- *Can You Feel the Force?* by Richard Hammond (Dorling Kindersley)
  Information about forces is enhanced with examples. How do planes stay in the air? How is it that a person feels no pain when on a bed of nails? There is also an introduction to the theory of relativity.

- *What Makes Me?* by Robert Winston (Dorling Kindersley)
  A book written in mature report style, for older primary aged children and beyond, tacking all aspects of body and mind and managing to explain the principles of genetics in an accessible way.

Figure 29.4 *Information texts, roughly in order of challenge*

instrument across the world from its beginnings in the Caribbean. There is quite a lot of text, but the pages are enlivened by vibrant photographs and drawings. Young readers will also enjoy listening to the accompanying CD of steel band performances.

After about age nine children can take on texts more grounded in report writing, but these need to be inviting and have quality visual information in the form of diagrams and photographs. Dorling Kindersley's Eyewitness Guides fall into this category; this is a huge series with over a hundred titles, well-illustrated and with written text informed by experts. Simon Adam's *World War II*, for example, shows photographs of people and events and draws in the written text on input from experts at the Imperial War Museum.

Texts on the history of art for children are often written as reports and take young learners a step further in controlling the more mature kind of writing. *The Usborne Introduction to Art* by Rosie Dickins and Mari Griffiths has the systematic but accessible organization of the best report and covers the main painting genres. This is a book that teachers could share with the class so that if children were studying portraiture or landscape relevant sections could be read aloud from the relevant pages. Like so many modern books, this one has useful links to websites via the publisher's site. Another interesting and stimulating series of art books is the Look! series; see, for example, *Look! Body Language in Art* by Gillian Wolfe.

Jan Mark's *The Museum Book*, illustrated by Richard Holland, starts by inviting readers to imagine what it would be like to enter a museum without knowing its purpose. Then the history of museums is covered and the array of different objects and artefacts museums store explored. This is a book for older primary children to dip into and share with teacher and other children. It is certainly a model of strong and interesting writing in the report genre.

Michael Rosen's books *What's So Special about Shakespeare?* and *What's So Special about Dickens?* put these authors in the context of their times, using quotations from their work. This is the sort of book teacher and children could share to enrich study in English and history.

SUMMARY

- Report texts are non-chronological (or non-narrative), hierarchically organized accounts, usually in the present tense, which describe, inform, compare and contrast.
- Report texts tend to be on generic subjects like the history of aviation or mammals.
- In their mature form they follow logical steps in the presentation of facts, ideas and information, using non-chronological connectives like 'therefore', 'so that' and 'but'.
- Texts for primary aged children are usually 'transitional' genres with only some of the features of the mature forms. Illustrations – diagrams, charts, photographs and drawings – as well as written text play their part in helping children understand ideas and concepts.
- In children's books, report is often placed alongside other text types like explanation or argument.
- While the basic categories of design, coverage and language and illustration provide a framework for judging the worth of a report text, we also look for that ability of the best books and CD-ROMs to involve and interest young readers and to make them want to find out more.

Chapter 30

Explanation texts
Choosing texts and resources

INTRODUCTION

Information texts for children often include both report and explanation and, as I have mentioned earlier, explanation can be regarded as a type of report. However, because explanation is such an important and useful genre, I have given it separate treatment. Texts and materials in this category are particularly important in gaining understanding in mathematics, science and geography because they can illuminate how structure affects function and how processes work. We might, for example, have an annotated diagram showing how an animal's skeleton and muscle groups affect the way it moves. A process might be shown through pictures and writing, indicating cause and effect, such as how a volcanic eruption occurs. Food chains, water cycles and machinery working are all processes that children need to learn about in the primary years. Print diagrams often use arrows to indicate how a plant or machine moves, but moving images have brought new power to explaining all manner of processes. So, for example, a CD-ROM can show with new dynamism how the digestive and blood systems work.

FEATURES OF EXPLANATION TEXTS

Explanation texts have a global organization which aims to show cause and effect. Typically, through a combination of written text and diagrams and in a series of logical steps, they provide an explanation of a structure or process. This means that children need to become able to control cause and effect connectives when it comes to writing or to annotating drawings. So we would expect, as children get older, to find them becoming more confident in using time connectives – for example 'first', 'then' and 'after that' – and causal connectives – words like 'in order to', 'resulting in', 'with the effect that', 'because' and 'therefore'. Explanation texts are usually written in the present tense and typically combine a diagram, perhaps a cross-section, with written annotation. The combination of design, illustration and writing that so often governs such texts makes them multimodal.

CHOOSING EXPLANATION TEXTS FOR DIFFERENT AGE GROUPS

The broad criteria for judging the quality of information texts of all kinds, good design, coverage and language and illustration, serve in considering the quality of explanation texts.

Many of the texts recommended in this chapter are transitional: they have only some of the features of mature explanation text. Those for younger children are likely to have an inviting, conversational tone and bright, interesting illustrations, often with a touch of humour. The best writers use analogy, imagery and comparison to help children understand and relate information to things they already know about. Dorling Kindersley's *Plant* helps children understand the size of the huge seed of the coco de mer tree by comparing its size with that of a beach ball.

In school, teachers bring in explanation texts to support and extend what is being learnt in lessons across the curriculum. This means that children are introduced to this kind of literacy in a way which is embedded in a supportive context.

Most publishers of reading programmes and schemes for children, for example Oxford University Press, Heinemann, Ginn, HarperTrophy and Usborne, offer strong non-fiction strands. Their books on science and geography generally link with National Curriculum programmes organized within age ranges and often come with notes for the teacher. However good the books to be found in a strand of a larger programme, there is a case for teachers selecting what is the best from different programmes and supplementing their collection with trade books. The age-related books recommended below draw freely on what is available and include some individual and original texts which I have found to have special appeal.

Pre-school and nursery, 3–5-year-olds

Very young children are likely first to hear and use the language of explanation when they ask questions in everyday conversations: 'How does that work?' 'Why is it like that?' In his book *The Growth of Scientific Concepts in the Young Child*, Navarro relates how his pre-school son asked constant, intense questions to find answers to his wonderings. On one occasion he asked why snow melted first on the sunny side of his garden (Navarro, 1955). In my own research I found that at just under age four, Orla thought deeply about something her aunt had said; it was about a relative dying and 'going up to heaven, which is in the sky'. Orla told her mother about her two theories. Perhaps, she thought, giants (she had recently had the story of *Jack and the Beanstalk* read to her) might lift people up in their long arms. Or perhaps people climbed to Heaven on long ladders. Orla carefully drew her own annotated map of the ladders reaching up to the sky (Mallett, 2003: 56). So sometimes children create their own explanation texts in talk or writing before being exposed to this kind of reading material. The best texts explain things in an appealing and sometimes entertaining way and, of course, include a big visual element.

Children certainly ask questions to begin to learn about how their own bodies work. A witty introduction to the senses, which I noticed in the Tate Gallery shop, is Herve Tullett's *The Five Senses*. It is an interactive book with things to touch, the Braille alphabet, which shows how blind people can read by touch, and a lovely page showing lots of specially adapted forks to make eating peas easier. Claire Llewellyn and Simone Abel, illustrator, keep things simple and lively in *The Best Ears in the World: A First Look at Sound and Hearing*, showing pictures of the organs of hearing together with explanatory text. Blue Apple Books' titles on the five senses have simple colourful illustrations and witty titles – for example *You Can't Taste a Pickle with Your Ear*, which is written by Fred Ehrlich and Harriet Ziefert, with pictures

314

by Amanda Haley. Another book that uses humour to teach and explain is *Sounds All Around* by Wendy Pfeffer. Children learn how sounds are made and how important they are in helping both animals and human beings to communicate. The older end of this age group would find Aliki's *My Five Senses* helpful to support lessons on the theme of 'Ourselves'.

There are a number of books to help parents to respond to children's questions about babies – where they come from and how they grow. My favourite of all those I know is *How Did I Begin?* by Mick Manning and Brita Granström. It goes carefully through the stages of pregnancy through to birth using cartoon pictures and its friendly tone invites discussion.

Some young children are beginning to think about how machines work. I had a trawl around some book shops to refresh my memory and found a lot of colourful little books about cars, tractors and trains. Some were more likely than others to help an adult to explain the workings of cranes, wheels and engines. For example, the board book *Dig, Dig, Digging* by Margaret Mayo and Alex Ayliffe has an excellent double spread showing cranes in action – both lifting and lowering materials, with a simple text 'Up go the bricks' and 'Down go the pipes'. Some board books are both toys and books; for example, Dorling Kindersley's *Fire Engine* is in the shape of a vehicle with plastic, movable wheels. The book encourages discussion of the turn-table ladders and hydraulic platforms that are essential to the vehicle's functioning. *Carl's Crane* by James Croft in Little Tiger Press' Mini Machine series is an information story explaining how cranes function. It has an appealing cover with the moving parts of a crane, complete with a hook to carry bundles of bricks and stones. Tony Mitton and Ant Parker are known for their brightly coloured, energetic little books on all manner of machines. *Amazing Aeroplanes* has an animal crew and explains how a plane flies for the very young. *Amazing Machines* is a pack of four of the series and in rhyming text the appealing animal characters show the actions of diggers, rockets, fire engines and trains. Like similar books, words to help explain the movement of the machines are used and emphasized in large print – 'scoop', gouge' and 'lift' – but, an adult's mediation would be needed to help children understand.

Some forward young learners might be ready to look at the illustrations in a book from the Franklin Watts' Wonderwise series called *Wheels Keep Turning* by Mick Manning and Brita Granström. This gives a simple history of how the wheel was invented – probably the first notion was a rolling log, going on to wheels on vehicles, wheelbarrows, the potter's wheel.

By the end of this age phase we would expect children to be able to talk through an explanation of how a simple process works – perhaps the stages through which the classroom tadpoles turn into frogs. This talk around first-hand experience is a good basis on which to build the ability to understand and learn from explanations in books.

5–8-year-olds

There are a large number of explanation texts for this age group to support lessons in science and nature study – many of which tell about the workings of machines, the body and about plant and animal structure. There are also a number of texts on geographical explanation, for example how the water cycle works. There are fewer books for this age range which include historical explanation.

Science and nature study

Have you come across HarperTrophy's Let's Find Out Science titles? Some of these have gone into new, updated editions; examples are *Air Is All Around You* by F.M. Branley, illustrated by John O'Brien, and *Forces Make Things Move* by K.B. Bradley, illustrated by Paul Meisel. The very successful titles in First Discovery from Moonlight Publishing use transparent overlays to explain changes and processes. This small independent publishing house concentrates on beautifully illustrated non-fiction for children. *Light* by Gilbert Houbre *et al.* and translated by Sarah Matthews uses pictures and cleverly designed overlays to explain the secrets of shadows and rainbows and shows how the world is lit up after dark.

Overlays and pictures are also used to fine effect in the Technology series, which includes books on the internet, wheels, boats and the telephone. *Pictures*, illustrated by Pierre-Marie Valat, explains what happens when we press the button on a camera.

Geoff Waring is another author who has found imaginative ways of explaining concepts like light and dark, moving and rolling and sound. In *Oscar and the Moth: A Book about Light*

Figure 30.1 *'The Blood System', diagram from pages 16 and 17 of* My Body Book *by Mick Manning and Brita Granström*
Reproduced with the permission of the publishers Franklin Watts. Copyright Franklin Watts 2006

and *Dark* the young cat learns about why there is light and dark on Earth and about creatures that manufacture light in their bodies.

In *A Ruined House* Mick Manning takes young readers on an imagined visit to an abandoned house. He explains some of the processes which cause the deterioration of old buildings. Dampness starts to take over when an unheated and uncared for house is left. This encourages the growth of fungi which break down old wood, and then beetles tunnel into the wood causing further destruction. Here the cause and effect sequence which is a major feature of explanation text is shown in a way children can understand.

There are a number of books on how food chains work, showing the roles of predator and prey. *Yum-Yum: A Book about Food Chains*, by Mick Manning and Brita Granström, is all about creatures eating and being eaten. These authors use arrows skilfully to show orientation and process, but in some other books children can be confused if the purpose of the arrows is not made clear. The annotated diagram is a strong feature in books that explain. The cross-sections of the heart, the ear and the digestive and blood systems in Manning and Granström's *My Body Book* are wonderfully clear and show children how the written annotation works

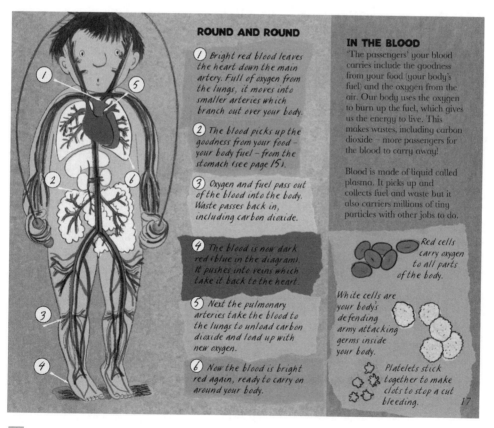

ROUND AND ROUND

1. Bright red blood leaves the heart down the main artery. Full of oxygen from the lungs, it moves into smaller arteries which branch out over your body.

2. The blood picks up the goodness from your food – your body fuel – from the stomach (see page 15).

3. Oxygen and fuel pass out of the blood into the body. Waste passes back in, including carbon dioxide.

4. The blood is now dark red (blue in the diagram). It pushes into veins which take it back to the heart.

5. Next the pulmonary arteries take the blood to the lungs to unload carbon dioxide and load up with new oxygen.

6. Now the blood is bright red again, ready to carry on around your body.

IN THE BLOOD

'The passengers' your blood carries include the goodness from your food (your body's fuel) and the oxygen from the air. Our body uses the oxygen to burn up the fuel, which gives us the energy to live. This makes wastes, including carbon dioxide – more passengers for the blood to carry away!

Blood is made of liquid called plasma. It picks up and collects fuel and waste but it also carries millions of tiny particles with other jobs to do.

Red cells carry oxygen to all parts of the body.

White cells are your body's defending army attacking germs inside your body.

Platelets stick together to make clots to stop a cut bleeding. 17

Figure 30.1 *continued*

with the images to communicate meaning (Figure 30.1). Another thing we look for in explanation texts is the use of analogy to make the concepts come alive for children. In the explanation of the blood system in *My Body Book*, the white blood cells are likened to an army attacking germs inside the body. In the section on the digestive system the mouth, with its mixing of food with saliva using teeth and tongue, is likened to 'a food blender'.

Another kind of text which aims to explain all manner of things about our world is the 'I wonder . . .' sort of book structured around questions. The best of these books go into enough detail in word and picture to explain structures and processes. They are very prevalent in the children's reference section of bookshops. A favourite on my bookshelf is Carole Stott's beautifully illustrated *I Wonder Why Stars Twinkle and Other Questions about Space*, which explains the differences between stars and planets, attempts to illuminate black holes and gives intriguing information – for example it tells young readers that 'you are made of the same stuff as a star'.

Geography

What's Under the Bed by Mick Manning and Brita Granström is a narrative which explains, amongst many other things, how caves are formed and the processes leading to a volcanic eruption. A teacher writes in a customer review on Amazon UK that his class of six-year-olds were fascinated by the book: 'They were amazed at all the things going on literally under their feet. They wanted to know more and talked for forty minutes.'

Splish Splash Splosh! is another book in the same series by the same authors introducing children to the water cycle. Again carefully annotated cross-sections show young readers the journey water makes from a reservoir to people's sinks and toilets and finally into the sewage system. Another favourite account of the water cycle is *Drop Goes Plop: A First Look at the Water Cycle* by Sam Godwin and illustrated with skill and humour by Simone Abel. I know from experience that this book appeals with its question and answer format: a baby bird asks mum about clouds and how they suck up water. It generates copious comments and questions as young as four.

Moving image texts have a strong place in explaining structures and processes. Usborne have helped here by producing their internet-linked series of print titles, which have useful links accessed from their website (www.usborne.co.uk). These links, which include the BBC Schools site and that of the National Geographic Association, make available video-film showing how, for example, earthquakes, hurricanes and wildfires come about. *Volcanoes* by Stephanie Turnbull is a colourful print book in this series allowing the young reader to use it on its own or to extend their understanding by accessing moving images via the quicklink to other websites. The explanatory voice is American, I should mention. The moving images show the force with which the lava is pushed up and out of the volcano (www.usborne-quicklinks.com/uk/).

8–11-year-olds

As children move into the later primary years explanation texts become more detailed and the annotation of diagrams more involved.

Science and nature study

There are an enormous number of texts for this age group about the structure of the human body and the way its systems function. *How Your Body Works* by Judy Hindley explains in intriguing diagrams how the body carries out so many important jobs all the time. *See Inside Your Body* by Katie Daynes and Colin King takes readers on an information-rich journey around the body with flaps revealing the hidden detail. The younger end of this age group would be enthused by the dynamic, functional approach which looks at processes like 'eating and excreting' and 'pumping blood'. Other books on this topic make full use of sophisticated paper engineering. Of course teachers need to seek out those books whose devices genuinely reveal valuable information. Worth a mention for older readers is Anita Ganeri's *Alive: The Pop-Up Human Body Book* which offers a 3D chest with lungs and heart and even the sound of a heart beating as you open the page. And then there is Richard Walker's *How the Incredible Body Works*, which uses the device of little people called 'Brainwaves' to explain things as challenging as the microstructure of a cell.

There is a simply splendid and hugely demanding book on the market entitled *Body: An Amazing Tour of Human Anatomy* by Robert Winston. Many of the illustrations come from scans of the human body and both the text and the illustrations give much detail. It comes with an interactive CD-ROM which enables the reader to move the virtual human around and even 'remove' layers of muscle to see what lies beneath. Excellent as it is, I think this book might overwhelm all but the most forward young readers in the final primary school year and even they would need some adult help.

For books explaining the structure and processes of animals and plants, Dorling Kindersley's Eyewitness series is hard to beat in terms of quality of illustration and information.

BOX 30.1 *THE WAY THINGS WORK* AND *THE NEW WAY THINGS WORK* BY DAVID MACAULAY (DORLING KINDERSLEY)

David Macaulay is a brilliant 'explainer' of how the structure of all manner of things dictates their function. So in the first edition of the books we have wheels, levers and magnets shown in large clear diagrams with helpful annotation. Macaulay groups his machines together according to the principles that decide their actions: one group includes a toilet, a carburettor and a fire extinguisher. The humour of his work comes mainly from the ever-present woolly mammoth – a symbol of those of us who are technologically unsophisticated!

The New Way Things Work includes much new material on digital technology. So young readers confront the working of compact discs, digital cameras and modems. The woolly mammoth is still a lumbering and endearing presence. These are inspirational texts whether in their print or electronic format, but of course the CD-ROM can show the different parts of machines actually working. Retrieval devices are excellent: there is a comprehensive glossary and index. These texts are often recommended for age nine and above, but I have seen them being shared by an adult with children as young as four years. And one customer reviewer on Amazon UK comments, 'These are not just books for children but also for inquisitive adults.'

Explanation is a major element in science books about the properties of materials and how these properties can be used and exploited. *Water Science Explorers* by Jane Harris and Nicola Edwards explains what happens to things made of different materials when they are put into water. It encourages children to think about all this and to form their own questions.

Science and technology combine when it comes to explaining the way machines of all sizes and kinds work. Here we have two outstanding texts, the first of which came out in the 1980s but which has remained an important text which has been updated and put into print and electronic formats. I am referring of course to David Macaulay's books *The Way Things Work* and *The New Way Things Work*, both of which benefit from his time as an architect and a teacher (see Box 30.1).

Geography

There are two books by Kate Petty and Jenny Maizels that use pop-ups and pull-outs most imaginatively to explain the structures and processes involved in volcanic eruptions. These are *The Amazing Pop-Up Geography Book* by Kate Petty and Jenny Maizels and, by the same authors, *One Wonderful World*. The latter has a 3D globe. Another book that entertains as well as providing quality explanations for phenomena is Anita Ganeri's *Earth-Shattering Earthquakes and Violent Volcanoes*, a title in the lively Horrible Geography series. Even less forward older primary children would enjoy the approach here. Organized in ten chapters, the book uses dramatic diagrams and clear text and includes details that will entertain children; for example, we hear about a hamster that was shaken out of its cage during an earthquake.

History

An author/illustrator who creates books enjoyed by readers of different age groups is Stephen Biesty, who has used magnificently detailed cross-sections to explain the structure of ancient buildings, including the pyramids, castles and ships. His book with Andrew Solway, *Rome in Spectacular Cross-Section*, uses his distinctive cutaway illustrations to reveal the interior of buildings in ancient Rome, including a house, public baths and the Temple of Jupiter.

SUMMARY

* Explanation texts tell us about the structure of an animal or a machine, a process like paper making or the working of the digestion system.
* They are sometimes seen as a sub-category of 'report' and are often found alongside other kinds of text in children's books and CD-ROMs.
* Explanation text is organized in a rhythm of 'cause and effect'.
* It is 'multimodal' because it combines design, writing and illustration.
* Multimedia explanation texts are dynamic and can, for example, show the functioning of a machine or of the heart.
* Like other information texts, explanation can be judged by taking account of the quality and age appropriateness of its design, coverage and language and illustration.
* These criteria should be used flexibly so that original and ground-breaking books are not ruled out – these so often are the texts which get children questioning and 'wondering'.

Chapter 31

Using report and explanation texts

INTRODUCTION

Starting with a text and examining its features might not be the best way to enthuse young learners. In fact it could be an extremely dreary and dispiriting start! Here I look at some ways of making report and explanation enjoyable and relevant to children's thinking and enquiry. These thoughts apply to children as they move from the nursery and Reception classes to the end of the primary years.

WAYS OF ENTHUSING YOUNG RESEARCHERS

Starting with first-hand and practical experience

Where children have started a project or series of lessons with first-hand experience or practical work, they often turn to texts with much more enthusiasm than if the texts were the starting point. This is particularly true of the under sixes. In geography early years teachers often take children out of the classroom – to farms, the seaside or to woodland. Back at school they can think about what they saw together, discover what questions they have and then take their questions to the texts. Early map work is also often best introduced by a foray into the local area to note its features and then to make simple maps. Here a look at maps can help them get to know about the conventions like using symbols and keys. Older children also benefit from geographical fieldwork in developing a sense of place and understanding how geographical enquiry can be about the way people live their lives. In science, investigations in the school grounds or at a nearby pond or park can lead to children wondering and questioning, and taking this enthusiasm into secondary sources.

Speaking and listening

Talking about new information and ideas in class discussion, in groups or with a response partner energizes learning in every lesson. Often a good way into books and resources is the questions children want answered after they have discussed and organized their existing knowledge. These questions put children in the driving seat when making their first foray into the texts. And once they start using the texts, talk is the best way to help children make the necessary links between first-hand experience and information from secondary sources. The teacher has a crucial mediating role here.

Thinking about history lessons, I find that, given some warning and support, children are very willing to research an aspect of a topic, to give an oral presentation and answer questions from the class or group. These talks may draw on first-hand enquiry like visits and on interviews and also on information from museums, books and websites. Let us not underestimate the effort needed to weave together information from different sources into a coherent whole. These oral presentations and the notes or lists of headings that act as mnemonics can be the basis of children's written accounts. Thinking about history, part of getting to grips with this subject involves understanding chronology. Children need to learn how a sequence of events might be linked. Evidence needs to be interrogated and cause and effect discovered and made explicit.

CASE STUDY 31.1 A NURSERY CLASS USE A TEXT TO EXTEND THINKING ABOUT COLOURS

After noticing during a nature walk that a lot of creatures are brown in colour, four-year-olds were shown a double spread about tawny owls from Sue Malyan's book *Look Closer: Birds*. One of the children remarked that the tawny owl in the picture was not really brown but 'speckled'. The children said this would help the owl to be 'hidden' from its enemies even more than if it had been plain brown. They were pleased to find when the teacher read aloud from the book that it said that the owl's feathers were 'mottled' to help keep them from being seen. The concept of camouflage had already been noted during the walk when the children saw the brown beetles and birds. This was reinforced by the book, which helped them see a connection between first-hand experiences and what books tell us.

Figure 31.1 'The Tawny Owl', text and images from page 18 of Look Closer: Birds
by Sue Malyan
Copyright Dorling Kindersley 2005

Talk also helps children draw on experience in their own lives, which may help their learning in every lesson. Holiday experiences and family links may inform and enrich study of particular countries in geography lessons. One way in which home–school links can be fostered is by asking children to give talks about their hobbies, whether these are to do with sport, caring for pet animals or making collections of things like fossils or coins. These talks are oral information texts. To bring in written texts, children could be asked to recommend some reading for their classmates – both print and screen-based – to extend their understanding.

The teacher's role: into writing

The reports and explanations children are asked to write are an important feature of lessons across the curriculum. Younger children will write using some of the structural and linguistic features of report but using an informal or 'expressive' voice.

Teachers sometimes carry out shared writing using a whiteboard, asking children to create a text jointly. This is an opportunity for genre features of texts to be pointed out. In my view this should be done with a light touch with younger children. Children often find it helpful to plan their account under paragraphs, perhaps being given sub-headings to help them become more confident in structuring their account. And we must remember, as Barrs argues, that more accessible kinds of writing are likely to help young learners use language as a tool for thinking (Barrs, 1987: 2). As children move to the later primary years they can be helped to make their understanding of text types, as readers and writers, explicit. Examples of successful report writing can be displayed. Explanation texts are by their nature likely to be multimodal, involving design of the pages, illustrations and writing. Perhaps we have not always given children credit for the annotated diagrams they have created to explain structures and processes. These texts combining modes are valued more now and there are efforts to find ways of assessing them (Evans, 2004: 10). Children could discuss in groups or with a response partner the sort of tables, pictures and diagrams that will help get the information across.

Book-making, either on paper or on the screen, is a good way of helping children experience satisfaction in their writing. They will have learnt about the global structure of a non-chronological information text and how pages can be designed and illustrations and

CASE STUDY 31.2 A YEAR 6 CLASS WRITE REPORTS IN A SERIES OF COMBINED LITERACY AND GEOGRAPHY LESSONS ABOUT A COUNTRY THEY WOULD LIKE TO VISIT OR REVISIT

A Year 6 class had written reports on a country they would like to visit or revisit, using the internet and paper texts to do their research. They were asked to read their first paragraphs aloud. One comment by a child on another child's opening paragraph was: 'He has started to give us the facts, but he has made it interesting by asking questions.' The child commenting read out the bit he liked to support his point. 'Italy is a warm Mediterranean country and a favourite holiday place because of its beautiful building and good food. Do you have a favourite Italian meal? You might start with . . .'

323

CASE STUDY 31.3 CHILDREN MAKE A PHOTO BOOK ABOUT THEIR NURSERY

A nursery teacher and her two early years colleagues helped the children use their developing skills in digital photography to make a book. The children were told that their book would help children joining at age three years to settle into the routines and activities of the nursery.

Making the book involved the children in planning the layout and in helping to decide on the sections. What better way is there into understanding how books work! Then it was time to take the photographs and for the children to tell the nursery team, who acted as scribes, what they wanted to say about each one. Once laminated and bound, the book went into the book corner.

The nursery staff found that all the children and some of the parents enjoyed reading the book, as well as the 'new starts'. Being involved at every stage of the making of the book, and having a clear purpose and audience for it, make it more likely that these children will have a positive approach to their future reading and writing.

More exciting book-making is planned: the nursery children will be helped to use an interactive whiteboard to produce an interactive book with photographs and video-clips.

Figure 31.2 All about Claremont Nursery *by the children of Claremont Primary School*
Image reproduced with the permission of Claremont Primary School and Clackmannanshire Council and with acknowledgement to the nursery class, staff and children and to Kirsteen Carmichael, Early Years Development Officer, who took the photograph

writing combined to communicate information. A glossary and retrieval devices like contents page and index can be added.

SOME ISSUES

These issues are relevant to all forms of non-fiction writing, but I find them particularly pertinent to the report and reference kinds of reading and writing.

Are writing frames useful?

These are frameworks of headings to help children structure their writing. If children were writing an explanatory account, they might be launched into their writing by 'sentence starts' like 'I want to explain why' and supported by connectives such as 'moreover', 'next' and 'however'. This strategy became widely known through the work of Wray and Lewis on the Exeter Extending Reading Project in the 1990s and their books on writing frames, which include *Writing Frames: Scaffolding Children's Non-Fiction Writing in a Range of Genres*. These researchers do not recommend that writing frames are used to teach in a direct way about genre. They believe, however, that when it comes to a new genre, having a skeleton structure, often with a vocabulary that drives the writing on, leaves children freer to concentrate on the content, on what they want to communicate. The frames are intended to be used for meaningful writing tasks where there is an understanding of purpose and audience and abandoned when children become confident enough to make their own plans.

I believe that some children, particularly those who find a blank page daunting, can benefit from using the frames. Nevertheless there is some concern that too enthusiastic a use of them might dull a young writer's spontaneity and delay their making an effort to structure their writing themselves.

More recently, Sue Palmer has designed 'skeleton frames' which draw on and develop visual memory skills to help children plan their writing of different text types. There are timelines to help organize chronological writing, flow charts to help with instruction and a spider diagram for helping to structure reports. These frames can be easily used with interactive whiteboards and their potential for integration with ICT makes them compatible with the increasing emphasis on digital kinds of literacy. The emphasis on using pictures and ICT texts seems to motivate less confident young male writers. You can read about these resources in Sue Palmer's *How to Teach Writing Across the Curriculum* books for Key Stages 1 and 2 (Palmer, 2003).

Teachers need to use their professional judgement about if, and when, a young learner might benefit from a frame, whether published or one made by teacher and pupil for a specific task.

What can we do about children copying or closely paraphrasing material out of texts?

This can be a problem with any kind of informational writing which is at least partly dependent on secondary sources, but is often an issue when it comes to report or a reference text like an encyclopedia. Here are some suggestions:

CASE STUDY 31.4 LINKING INTERNET INFORMATION WITH WHAT WE LEARN FROM BEING TOLD

Eight-year-old Orla worked on a home–school project called 'My Family' and structured it by writing down some questions which served as sub-headings. Where are the W . . . family from? Where are the C . . . family from? Were there any famous people in my family? What countries are in me? Creating her own organization put her in the driving seat and she used secondary sources to serve her purposes. Her parents helped her track down information from the internet and told her what they knew about their parents and grandparents. The page reproduced from her project booklet in Figure 31.3 gives us a sense of a young writer developing her own 'voice' for report writing. She has some awareness of her readers' needs: she mentions that there is a picture of her ancestor on the next page, explains he is 'from my Dad's side' and directs them, by using an arrow, to the next page. Figure 31.4 shows the front cover of the project designed by Orla. Here we have the three elements of a print multimodal page: a picture of Orla with her younger sister, words in the title and the annotation on her family tree, and the designed cover with the family tree bounded by a tree shape.

Were there any famous people in my family?

The anser is yes there were three well known famous people. the first was called Frederick Hooper. He was the first to reach the south pole. He went with a very famous explorer called Sir Robert falcon Scott. Sir Robert falcon Scott was not my ancestor but Frederick Hooper was. After they made the amazing Adventurers journy, There was a moutain named after Frederick Hooper. There is a picture of him on the next page. He was from my Dads side.

4.

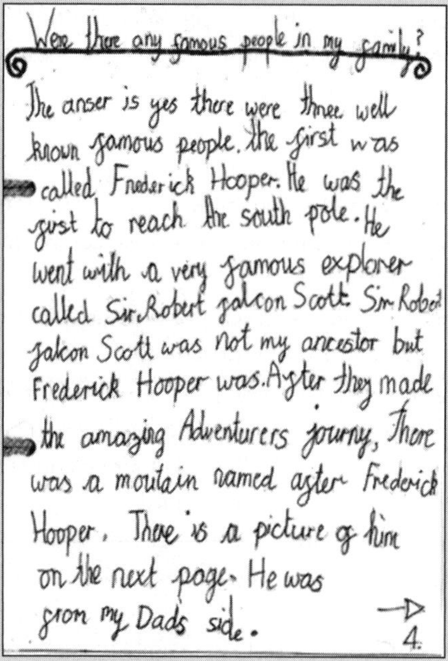

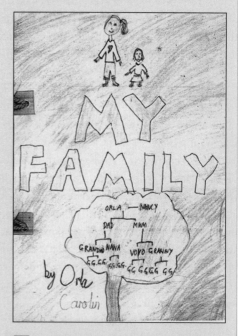

Figure 31.3
A page from Orla's 'My Family' project book

Figure 31.4
Front cover of 'My Family' designed by Orla for her project book

- Feed in new experience relevant to the topic – an outing, a visitor's input or some practical work to enrich their writing.
- Spend some time discussing what children already know about a new topic so that their 'prior knowledge' is organized into a framework ready to receive the new information actively.
- Suggest they take some of their own questions to the secondary sources. Some joint work on grouping and refining questions is helpful.
- Talk to children often about their developing ideas.
- Make notes from several sources and write the final account from the notes.
- Make notes from diagrams and illustrations as well as from written sources.
- Provide opportunities for oral presentations using headings as mnemonics from their reading.
- Sometimes change the text type of the books read to another text type – write a diary in the role of a Tudor maid or page, transforming the information in the book, thus helping make writing tasks interesting and appropriate.

ASSESSING AND RECORDING PROGRESS

There are two sides to assessment: first, progress in learning about a subject or topic and, second, progress in becoming young researchers able to learn from a range of resources and developing library and study abilities and skills.

When it comes to the second of these, teachers look at a child's ability to read, write and illustrate increasingly demanding texts, a developing understanding of the text type or genre and an ability to take the audience for oral and written presentations into account. The following help achieve a record, held in either a print or electronic portfolio, of children's progress in controlling report and explanation texts as readers and writers:

- Dated observations of children's 'finding out' strategies from print and electronic texts. A good opportunity for this kind of observation is during children's library times.
- Examples of children's notes from any lesson, with date and teacher's brief comment.
- Brief dated notes on presentations for which children have used information from report and/or explanation texts. Part of making progress through the primary years is to do with adapting a presentation for a particular purpose and to a particular audience.
- Dated examples of children's non-chronological report writing and annotated explanation diagrams from any lesson. We would expect the writing of younger children to be less formal and more 'expressive' than that of older children and adults.
- Children's reports on fieldwork in geography and history.
- Dated examples of children's multimodal texts combining design, writing and illustration.
- A copy of a book made on a topic. Having the opportunity to make books helps children show how far they have learnt to control writing report and explanation and to use glossaries and retrieval devices like contents pages and indexes.
- Dated examples of children's written evaluations of the report and explanation texts they have been using in lessons across the curriculum.
- Increasing understanding of the purpose of report and explanation – the latter explains rather than just describes – is a sign of progress.

EVALUATION OF RESOURCES

Towards the end of a series of lessons or a project, teacher and children can usefully talk about and evaluate all the resources they have been using. Quite a number of these will belong to the 'report' and 'explanation' genres which are the subject of this chapter and will include print and electronic resources and, of course, the internet.

Teachers need to bring both subject knowledge and pedagogical understanding to their assessment. And the worth of children's evaluative comments is also significant in deciding which resources will be used in future work. These conversations help children to think about both the quality of the information they have found and the appropriateness of particular kinds of texts and information resources to enhance and support particular kinds of learning. So a 'moving image' text is often the best kind to explain how a machine works or to demonstrate an animal's digestive system in action. This deep reflection helps children to become more aware of themselves as learners too. As Mallett comments, 'Searching for information is an area in which metacognitive abilities are particularly useful' (Mallett, 2008: 213).

When inviting children to comment on what they found useful or otherwise, we should include the texts some of them have used at home. Case Study 31.4 shows the value of children collaborating with members of their family over texts to link with and extend school learning.

Now that the repertoire of resources is so rich and varied in mode and media, teachers are developing ways of assessing new kinds of text. Attention is turning to the quality of electronic resources and of children's widening range of written and illustrated responses when using them (Bearne, 2009; Bearne *et al.*, 2004).

SUMMARY

- The widening of the library and classroom collections to include electronic texts – the internet, software and CD-ROM – and the increasing use of ICT, often using interactive whiteboards, have energized learning from report and explanation texts – not least when moving images show processes and systems.
- Nevertheless, children continue to use and be inspired by print texts. These have benefited from new technologies which enhance their format and the quality of illustrations, including photographs.
- Younger children will cope best with transitional versions of the genre, moving towards versions with mature structural and linguistic features by the end of the primary years.
- Report and explanation texts need careful mediation from the teacher if children are to enjoy and learn from them. Where possible, planning needs to include some practical work or some first-hand experience before or alongside the use of secondary resources and much speaking and listening as well as writing and drawing.
- Towards the end of a series of lessons children can be helped to assess what they have learnt and to evaluate the resources they have been using.
- Children show they have made progress in controlling report and explanation when they are able to take account of purpose and audience when they present information orally and in writing.

Chapter 32

Argument
Discussion and persuasion texts

INTRODUCTION

If you want to bring children's thinking and learning into top gear, the spoken and written texts that we call 'discussion' and 'persuasion' will help enormously. Both are to do with argument and because their structure is logical rather than chronological they are often thought to be challenging for younger learners. In their mature, written form they are likely to be difficult for the under elevens. But even very young children can argue for a viewpoint orally, especially if they are talking about things they care about – issues that arise in everyday contexts at home and in the classroom. As children move through the primary years, they encounter different points of view in a variety of lesson topics. Exploring these makes learning exciting and gives real point to children's discussion, to their research in books and to their investigations on the internet. Of course, children are not going to get excited by the bland or commonplace. They need to be fascinated, provoked, sometimes even shocked to bring their thinking into top gear. It was Jean Piaget who most powerfully suggested that learning occurs when we feel unsettled by a situation or by some information. He calls this unsettled state of mind 'disequilibrium' and believes that seeking out answers to our questions restores that balance of mind he terms 'equilibrium' (Piaget, 1952). How do teachers bring about situations in which children genuinely and passionately want to find out? I believe that it is by helping them to seek out the controversial, mind stretching issues that lie at the heart of so many topics and then to explore those issues through reading, talk and writing. Thinking about different points of view and encouraging open ended tasks helps develop flexible and creative thinking and their ability to make new connections. And children's interests and activities outside the classroom can be drawn on to energize learning. They can bring much knowledge to school – gleaned from websites, films and television programmes as well as from print material. The trigger for children's engagement with a controversial topic is sometimes not an information text, but a story, poem or picturebook which raises compelling issues, and this is recognized in this chapter.

FEATURES OF DISCUSSION AND PERSUASION TEXTS

In a nutshell, discussion texts involve setting out different points of view, while persuasion texts tend only to present one favoured viewpoint.

Discussion texts

These offer different 'takes' on a topic, providing evidence for each point of view, and tend to end with a conclusion leaning strongly in one direction. A discussion text typically begins with a short presentation of the main competing arguments. After this, the organization varies, but often the traditional debating structure is followed: the arguments for one position are stated with supporting evidence, including quotations from experts and often facts and figures. Then the arguments for another point of view, or of several other points of view, are set out – again with supporting evidence. The rhythm of a discussion text, and indeed of persuasion text too, is point and elaboration. The conclusion draws on evidence to make a final plea for the preferred viewpoint.

What are the linguistic features of discussion texts? There are probably three main ones. First, in its mature form at least, discussion text is written in impersonal language to give a sense of objectivity. Second, the competing arguments are usually set out in the present tense. Third, there is a distinctive use of connectives – words or phrases to link different parts of a sentence – to secure the logic of the argument. Simple chronological connectives include words and phrases like 'first of all', 'then' and 'afterwards', while the logical connectives we would expect to find in argument might include 'but', 'and', 'on the other hand', 'as a result', 'however' and 'some people think'.

Other modes can be used in combination with writing. Print texts may use diagrams and pictures to strengthen the arguments, while multimedia texts can use sound and the moving image to help.

Persuasion texts

Texts that fall into the persuasion category, whether spoken or written, make the case for a particular opinion and accordingly stay closer to the writer's viewpoint than would be the case in a discussion text. Mature persuasion text starts with a clear, brief statement of the writer's position on a subject. Then the main points to establish the argument are set out, each point being accompanied by supporting evidence. Persuasion texts have several things in common with discussion texts – both follow a broad pattern in which a point is stated and then elaborated. So both text types tend to move from general points to specific examples. Both are in the present tense and use logical rather than simple chronological connectives; and both end with a summary of the main argument. Of course like discussion text, persuasion text aims to convince the listener or reader that one viewpoint is superior. But when it comes to linguistic features, persuasion text is more likely to use dramatic or emotional language to help drive home the case. An advertisement might include phrases like 'only . . . brings long-lasting relief' and 'for those who want the purest, tastiest . . .'. Rhetorical questions are used to manipulate; for example, 'Do you want to do the best for your family?'; 'Did you know that 9 out of 10 people asked said they preferred . . .?' Humour and alliteration to make slogans more punchy also help make the case. Pictures can manipulate too. I remember children being very moved by a photograph of a bird black with fuel oil in a book about sea and beach pollution.

In coming to understand these features children need to have the opportunity to talk: this talk needs to be flexible and free flowing, with points made, revisited, dismissed or embraced.

They may need help in listening and responding to what others have said and to raise new ideas and backtrack to previous points. The main thing is that both discussion and persuasion texts should be interesting and enjoyable at the point at which they are read, created or used. Making progress in controlling them also prepares children for the evidence-based kinds of thinking required to do well in the secondary school years and beyond.

CHOOSING TEXTS WHICH INCLUDE OR PROMOTE ARGUMENT FOR DIFFERENT AGES

Pre-school and nursery, 3–5-year-olds

One type of non-fiction text likely to get very young children thinking about different viewpoints is the information picture book. 'Experience books' which reach out to everyday activities – meal times, shopping, school activity and visiting the doctor – often wind a text around photographs or pictures of young children carrying out the activities. Where does 'argument' come in here? Issues like getting along with others, the case for sharing toys and so on are typical themes and discussion can help develop a point of view. The very large number of stories about starting school remind us what a big step this is for many children and about the mixed feelings they may have about it. In *I Am Too Absolutely Small for School* Lauren Child shows, with her usual humour, how Charlie persuades his little sister, Lola, that school is fun. *A First Look at Starting School*, by Pat Thomas and illustrated by Lesley Harker, tells a story and asks: 'Why do you think there are rules at school?' Where there seem to be too many squabbles in a nursery class, a book can distance a discussion from raw actuality, where feelings may be intense, so that calm and constructive discussion can take place.

I Want a Friend by Tony Ross introduces the issue with a light touch. Stephen Cartwright and Anna Civardi's First Experiences series would also get children talking about what we should do in certain circumstances. Titles include *Going to a Party* and *Moving House*. The theme of why we should treat animals well is taken up in Margaret Chamberlain's picturebook *Tootsie* and the tensions that the arrival of a new baby in the family can cause children is another theme explored in many books, for example in *Sophie and the New Baby* by Catherine and Lawrence Anholt.

For a first introduction to the arguments for recycling rubbish Lauren Child's *Look After Your Planet* is well worth considering. Charlie tells Lola why plastic, paper and cans should be separated and recycled and Lola in turn explains to her friend, in her inimitable way, why they should collect paper and recycle it to save trees.

5–8-year-olds

The information story continues to be a useful form to get this age group thinking and discussing in lessons across the curriculum. Food for discussion also comes from illustrated information books written as report, but including some discussion or persuasive text. Some of these books are too bland. We do well to seek those texts which are lively and sometimes include the controversial; children thrive on the unusual and unexpected popping up in their reading. Illustrations, or some of them at least, need to stimulate, challenge or even upset.

Science and nature study

Most dinosaur books are sound – they have to be to survive amongst so much competition. Try, for example, *What Happened to the Dinosaurs?* by Jon Hughes and ask children which theory they find most convincing. *Dinosaurs* by Jonathan Sheikh-Miller, illustrated by Rachel First, shows how evidence is pieced together and, like Usborne's other information books, is internet-linked so that children can easily access websites with sound, animation and video-clips to further their knowledge. Space is another topic to which most children in this age group feel drawn. *Let's Go to Mars* by Janice Marriott takes young readers on a journey, using the story framework to give a lot of information, including how astronauts meet their need for oxygen and the effects of weightlessness. A book like this can lead to children's talk and writing about, for example, how far are these journeys into space a good thing? A class hooked on space would enjoy Jane Hunter and Mark Turner's story *Star Boy's Surprise*: not only do young readers find out about the space travels of Star Boy and his dog Ace, they also learn about the importance of friendship, particularly when on dangerous missions. All this can contribute to debate about whether or not space travel is 'a good thing'.

It is worth looking through the titles of reading scheme and reading programme publishers like Oxford University Press, Collins, Franklin Watts, A&C Black and Usborne for texts to raise issues and therefore to get children thinking and debating. Collins Big Cat non-fiction series includes *At the Dump* by Claire Llewellyn, a lively information story describing a family's trip to the local dump. The cartoon-like illustrations by Ley Honor Roberts are likely to appeal to children. The book could support science or geography lessons and, while it is basically a recount, it raises the issue of who should take responsibility for the management of litter, providing the evidence to nourish discussion.

Geography

Environmental and global issues are currently very much in people's minds and this is reflected in the prevalence of books on these topics in the lists of publishers of children's books under both science and geography. In fact it is when we tackle these topics that the two disciplines meet. The texts on offer range from inspirational and original to dull and banal. In the latter category are books which trot out the same old things in unimaginative ways about the benefit of organic food and the environmental harm too much air travel causes. Of course children do need to find out about 'green issues' and to know something about rubbish disposal and recycling. I think *Rubbish and Recycling*, a title in Usborne's Beginners series by Stephanie Turner, fits with geography and with PSHE lessons as it raises environmental issues about where waste water goes and where our rubbish ends up after the dust cart takes it away. Children could argue the case for responsible citizenship. A jolly little information story – *Tec and the Litter* by Tony Mitton and illustrated by Martin Chatterton – follows Tec and his dog's search for someone who has dropped litter. They trace the culprit by following the trail of litter. The pictures invite discussion about how to keep our environment litter free. Mick Manning and Brita Granström's information books about the natural world often include some consideration of environmental issues. Their *Voices of the Rainforest* shows first the rich and unique plant and animal elements of these special environments and then explains that these are in danger if the destruction of the rainforests continues. What we could or should do about this could lead to further research and discussion. Another book which celebrates the variety of life on our planet is *The Tree of Life* by Rochelle Strauss and illustrated by Margot Thompson and the same team who created for older children that boundary-breaking book *If the World Were a Village*. Young readers are invited to think of all the species in the world as leaves on a tree. There would be over two million of them and the book explains how all living things are interconnected so that what happens to one species affects others.

Nearly every geography book or CD-ROM has within it the seeds of a debate. *Planet Earth* by Leonie Pratt and *Volcanoes* by Stephanie Turnbull have the beginnings of evidence about issues like global warming and how we can predict volcano eruption to avoid disaster.

I think children in this five to eight age range would be inspired to discuss such issues as climate change and global warming by Katie Daynes' book *See Inside Planet Earth*, vibrantly illustrated by Peter Allan. This has flaps which reveal the Earth's structure and illustrations which show us how global warming happens. The Earth is shown in all its variety and beauty so that is seems worth looking after. As is the case with so many non-fiction books, some help from the teacher would be needed with reading and thinking about the information. Children also need guidance on using the information on the linked websites.

History

There are a lot of interesting debates around the character and behaviour of people in history. Were the Vikings, for example, as bad as they have been portrayed? Children would find evidence to support or refute this in books like Scoular Anderson's *How to Be a Viking* and Mick Manning and Brita Granström's *Viking Longship*. They would like the humour in the writing and illustration of John Malam's You Wouldn't Want to Be . . . series. *You Wouldn't Want to Be a Victorian School Child*, like the other titles, makes some serious points in an entertaining way and could lead to children's own debate and writing.

BOX 32.1 *GROWING GREEN: A YOUNG PERSON'S GUIDE TO TAKING CARE OF THE PLANET* BY CHRISTINA GOODINGS AND MASUMI FURUKAWA (LION HUDSON)

This book sets out the argument for us all taking more care over everyday choices that could, if enough people co-operated, help the planet. The text encourages a questioning approach: 'Could you have chosen a better path, one that treated plants more gently?', 'When you plan a journey, how can you travel lightly?'

Children are also introduced to global issues, for example about how we can make it more likely that people will be paid a fair wage for their work. Good talking points are provided in words and pictures.

The more recent past is a favourite theme in history books for the five to eight age range. Franklin Watts titles include *When Your Mum Was Little* and *When Your Grandad Was Little* by Jane Bidder and illustrated by Sheila McNicholas. Reading these could lead to a debate about which time to be young was best – the earlier time or nowadays.

English and PSHE

When it comes to debate and discussion nothing can compete with powerful fiction as a starting point for reflection on such universal issues as how human beings should live their lives, behave towards others and care for their environment. All this is taken up later in this chapter. Some teachers feel resistance to using stories for a narrow purpose – rather than for enjoyment and reflection. Nevertheless it is worth considering some of the 'argument through story' approaches. Take the Berenstain Bears First Time books by Stan and Jan Berenstain, for example. While these have some American expressions needing explanation and they do vary in quality, each story explores a principle using words and amusing pictures on topics like teasing, blaming and eating healthily. It is the way reasons and evidence are set out that nudges children towards the sort of thinking and writing that establishes an argument. *Berenstain Bears and the Truth* uses the story of the bears breaking their mother's favourite lamp to suggest owning up might be best in the long run even if difficult at the time. Some reviewers have felt that punishing young children by making them do chores, as happens in *Berenstain Bears Mind Their Manners*, is unwise. Doing everyday things alongside their parents and others should be for sheer satisfaction and enjoyment.

Robert Fisher is well known for his story approach to encouraging children's philosophical thinking. For this age group teachers find it helpful to read aloud to the class the stories from his anthology *First Stories for Thinking*. Some of the questions he includes to stimulate discussion have the flavour of a comprehension exercise. Others, however, have the potential to lead to deeper thought.

Another series using the 'story' approach is But Why? from Network Educational Press, which includes *Pinocchio: The Cricket's Tale* – unsurprisingly about timeless questions like telling the truth – by Sara Stanley and illustrated wittily by Nigel Potter. Teachers can read more about this approach in *Philosophy Bear: Developing Philosophical Thinking in the Classroom* by Sara Stanley with Steve Bowkett.

8–11-year-olds

Children in this age group are able to take on more subtle argument, but still need to get their thinking straight through discussion before writing. Almost every topic in lessons across the curriculum has a controversial aspect which can lead to debate and often it is a text which sparks off interest.

Science and nature study

Children at the younger end of Key Stage 2 are often fascinated by dinosaur books, not least those that provide evidence for the theories about how they became extinct. This puzzle is explored in *Great Dinosaur Search* by Rosie Heywood and in Robert Firth's book *Discovery:*

Dinosaurs. In the latter young readers are directed to related websites where the moving image contributes to how convincing or otherwise a particular theory seems to be. Space also continues to interest children in this age range. Another twist to investigating space travel is the possibility of there being life on other planets. Are we alone in the Universe? Nic Bishop, a wildlife and science author, explores this in his book *Is There Anyone Out There?*

Science meets PSHE in Kate Knighton and illustrator Adam Larkum's *The Case for Healthy Food*, which sets out the case against junk food, why we still eat it although we know it is not good for us (it tastes nice!) and what is the case for and against organically farmed food.

As we have seen, texts can be used to introduce younger children to the issues around global warming, animal extinction and rainforest destruction. Publishers still like the 'double spread' organization in their non-fiction series. Often the ethical and controversial issues in a topic are given just one double spread. Older children need to be helped to take on the complexity of the topics. *Animals Like Us: The World's Endangered Species Speak Out* by Andrea Mills devotes a whole large format book to the evidence and takes the arguments to a more mature level. There are 'how can you help?' pages with copious websites and addresses of the many organizations which try to support animals at risk of extinction. Dorling Kindersley's *Encyclopedia of Animals* edited by Charlotte Stock would be accessible to the younger readers in this age group and makes an appeal to the heart as well as the mind. It includes the constructive things that are happening – for example, the golden Tamarin monkey has been saved from extinction by a captive breeding programme. The United Nations are also eager to help avoid animal extinction. They have banned the use of long drift nets for fishing to save whales, dolphins and turtles from perishing by being caught up in these. The eyewitness *Whale* book by Vassili Papastavrou, with photographs by Frank Greenaway, includes a section that could support children's talk and writing in the 'discussion' genre, as different viewpoints can be argued.

Geography

Texts on disasters like earthquakes and volcanic eruptions leading to discussion about how these might be avoided and texts on global environmental issues and endangered species are on the websites of the main publishers of children's non-fiction. The Collins Virtual Geography materials cover environmental issues like pollution and recycling and use the moving image to help. Take the 'Dealing with Waste' topic – on this CD-ROM the moving image shows a factory dealing with waste and another image of a moving tipper on a landfill. The size of the lorry and driver reveals the mountain of waste and shows the sheer scale of the problem. Some images from the photo bank, which teachers can use for information and discussion, appeal to the heart as well as the mind. One is of an oil-soaked, bedraggled and forlorn bird – the victim of an oil spillage.

David Smith's book *If the World Were a Village* is inspirational and boundary-breaking in its contribution to children's understanding of global issues (www.acblack.com/globalvillage). It contracts the world to the scale of a village and uses this device to get children thinking about the issues and problems of poverty and food and water shortages in our world. It is an interactive book with exciting ideas for follow-up work and it helps children move up a gear in thinking about these large and complex issues.

By this age children are becoming able to understand that flyers and advertising material from holiday companies are likely to give a rosy picture of the countries they want us to visit. Food for thought is supplied by Gillian Doherty and Anna Claybourne's book *Peoples of the World*. The spread on the Caribbean compares tourist impressions with the realities of life for the inhabitants of the poorer areas like Haiti where unemployment is high. This mismatch between the pictures in holiday advertisements and the realities for the inhabitants of some countries could be explored by looking at books like this and the publicity material for tourism.

With some support, able children at the older end of this age group would discover issues to discuss in Franklin Watts' Countries in the News series. These titles draw on the history as well as the geography of countries constantly in the newspapers and titles include *Iraq*, *Israel* and *Afghanistan*.

History

Have you come across Fergus Fleming's history series in newspaper format? All the titles, including *Greek Gazette*, *The Medieval Messenger* and *The Viking Invader*, have news items and advertisements with more than a touch of humour. Young readers will learn something about journalistic kinds of writing and illustrating from them. A theme running through *Greek Gazette* is: how civilized were the Greeks really? This encourages debate and possibly writing for Key Stage 2 children following an Ancient Greek unit in history.

Evidence-based information books help older children to build an argument. The DK Eyewitness guides offer a challenging but interesting read for them. *The Titanic* by Simon Adams includes sections on the controversial aspects of the ship's sinking on its maiden voyage. Why, for instance, were the crew not aware that the lifeboats could be lowered fully laden? And why did the captain of the Californian not come swiftly to the rescue? Children could debate or write under a heading like 'Who Was to Blame?' They would, of course, need more than one text to draw evidence from.

The titles in the Usborne Famous Lives in the Young Reading series, for confident readers in this age group, help children think about how reliable or otherwise the reputations of well-known historical figures like Nelson, Winston Churchill and Marie Antoinette are. In *Marie Antoinette* the author, Katie Daynes, suggests that the way she is perceived has been affected by how journalists have portrayed her. A debate about journalistic exaggeration might well be sparked off by this book.

English

Younger children will have come across, and even have helped make, posters and flyers to persuade people to come to school events like fetes, concerts and sports days. As they get older children explore advertisements, print and electronic, and these can be used to show how readers and viewers can be manipulated. The scope for debate is enormous and might include topics like: what makes a 'good' advertisement in a particular medium, why advertising needs to be monitored, why advertisements aimed at the very young need to be controlled and the analysis of the kinds of language devices and illustrations used to influence the intended 'audience'.

Print books to inspire debate in English lessons include a title from Terry Deary's Horrible Histories series, written with Neil Tonge and illustrated by Martin Brown – *Terrible Shakespeare: Did He Write the Plays?* Such a debate would need support from other books and perhaps information from websites.

Texts in the spirit of the 'thinking through story' approaches were mentioned as possible choices for the five to eight age group. Robert Fisher also has an anthology of stories to get older children thinking about philosophical issues, *Stories for Thinking*, including, for example, one which tells of the mystery of the Marie Celeste.

Support for the controversial kinds of discussions to stretch the debating skills of the oldest primary children comes from the Franklin Watts series In the News. Titles here include *Football and Its Followers*, *Drug Culture* and *Cruelty to Animals* by P. May, S. Adams, A. Smith and A. Hibbert respectively.

The Franklin Watts series on British Issues, which looks at key issues faced by Britain today, includes the titles *Future Energy*, *Sustainable Cities* and *Sporting Successes*, by Rob Bowden, Andrea Smith and James Kerr respectively, and could support debate across the curriculum and would certainly be a helpful resource in geography, English and citizenship and PSHE lessons. However, even able ten- to eleven-year-olds would need quite a lot of teacher support to benefit from these books.

The texts we term 'popular culture' texts can be brought in to support debate across the curriculum. But they have a particularly important place in the English lesson, where the range of topics can be broader. Children are more likely to be self-starters and to sustain interest in hard things like writing if we draw from their own interests in setting up discussions and debates. We can draw on information gained from the internet and from computer games. Caring for a virtual dog can lead to talk and writing about such issues as should dogs be kept in towns, allowed on beaches and so on. There is much material on the CBBC website which can be taken up and used in the classroom.

BOX 32.2 *WE ARE ALL BORN EQUAL* BY AMNESTY INTERNATIONAL, ILLUSTRATED BY 30 ARTISTS (FRANCES LINCOLN)

This book, published to celebrate the sixtieth anniversary of the signing of the Universal Declaration of Human Rights, sets out the thirty principles written in words children can understand. Each principle is superbly illustrated by an internationally renowned artist, adding greatly to the richness of the reading experience.

'The law is the same for everyone. It must treat us all fairly' is illustrated by Jan Spivey and shows a vast figure holding a balanced set of scales. On one side are boys from different ethnic groups and on the other side are girls from different ethnic groups, ingeniously illustrating the principle of sexual and racial equality. Older children could present the case for each principle as part of discussion or argue for which principles are the most important ones in making for a fairer world.

These comments draw on a review to mark the presentation of *English 4–11's* Awards for the Best Illustrated Books of 2008 (Mallett, 2009).

FICTION CAN THROW UP EXCITING THEMES FOR ARGUMENT

The best children's fiction has the power to make children think and care about important issues and to see their complexity. Confronting sensitive themes in stories allows children to think about issues 'at a distance'. The best picturebooks have at their heart something about our world and our place in it and so they have the potential to get children talking and thinking. In often subtle and interesting and, above all, visual ways some picturebooks explore themes of environmental concern. Long well liked is Jeannie Baker's wordless book *Window*, which shows the effect on human beings' quality of life of unrestrained development. Picturebooks can take up almost any theme, including the consequences of conflict and aggression. Nikolai Popov's *Why?* begins with a mouse attacking a frog for no reason. Debate develops around themes such as why violence and oppression is wrong and what we can do to avoid it.

The best children's novels raise difficult questions such as those about our behaviour towards others. With care and a sensitive approach, that values the story for its own sake and not just as a vehicle for discussion, novels can give rise to impassioned debate and much more than superficial thinking. Many of Michael Morpurgo's novels stir children into caring about things. *The Dancing Bear* is an involving story for the over eights and, more powerfully than any information text could, shows how people use animals for their own purposes.

Another Morpurgo book, *The Wreck of the Zanzibar*, raises a particularly difficult issue. Laura finds a turtle and feeds it secretly with jellyfish. She knows if other islanders found the creature it would be eaten. Should she have hidden the turtle when human beings were hungry? This dilemma is particularly suited to presentation as an oral or written discussion text.

USING TEXTS TO THINK ABOUT ISSUES AND TO ARGUE A CASE

Unless otherwise stated, these suggestions can be adapted for different age groups.

Using practical work and drama

- Pre-school and nursery children can build role play, using some simple props, around issues like keeping the classroom litter free. *Look After Your Planet*, a Charlie and Lola book by Lauren Child, is one of a number of books to help ignite young imaginations.
- When it comes to ways of thinking linked to 'discussion' texts, situations can be created where different characters are required to argue different points of view.
- Children of all ages could be helped to use *We Are All Born Free* by Amnesty International as a starting point for discussion.
- Making a class newspaper or magazine, print or electronic, has always provided, for over eights, a strong 'hands-on' context for writing and presenting all kinds of writing, including 'argument'. The following might awaken interest and give some hints: *First News*, a newspaper for children published monthly by Newsbridge; *Making Books* by Paul Johnson; Fergus Fleming's history series in newspaper format, for example *Greek Gazette*.
- Creating a 'conflict' situation. I have seen teachers use different versions of the following idea. Teacher and children create an imaginary village and make a map on paper or using

an interactive whiteboard. Perhaps the village has a small wild area with some seats around a pond. One day a group of children find a new notice. A developer wants to buy the land and build houses/hotel/supermarket on it. The teacher writes up points for and against the development and the children write a petition in the role of villagers. Talk centres on how to make the petition powerful verbally and visually. Text messages and emails could be included, as well as the creation of a pretend website on the issues.

Talking and thinking together

- Setting up 'response partners' makes it possible for children to rehearse an argument in pairs before giving their main points to the group or class.
- Using circle time with younger children and discussion time with older children can develop spoken argument based on children's current activities and preoccupations. The point and elaboration principle can be used about something like 'why our assembly/ school outing/sports day was a success'. A 'point' might be 'because we all worked together as a team' and the 'elaboration' something like 'this meant that everyone's ideas were used'.

Texts as a focus for discussion

- Pictures can give rise to passionate discussion. I remember eight-year-olds doing a geography project on 'Litter' being upset by a photograph in an information book of a hedgehog caught in a carelessly discarded jagged edged tin can. This led to talk about how our own behaviour could prevent this happening.
- Internet materials. Younger children would enjoy playing the Recycling game with Barnaby Bear (www.bbc.co.uk/schools/barnaby bear/games/recycle/) as a way into a discussion on the reasons for recycling waste. Children aged about eight years and under would enjoy reading *Snow Leopards* by Nicole Poppenhager, illustrated by Ivan Gantschev, an involving story about two young leopards who get lost in harsh terrain.
- *Planet Patrol* by Mick Manning and Brita Granström is about a group of children who have formed their own eco-group on the internet called 'the Planet Patrol'. The site would be an inspiration for children's discussion (www.theplanetpatrol.com).
- Reading aloud from inspirational information books can help nudge children towards persuasive uses of language. Pre-school and nursery aged children would find a book on endangered animals, for example *Animals in Danger*, a pop-up book by Thando McLaren and Christopher Gilvan-Cartwright, helpful in starting to think about this.
- For about age eight and over we need texts that give the evidence and leave young speakers and writers to decide on a viewpoint so that they can create their own 'discussion' text. *Robots: Friend or Foe?* by Sarah Fleming, one of the Oxford TreeTops series, allows readers to look at the evidence and to decide for themselves if the impact of robots is likely to be good or problematic.
- Older children find food for thought in books of a philosophical nature, for example, Nicolai Popov's *Why?*
- Newspaper and magazine articles brought in by teacher or pupil can be the starting point for debate in English or across the curriculum.

Figure 32.1
*Text and illustration
from page 6 of*
Robots: Friend or Foe?
by Sarah Fleming
Reproduced with the
permission of the
publishers Oxford
University Press

- 'Popular culture' materials to energize discussion include football and pop music magazines and comics. These can lead to children' own attempts at 'discussion' or 'persuasion'. Print books can help too – Franklin Watts' *Football and Its Followers* by P. May, from the In the News series, looks at the dark as well as the positive side of the game.
- Fiction, for example the class novel, can inspire children of different ages and interests to think and argue deeply about issues of human importance.
- An interesting English focus for older children is speeches by the great characters in literature. Speeches from Shakespeare are challenging but some, for example those by Portia and Mark Antony, can be used to show how metaphor, lists and paired synonyms can be used to persuade. Ron Norman calls these 'The Great Persuaders' (Norman, 1998: 231).

Into writing

- Please see Chapter 34 on library and study skills for a discussion of note-taking.
- Making print advertisements and posters helps children understand how design and language and illustration work together to get points across. Children need teacher support

to take account of factors like the size, orientation, style and colour of print and the use of punctuation and to understand how all these help make an impact.

- Making multimedia advertisements helps children combine sound, music and the moving image with writing to persuade.
- Making lists of pros and cons of two different viewpoints helps towards the writing of a discussion text. In an interesting case study built around a 'Living Things' science unit children are inspired by Anthony Browne's picturebook *Zoo*. The teacher helped seven-year-olds make notes under columns headed 'zoos are good for animals' and 'zoos are bad for animals' (see Riley and Reedy, 2000: 147–60).
- Teachers find that some young writers can be helped to organize the global structure of an account by using a writing frame with guiding headings. Published frames can be used – Wray and Lewis (1997) include writing frames for discussion and persuasion in their books on non-fiction or child and teacher can construct a frame tailored to the needs of the child and the topic.
- Children can be helped to use the full range of visual as well as written forms, deciding on which of these will help demonstrate information and evidence for their argument best, including digital photographs, pie and bar graphs, charts, posters, drawings and diagrams like cross-sections.

CASE STUDY 32.1 A YEAR 2 CLASS MAKE AN ELECTRICITY SAFETY FILM

A Year 2 class who had been following a science unit on electricity were helped to make a film about the dangers of electricity. First they were shown a road safety film and encouraged to talk about how it had been put together and how language and moving images were used to persuade the viewers to act sensibly. Then a rap structure – a 'popular culture' text – was used in their own short film. Groups of children worked with one of three main topics: danger near sub-stations and pylons; danger in the kitchen; danger from appliances. The editing team brought together the work of each group as a rap poem, adding titles, music, transitions and surging images of electricity. The teaching team felt it was the collaborative nature of the work and using an exciting mixture of media which helped children make a good start in understanding how to use language and image to persuade and influence behaviour.

Keep safe in the kitchen!
When you use the cooker,
Remember it gets very hot.
Follow our advice and keep safe.

Never mix water and electricity
– water conducts electricity.
Follow our advice and keep safe.

Figure 32.2
*'Keep Safe in the Kitchen',
a rap*

CASE STUDY 32.2 A YEAR 5 CLASS EXPLORE THE PROS AND CONS OF TOURISM IN A VULNERABLE ENVIRONMENT

In 'Talk and Pictures in Key Stage 2 Geography', Margaret Mackintosh describes some classroom work on Antarctica to help children understand more about environmental issues but also to show them that people have different points of view. This was brought to a practical level by asking children to read and talk about the impact of tourism on Antarctica and to think about the differing perspectives on this of tour companies, tourists and an imaginary environmental group called 'the Bright Greens'. The children read relevant articles the teacher had found from newspapers and magazines and also some publicity material for tourists. They were asked to take turns at presenting both arguments for and against further tourism. One outcome was the creation of posters, an example of which is shown in Figure 32.3, to argue for a particular viewpoint (Mackintosh, 2004).

Figure 32.3
'STOP!' Child's poster about protecting Antarctica
Reproduced with the permission of Margaret Mackintosh and PEM and with acknowledgement to Karen O'Toole, Sean Millar and the young writer

MAKING PROGRESS

What do we hope children will have achieved in controlling the text types we call 'argument' in the form of persuasion and discussion by the time they reach the end of the primary years? We would look for increased 'generic control' – understanding as speakers, readers and writers of the structure and pattern of the argument being made. This would mean, for instance, that they will be able to make points coherently and elaborate them by giving examples and evidence. They will also be increasingly able to keep the purpose of the text and audience for whom the argument is intended in mind when presenting a case orally or when organizing, writing and illustrating their account.

When it comes to control over the linguistic features of argument, we would look for developing insight about the vocabulary or lexis and its impact. The syntax or grammar used can also affect the audience. Short sentences with exclamation marks might make an advertisement pithy or perhaps the accumulation of clauses might build to a climax. Also involved is an improved understanding of register, for example whether a text is formal or informal.

Experience of making a case in discussion and oral debate, with teacher support, helps hone children's sense of purpose and audience. This is the underpinning to children's understanding of the devices that can be used to make their writing powerful and successful. The aim, of course, is to help young speakers and writers become able to control more subtle and complex arguments, using more sophisticated language and becoming able to anticipate and cope with counter arguments.

Gaining increasing control over argument as speakers and writers helps children become critical readers of the writing of others. Most importantly, they will become increasingly able to distinguish between fact and opinion and to know when and how they are being unreasonably manipulated.

ASSESSING AND RECORDING PROGRESS

Here are some suggestions for what might be included in children's English, language and literacy portfolios:

- lists of some of the texts (with dates) they have read and discussed to help their progress in controlling discussion and persuasion text types in school;
- dated lists of children's oral presentations to argue a case with short evaluative comment;
- examples of writing, chosen by teacher and child, evaluating different viewpoints on a topic (annotated with date, context and brief comment by teacher and/or child);
- examples of writing and illustrating to persuade, including print multimodal texts such as posters, pamphlets, petitions and advertisements (see Figure 32.3);
- digital photographs of displays which the pupil has helped to design and label and which present an argument.

SUMMARY

- Discussion and persuasion are text types that fall under the larger category of argument. These forms make possible the formulation of a logical argument structured around a series of points and elaboration of these points.
- Discussion and persuasion texts for children are, particularly for younger children, transitional genres and often appear alongside other kinds of writing.
- Discussion and persuasion are found in print books, multimedia resources and websites and non-book print like newspapers, magazines, posters, flyers, advertisements and letters.
- As children get older they can understand and make explicit the structural and linguistic features of text types to do with discussion and persuasion.
- Progression is partly to do with the increasing ability to grasp the counter arguments to the preferred viewpoint, talk about them and put them into practice in both spoken and written language.
- Constructing spoken argument, through debate and dramatic improvisation, generally comes before and aids writing.
- Sometimes it is fiction texts – picturebooks, stories and poems – which inspire these strong feelings and 'wonderings' about topics and issues and which lead to a search for evidence to help sustain and enrich argument.
- If we want to awaken children's interest and sustain it through challenging activities like writing we need to draw imaginatively on their lives and interests outside school: sport, comics, websites, television programmes and computer games all throw up exciting possibilities for all kinds of discussion and writing.
- Evidence of progress in controlling argument can be stored in the language and literacy section in a paper or electronic portfolio.

Chapter 33

Reference texts
Choosing texts and resources

INTRODUCTION

Not so very long ago when 'children's reference texts' were mentioned, rather uninviting, traditional looking dictionaries and predictable, formulaic entries in encyclopedias came to mind. This picture is very far from the case today. Currently texts in the reference 'stable' – dictionaries, thesauruses, atlases and encyclopedias – are full of colour and interest and carefully designed. The best are valuable aids to children's research, learning and writing in every lesson.

Print versions continue to hold an important place and new technology has enhanced their format and presentation enormously. But, of course, the repertoire is increasingly extended by multimedia texts: the combination of text, sound and image in these makes them potentially a rich and distinctive reading experience. They also have the advantage of being easily stored on CD-ROMs. Another great plus is the potential of screen-based texts in linking home and school literacy experiences. All reference material for children and for adults needs constant updating to reflect new vocabulary, new knowledge and changing attitudes to existing knowledge. This updating is easier when resources are online.

Particular titles are mentioned in this chapter as being quality texts for each age group. These represent only a small selection of all those I know and have looked at. They are used as examples and the omission of texts does not imply any judgement on their quality. What is available changes and develops constantly, and so teachers updating the reference collection will find it helpful to look on the websites of the main publishers. These include Chambers, Collins, Dorling Kindersley, Global Software Publishing, Kingfisher, Ladybird, Longman, Macmillan, Oxford University Press, Philips (Heinemann) and Usborne. Where I hope to help is in suggesting some criteria for quality texts: it is easy to become overwhelmed by the sheer choice and the array of colourful and dynamic reference resources. The very best books have that spark of originality that is difficult to pin down and exciting, boundary-breaking books might be missed if we stick too inflexibly to lists of 'desirable features'.

FEATURES OF REFERENCE TEXTS

The structure of reference texts, their global organization, varies from an alphabetic list giving meanings and sometimes roots of words, sample sentences and synonyms, as in a dictionary or thesaurus, to the topic-based organization of an atlas and of some encyclopedias for the very young. We must remember that reference texts for the youngest readership are likely to be 'transitional genres'. This is a term first used in *Children's First School Books* (Baker and Freebody, 1989) and refers to texts that have only some of the features of the mature versions; in this way young readers are introduced gradually to the typical text conventions. So very early dictionaries, often called 'word books', may be organized by theme (words to do with the different rooms of a house in turn) rather than alphabetically. The same is true of some early encyclopedias which are theme-structured under headings like 'Our World', 'Animals and Plants', 'Space' and 'Famous People'. Transitional texts are often highly original and vibrant and sometimes at risk in a genre-dominated approach to expanding children's reading repertoire.

Encyclopedias often contain many different types or genres of writing. The writing under the headwords is usually in the form of a report or short article organized to suit the needs of the topic and not chronologically. Christine Pappas has provided a helpful analysis of the structure of report (Pappas, 1986). It typically begins with a presentation of the topic ('a spider is . . .'), proceeds to attributes and characteristics ('spiders have eight legs and most spin webs and produce poison to paralyse their prey') and then outlines characteristic events like life cycle, food and hibernation. Of course children 'read' a CD-ROM enclyclopaedia or information source on the internet differently to a print one. They can choose to access particular sub-topics at the click of the mouse and learn from the moving image in video-clips. But I think the elements that Pappas has pinpointed as being 'obligatory' would still be evident. A small-scale study found that children competent in using the internet at home were ahead of their peers in their information retrieval abilities, whether applied to print or electronic sources. So competence in one medium may transfer to another (Burnett and Wilkinson, 2005: 159).

As well as report, encyclopedias may include some chronologically organized text, for example biographies of famous people or snippets of autobiography and some 'explanation' writing and illustration.

As children make their way through the primary years they learn to cope with more specialized vocabulary and more demanding syntax. There may be a conversational tone in books for younger readers, using rhetorical questions and the friendly second person: 'Have you ever seen a chrysalis?' or 'How do you keep cool in a hot country?' By the end of the primary years children are encountering more formal styles to prepare them for the demands of the secondary years.

Another couple of things to do with genre are worth mentioning. The best reference texts have carefully thought out retrieval devices – indexes and glossaries and 'how to use this book' sections. Often the links between different parts of the text are particularly user-friendly when the text is electronic. And illustrations – the photographs, diagrams, drawings and graphics – identify the text with a particular genre. Most modern encyclopedias are visually alive and offer a huge variety of illustrations, energizing each page. They are certainly strong examples of multimodality with their careful design and annotated illustrations and pictures. Many are also multimedia resources, with all the variety of communication methods which this implies.

Two things are necessary if we want children to have a positive experience of reference texts. The first is to do with provision: a varied selection of quality resources is needed in both classroom and library collections. The second gets to the heart of what teaching is about:

there needs to be skilful and imaginative teaching which uses the texts to nourish and extend children's activities and research tasks. The urge to know is a powerful energizer.

SOME CRITERIA FOR CHOOSING

The rich variety of reference texts, both print and electronic, and the varied media through which information can be received demands that children develop multiple literacies, and as Eve Bearne suggests, a 'repertoire of approaches' so that they can choose the mode and medium best suited for the task (Bearne *et al.*, 2004: 16). But what about the quality of the texts themselves? Are there some things we can ask of any reference and of many information texts? Here are three fundamental criteria which have been used to begin to evaluate all the non-fiction text types in this part of the book, taking account of the age of the intended readers:

- *Design*: good design makes a text appealing and easy to read and use.
- *Coverage*: content and ideas that children will be covering in lessons across the curriculum and beyond it need to be presented in a way that helps them reflect, feel and want to find out more.
- *Language and illustration*: we look for clear, accurate and interesting text – both written and visual – that illuminates concepts and ideas.

How do practitioners judge particular books on these criteria? Journals like *Books for Keeps*, *The School Librarian* and *English 4–11* include reviews of reference books, both print and online, and there are websites with reviews by teachers and sometimes by pupils too. But, in my experience, nothing beats the opinions of a group of teachers looking at some competing texts 'on approval' and judging their suitability for their classes. What about making sure about a text's accuracy? I think that judging the accuracy of reference books, particularly encyclopedias for older primary children, is challenging. As a generalist primary school teacher whose curriculum strength is not science, I have relied on the experts who are usually part of the team when encyclopedias for the over eights are produced. *Books for Keeps* have some reviewers with science knowledge who sometimes pick up copious inaccuracies in books that seem superficially fine. We must also keep an eye on the quality of the dedicated websites included in some packages and on the quality of the sites that links lead to.

There now follows a consideration of each of the main groups of reference texts: dictionaries and thesauri, atlases, encyclopedias and study guides.

DICTIONARIES

Dictionaries for children, today created with the help of education consultants and teachers as well as lexicographers, came into being only at the beginning of the twentieth century. Publishers of children's dictionaries, for example Oxford University Press, Collins and Usborne, carry out careful research in schools, about the words young children come across and need explained. But how is it decided which words children at different stages need explained? Bringing in new words, for example those relating to computers and IT or those associated with curriculum changes, means that other words are likely to be dropped to make space. Sue Unstead comments on the 'vehement response' of some people to the decision of the publishing team of a new *Oxford Junior Dictionary* for age seven and above to miss out some words relating to religion and church architecture – 'abbey', 'bishop', 'monastery' and 'psalm'. The response, which strongly criticized the omissions – on the grounds that young users were being denied access to British heritage – was, Unstead feels, the result of some people misunderstanding what dictionaries for young children are for. Where young children are concerned a major role of the dictionary is for it to be a 'tool for the classroom', prioritizing those words which are needed most (Unstead, 2009: 8). Oxford's *Primary Dictionary* for older primary children from eight upwards does include the missed out words.

Another thing to keep in mind when deciding on the headwords is that children are writers as well as readers and need their vocabularies to be nourished by encountering not just nouns but also interesting words that describe objects, people and feelings – 'enchanting', 'charming', 'forlorn' and 'joyful'.

Publishers specializing in dictionaries usually produce a series of books of increasing challenge. Sticking to the same publishing house means that children can tune into the format of the books as they move through the school years. But we should keep in mind that dictionaries should sometimes 'invite and enable leisurely wanderings' and, as Robert Hull argues in *Books for Keeps*, that means having a wider range of dictionaries available on the classroom or school library bookshelf (Hull, 2009: 8).

Pre-school and nursery, 3–5-year-olds

Some of the first texts to help children develop an interest in words are the lively 'word books' which appeal in the pre-school years and beyond. While these are not, strictly speaking, dictionaries – they are thematically and not alphabetically organized – they offer familiar and new vocabulary in settings like 'our house', 'the farm' and 'people who help us'. Richard Scarry's timeless classics are full of colourful, detailed pictures which have an energy and humour about them. His *Busiest People Ever* takes us to Busy Town and shows us the jobs people do, while *Richard Scarry's Best Word Book Ever* has pages on 'Tools', 'At the Playground' and 'Supermarket'. The books are frequently updated for new generations of children and rarely out of print. Another favourite word book is Janet and Allan Ahlberg's *The Baby's Catalogue*, which lists and illustrates all the things babies use and play with. This author and illustrator saw that their daughter, Jessica, loved playing with the Mothercare catalogue when she was a toddler and this gave them the idea to produce their own catalogue, which shows so effectively how illustration and written text link to make meaning. *Collins First Picture Dictionary*, written by Irene Yates, has eye-catching pictures with illustrator Nick Sharratt's distinctive bold line and vivid colours. The dictionary is arranged thematically under everyday topics like 'Birthdays', 'In the Garden' and 'The Supermarket'. There are spreads on colour, shape and number and the themes in this book, as in other word books, can be linked with what the children are learning about at a particular time. The 400 words introduced under the themes are also organized in an A–Z index.

CD-ROM word books combine animation, sound, games, rhymes and word families. The Oxford University Press' *My Oxford Word Box CD-ROM* for children aged three plus (with help, of course) has all these features and is a considerable resource with its 1,000 words

Figure 33.1
Front cover of Oxford Reading
Tree Dictionary *by Roderick Hunt
and Clare Kirtley and Alex Brycha
(illus.)*
Reproduced with the permission of the
publishers Oxford University Press

and 700 animations; it enables children to navigate easily and to click on words to hear the word and its context read aloud.

The placing of words in context is the strength of the thematic organization typical of word books. But it is important that children are introduced early to alphabetically ordered books. So simple but alphabetically organized dictionaries are also part of the collection for children approaching age five. Adults can help children begin to use the dictionaries to check spelling, clarify meanings and reinforce teaching about alphabetic ordering.

There is a large number of first dictionaries on the market. It can be confusing for purchasers as so many seem to be called just that – 'First Dictionary' – and yet some are much more detailed and challenging than others. It is quite difficult to find one without merit. Nearly all have the alphabet displayed in both upper and lower case on each page. *Ladybird First Picture Dictionary*, by Gaynor Berry, also highlights the letters dealt with on each double spread. Most early print dictionaries are copiously and often imaginatively illustrated and use carefully thought out design and colour to add interest and variety to the pages. For group-based work on dictionary skills with children aged about four to six years, I recommend *Oxford Reading Tree Dictionary* in big book format. It has 300 headwords, simple definitions and helpful pictures. *My ABC Dictionary* by Irene Yates and Chris Fisher is for the same age group and has large letters and amusing illustrations.

Advanced young learners towards age five or six years might manage the *Oxford First Dictionary* with some help. It has 1,500 words, clearly defined, and with words placed in full sentences. Like most other alphabetic dictionaries for young children this one has a thematic section at the end providing words and pictures on colour, animals and fruit. Teachers of this age group know how searching and interesting children's questions can be and it is as well to have an adult dictionary (and encyclopedia) to hand.

5–8-year-olds

By this age most children have a grip on alphabetical ordering and are ready to learn about some other features of dictionaries, including the provision of several word meanings, plurals and synonyms. The *Oxford Very First Dictionary*, by Clare Kirtley and illustrated by George Birkett, has only 300 words and could be used independently by most six- to seven-year-olds; it supports early attempts at writing, providing pages on verbs, words we use a lot, numbers and the alphabet. If I have a criticism of illustrations in children's reference books generally, it is that sometimes rather static and overused images are shown. This dictionary has some more interesting and dynamic pictures: for example, to illustrate 'grow' and 'growing' we have a small and big flower with a ruler alongside.

Moving up to the seven to rising nines, teachers select dictionaries that cover the vocabulary children are likely to need across the curriculum. Dictionaries also help children develop and refine their language knowledge, for example about parts of speech and plurals. There are some good print dictionaries for this age group by the main publishers of children's reference books and an increasing number of electronic versions. The *Oxford First Dictionary* is a clear step up from the *Oxford Very First Dictionary*, with 1,500 words and pages with place and position words and some collections of words to do with time, measurement and seasons. The *Usborne First Dictionary*, written by Rachel Wardley, includes puzzles and spelling tips. Any dictionary with 'first' in the title is likely to be illustrated and some children continue to feel comfortable with these even as they move to the upper part of the primary school. Such pupils might like the *Collins Primary Illustrated Dictionary*, which has pictures but also some mature features – for instance, example sentences for each synonym and a splendid index. Also intended for pupils in the middle years of the primary school is the 2006 edition of *Oxford Children's Colour Dictionary* by Rosemary Sansome *et al.*, based on *Oxford Junior Illustrated Dictionary* by Sheila Dignen. This is a 'pop in your school bag' dictionary. If a young learner wants a quick guide about spelling and meanings this would be a good choice. It keeps everything clear and simple, with bold headwords in blue, word class information and example sentences. Let us look at this dictionary in a little more depth. A quick spin through shows the compilers have included good entries on modern technology; for example the DVD definition is 'a small flat disc on which music, pictures or film can be stored – short for digital versatile disc'. Some illustrations are of the familiar – flower, dragonfly and so on. Better are the labelled diagrams – for example, a head of a fish showing the gills and a diagram showing a line across a circle to show diameter. If you want an easy-to-use, fairly basic dictionary with succinct definitions this would be fine.

I do find it odd that many of the dictionaries for this age group have minimal information to explain important mathematical concepts like 'graph'. One well-known dictionary has: 'shows information about something'. This does not take the reader very far; what about the different kinds of graph – pie, line – and the kind of information you might show? Vocabulary about film and film making, now such an important element in the primary programme, is mostly absent.

Ladybird reference and information books are very good value for money. *School Dictionary: First Reference for Young Readers and Writers* is easy to use and has 1,000 headwords, in clear bright blue, and their meanings. The pictures are good too: there is a simply splendid diagram of a computer on page 128. Collins' series of dictionaries for every age range within the primary years have headwords and meanings that are generously spaced. *The Collins Junior*

Dictionary, by Evelyn Goldsmith and recommended for children of age seven and over, is lightly illustrated and has 'Top Tips for Tricky Words' as well as plurals, tenses and parts of speech.

For those ready to cope with a good dictionary without illustrations, the *Oxford Young Readers' Dictionary* by Rosemary Sansome *et al.*, for the over sevens, has 6,000 entries; like most dictionaries for the primary school stage this one has 'bold print' headwords, and includes phrases and parts of speech. It is particularly user-friendly because of the choice of bold print on cream coloured paper and the 'using this dictionary' page, which is lucid and inviting. Dorling Kindersley have led the way in CD-ROM dictionaries. Their *My First Incredible Amazing Dictionary* has become a favourite with Key Stage 1 children and their teachers. Access to words is made easy by clicking on the letters of the alphabet at the top of the screen page. The hypertext links to words across the dictionary and the spoken definitions are two strong features. It has fewer headwords at 1,000 than, for example, *The Oxford Young Readers' Dictionary* but is full of games and puzzles to practise dictionary skills. *Word Bank* and *Crossword Creator* (which includes a thesaurus) help children compile their own personal dictionaries.

8–11-year-olds

What do we want children to have achieved in their use of dictionaries by the later primary years? They will now cope with dictionaries with more headwords and fuller definitions. We hope they will understand some of the main genre features and how to control them. For example they will have become familiar with the use of phrases as well as sentences to explain meanings, with the provision of several often numbered meanings and with abbreviations. Sheila Dignen's *Oxford Junior Illustrated Dictionary* helps with all this and also encourages children to apply themselves to their reading and writing by using example sentences by well-known authors like Jacqueline Wilson, Roald Dahl and Dick King-Smith. *Collins School Dictionary* and *Collins Concise School Dictionary*, both by John McIllwain, are both appropriate for abler children as they approach eleven and give helpful information on grammar and pronunciation. Etymologies for words, and synonyms and antonyms are highlighted and vocabulary likely to be useful across the curriculum is included. I like the generous spacing in these dictionaries; each 'sense' of the word is given a new line. The *Oxford School Dictionary* by Andrew Delahunty will help children in the last year of the primary school and see them into the early years of the secondary school. It has 40,000 headwords, with plurals, tenses and word origins for all root words. 'Internet' and 'virtual reality' are well explained. Some children, particularly those with special educational needs, are happier with an illustrated dictionary until the end of the primary years. The *Usborne Illustrated Dictionary* by Jane Bingham has visual appeal and gives a helpful user's guide to such things as how plurals are formed and how apostrophes are used. For good support with homophones – words that sound the same but are spelt differently and mean different things – the *Oxford Primary Dictionary*, another dictionary from Andrew Delahunty, has advice in boxes, for example 'Take care not to confuse "currant", a dried fruit, with "current" which means a flow'. It then goes on to explain the history of the word. 'The word "currant" comes from the name "Corinth", a city of Ancient Greece where currants were first used' (www.oup.com). This is a very user-friendly dictionary with headwords in blue and explanations in black.

351

By the later primary years children will have used electronic dictionaries on CD-ROMs, software and the internet. *Franklin Children's Dictionary* is an interactive children's reference resource which includes *The Oxford Children's Dictionary*. The Oxford *Dictosaurus* is a combined dictionary and thesaurus which offers support with writing and spelling across the curriculum. Older children also find useful dictionaries online. With some teacher or parent support many children will be able to use *The Oxford English Dictionary for Schools*, edited by Robert Allen, and/or *The Concise Oxford English Dictionary* either in print, on CD-ROM or online. The advantage of the online version is that it is responsive to the changes that happen all the time. This dictionary gives information about the roots of words and whether they come from foreign languages or some other source. Etymology and morphology – partly to help spell new words – are part of language study for older primary children. These dictionaries give some help with word structure, place names and with the origins of words. All this helps the young users understand how language changes and how meanings become refined.

Specialist dictionaries include those on particular subject areas like space, science and geography. Peter Patilla's *Oxford First Maths Dictionary* is, like the others in the series, alphabetically ordered and has helpful and appealing artwork. Young word games enthusiasts would like Evelyn Goldsmith's *Collins Scrabble Dictionary*, which has a spellchecker and help over word meanings in sentences. There are quite a lot of rhyming dictionaries too, to help young verse writers. *Black's Rhyming and Spelling Dictionary* by Pie Corbett and Ruth Thomson nurtures a love of words and has some jolly nonsense rhymes for children to enjoy. A nice book for browsing is John Foster's *Oxford First Rhyming Dictionary*, which provides words that rhyme, rhyming families and rhyming sounds. There is attention to words that rhyme, but are not spelt in a similar way – 'mole' and 'goal' for example.

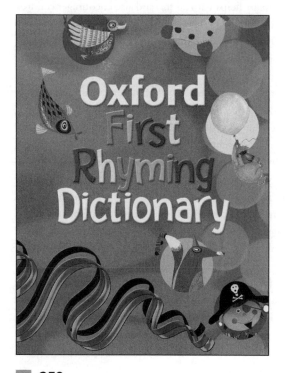

Figure 33.2
Front cover of Oxford First Rhyming Dictionary *by* *John Foster*
Reproduced with the permission of the publishers Oxford University Press

Summary: things to look for when choosing dictionaries, keeping the intended age range in mind

These include:

- *Design*: clear structure and easily visible headwords.
- *Coverage*: meets needs across the curriculum and beyond.
- *Language and illustration*: lucid written explanations that are well contextualized and in enough detail for the age group. Illustrations that are dynamic and which extend understanding. Diagrams that are appropriate, clear and well annotated.

and

- Clear print in paper books and the clear communication of non-linear information in electronic books.
- Technological concepts included, like 'homepage', 'image map' and 'hypertext links'.
- New and interesting words to extend children's vocabularies and nourish an interest in language.

THESAURI

A thesaurus presents a key word and then lists its antonyms and synonyms. It can be organized either thematically or alphabetically. The design needs to be clear and inviting and care needs to have been taken over the meanings of synonyms, which may differ in subtle ways from words that seem to mean the same. The main publishers of children's dictionaries nearly always include thesauri for different ages and stages in their title lists, although there are

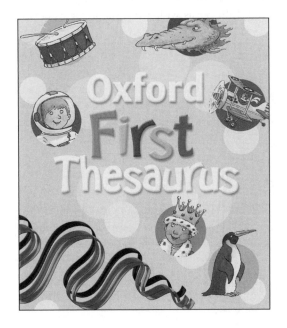

Figure 33.3
Front cover of Oxford First
Thesaurus *by Andrew Delahunty
and Steve Cox*
2007 edition, reproduced with the
permission of the publishers Oxford
University Press

some texts combining a dictionary and thesaurus both in print and online. I find children from about age five like looking through *Oxford First Thesaurus*. It has a spacious, uncluttered format and entertaining illustrations. Under 'sound', synonyms – 'bang', 'bleep', 'buzz' through to 'whirr' and 'whistle' – are arranged alphabetically along an imaginary machine.

The encouragement to be an active 'word explorer' continues with *Oxford Primary Thesaurus* for age about eight upwards. It has 50,000 words and keeps things clear and simple, with bright blue headwords and sentence meanings in black.

Whether a thesaurus is in print form or built into a word processing package its function is to offer an exciting range of options to express our meaning. A lot of thesauruses are aimed at the nine plus age group. Sheila Dignen's *Oxford Junior Illustrated Thesaurus* has 20,000 synonyms with example sentences which, like the companion dictionary, draw on the writing of favourite childrens' authors. The *Oxford Children's Thesaurus* by Alan Spooner and Robert Allen has a nine to twelve age frame. This has simple, clear and effective explanations and some special attention to words supporting lessons on projects like 'weather' and 'the farm'.

For children of age ten and over, the *Usborne Illustrated Thesaurus* by Jane Bingham has 60,000 words and the added interest of beautiful and imaginative illustrations, some of which are carefully labelled. Pictures make the page more varied and less daunting than huge blocks of written text. Some words are picked out for special attention – there are 100 synonyms for nice! Alongside a panel about weather words is an oval picture showing 'snow-laden trees'. So children are encouraged to enjoy and vary the vocabulary in their writing.

The absence of illustrations in John McIlwain's *Collins Primary Thesaurus* flags that it is a stretching resource for upper primary school children. It has a full and helpful index and 'word power' boxes to support young writers' efforts to vary their vocabulary.

Dictosaurus, a combined electronic dictionary and thesaurus from Oxford University Press, is recommended as an interesting and effective writing support for children from age seven upwards and still serves children well as they reach the oldest class in the primary school and beyond. *Chambers School Thesaurus* is an advanced thesaurus with a rich supply of synonyms

Figure 33.4
Front cover of Dictosaurus
CD-ROM, reproduced with the
permission of the publishers
Oxford University Press.
Copyright Oxford University
Press and Polderland Language
and Speech Technology 2006

that abler primary school children could use with help from the teacher. The concise edition of *Collins English Dictionary and Thesaurus*, with each of its synonyms embedded in a sentence, is a handy reference book for teachers.

I find, when listing 'criteria or things to look for' in texts, that the things that make a book exceptional of its kind are hard to pinpoint. So it is with the best thesauri. You have to look at a book like the *Usborne Illustrated Thesaurus* to appreciate its charm and appeal and its ability to enthuse and inspire young writers. Nevertheless, here are some suggestions.

Summary: some things to look for when choosing thesauri

Bearing in mind the age and ability of the children they might include:

- *Design*: making it inviting and easy to use, providing some humour and illuminating examples.
- *Coverage*: offering a wide enough vocabulary to provide an increase in the range of options from which children can select as writers.
- *Language and illustration*: good contextualization of the vocabulary through example and pictures.

and

- Interesting enough to ensure browsing is thought-provoking.
- Reinforcing a belief that language is essentially creative.

ACTIVITIES TO SUPPORT AND ENCOURAGE THE USE OF DICTIONARIES AND THESAURI

- Class- or group-based work, looking up vocabulary being used in a lesson.
- Make a language thermometer. A class of eight-year-olds created a huge thermometer with silver paper, oriented horizontally on the back wall of the classroom. Starting with 'freezing' they arranged words about temperature along the thermometer right through to 'scalding'.
- Talk about the different dictionaries and thesauri provided under headings like 'design', 'coverage' and 'writing and illustration'.
- Make lists, perhaps with a partner, of all the words they can think of for overused words like 'said' and 'boring'.
- Make simple crosswords.
- Play Scrabble in groups.
- Talk about homophones – words that sound the same but have different meanings.
- Talk about the subtle difference between words which have broadly the same meaning.

ATLASES AND MAP BOOKS

Atlases, both print and electronic, are important reference texts as they help children get to the heart of geographical thinking. They cover physical features of land masses and oceans and give information about lifestyles of peoples in different countries, including land use, occupations and population data. This information is communicated through the visual — diagrams, photographs and drawings — as well as written accounts and annotation. Children need help — even into the secondary years — with distinctive ways of organizing information in atlases, with the interpretation of keys and the use of grid references and geographical indexes. The print atlas continues to hold its place in school collections, but now it often has links to websites. The electronic whiteboard is a powerful tool for showing parts of atlases to meet the needs of a lesson. (ICT resources that are SMARTBoard accredited are suitable for use with an electronic whiteboard.)

Pre-school and nursery, 3–5-year-olds

What do we look for when choosing a very first map book? The best place to start is with something familiar like the spatial arrangement of features in children's bedrooms, a classroom or the school grounds. Lani Yamamoto's intriguing information story for about age three to five years, *Albert*, starts with a picture plan of Albert's bedroom and then extends to his family's street, the nearby park, the town and then gets progressively bigger, showing the town is in the country, the country on Earth and Earth in the universe. These early maps have just the right amount of information for a young child.

When it comes to early map books a good place to start is with maps of children's own area — ordinance survey or road maps. Then we move them on to maps books and first atlases showing the countries of the world, we look for help with interpreting simple maps and a good introduction to geographical concepts like climate and lifestyle. These features are to be found in most of the early map books from the usual publishers of children's reference books. I find particularly appealing Ruth Brocklehurst *et al.*'s *The Usborne Children's Picture Atlas*. Young readers are taken on a pictorial journey, using maps and drawings, from hot regions like India and Africa to the frozen areas in the Arctic and Antarctic. There is good input on the use of colour in map making. So pre-schoolers learn that white is used to indicate ice and snow, yellow to show deserts and blue lakes and seas, and the concept of a key is introduced.

in the town...

Figure 33.5
'In the Town', a map from Albert *by Lani Yamamoto*
2004, reproduced here with the permission of the publishers Frances Lincoln Ltd

5–8-year-olds

Good atlases for this age group will have helpful support over using keys and understanding grid marks and geographical data. Dorling Kindersley's *Picture Atlas* by Anita Ganeri and Chris Oxlade has maps of the different countries and continents of the world which are full of life and colour. Take the map showing Africa – this has pictures of the animals that inhabit each region and also helpful annotation about the different landscapes like the Savanna grassland which covers so much of the continent. The cover says 'for young readers and writers' and I think the rich illustrations showing animals and the lifestyles of people would help with children's early geographical writing.

Oxford Infant Atlas for the four to seven age group demonstrates well the use of keys, using child-friendly symbols for mountains, rivers and deserts. It has a good index with place names. Above all it is visually interesting with colourful maps and some satellite images. Teachers looking for good coverage of the UK will find this a useful resource which is available in both print and CD-ROM.

Less forward young readers will be helped by the narration which is a main feature of the *Oxford Talking Infant Atlas* by Patrick Wiegand. Recommended for five- to seven-year-olds, this resource allows children to explore at their own pace.

8–11-year-olds

By about seven to nine years children are becoming able to appreciate the more subtle and detailed information provided by aerial photographs and satellite images. Good atlases from the main publishers for older children also have input on extra topics like weather, land use and journeys. Indexes need grid references as well as place numbers. *Oxford First Atlas* written by Patrick Wiegand has all this and good, clear mapping. The *Oxford Primary Atlas* by the same author has a number of excellent features. Bright, colourful maps are accompanied by relevant photographs which give information about geographical features. The generous size of the keys in this atlas helps with the teaching of map-reading skills.

From about eight or nine years children are ready to use a world atlas like, for example, *Philip's Children's Atlas* by David and Jill Wright. It has clear maps, lucid text and helpful photographs.

Oxford Junior Atlas for nine- to eleven-year-olds has much Key Stage 2 curriculum linked content. For Year 6 and beyond the *Oxford School Atlas* offers, as well as the usual maps and information atlases for older children, case studies on tsunamis, volcanos and earthquakes. Both these are written by Patrick Wiegand. Most ten-year-olds would need support to use these resources.

Good print atlases continue to have a strong place in the collection. However, quality CD-ROM atlases can provide illuminating topographical mapping giving 3D impressions from different angles and therefore excellent information about the physical features of landscapes. Simon Catling's *Collins Primary World Whiteboard Atlas* is a CD-ROM based on the print atlas *Collins Primary World Atlas* for use with digital whiteboards. Both print and electronic versions of this atlas have clear, colourful maps of the UK, Europe and countries across the world. There is help over map-reading skills and the meaning of scale. The index provides simple grid references and directs young geographers to web addresses for further information and research. This atlas should see children at least to the end of the primary years.

Criteria for choosing atlases and map books

- *Design*: appropriate to an age group, with growing complexity while still remaining accessible and inviting.
- *Coverage*: taking account of the child's developing understanding and draws them through the expectations of the curriculum.
- *Illustration and language*: accuracy and clarity are essential, but we also look for perspectives and narration which intrigue and encourage thinking and a wish to find out more.

Using atlases and map books

Help children to:

- make maps of the classroom, their bedroom and the route to school;
- use a large map of their town to plan routes to their family and friends;
- again, use a large map (perhaps a photocopy or tracing) to annotate with comments on places they know;
- use grid references from the indexes of atlases and then ask them to practice finding familiar towns and places;
- build up a collection of digital photographs to build and develop an understanding of a landscape or environment, encouraging their contributions to the collection;
- make relief map models;

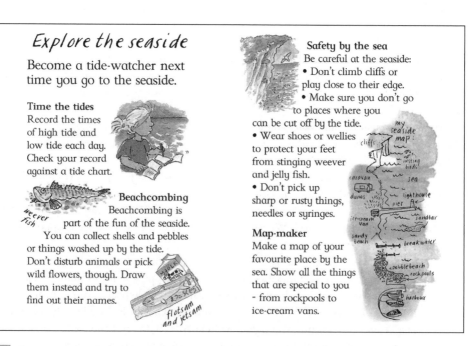

Explore the seaside

Become a tide-watcher next time you go to the seaside.

Time the tides
Record the times of high tide and low tide each day. Check your record against a tide chart.

weever fish

Beachcombing
Beachcombing is part of the fun of the seaside. You can collect shells and pebbles or things washed up by the tide. Don't disturb animals or pick wild flowers, though. Draw them instead and try to find out their names.

flotsam and jetsam

Safety by the sea
Be careful at the seaside:
- Don't climb cliffs or play close to their edge.
- Make sure you don't go to places where you can be cut off by the tide.
- Wear shoes or wellies to protect your feet from stinging weever and jelly fish.
- Don't pick up sharp or rusty things, needles or syringes.

Map-maker
Make a map of your favourite place by the sea. Show all the things that are special to you - from rockpools to ice-cream vans.

my seaside map: cliffs, nesting birds, caravan, dunes, lighthouse, pier, sea, ice-cream van, sandbar, sandy beach, breakwater, pebble beach, rockpools, harbour

Figure 33.6 *Map of shoreline from page 29 of* High Tide, Low Tide *by Mick Manning and Brita Granström. This map could be used to inspire children aged up to about age eight to make their own maps of favourite places*
2003 edition, reproduced with the permission of Franklin Watts.

- make a video-film of an area like a riverbank or seashore looking at patterns, processes and changes;
- prepare their own annotated maps of, for example, land use or the distribution of retail outlets in their locality or, on a global basis, of population density;
- use information from maps to inform their geographical discussions and writing;
- discuss the maps they have been using – what have they found useful or less helpful.

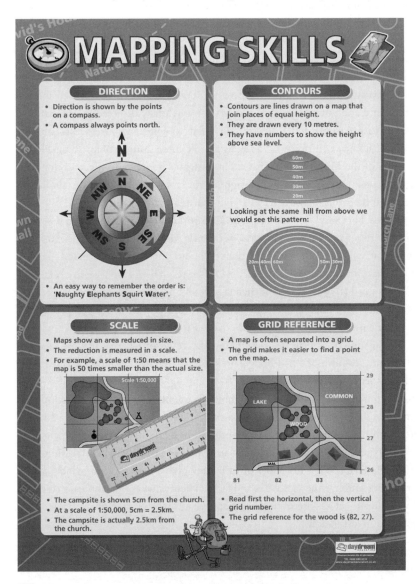

Figure 33.7 *Chart 'Mapping Skills GE 024'. Posters and charts with advice about map reading are accessible and encourage group discussion. This one would be suitable for the over nines with some teacher support*
Chart reproduced with the permission of the publishers Daydream Education.
© Daydream Education 2003.

ENCYCLOPEDIAS

Because of limits on space this book has not included chapters on the history of children's literature. But here I would like to mention two books which are the forerunners of the modern encyclopedia. *Orbis Sensualium Pictus* (1658) by John Amos Comenius described and celebrated the natural world and human achievement in text and illustration. Much later, Arthur Mee's *The Children's Encyclopedia* (1905) provided information to increase knowledge about all aspects of the world. Both of these works stirred the imagination as well as providing 'facts', a principle we do well to keep in mind.

There is a huge international market for encyclopedias, as anyone who attends the big book fairs like those at Bologna and Frankfurt knows. The good thing about this is that there can be a great sharing of expertise between countries. However, it does mean that encyclopedias often have a 'global' look and content so that they are not too obviously directed at one national market. Even so, British parents and teachers will want to select resources that support children's school and homework projects here. In a very interesting article, 'Non-Fiction Publishing: The Facts of the Matter', Sue Unstead investigates how children's encyclopedias are created and stresses that editors and designers must be knowledgeable about the international market if their businesses are to survive (Unstead, 2003).

Both parents and teachers need to look carefully at resources before buying them to ensure they cover the topics required. If, like me, you frequently visit children's book sections in quality bookshops you will be confronted by shelves of brightly coloured, mainly single-volume, encyclopedias with vibrant covers or CD-ROM boxes. These resources are relatively costly and purchasers need to be clear about their needs and priorities. However impressive the scope of information and quality of illustration seem in a particular encyclopedia, it is essential to check the entries on topics you want covered in some depth. A parent reviewer on Amazon UK found the Great Fire of London and the reign of Charles II were covered only superficially in the resource she had bought to support a child's homework research.

Refreshing the information in encyclopedias by bringing out new editions at regular intervals helps justify purchasers' confidence. Britannica frequently update their encyclopedias for children, for example their *Encyclopedia Britannica: Children's Encyclopedia CD, 7–14*.

For each age group the collection needs to include some texts that most of the children can use independently and others which they can use with some help, when tackling their projects. Encyclopedias are often a first port of call: they give a basic outline which can be built on by other reading and by other activities and tasks. Their value as a preliminary resource is that, hopefully, children get a sense of the 'big shape' of a topic before embarking on more in-depth research and investigation.

Pre-school and nursery, 3–5-year-olds

In a thematic encyclopedia there can be some coherence about the main topics of interest to young children. But an alphabetic organization gets you quickly to information to help answer your questions swiftly. It may, however, have some overlap and miss out the unity of the bigger topics.

Catalogues are early introductions to the way encyclopedias are organized and many nursery classes have Mothercare and Early Learning catalogues in the home play area. I know a nursery class which has this sort of catalogue alongside *The Baby's Catalogue*, a classic from Allan and Janet Ahlberg. This groups everyday things by theme and follows five different families and their babies through twenty-four hours.

Two encyclopedias from the Usborne First Encyclopedia series – *First Encyclopedia of Our World* by Felicity Brooks and *First Encyclopedia of Animals* by Paul Dowswell – have sixty-four pages and so are not too daunting. The print is clear and there are interesting pictures for this age group to share with an adult.

5–8-year-olds

There are a number of brightly illustrated encyclopedias with the words 'first' and 'illustrated' in their titles, published by Kingfisher, Collins and Oxford. Andrew Langley's *Oxford First Encyclopedia*, which is in a generous format, deals with topics with just the right amount of detail for this age group. There is clearly written information on all topics including space and computing, lively illustration which includes photographs and annotated diagrams and, where appropriate, suggestions for experiments. The cross-referencing and good index help with developing reference skills. The *Oxford First Encyclopedia* is now in CD-ROM format. Pictures and text can be pasted into other software packages to support school projects on – body, people, places, animals and plants.

The best specialist encyclopedias have the power to interest and inform young readers who already have a foothold in a topic. David Burnie's *The Kingfisher Illustrated Dinosaur Encyclopedia* has clear written information likely to answer most of the questions of young palaeontologists about dinosaurs and the other reptiles living on land and in the sea at the same time.

8–11-year-olds

Older children are expected to control more difficult kinds of reading and writing and part of this is to do with dealing with longer sentences and more technical vocabulary. However, long passages of print can be off putting (Littlefair, 1991: 38). And this is why writers and illustrators of encyclopedias try to achieve some variety on the page. The writing and illustration must, of course, be linked coherently. The *Kingfisher Children's Encyclopedia* would be suitable for younger Key Stage 2 children, around seven or eight years, with some adult help, while older children could manage it independently.

For the last two years of the primary school a stretching and challenging choice would be Dorling Kindersley's *Children's Illustrated Encyclopedia*, which has 500 entries alphabetically organized. It is up to date on technology, scientific discovery and so is a good support for projects and homework. There is a lot of lively artwork – drawings and photographs – and a thirty-page fact finder for quick reference, including historical dates, places and discoveries. But perhaps the most visually enticing and innovative DK encyclopedia for this age group is *Pick Me Up: Stuff You Need to Know* by David Roberts and Jeremy Leslie and first published in 2006.

361

BOX 33.1 *PICK ME UP: STUFF YOU NEED TO KNOW* BY DAVID ROBERTS AND JEREMY LESLIE (DORLING KINDERSLEY)

The dramatic 3D effect front cover will ensure older primary school children pounce on this book. Then the invitation to the encyclopedia – 'I'm information for the iPod generation' – promises to help the reader navigate through the pages as if at a computer screen and it directs them to linking topics. So the philosophical underpinning is that everything connects. The rich variety of illustrations, including drawings, maps, diagrams, cartoons, photographs and charts, will appeal to young readers who learn well through visual input. But the written text also teaches and intrigues, sometimes with unsettling questions like: 'Can you imagine a world without printed text?' Then there are the sort of questions that young browsers like to puzzle over. How many people are using the internet at any particular time? The book gives in-depth information on issues like war, relations between the sexes and drugs and so would take young readers beyond the later primary years into the secondary school. Just one thing: a few people have remarked to me that the written text has an American flavour. But this could be a talking point for young readers.

Figure 33.8
Front cover of Pick Me Up: Stuff You Need to Know *edited by David Roberts and Jeremy Leslie*
Copyright Dorling Kindersley Ltd 2006.

Usborne reference books are liked for their distinctive approach: not too formulaic and particularly good on illustration. Kirsteen Rogers' *Usborne Science Encyclopedia* has exceptionally good diagrams and helpful internet links. This is a demanding text for a child to use at home or school with adult help.

Many print encyclopedias are now offered also in CD-ROM format with the addition of some multimedia features such as sound and animation. The DK Eyewitness *Children's Encyclopedia* is closely linked to subjects across the curriculum at Key Stage 2. This and other CD-ROM encyclopedias also help improve children's IT skills and abilities.

Another lively CD-ROM encyclopedia is the *Oxford Children's Encyclopedia*, with text, pictures, video-film extracts, animations and games (www.bluemooneducation.co.uk).

Online encyclopedias are becoming popular for home use – with all the potential for family members to support and share each other's research, as well as for use in school. A strong contender for help with homework across the curriculum as well as for more general information is the 2008 *Children's Britannica* with its range of digital and online resources, including an A–Z browser and a Homework help desk. The resource is advertised from age six, but I think even ten-year-olds would need adult support to use all the resources of this encyclopedia.

There are a large number of single topic guides and encyclopedias on almost every topic you can think of, but particularly on science, history and space. Caroline Bingham's *Space Encyclopedia*, published by Dorling Kindersley, has a good global organization and includes sections on 'What is space?', 'Exploring space', 'The solar system' and 'Comets and meteors'. The section on 'Mysteries of space' covers aliens, UFOs and 'Are there other earths?' So there is a great deal of useful information and encouragement to argue the case for and against the possibility of human life on other planets.

Dorling Kindersley's *e.Encyclopedia Science* is up to the usual high standard of illustration and organization of material of this publishing house. But Felix Pirani is concerned about the spread on the Universe, in which 'dark matter and dark energy are hopelessly mixed up' (Pirani, 2005: 28). This book has a dedicated website with links to other sites, but of course teachers have to be alert to the quality of the websites to which this and other encyclopedias direct children.

The Usborne Internet-Linked Encyclopedia of Science, written by Judy Tatchell, has a splendid A–Z dictionary of scientific terms. One reviewer on Amazon comments that the print text gives 'the basics' while the websites are 'in-depth and detailed'. *Books for Keeps* gave *The Way the Universe Works* by Robin Kerrod and Giles Sparrow the accolade of four stars. This large format book is a hugely interesting and challenging book for able children in the last year of the primary school and beyond.

Dorling Kindersley's Eyewitness guides are technically good, have high-quality colour illustrations and show us new ways of presenting information. *Ancient Rome* by Simon James includes a large wall chart, an interactive clip-art CD and has a dedicated website. Children can see virtual sea battles and aspects of the Roman lifestyle like visits to the Roman Baths. However, as with all publications for children, we have to keep our critical hats on and, as we would expect from such a huge publishing enterprise, some titles work better than others.

STUDY GUIDES

Study guides sit with reference texts and topics range from map reading to books on grammar and punctuation. 'Study guide' seems too sober a categorization for Kate Petty and Jenny Maizels' exciting multimodal book *The Great Grammar Book*. This is the first of a ground-breaking series which have pull-outs, pop-ups and ingenious paper engineering. Nouns, verbs, adjectives, pronouns, prepositions and conjunctions are all covered and explained, but the young reader is in control in this interactive book. In their *The Perfect Pop-Up Punctuation Book* young readers pull tabs to lift commas and apostrophes into the right place. Children will like the amusing devices; for example, little tadpole commas are rescued from extinction from the jaws of scary pike! Another book which uses humour to teach about language, solely about commas in fact, is *Eats Shoots and Leaves: Why, Commas Really Do Make a Difference* by Lynne Truss. More conventional, but still amusingly illustrated, are the Usborne Study Guides which cover spelling, punctuation and grammar; see, for example, Nicola Irving's *The Usborne Guide to English Punctuation*.

THE IMPORTANCE OF 'WONDERING'

Sometimes bright new encyclopedias with beautiful photography and impeccable indexes and glossaries can suggest everything is 'out there' and not negotiable. They may not awaken or reinforce the capacity 'to wonder' that Margaret Meek thinks so important in learning and the development of critical thinking and reading. We must include the potential for 'the imaginative interpretations most children bring to their book learning' (Meek, 1996: 46).

There is also a need for quirky, original books that encourage children to think and speculate. Books on hobbies are often like this and I have found that children, if encouraged, bring into school their own favourites on science, space and history to show and share with other children. Charlotte Voake's *A Child's Guide to Wild Flowers* certainly gets children involved and wondering. The drawings of the wild flowers are beautiful and sufficiently detailed to make identification easy. The annotation is helpful, giving hints about distinguishing between flowers that seem superficially similar. The very best encyclopedias have the features mentioned below, but also have that special something that makes them precious and memorable.

Criteria for choosing print encyclopedias

*   *Design*: including a good global structure and easy to use retrieval devices. Uncluttered pages are most likely to make for clarity and have aesthetic appeal. Devices like 'find out more' direct young readers to other relevant entries but if there are too many complicated devices they can be counterproductive.
*   *Coverage*: an appropriate core of entries, some of which extend children's thinking about the familiar and about curriculum areas, and others which will introduce the new, the fascinating and the thought-provoking.
*   *Language and illustration*: setting out information and ideas clearly, accurately and in an interesting way that makes the young reader want to find out more.

and

*   An authorial voice which distinguishes between fact and opinion and which approaches knowledge as something which grows and changes as more information is discovered.
*   Illustrations which work with the written text to explain the topics and ideas accurately and well.
*   Enough interest and liveliness to encourage children to browse through the text for sheer enjoyment.

When checking coverage of 'one-volume' print encyclopedias for younger children, it is important to make sure that each topic is covered to the right sort of depth. Too many entries might mean rather superficial coverage of a lot of things so that children's curiosity is not awakened and their questions not answered. These general criteria apply to print and electronic encyclopedias. Here are some extra things to consider when looking at multimedia packages.

Criteria for choosing multimedia encyclopedias

The best are not just books on screen, but allow users to explore pathways and make effective use of sound and moving image. Being able to see function as well as structure – for example plants growing, machines working, arterial systems functioning and animals moving – is motivating and often more illuminating than a print picture. What are some of the things to look for in judging the worth of a CD-ROM? How far does it:

- make imaginative use of the technology by offering good images and audio experiences?
- offer quality content, taking account of accuracy, comprehensiveness and creativity?
- enable the user of the age it is intended for to navigate easily?

NON-BOOK PRINT

One of the most traditional kinds of non-book print used in classrooms has been the print wallchart. The best of these charts encourage children to look and talk about the information set out. There are charts covering every possible subject and topic across the curriculum. The same general criteria for choosing apply here – good design, coverage and language use for a particular age group. Autumn Publishing have a clear, uncluttered, laminated series,

---

Here are named the sort of distinctive and original books that turn some children into readers and researchers.

- *My Map Book* by Sara Fanelli (HarperCollins)
  Includes maps with emotional significance – 'maps of my heart' and 'a map of my dog'.

- *The Book about Books* by Chris Powling (A&C Black)
  This covers the history of book publishing, design, illustration and writing. It also speculates about the future of books.

- *Kings and Queens* by Tony Robinson (Red Fox)
  I noticed that a young reader was chuckling over the illustration of deeds, achievements and disasters of English monarchs while I was perusing some of the more sober books on the shelf at the Kensington branch of Waterstones.

- *Bugs: A Close-Up View of the Insect World* by Chris Maynard (Dorling Kindersley)
  This is a large, good value for money book with colourful illustrations and clear text about the lifestyles, habitats, friends and predators of the insect world.

Figure 33.9 *Unusual reference books*

including *My First World Map Wall Chart* (www.autumnpublicating.net/pdfs/wallcharts). Daydream Education have charts entitled 'Adjectives, Verbs and Adverbs', 'Clichés, Idioms and Proverbs' and 'Antonyms'. The geography selection from this publisher is also comprehensive with charts on 'Map Symbols' and 'Mapping Skills' (see Figure 33.7). There is a chart showing the British Isles (GE 026 depicts the Sahara Desert) and human geography topics like population and tourism.

As we might expect, there has been development of e-learning applications and the print wallcharts are mostly now available as interactive whiteboard charts.

SUMMARY

- Different reference texts serve different functions in children's learning. Dictionaries and thesauri are companions to keep handy for writing tasks, map books and atlases are central to finding things out in geography lessons and encyclopedias are often a 'first port of call' whenever a new topic is started in any lesson.
- A first step to evaluating reference texts, whether print or electronic, is to consider the quality of design, coverage and language and illustration.
- These elements need to work together to help children think and learn.
- Teachers seek to make a collection of good-quality, age-related and exciting print and multimedia reference texts for the classroom and central library collections.
- Encyclopedias that stand out draw children into the topics they explain and make young readers start to 'wonder' and to want to find out more.
- Use of reference books is more meaningful when well embedded in the bigger shapes of learning and in topics in lessons across the curriculum.
- Children often come to reference texts with new insight if they have had the opportunity to make their own.

Chapter 34

Using the school and classroom libraries

INTRODUCTION

One sign that a primary school has a good library is the presence of children engrossed in books and computer activities throughout the day. This is more likely to be the case if there is enough room for a whole class to use the library together and sufficient books and ICT resources for them all to use them at the same time. If you are fortunate enough to be setting up a new library you would find 'Our Beautiful New Library', an article by Ann Leeming, helpful (Leeming, 2008: 15–16). She describes the setting up of the library, called the Michael Rosen Library, at Milton Road Primary School in Cambridgeshire. This was made an exciting room with internet café style computers and high stools. The creative design also includes the provision of play tunnels for the younger children where they can enjoy reading their books and seeing their reflections in the mirrors. Even if you are improving and refreshing an existing library you could take up some of the ideas: making the library a pleasant space to walk through with interesting displays; working towards providing a good balance between books and IT. This chapter looks at library provision and at how children can be helped to use the books and resources.

USING THE CLASSROOM AND SCHOOL LIBRARY

Non-fiction texts are a central part of both the classroom and school collections as they support learning in every lesson. Good library provision has three features: quality resources covering the whole range of print and multimedia texts for different ages and abilities, good availability during the school day and outside it and carefully managed help by the Library Manager in how to use the search facilities. The School Library Association campaigns for these three essential features and the funding that makes them possible. The first has been considered throughout this book, while the second is, at present, up to the judgement of the management team in each primary school. Of great importance is the third essential: the competence of the person in charge of the library. Library Managers certainly need a good knowledge of children's literature and ideally a library qualification. If the person is a member of the school staff, they need some designated library time to carry out this additional task.

A simplified Dewey system has long been the preferred way of organizing non-fiction materials in the primary school library. Those setting up a school library or reorganizing an existing one would find helpful *The Primary School Classification Scheme* (SLA, 2004). This package

367

includes a Subject Index and a simple database on a CD-ROM together with a Practical Guide and a poster with classification numbers. Advice on all aspects of stocking and running a school library is available on the School Library Association website (www.sla.org.uk).

When a class is working in the library teachers have a good opportunity to observe, assess and record children's developing abilities to use all the facilities. How well are they getting on with finding texts using the Dewey system and are they developing useful skills like skimming (to get the gist of an argument) and scanning (to seek a date or name), use of retrieval devices and note-taking strategies? In her talk to the Write Away conference in May 2008, Nicola Davies remarked that 'a child who learns to use an index is equipped with a crucial research strategy for life' (Davies, unpublished paper given on 22 May 2008). Interestingly, Bakewell, of the Society of Indexers, found in a small-scale study evidence that children confident in using indexes for print resources transferred this skill in finding their way around electronic sources and the internet (Bakewell, 2000). Older children as well as the teacher or Library Manager can help by demonstrating how to use an index as well as how to browse and how to 'scan' for facts and how to 'skim read' to get the gist of a passage or chapter. Some schools encourage older children to volunteer to be trained to be school library assistants; often a certificate is awarded to those who have learnt a core of skills: putting books into alphabetical order, using retrieval devices, explaining how to use electronic search engines and supporting younger children.

The library supports learning in every subject, but it is usually the English Manager who, with the help of colleagues, develops a structured programme of library and research strategies as part of the English Communication and Languages policy (Rose, 2009).

As well as a central library, most schools have classroom collections of books and resources. A designated area for language and literacy supports informational kinds of literacy by providing a core collection of reference texts, print and electronic, including dictionaries, thesauri and encyclopedias. Non-book print like magazines and posters also has a place. From time to time resources to support lessons across the curriculum may be borrowed from the central library. Display areas can reflect the work in hand and include a message board and posters with advice about using particular kinds of texts and resources. The most useful language and literacy areas also provide listening points with CD players and headphones and an area for discussion, group work and role play. The emphasis of the area will change as children move through the primary school. The texts will be more demanding and children will be more experienced at using the area independently and creatively. At every age the area is central in teaching about study and research skills which will be reinforced during designated library time.

STUDY AND RESEARCH SKILLS

We hope that by the end of the primary years children will be able to access and use a wide range of non-fiction including both print and ICT resources and that they will be able to use these to explore information and ideas in-depth. There is a need for a structured programme, each year group's work building on the one before. There has to be some direct teaching too, but this can nearly always be linked with what children are actually learning at a particular time. They are unlikely to be set alight by mechanical exercises unrelated to anything else

CASE STUDY 34.1 YEAR 5 AND 6 CHILDREN TAKE ON THE ROLE OF LIBRARY MONITORS

Children at a London primary school who had volunteered to help in the school library were given some training by the English Manager and awarded badges to show their status. They used part of their lunch hours on designated days to help a teacher. Their responsibilities included:

- marking new books with the school stamp;
- helping with library displays;
- creating charts giving advice about using print resources and software and the internet;
- arranging books on the shelves and generally helping to keep the library tidy;
- helping younger children find texts and resources;
- attending meetings about library matters.

they are doing or thinking about. So if learning about retrieval devices is one of the things to be covered in Year 2, they can be helped to look at the print books they are using in science, history or geography. And then they would enjoy making their own little fact books with contents page, index and glossary. Children need to know what it is like to care passionately about a subject or issue, to talk about developing ideas and to feel their teacher supports and really cares about their progress as readers and writers. These bigger shapes frame all classroom learning: information seeking strategies are not an end in themselves.

Note-taking

Making notes from secondary sources – print books, non-book print, electronic sources and film – is usually seen as part of the quiver of study skills. But we need to keep in mind that becoming competent demands the interaction of a number of different skills and abilities. It needs children to come to understand the hierarchical structure of information. Picking out the main idea in a passage, for example, is an intellectual and not just a mechanical achievement. Becoming able to produce clear, useful notes as a basis for writing makes a young researcher more likely to find their own 'voice' and less likely to produce very close paraphrases of what is in the texts they are reading. The purpose of the notes and the audience they are aimed at are the main guides to the best structure and content.

The purpose of a particular note-taking task is well worth clarifying. Having bigger purposes makes it more worthwhile and interesting and so pupils are prepared to put in the concentrated effort needed. The notes may be to answer some questions a child or the children in a group have about a topic. This is a very good way into using secondary sources as the pupil is in the driving seat of the research. These questions help a pupil decide which resources are most likely to be helpful. With some adult support, quite young children can be helped to 'scan' contents pages and indexes to see if relevant information is promised. The quality of the resource and its usefulness for a particular task are only evident when children use contents and index to find the relevant part of the book. Then we ask: is the information detailed enough to help with the question?

Questions give a focus, but a child also needs to take account of how the notes will be used. Their purpose may be to support a speaking and listening context – an oral contribution, for example, or to prepare for a focused discussion or to give input to a lesson. Or they may be intended to enrich a written account, linking information gained from first-hand experience and observation with information from secondary sources. After a walk around the school grounds to observe and draw spiders and their webs, seven-year-olds were then helped to read books about web making and to jot down some facts to integrate into their writing. At other times notes might be a mnemonic or provide a record, for example of a reading task showing how it fed into study of a topic.

The sense of audience needed when you write notes is closely linked to purpose. Notes that serve as records or mnemonics are clearly for the writer's use. Oral and written presentations are usually for a known audience in primary school and it is wise to keep that audience in mind at the note-taking stage. To illustrate this an example helps. I remember a ten-year-old giving some input from notes from an encyclopedia to a lesson about Tudor food. When the children were asked if they had found the talk useful, one child said: 'I like the way he told us about food for the wealthy and poor and gave us some examples . . . showed us some pictures . . . of real Tudor meals and feasts to make it interesting.'

Some suggestions to support note-taking

(This draws on a list in *Active Encounters*, Mallett, 2007a: 24.) Different strategies work for different children and teachers and so the ideas here – all examples of what I have used myself or seen others use successfully – are offered for consideration. Good note-taking is linked to general intellectual development and so younger children and those with special educational needs require more support.

Pre-school and nursery, 3–5-year-olds

At the pre-school and nursery stage oral work prepares children for note-taking later on. The sort of conversations parents, nursery teachers and children have around early fact books are the precursor of the kind of organized thinking that subsequently leads to note-taking.

5–8-year-olds

- Scribing: which allows struggling writers to articulate their points and see them written down.
- Making joint notes with a partner: being paired with a 'response partner' to help make their thinking explicit.
- Shared note-taking: teacher demonstrates note-taking from a text on the whiteboard, preferably a text relevant to a current history, geography or science theme. The text needs to be rich enough to summarize. Ask children to say which are the most important sentences. Simplify these and place on a flipchart or notepad on the whiteboard. Children have the opportunity to internalize the thinking and reasoning of a mature reader and writer.

CASE STUDY 34.2 A NURSERY CLASS TALK ABOUT WHAT HAS BEEN LEARNT ABOUT COLOUR

A nursery teacher asked a class of four-year-olds what they could remember about the colour of the week – brown. In their responses the children drew both on their first-hand experience of looking at brown plants and creatures in the school grounds and on the books they had used. They remembered that: brown is the colour of mud and earth, that a lot of birds and small animals are brown so that they cannot be seen by their enemies against a brown background, and brown is the colour of some favourite foods like meat, chocolate and mushrooms. This kind of talk and remembering what they have learnt gives children a structure in which to make mental 'notes', creating the foundation for note-taking later on. A 'next step' would be for the teacher to scribe the main points the children mentioned on an interactive whiteboard or print flipchart.

- Using a highlighter pen or electronic tool to mark key sentences, phrases and then presenting them as bullet point notes; this can be a shared task.
- Making a diagram: texts explaining processes or a journey lend themselves to being recorded as annotated pictures rather than always using written notes.
- Creating a table: sometimes it helps to organize research under sub-topics. Each sub-topic can be named at the head of a column, for example: a plant's habitat, structure, life cycle and uses. This helps with global organization and with achieving balance.
- Using a notepad: software and CD-ROMs often provide this.
- Using Sue Palmer's visual approach to note-taking – see her large format *Skeleton Poster Book*. Her spider diagram helps plan report writing; each leg has a note written along it and can become a sub-heading in the written account (Palmer, 2004).

8–11-year-olds

Older primary children continue to use some of the strategies above and, in addition, will find useful:

- Listing: putting main information in a list or in bullet points.
- Focused work on the internet, so they do not end up with pages of notes downloaded from websites. The focus might be some questions or headings arrived at during a class or group discussion.
- Constructing questionnaires in science and mathematics using software to help with design.
- Highlighting: after experience of shared note-taking some children will become able to highlight the main point on photocopies of texts. Different colours can be used to indicate main points, subordinate points and examples. Information that seems puzzling can be marked with a symbol.
- Assessing their own notes, perhaps reshaping them by putting in sub-headings or 'bullet points' some information – easier when the notes are on the computer.

CASE STUDY 34.3 A YEAR 4 CLASS USE BULLET POINTS TO SUMMARIZE WORK ON FORCES IN SCIENCE AND LITERACY

The children had acquired information in the following ways: demonstrating the concept of 'force' by pulling and pushing; using and talking about an instrument to measure force called a Newton metre or a Force metre; looking up information on the internet and using books from the non-fiction shelf in the classroom. After class discussion to help weave together insights from all these lines of investigation, the children made bullet point notes in their workbooks. The teacher put up some of the children's lists on the whiteboard. In Figure 34.1 below is Taylor's bullet point summary, followed by Figure 34.2 which shows the amendments made during the teacher's discussion with the class. They decided that short bullet points needed no full stops, the symbol (N) needed to be in brackets and the last bullet point needed to be shortened.

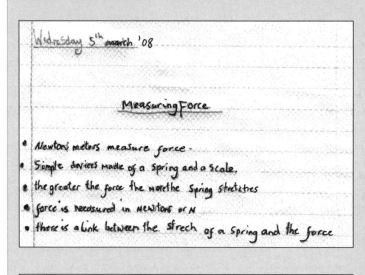

Figure 34.1
Taylor's bullet point notes

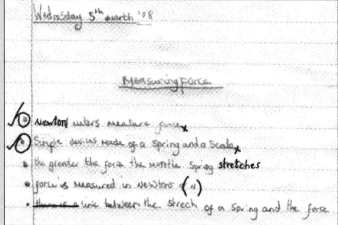

Figure 34.2
Taylor's bullet point notes amended after class discussion

SUMMARY

- Good library provision has three elements: quality resources, accessibility and carefully managed help to search the facilities.
- This needs to be supported by a structured programme of teaching library and study skills.
- Such programmes are best placed within the context of the bigger shapes of learning that give children the will and interest to concentrate and make progress.

Chapter 35

Conclusion to Part II

As Part II nears its end, let me leave you with some last thoughts. Children need to be at the controls when it comes to using reference and indeed all information texts. We encourage this by making critical reading important from the earliest stages so that children can develop their own viewpoints and their own 'voice' when they speak and when they write. Of course we need to provide children with quality resources and teach them the study skills and abilities that young researchers need. But we want them to know that 'the facts' are extended and amended constantly, as are our attitudes towards them. New theories about why the dinosaurs died out are constantly emerging and the discovery of new planets and stars modifies what is known about the universe. We want children also to come to realize that some texts are better than others for particular tasks. Children and adults often turn to internet encyclopedias – Wikipedia for example – for help with finding information and this sometimes helps. But many classrooms have a shelf or basket of print non-fiction encylopedias and books and, for many kinds of information gathering, perhaps checking a timeline for a historical figure or seeking a succinct definition of a phenomenon or concept, these prove quicker and better. This is why many teachers ask the class which resources they found most helpful at the end of a project or a series of lessons.

And finally I would like to draw attention to new and exciting research and thinking which applies Wolfgang Iser's notion of the 'implied reader' to children's non-fiction. A Canadian scholar, Patricia Larkin-Lieffers, finds that different 'factual' texts present the young reader as either active or passive (Larkin-Lieffers, 2010). This suggests that we should recognize the potential power of information texts, print and electronic, in shaping children's reading experiences and cultural understandings.

Bibliography

Alderson, B. (2001) 'Fairy Tales in the New Millenium', in *Books for Keeps* 131, November.

Alderson, B. (2004) 'Classics in Short 48: Lavender's Blue', in *Books for Keeps* 149, November.

Alderson, B. (2006) 'Classics in Short 59: The Jungle Books', in *Books for Keeps* 160, September.

Alderson, B. (2007) 'Classics in Short 64: The History of Aesop's Fables', in *Books For Keeps* 165, July. (There is an extension of this article which gives an overview of the progress of Fable Publishing for Children on the *Books for Keeps* website: www.booksforkeeps.co.uk, site accessed 31 May 2009.)

Alderson, B. (2008) 'Classics in Short 69: Picture History of Britain', in *Books for Keeps* 170, May.

Alderson, B. (2009) 'Classics in Short 75: Forty Years of Munching', in *Books for Keeps* 75, May.

Alexander, C. (2000) 'The Cymbeline Project' in *English 4–11* 9, Winter.

Alexander, R. (2009) *Children, Their World, Their Education: Final Report and Recommendations of the Cambridge Primary Review*. London and New York: Routledge.

Alston, A. (2008) *The Family in English Children's Literature*. London: Routledge.

Anstey, M. and Bull, G. (2004) 'The Picturebook: Modern and Postmodern', in P. Hunt (ed.), *International Companion Encyclopedia of Children's Literature*, 2nd edn. London: Routledge.

Applebee, A. (1978) *The Child's Concept of Story*. Chicago, IL: University of Chicago Press.

Arizpe, E. and Styles, M. (2003) *Children Reading Pictures: Interpreting Visual Texts*. London: RoutledgeFalmer.

Avery, G. (1995) 'Beginnings of Children's Reading to 1700', in P. Hunt, *Children's Literature: An Illustrated History*. Oxford: Oxford University Press.

Avery, G. (2004) 'The Family Story', in P. Hunt (ed.), *International Companion Encyclopedia of Children's Literature*, 2nd edn. London: Routledge.

Baker, C.D. and Freebody, P. (1989) *Children's First School Books*. Oxford: Basil Blackwell.

Bakewell, K.G. (2000) 'Indexing Children's Books'. An occasional paper for the Society of Indexers.

Barnes, C. (2008) 'Review of *The Savage*', in *Books for Keeps* 171, July.

Barrs, M. (1987) 'Mapping the World', in *English in Education*, London: NATE, 21: 3.

Barrs, M. and Cork, V. (2001) *The Reader in the Writer: The Links Between the Study of Literature and Writing Development at Key Stage 2*. London: CLPE.

Barrs, M., Ellis, S., Hester, H. and Thomas, A. (1988/95) *The Primary Language Record*. London: CLPE.

Barrs, M., Ellis, S., Hester, H. and Thomas, A. (1998) *CLPE Language and Reading Record*. London: CLPE.

Barrs, M. and Pidgeon, S. (2002) *Boys and Writing*. London: CLPE.

Barrs, M. and Thomas, A. (1991) *The Reading Book*. London: CLPE.

Bate, J. and Rasmussen, E. (eds) (2007) *The RSC Shakespeare: The Complete Works*. London: Palgrave Macmillan.

Baxter, J. (2001) *Making Gender Work*. Reading: Reading and Language Information Centre.

Bearne, E. (2002) 'Multimodal Narratives', in M. Barrs and S. Pidgeon (eds), *Boys and Writing*. London: Centre for Literacy in Primary Education.

Bearne, E. (2003) 'Playing with Possibilities: Children's Multidimensional Texts', in E. Bearne, H. Dombey and T. Grainger (eds), *Classroom Interactions in Literacy*. Maidenhead: Open University Press.

Bearne, E. (2004) 'Multimodal Texts: What They Are and How Children Use Them', in J. Evans (ed.), *Literacy Moves On: Using Popular Culture, New Technologies and Critical Literacy in the Primary Classroom*. London: David Fulton.

Bearne, E. (2009) 'Multimodality, Literacy, and Texts: Developing a Discourse', *Journal of Early Childhood Literacy*. Special edition Multimodality. London: Sage. August, 2009.

Bearne, E., Clark, C., Johnson, A., Manford, P., Mottram, M. and Wolstencroft, H. (2007) *Reading on Screen*. Leicester: UKLA.

Bearne, E., Ellis, S., Graham, L., Hulme, P., Merchant, G. and Mills, C. (2004) *More than Words: Multimodal Texts in the Classroom*. London: QCA/UKLA.

Bearne, E., Ellis, S., Graham, L., Hulme, P., Meiner, J. and Wolstencroft, M. (2005) *More than Words 2: Creating Stories on Page and Screen*. London: QCA/UKLA.

Bednall, J., Cranston, L. and Bearne, E. (2008) 'The Most Wonderful Adventure: Going Beyond the Literal', in *English 4–11* 31, Spring.

Bennett, J. (1991) *Learning to Read with Picture Books*. Stroud: Signal, The Thimble Press.

Bennett, J. (2008) 'Sounding Off! Some Noisy Picture Books', in *Books for Keeps* 173, November.

Benton, M. and Fox, G. (1985) *Teaching Literature, Nine to Fourteen*. Oxford: Oxford University Press.

Bereiter, C. and Scardamalia, M. (1987) *The Psychology of Written Composition*. Hillsdale, NH: Lawrence Erlbaum.

Bettleheim, B. (1988) *The Uses of Enchantment: The Meaning and Importance of Fairy Tales*. London: Penguin.

Bickler, S., Baker, S. and Bodmin, S. (2007) *Book Bands for Guided Reading: A Handbook to Support Foundation and Key Stage 1 Teachers*, 4th edn. London: Institute of Education.

Booker, C. (2004) *The Seven Basic Plots*. London: Continuum.

Booktrust survey (2007/8) 'The Best Children's Book of All Time'. www.booktrustchildrensbooks.org.uk. Accessed 2 February 2009.

Bottigheimer, R.B. (2004) 'Fairy Tales and Folk Tales', in P. Hunt (ed.) *International Companion Encyclopedia of Children's Literature*, 2nd edn. London: Routledge.

Bottoms, J. (2005) 'Shakespeare for Juniors: Introducing Playworlds', in *The Primary English Magazine,* 10: 3, February.

Bradley, M. and Bryant, P. (1983) 'Categorising Sounds and Learning to Read: A Causal Connection'. *Nature*, 301.

Bramwell, P. (2004) 'Feminism and History: Historical Fiction – Not Just a Thing of the Past', in K. Reynolds (ed.), *Modern Children's Literature*. London: Palgrave Macmillan.

Briggs, J. (1995) 'Transitions (1890–1914)', in P. Hunt (ed.), *Children's Literature: An Illustrated History*. Oxford and New York: Oxford University Press.

Briggs, K. (1991) *Dictionary of British Folk Tales*. London: Routledge.

Briggs, K. (2002) *The Fairies in Tradition and Literature*, 2nd edn. London: Routledge.

Brine, A. (1991) 'Faith in Story', in *Books for Keeps* 69, July.

Brinton, I. (2004) *Skellig by David Almond: Text and Context*. English Association Primary Bookmarks. No. I. Leicester: The English Association.

British Film Institute (2003) *Look Again! A Teaching Guide to Using Film and Television with Three- to Eleven-Year-Olds*. London: BFI Education.

Britton, J.N. (1970) *Language and Learning*. London: The Allen Lane Press.

Britton, J.N. (1977) 'The Role of Fantasy', in M. Meek, A. Warlow and G. Barton (eds), *The Cool Web: The Pattern of Children's Reading*. London: The Bodley Head.

Bromley, H. (2003) *Author Study Activities for Key Stage 2*. London: David Fulton.

Bromley, H. (2004) 'Storyboxes', *The Primary English Magazine*, 9: 5, June.

Bromley, H. (2004) *50 Exciting Ideas for Storyboxes*. London: Lawrence Educational Publications.

Brown, N. (1999) *Young Children's Literacy Development and the Role of Televisual Texts*. London: Routledge.

Brownjohn, S. (1994) *To Rhyme or Not to Rhyme?* London: Hodder & Stoughton.

Brownjohn, S. (1995) 'Rhyme in Children's Writing', in R. Beard (ed.), *Rhyme, Reading and Writing*. London: Hodder & Stoughton.

Bruner, J. (1967) *Towards a Theory of Instruction*. Harvard: Belknap Press.

Bruner, J. (1981) *Actual Minds, Possible Worlds*. Cambridge, MA: MIT Press.

Bryant, P. (1993) 'Phonological Aspects of Learning to Read', in R. Beard (ed.), *Teaching Literacy, Balancing Perspectives*. London: Hodder & Stoughton.

Bryson, B. (2001) *Shakespeare: The World as a Stage*. London: HarperPress.

Buckingham, D. (1999) 'Superhighway or Road to Nowhere?', *English in Education*, 33 (1).

Buckingham, D. (2003) *Media Education: Literacy, Learning and Contemporary Culture*. London: Polity Press.

Bunting, J., Nicholson, D. and Barrs, M. (2006) *Book Power: Literacy Through Literature, Year 6*. London: Centre for Literacy in Primary Education.

Burn, A. and Leach, J. (2004) *A Systematic Review of the Impact of ICT on the Learning of Literacies Associated with Moving Image Texts in English, 5–15*. London: EPPI Centre, Social Science Research Unit, Institute of Education, University of London.

Burnett, C. and Wilkinson, J. (2005) 'Holy Lemons! Learning from Children's Usages of the Internet in Out-of-School Contexts', *Literacy*, 39 (2).

Callow, J. (ed.) (1999) *Visual Images: Visual Texts in the Classroom*. Marrickville, Australia: PETA The Primary English Teaching Association.

Campbell, R. (1995/ 2002) *Reading in the Early Years Handbook*. Milton Keynes: Open University Press.

Carpenter, H. and Prichard, M. (1984) *The Oxford Companion to Children's Literature*. Oxford: Oxford University Press.

Carter, D. (1998) *Teaching Poetry in the Primary School*. London: David Fulton.

Chambers, A. (1991) *The Reading Environment: How Adults Help Children Enjoy Books*. Stroud: The Thimble Press.

Chambers, A. (1993) *Tell Me: Children Reading and Talk*. Stroud: The Thimble Press.

Chukovsky, K. (1963) *From Two to Five*. Los Angeles, CA: University of California Press.

Collins, F. and Graham, J. (eds) (2001) *Historical Fiction for Children: Capturing the Past*. London: Routledge/David Fulton.

Cook, E. (1971) *The Ordinary and the Fabulous: An Introduction to Myths, Legends and Fairy Tales for Teachers and Storytellers*. Cambridge: Cambridge University Press.

Cremin, T., Goouch, K., Blakemore, I., Goff, E. and Macdonald, R. (2006) 'Connecting Drama and Writing: Seizing the Moment to Write', *Research in Drama Education*. 11, 3.

Cremin, T., Bearne, E., Mottram, M. and Goodwin, P. (2007) *Teachers as Readers: Phase 1*. Research report on UKLA's website (www.ukla.org.uk – link is TARwebreport.LIJ).

Crossley-Holland, K. (1982) 'The Northern Myths', in *Books for Keeps* 16, September.

Culler, J. (1975) *Structural Poetics*. London: Routledge.

Culler, J. (2000) *Literary Theory*. Oxford: Oxford Paperbacks, OUP.

Davies, N. (2005) 'Adventures in the Real World', unpublished introduction to the conference on children's non-fiction at the Dylan Thomas Centre, Swansea Festival, 20 October.

Davies, N. (2008) 'Writing Non-Fiction for Children', unpublished paper presented to the 2008 Write Away conference 'Non-Fiction: More than Information' at the London Institute of Education, 22 May.

Department for Children, Schools and Families (2007) *Primary National Strategy: Letters and Sounds*. London: DCSF.

Department for Children, Schools and Families (2008) *Primary National Strategy: Early Years Foundation Stage Framework*. London: DCSF.

De Rijke, V. (2004) 'Horror', in P. Hunt (ed.), *International Companion Encyclopedia of Children's Literature*, 2nd edn. London: Routledge.

DfEE (1999) *The National Curriculum*. London: HMSO.

DfES (2006) *Primary National Strategy: Primary Framework for Literacy and Mathematics*. London: HMSO.

Donaldson, M. (1979) *Children's Minds*. London: Fontana Press.

Dymoke, S. (2003) *Drafting and Assessing Poetry: A Guide for Teachers*. London: Paul Chapman.

Elkin, J. (1983) 'Traditional Tales in a Multicultural Society', in *Books for Keeps* 20, May.

Evans, J. (ed.) (2004) *Literacy Moves On: Using Popular Culture, New Technologies and Critical Literacy in the Primary Classroom*. London: David Fulton.

Fellows, A. (2001) 'Stimulating the Historical Imagination: Working with Primary Age Children on Books about the Plague', in F.M. Collins and J. Graham (eds), *Historical Fiction for Children*. London: David Fulton/Routledge.

Fine, A. (2007) 'Write and Wrong', *Times* 2 p. 4 in *The Times*. 13 July.

Fish, S.E. (1980) *Is There a Text in this Class? The Authority of Interpretive Communities*, Boston, MA: Harvard University Press.

Fisher, A. (2008) 'Developing a Poetry-Friendly Classroom', in *English 4–11*, 33, Summer.

Fisher, F. (2004) 'Historical Fiction', in P. Hunt (ed.), *International Companion Encyclopedia of Children's Literature*, 2nd edn. London: Routledge.

Flynn, S. (2004) 'Animal Stories' in P. Hunt (ed.), *International Companion Encyclopedia of Chidren's Literature*, 2nd edn. London: Routledge.

Foreman, M. (2001) 'Flesh on the Bones', in F.M. Collins and J. Graham (eds), *Historical Fiction for Children*. London: David Fulton/Routledge.

Fox, C. and Hunt, P. (2004) 'War', in P. Hunt (ed.), *International Companion Encyclopedia of Children's Literature*, 2nd edn. London: Routledge.

Galton, M. (2007) *Learning and Teaching in the Primary Classroom*. London: Sage.

Gamble, N. (2004) 'Teaching Fiction' in P. Hunt (ed.), *International Companion Encyclopedia of Children's Literature*, 2nd edn. London: Routledge.

Gamble, N. and Yates, S. (2008) *Exploring Children's Literature*, 2nd edn. London: Paul Chapman Publishing.

Gee, J.P. (2004) *What Video Games Have to Teach Us about Learning and Literacy*. London: Palgrave Macmillan.

Glen, P. (1987) *Mr Togs the Tailor: A Context for Writing*. Scotland: Scottish Consultative Council on the Curriculum.

Gopnik, A., Kuhl, P.K. and Meltzoff, A. (1999) *How Babies Think: The Science of Childhood*. London: Phoenix, Orion.

Goswami, U. (1995) 'Rhyme in Children's Early Reading', in R. Beard (ed.), *Rhyme, Reading and Writing*. London: Hodder & Stoughton.

Goswami, U. and Bryant, P.E. (1990) *Phonological Skills and Learning to Read*. Hove: Lawrence Erlbaum.

378

Graham, J. (2005) 'Reading Contemporary Picturebooks', in K. Reynolds (ed.), *Modern Children's Literature*. London: Palgrave Macmillan.

Graham, J. and Kelly, A. (2003) *Writing Under Control*. London: David Fulton.

Graham, J. and Kelly, A. (2007) *Reading Under Control*, 3rd edn. London: David Fulton.

Graham, L. and Johnson, A. (2003) *Children's Writing Journals*. UKLA minibook. Leicester: UKLA.

Hallford, D., Zaghini, E. and Blake, Q. (illus.) (2005) *Folk and Fairy Tales: A Book Guide*. London: Booktrust.

Halliday, M.A.K. and Hasan, R. (1976) *Cohesion in English*. Harlow: Longman.

Hardy, B. (1977) 'Narrative as a Primary Act of Mind', in M. Meek, A. Warlow and G. Barton (eds), *The Cool Web*. London: The Bodley Head.

Harvey, S. (1998) *Non-Fiction Matters*. York, ME: Stenhouse Publishers.

Haymonds, A. (2004) 'Pony Books', in P. Hunt (ed.), *International Companion Encyclopedia of Children's Literature*, 2nd edn. London: Routledge.

Hendrickson, L. (2001) 'Biography and Autobiography', in V. Watson (ed.), *The Cambridge Guide to Children's Books in English*. Cambridge: Cambridge University Press.

Hobsbaum, A., Bickler, S. and Baker, S. (2004) *Bridging Bands for Guided Reading: Resourcing for Diversity at Key Stage 2*. London: Institute of Education.

Hobsbaum, A., Gamble, N. and Reedy, D. (2006) *Guiding Readers: A Handbook for Teaching Guided Reading at Key Stage 2*. London: Institute of Education.

Holifield, C. (2008) 'Where Have All the Poetry Books Gone?', in *English 4–11*. Autumn.

Hollindale, P. (2008) Review of 'Hazel's Phantasmagoria', in *Books for Keeps* 171, July.

Hoodless, P. (1998) 'Children's Awareness of Time in Story and Historical Fiction', in P. Hoodless (ed.), *History and English: Exploiting the Links*. London: Routledge.

Horn, C. (2008) 'Age Guidance', in *Books for Keeps* 171, July.

Hughes, T. (1967) *Poetry in the Making*. London: Faber & Faber.

Hull, R. (2009) 'Wandering Worth Encouraging', in *Books for Keeps* 176, May.

Hunt, P. (1994) *An Introduction to Children's Literature*. Oxford: Oxford Paperbacks.

Hunt, P. (1995) *Children's Literature: An Illustrated History*. Oxford: Oxford University Press.

Hunt, P. (ed.) (2004) *International Companion Encyclopedia of Children's Literature*, 2nd edn. London: Routledge.

Impey, R. (1990) 'Too Scary for Children?', in *Books for Keeps* 61, March.

Iser, W. (1978) *The Act of Reading*. Baltimore, MD: Johns Hopkins University Press.

Jarrett, P. (2008) 'Poetry in Schools: An Ofsted View', in *English 4–11* 31, Spring.

Johnson, A. (2006) 'Investigating the Use of Film to Improve Children's Literacy Skills', in *English 4–11* 26, Spring.

Johnson, C. (2000) 'What Did I Say?: Speaking, Listening and Drama', in R. Fisher and M. Williams (eds), *Unlocking Literacy*. London: David Fulton.

Koch, K. (1998a). *Rose, Where Did You Get that Red? Teaching Great Poetry to Children*. London: Random House, Vintage Books.

Koch, K. (1998b) *Wishes, Lies and Dreams: Teaching Children to Write Poetry*. London: HarperCollins.

Kress, G. (2003) *Literacy in the New Media Age*. London: Routledge.

Kress, G. and van Leeuwen, T. (2006) *Reading Images: The Grammar of Visual Design*, 2nd edn. London: Routledge.

Lankshear, C. and Knobel, M. (2007) *New Literacies: Everyday Practices and Classroom Learning*, 2nd edn. Milton Keynes: Open University Press.

Larkin-Lieffers, P. (2010) 'Images of Childhood and the Implied Reader in Young Children's Information Books', in *Literacy* (in press).

Lathey, G. (2004) 'Autobiography and History: Literature of War', in K. Reynolds (ed.), *Modern Children's Literature*. London: Palgrave Macmillan.

Leeming, A. (2008) 'Our Beautiful New Library: Planning a Primary School Library', in *The School Librarian*, 56: 1, Spring.

Lewis, D. (2001) *Reading Contemporary Picturebooks: Picturing Text*. London: RoutledgeFalmer.

Lewis, M. and Fisher, R. (2003) *Curiosity Kits*. Reading: Reading University.

Littlefair, A. (1991) *Reading All Types of Writing: Importance of Genre and Register for Reading Development*. Milton Keynes: Open University Press.

Longacre, R. (1976) *An Anatomy of Speech Notions*. Lisse: Peter de Riddes.

McArthur, T. (1992) *The Oxford Companion to the English Language*. Oxford: Oxford University Press.

McCaughrean, G. (1996) 'Nasty, Brutish and Short', in *Books for Keeps* 100, September.

Mackintosh, M. (2004) 'Talk and Pictures in Key Stage 2 Geography', in *Primary English Magazine*, Summer.

Macpherson, A. (2004) 'Listening to a Good Book', in *Books for Keeps* 144, January.

Mallett, M. (1992) *Making Facts Matter*. London: Paul Chapman.

Mallett, M. (1997) 'Genre and Gender: Reading and Writing Choices of Older Juniors', in *Reading* (renamed *Literacy*). UKLA, 31 (2), July.

Mallett, M. (2003) *Early Years Non-Fiction: A Guide to Helping Young Researchers Use and Enjoy Information Texts*. London: Routledge.

Mallett, M. (2004) 'Children's Information Texts', in P. Hunt (ed.), *International Companion Encyclopedia of Children's Literature*, 2nd edn. London: Routledge.

Mallett, M. (2006) 'Voices from the Classroom: Children and Their Non-Fiction Texts', in *English 4–11* 26, Spring.

Mallett, M. (2007a) *Active Encounters: Inspiring Young Readers and Writers of Non-Fiction 4–11*. Minibook 24. Leicester: The United Kingdom Literacy Association.

Mallett, M. (2007b) *The Lyrical Voice in Non-Fiction: Think of an Eel by Karen Wallace and Mike Bostock*. English Association Minibook 3. Leicester: The English Association.

Mallett, M. (2007c) 'Meeting Leigh Hobbs', in *English 4–11* 29, Spring.

Mallett, M. (2008a) *The Primary English Encyclopedia*, 3rd edn. London: David Fulton.

Mallett, M. (2008b) 'Marcia Williams' Books for Children: Classic Retellings and Innovative Information Picturebooks', in *English 4–11* 33, Summer.

Mallett, M. (2009) 'Review of *We Are All Born Equal*', in *English 4–11* 36, Summer.

Marcovitch, L. (2006) 'Diversity Matters', letter in *Books for Keeps* 161, November.

Marsh, J. and Millard, E. (2000) *Literacy and Popular Culture: Using Children's Culture in the Classroom*. London: Paul Chapman.

Martin, J., Christie, F. and Rothery, J. (1987) 'Social Processes in Education: A Reply to Sawyer and Watson (and Others)', in I. Reid (ed.), *The Place of Genre in Learning*. Victoria: Deakin University.

Martin, T. and Leather, B. (1994) *Readers and Texts in the Primary Years*. Buckingham. Philadelphia: Open University Press.

Maynard, S., Mackay, S., Smith, F. and Reynolds, K. (2007). *Young People's Reading in 2005: The Second Study of Young People's Reading Habits*. London: National Centre for Research in Children's Literature.

Medwell, J., Moore, G., Wray, D. and Griffiths, V. (2007) *Primary English: Knowledge and Understanding*. Exeter: Learning Matters.

Meek, M. (1988) *How Texts Teach What Readers Learn*. Stroud: The Thimble Press.

Meek, M. (1996) *Information and Book Learning*. Stroud: The Thimble Press.

Meek, M., Warlow, A. and Barton, G. (1977) *The Cool Web: The Pattern of Children's Reading*. London: The Bodley Head.

Melling, J. (2002) 'Briefing', in *Books for Keeps* 132, January.

Merchant, G. (2007) 'Writing the Future in the Digital Age', in *Literacy*, 41: 3.

Merchant, G. (2008) 'Out of the Classroom and into the World', in *English 4–11* 32, Spring.

Millard, E. (1997) *Differently Literate: Boys, Girls and the Schooling of Literacy*. London: Falmer.

Millard, E. (2001) 'Aspects of Gender: How Boys' and Girls' Experiences of Reading Shape Their Writing', in *The Writing Classroom: Aspects of Writing and The Primary School Child*. London: David Fulton.

Mills, R. (2009) 'Hal's Reading Diary', in *Books for Keeps* 176, May.

Morris, J. (2009) 'Picturebooks for Everyone', in *Books for Keeps* 174, January.

Moss, E. (1992) *Picturebooks for Young People, 9–13*, 3rd edn. Stroud: The Thimble Press.

Moss, G. (2000) 'Raising Boys' Achievement in Reading: Some Principles for Intervention', in *Reading*, 36.

Myers, J. and Burnett, C. (2004) *Teaching English 3–13*. London and New York: Continuum International.

Navarro, J.G. (1955) *The Growth of Scientific Concepts in the Young Child*. New York: Teachers' College, Columbia University.

Nikolajeva, M. and Scott, C. (2001) *How Picturebooks Work*. London and New York: Garland Publishing.

Nodelman, P. (1988, 1999) *Words about Pictures: The Narrative Art of Children's Picturebooks*. Athens, GA and London: University of Georgia Press.

Nodelman, P. (1996) *The Pleasures of Children's Literature*. White Plains, NY: Longman.

Norman, R. (1998) 'The Great Persuaders', in *English Language and Literature: An Integrated Approach*. Cheltenham: Nelson Thornes.

Ofsted (2007) *Poetry in Schools: A Survey of Practice*. London: HMSO.

Opie, P. and Opie, I. (1959) *The Lore and Language of Schoolchildren*. Oxford: Oxford University Press.

Opie, P. and Opie, I. (1993) *The Oxford Nursery Rhyme Book*. Oxford: Oxford University Press.

Opie, P. and Opie, I. (1997) *The Oxford Dictionary of Nursery Rhymes*, revised edn. Oxford: Oxford University Press.

O'Sullivan, O. and McGonigle, S. (2009) *The Power of Reading*. London: CLPE. (See summary of the 2005–9 phase at www.clpe.co.uk.)

Pahl, K. (1999) *Transformations: Making Meaning in Nursery Education*. Stoke on Trent: Trentham Books.

Palmer, S. (2003) *How to Teach Writing Across the Curriculum at Key Stage 1; How to Teach Writing Across the Curriculum at Key Stage 2*. London: David Fulton.

Palmer, S. (2004) *Skeleton Poster Books*. London: TTS Group. (These are poster size.)

Pandit, S. (2006) 'Diverse Matters', in *Books for Keeps* 160, September.

Pappas, C. (1986) 'Exploring the Global Structure of Children's Information Books', paper presented to the Annual Meeting of the National Reading Conference, Austin, Texas.

Percy, T. (2008) 'Review of *The Beeman*', in *Books for Keeps* 170, May.

Percy, T. (2008) 'Review of *How to Turn Your Parents Green*', in *Books for Keeps* 169, March.

Philip, N. (2008) 'Why Do We Really Tell Stories?', in *Books for Keeps* 168, January.

Piaget, J. (1952) *The Origin of Intelligence in the Child*. London: Routledge. (There is a later edition translated by Margaret Cook, Penguin 1977.)

Pirani, F. (2000) 'Review of *The DK Space Encyclopedia*', *Books for Keeps* 121, March.

Pirani, F. (2005) 'Review of *The DK e.Encyclopedia Science*', in *Books for Keeps* 150, January.

Pizzi, K. (2004) 'Contemporary Comics', in P. Hunt (ed.), *International Companion Encyclopedia of Children's Literature*, 2nd edn. London: Routledge.

Pullman, P. (1995) 'Partners in a Dance: Philip Pullman on his Enthusiasm for the Graphic Novel', in *Books for Keeps* 92, May.

Ray, S. (2004) 'School Stories', in P. Hunt (ed.), *International Companion Encyclopedia of Children's Literature*, 2nd edn. London: Routledge.

Reid, I. (ed.) (1987) *The Place of Genre in Learning*. Victoria: Deakin University.

Reynolds, K. (ed.) (1996) *Young People's Reading at the End of the Century*. London: Roehampton University National Centre for Research in Children's Literature.

Reynolds, K. (comp. and ed.) (1998) *Childhood Remembered: Proceedings from the 4th Annual IBBY/MA Children's Literature Conference at Roehampton Institute*. London: Roehampton NCRCL Papers, 3.

Reynolds, K. (ed.) (2004) *Modern Children's Literature: An Introduction*. London: Palgrave Macmillan.

Riley, J. and Reedy, D. (2000) *Developing Writing for Different Purposes: Teaching about Genre in the Early Years*. London: Paul Chapman Publishing.

Robins, G. (2009) 'Contemporary Approaches to Classic Texts: H.G. Wells' *War of the Worlds*', *English 4–11* 35, Spring.

Rose, J. (2009) *Independent Review of the Primary Curriculum: Final Report*. London: DCSF.

Rosen, M. (2007) Speech at Michael Rosen's inauguration as Children's Laureate at Bafta on 11 June 2007.

Rosen, M. and Ingpen, R. (illus.) (2001) *Shakespeare: His World and His Work*. London: Walker.

Rudd, D. (2001) 'Enid Mary Blyton', in V. Watson (ed.), *The Cambridge Guide to Children's Books in English*. Cambridge: Cambridge University Press.

Rustin, M. (2004) 'Pullman's Daemons', in *Books for Keeps* 145, March.

Safford, K. (2008) 'Reading in the Middle Years, 9–11', in *Books for Keeps* 170, May.

Safford, K., O'Sullivan, O. and Barrs, M. (2004) *Boys on the Margin: Promoting Boys' Literacy Learning at Key Stage 2*. London: Centre for Literacy in Primary Education.

Sainsbury, L. (2005) 'Picturebook Case Study: Politics and Philosophy in the Work of Raymond Briggs', in K. Reynolds (ed.), *Modern Children's Literature*. London: Palgrave Macmillan.

Saxby, M. (2004) 'Myth and Legend', in P. Hunt (ed.), *International Companion Encyclopedia of Children's Literature*, 2nd edn. London: Routledge.

School Library Association (SLA) (2004) *The Primary School Classification Scheme* (includes Subject Index, CD-ROM, Practical Guide and Poster, www.sla.org.uk).

Sedgwick, F. (1999) *Shakespeare and the Young Writer*. London: Routledge.

Shakespeare, W., Bate, J. and Rasmussen, E. (eds) (2007) *The RSC Shakespeare: The Complete Works*. London: Palgrave Macmillan.

Shakespeare, W., Wells, S., Taylor, G., Jowett, J. and Montgomery, W. (eds) (2005) *William Shakespeare: The Complete Works*. Oxford: Oxford University Press.

Skidmore, D., Perez-Parent, M. and Arnfield, D. (2003) 'Teacher–Pupil Dialogue in the Guided Reading Session', in *Reading, Literacy and Language*, 37: 2.

Smith, F. (1982) *Writing and the Writer*. London: Heinemann.

Smith, L. (2004) 'Domestic Fantasy: Real Gardens with Imaginary Toads', in P. Hunt (ed.), *International Companion Encyclopedia of Children's Literature*, 2nd edn. London: Routledge.

Steele, M. (1989) *Traditional Tales*, 2nd edn. Signal Book Guide. Stroud: The Thimble Press.

Stones, R. (ed.) (1999a) *A Multicultural Guide to Children's Books 0–12*, 2nd edn. London: Books for Keeps.

Stones, R. (1999b) 'Briefing', in *Books for Keeps* 116, May.

Stones, R. (2002a) 'Editor's Page', in *Books for Keeps* 137, January.

Stones, R. (2002b) 'News Briefing', in *Books for Keeps* 134, May.

Stones, R. (2006a) 'Editor's Page', in *Books for Keeps* 160, September.

Stones, R. (2006b) 'Diversity Matters – Multi-Cultural Publishing: What It Took to Get Where We Are', in *Books for Keeps* 161, November.

Styles, M. (1994) '"Am I That Geezer, Hermia?" Children and "Great" Literature', in M. Styles, E. Bearne and V. Watson (eds), *The Prose and the Passion: Children and Their Reading*. London: Cassell.

Styles, M. (1998) *From the Garden to the Street: 300 Years of Poetry for Children*. London: Cassell.

Styles, M. (2004) 'Poetry', in P. Hunt (ed.), *International Companion Encyclopedia of Children's Literature*, 2nd edn. London: Routledge.

Styles, M., Bearne, E. and Watson, V. (1992) *After Alice*. London: Cassell.

Styles, M. and Triggs, P. (1988) *The Books for Keeps Guide to Poetry 0–16,* London: Books for Keeps.

Sullivan, C.W. (2004) 'High Fantasy' in P. Hunt (ed.), *International Companion Encyclopedia of Children's Literature*, 2nd edn. London: Routledge.

Swann, J. and Graddol, D. (1988) 'Gender Inequalities in Classroom Talk', in *English in Education*, 22 (1).

Taylor, H. (2006) 'Ted Hughes: Collected Poems for Children', in *Books for Keeps* 157, March.

The Times (2010) 'News report on the Cambridge/Homerton Research and Teaching Centre', 5 February.

Townsend, J.R. (1990, 1995) *Written For Children: An Outline of English-Language Children's Literature*. London: The Bodley Head.

Townsend, J.R. (1998) 'The Years of Challenge', in *Books for Keeps* 109, March.

Tucker, N. (1981) *The Child and the Book: A Psychological and Literary Exploration*. Cambridge: Cambridge University Press.

Tucker, N. (1989) 'Which Book for Which Children?', in *Books for Keeps* 58, September.

Tucker, N. and Gamble, N. (2001) *Family Fictions: Contemporary Classics of Children's Fiction*. London: Continuum.

Tucker, N. and Reynolds, K. (eds) (1997) *Enid Blyton: A Celebration and Reappraisal*. Roehampton University NCRCL Papers 2.

Twist, L., Shagen, I. and Hodgson, C. (2006) *PIRLS: Progress in International Reading Literacy Study*. Slough: NFER.

Unstead, S. (2003) 'Non-Fiction Publishing: The Facts of the Matter', in *Books for Keeps* 139, March.

Unstead, S. (2009) 'A Question of Words: How Do Children's Dictionary Publishers Establish Criteria for Lexicons?', in *Books for Keeps* 175, March.

Vygotsky, L. (1986) *Thought and Language*. Cambridge, MA: Harvard University Press.

Warrington, M., Younger, M. with Bearne, E. (2006) *Raising Boys' Achievement in Primary Schools: Towards a Holistic Approach*. Milton Keynes: Open University Press.

Watson, V. (2001) *The Cambridge Guide to Children's Books in English*. Cambridge: Cambridge University Press.

Weir, R.H. (1962) *Language in the Crib*. The Hague: Mouton.

Wells, S. (2005) *William Shakespeare: The Complete Works*. Oxford: Oxford University Press.

Whalley, J.I. (2004) 'The Development of Illustrated Texts and Picturebooks', in P. Hunt (ed.), *International Companion Encyclopedia of Children's Literature*, 2nd edn. London: Routledge.

Whitehead, M.R. (1995) 'Nonsense, Rhyme and Word Play in Young Children', in R. Beard (ed.), *Rhyme, Reading and Writing*. London: Hodder & Stoughton.

Whitehead, M. (2004) *Language and Literacy in the Early Years*, 3rd edn. London: Sage.

Wilson, A. (2001) *Language and Knowledge for Primary Teachers: A Guide to Textual, Grammatical* and *Lexical Study*, 2nd edn. London: David Fulton.

Wilson, A. (2006) *Language Knowledge for Primary Teachers*, 3rd edn. London: David Fulton.

Wilson, A. and Hughes, S. (1998) *The Poetry Book for Primary Schools*. London: The Poetry Society.

Winnicott, D. (1971) *Playing and Reality* (UK pbk edn 1991). London: Routledge.

Wray, D. and Lewis, M. (1996) *Writing Frames: Scaffolding Children's Non-Fiction Writing in a Range of Genres*. Reading: Reading University National Centre for Language and Literacy.

Wray, D. and Lewis, M. (1997) *Extending Literacy: Children Reading and Writing Non-Fiction*. London: Routledge.

Wyse, D. and Jones, R. (2007a) 'ICT and Multimedia', in D. Wyse and R. Jones, *Teaching English, Language and Literacy*. London: Routledge.

Wyse, D. and Jones, R (2007b) 'Assessing Writing', in D. Wyse and R. Jones, *Teaching English, Language and Literacy*. London: Routledge.

Yates, J. (2004) 'Science Fiction', in P. Hunt (ed.), *International Companion Encyclopedia of Children's Literature*, 2nd edn. London: Routledge.

Zipes, J. (2002a) *Breaking the Magic Spell: Radical Theories of Folk Tales and Fairy Tales*, revised edn. Kentucky: University Press of Kentucky.

Zipes, J. (2002b) *Sticks and Stones: The Troublesome Success of Children's Literature from Slovenly Peter to Harry Potter*. London: Routledge.

Zipes, J. (2006a) *Why Fairy Tales Stick: The Evolution and Relevance of a Genre*. London: Routledge.

Zipes, J. (2006b) *Fairy Tales and the Art of Subversion*. London: Routledge.

Useful information and websites

Aventis Junior Prize for Science Books: www.royalsociety.org/bookspage. For the best science writing, chosen from a short list by panels of children.

BBC audio resources: www.bbc.co.uk/schoolsradio/english/. Resources for English, for example 15 minute 'Meet the author' interviews with authors including Anne Fine, Jacqueline Wilson and Michael Morpurgo.

BBC Bitesize: www.bbc.co.uk/schools/ks2bitesize/english. Interactive pages for active revision.

BBC graphically illustrated moving image version of *A Midsummer Night's Dream* with quotations from Shakespeare's play, www.bbc.co.uk/cbeebies/stories.

BBC Schools: www.bbc.co.uk/schools/. For information about the programmes and resources available from the BBC.

Blue Peter Book Awards: www.bbc.co.uk/cbbc/bluepetersbookclub. Include 'Most Fun Book with Pictures' and 'Books with Facts'.

Books for Keeps: www.booksforkeeps.uk. The print journal ended in 2010 but the website will continue with an e-version and archive and is a rich resource for anyone interested in children's literature both past and current.

Booktrust: www.booktrustchildrensbooks.org.uk. Has projects and resources to do with all aspects of children's books.

British Council: www.britishcouncil.org/kids-stories. Has animated fairy stories with graphic-style pictures.

British Film Institute, Education Department: www.bfi.org.uk/education. Teachers can learn about all aspects of the use of film.

The Cambridge/Homerton Research and Teaching Centre for Children, Literature: www.educ. cam.ac.uk/centres/childrensliterature. Critical attention is given to film, television programmes, cartoons and video-games as well as the established texts of children's literature.

Carnegie and Kate Greenaway medals: www.carnegiegreenaway.org.uk. Both are awarded by children's librarians for an outstanding book of the previous year – Carnegie for a book, Kate Greenaway for a book with illustrations.

Centre for Literacy in Primary Education: www.clpe.co.uk. This is a major London-based resource centre which provides courses on all aspects of language and literacy and publishes professional books for teachers.

Children's Laureate: www.childrenslaureate.org.uk. Gives voice to the views and activities of the current laureate; some pages are interactive.

Children's Literature in Education. Information about this international quarterly, published by Springer Netherlands, is available on www.springer.com.

Children's Poetry Bookshelf: www.childrenspoetrybookshelf.co.uk. Helps teachers find out about new children's poetry anthologies.

Classic Stories online: www.bygosh.com. Includes original versions of children's stories, for example the whole of Carroll's *Alice's Adventures in Wonderland* with John Tenniel's illustrations.

Diversity in Publishing: www.diversityinpublishing.com. Includes reviews of children's books by ethnic minority authors.

Dramatic Media: www.dramaticmedia.net. Details of film dramas to support Primary Literacy from 8–11 years.

The English Association: www.le.ac.uk/engassoc. An informed voice on all aspects of English teaching from the primary and early years right through to higher education. The website gives information about issues to do with English in the primary school years, the association's primary journal *English 4–11* and the annual awards for the best-illustrated books of the previous year.

English Space: www.englishspace.org. Teachers can enjoy free membership of this site sharing ideas for teaching.

Fairy-Tales-Online.com. A helpful site for teachers as you can browse stories from all over the world. Like some other sites of this kind it does have advertising material.

First News: www.firstnews.co.uk. A newspaper for children covering current affairs and issues.

Guardian Children's Fiction Prize: www.guardian.co.uk/books/guardian-childrens-fiction-prize. Judged by children's authors.

ICUE: www.i-cue.co.uk. An invention that allows a user to store and read books on their mobile phone. Up to about 400 books can be stored on a phone memory card.

Libraries Matter: www.oup.com/uk/librariesmatter. The downloadable catalogue sets out annotated lists of OUP's books and resources under fiction and non-fiction.

Love Reading: www.lovereading4schools.co.uk. Age-related recommendations for children's books.

National Association for the Teaching of English (NATE): www.nate.org.uk. Promotes excellence in English teaching from early years to university. It aims to be an informed national voice on all relevant issues and encourages research which has practical classroom value.

National Centre for Language and Literacy: www.ncll.org.uk. Houses 15,000 children's books in print, video-films, DVDs, cassettes, educational software and professional books and journals for teachers and offers courses for teachers and research projects, including the project called 'Literacy Learning in Chinese and Sikh Communities'.

National Centre for Research in Children's Literature (NCRCL): www.roehampton.ac.uk. This organization promotes critical debate and enquiry in the field of children's literature.

National Literacy Trust: www.literacytrust.org.uk/. Offers a site for research and ideas to promote children's reading and writing.

Nestlé Smarties Book Prize. A well-established award for the best story, novel or poetry book of the previous year. Details are available on www.booktrustchildrensbooks.org.uk.

Nursery Rhymes: www.rhymes.org.uk.

Oxford University Press: www.oup.co.uk. Visit their site's education pages for age-related ideas for improving dictionary and thesaurus skills.

Poetry Right Now!: Michael Rosen's poetry project – details at www.clpe.co.uk.

Poetry Society: www.poetrysociety.org.uk. Founded 1909, this society's website has a section on education which provides information about the Poets in School scheme.

Power of Reading project: www.clpe.co.uk.

Scholastic Book Club: www.mybooks.co.uk. This free site provides children with an online questionnaire to find which books they may like.

School Library Association: www.sla.org.uk. Linked with the SLA journal, this site offers information about libraries and the Association's Librarian of the Year Award. The journal includes articles about children's books and libraries and includes substantial review sections on children's fiction and non-fiction and on ICT and electronic books.

Science Museum: www.sciencemuseum.org.uk. Provides information about the museum and supports children's developing informational literacy.

Seven Stories Centre for Children's Books: www.sevenstories.org.uk/home/. Has a fine collection of children's books of all kinds and regularly offers courses for teachers and students and presents exhibitions of authors' and illustrators' work.

Standards site: www.standard.dfes.gov.uk/primaryframeworks/literacy.

The Story Museum: www.storymuseum.org.uk. Starting as a 'virtual' museum about children's stories, a physical presence is to be established in Oxford.

Teachernet: www.teachernet.gov.uk/teachingandlearning/.

Teachers Evaluate Educational Multimedia (TEEM): www.teem.org.uk/.

Teaching Ideas for Primary Teachers: www.teachingideas.co.uk. Includes ideas for a critical response to books. Site visitors need, as always, to be selective.

Times Educational Supplement: www.tes.co.uk/reviews-and-resources. Reviews of children's books are now mostly on-line rather than in the print journal.

The Wee Web: www.theweeweb.co.uk/ladybird/. This site carries the history of Ladybird books over sixty years.

Write Away: www.writeaway.org.uk. Reviews children's books organized in age ranges, mostly fiction.

Young Times: www.timesonline.co.uk/youngtimes. Section of *Times 2* which includes news, information about hobbies and places of interest for age eights and over.

Index